CLEANER PRODUCTION

Sustainable Trade & Industrial Ecology

CLEANER PRODUCTION
Sustainable Trade & Industrial Ecology

H D Kumar

&

Enakshi Kumar

Vitasta

Vitasta Publishing Pvt. Ltd.

New Delhi

Published by
Vitasta Publishing Pvt. Ltd.
2/15, Ansari Road, Daryaganj,
New Delhi - 110 002

ISBN 978-81-89766-66-5

Typeset and cover design by Vitasta Publishing Pvt. Ltd., New Delhi
Printed by Vits Press, New Delhi

Contents

Preface

All over the world it has become very clear that pollution and degradation of air, water and land, together with a wasteful lifestyle involving overconsumption of depleting natural resources, are damaging and even limiting the planetary resource-base needed for human survival and for future socio-economic development. The 'throw-away' century that ended less than a decade ago left behind mountain-loads of industrial, agricultural, pharmaceutical, hazardous and non-biodegradable wastes that chemicalized the global environment to the detriment of human health and well-being. It underlined the urgent need to manage the environment with the least possible disturbance by adopting cleaner production processes based on sound ecological principles. A rigorous "cradle to grave" life cycle analysis of industrial materials and processes by using scientific and technical analysis can facilitate identification and critical specification of "least harm" technologies and the formulation of policies that can promote socially responsible environmental management and economic development. Such "sustainable" management must form a core element of economic and industrial development worldwide.

Besides processes, clean products are just as important as clean processes. In fact, the products may be even more important than the processes. In view of the important non-point source pollution and dissipative material flows, manufacturers should ensure that the hazard is not simply transferred from the process waste stream to the product. With industrial systems showing a clear trend of moving towards preventive solutions, there is a need for environmental considerations to be effectively integrated within the design of production processes and product life cycles. Two crucial aspects of this integrative character of clean production are (a) clean production calls for process-integrated solutions rather than add-on (end-of-pipe) ones and (b) it calls for integrated life cycle assessments in which attention is focussed on both processes and products. The entire product life cycle is so designed as to reduce the generation of hazardous wastes.

Integrative prevention of hazard has posed a formidable challenge for clean production because corporate responsibilities and national procedures are intimately tied geographically, institutionally and economically. This necessitates solutions that can cross these boundaries. Substitution can be attempted not merely at the level of the individual substance, where one hazard is simply replaced with another, but also at the levels of the process, the system, and the economic, the social and the technical infrastructures.

In today's deeply contradictory, strongly turbulent and very unequal world, many people are increasingly affected by the state of humanity and are genuinely concerned about the worrying damage being done to the planet Earth. A marked social churning, disorder, proneness to violence, economic uncertainty and decline are manifesting in many countries. The fault lies not between the global North and the global South—it runs between different classes and social groups in both First and Third Worlds. Some feel that development and economic growth have led us to a dead end. Others opine that the problem has little, if anything, to do with development and economic growth as such, rather it tends to arise from mismanagement, whereas in some parts of the world growth has been too slow or unevenly shared, elsewhere politicians or private interests have promoted a dubious or biased kind of development. What is really needed is to differentiate clearly between the ideal of development which brings well-being and joy to all, and the development that actually takes place. The negative effects of the latter are often seen everywhere. In the face of an ongoing general transformation and destruction of the natural environment and social relations, today development merely reflects the general commodification of nature and social relations.

In the era of globalization, our ecological enemies endanger our living conditions. The greenhouse effect, the depletion of stratospheric ozone, deforestation, acute water shortages, climate change, and runaway depletion and exhaustion of mineral as well as living resources all are the consequences of the development paradigm. They pose real threats that have been underestimated. The time has come to earnestly focus on the pressing issues of global concern and concentrate our energy more on commonly shared problems.

Flawed or lop-sided economic thinking has trapped people in an 'Abhimanyu' style maze. Certain basic assumptions are shared and perceived as 'minor beliefs' by most hardcore (mainstream) economists beliefs which not only form an integral part of development but also reinforce it. This is best exemplified by the long-held assumption that humans have always lived in a condition of natural scarcity, constantly eking out a living and failing to satisfy their never-ending 'unlimited' wants and needs. This doctrine was proven wrong long ago by economic anthropology (M Sahlins, *Stone Age Economics*, Aldine, Chicago, 1972). It is nevertheless still being taught to students taking diverse economics courses. The economists adhere to this outmoded doctrine, believing that if scarcity is natural (rather than socially created by the market system combined with private ownership regulations) and humans have unlimited wants, only unlimited growth can satisfy these wants, and division of labour and market exchange may be well-suited to increase production. Conversely, the need for growth arises from the root of the continued fabrication of new wants or needs. Little wonder, therefore, that the economic system churns out simultaneously both affluence and scarcity!

We have attempted to discuss some of the above topics, placing special emphasis on cleaner production, wastes and their management, industrial ecology with special reference to energy-related matters, trade, globalization, marketing, commerce and green business—all under the overarching umbrella of sustainable development in the century of the environment.

Acknowledgements

We thank the Stockholm Environment Institute, the Dag Hammerskjöld Foundation Uppsala and the Indian National Science Academy, New Delhi, for providing background literature for this book. We are obliged to all those who kindly provided reprints or gray literature.

We are especially indebted to our friends O N Srivastava, Ashok Kumar, Vinay Sharma and T S Misra for helping us from time to time. Thanks is also due to fellow members and Chairman of the United Nations Environment Programme (UNEP) Panel on Environmental Effects for their suggestions and support.

We are thankful to Rang Nath Singh for composing the manuscript.

Last but not the least, recognition is due to Mrs Renu Kaul Verma, Managing Director, Vitasta Publishing and her team for taking keen interest in this volume.

Abbreviations and Acronyms

BARC	Bhabha Atomic Research Centre
BAT	Best Available Technology
BCA	Benefit–Cost Analysis
BCSEF	Business Council for a Sustainable Energy Future
BFF	Beyond Farmer-First
CCS	Carbon Capture and Storage
CDFC	Community Development Carbon Fund
CDM	Clean Development Mechanism
CERs	Certified emission reductions
CESR	Corporate environmental and social responsibility
CFCs	Chlorofluorocarbons
CF-SEA	Carbon Finance for Sustainable Energy in Africa
CGIAR	Consultative Group on International Agricultural Research
CIS	Commonwealth of Independent States
CMS	Cytoplasmic Male Sterility
CPCB	Central Pollution Control Board
CSOs	Civil society organizations
CSP	Concentrating solar power
CSR	Corporate social responsibility
DFE	Design for the environment
DP	Dual-phase
DSM	Demand-side management
EC	European Community
EHS	Environmental health and safety
EIA	Environmental impact assessment
EMAS	European Eco-Management and Audit Scheme
EMD	Environmental management of development
EMQ	Economic Manufacturing Quantity
EMS	Environmental Management Systems
EnTA	Environmentally Focused Technology Assessment
EOP	End-of-pipe
EPDs	Environmental Product Degradations
EST	Environmentally Sound Technology
FAO	Food and Agriculture Organization
FF	Farmer-first
FFS	Farmer field school
FPR	Farmer participatory research
FRA	Forest Resource Assessment

FS	Faecal sludge
GAEZ	Global Agro-Ecological Zones
GDP	Gross domestic product
GHG	Greenhouse gas
GM	Genetically modified
GMOs	Genetically modified organisms
GNP	Gross national product
HDPE	High density polyethylene
HFC	Hydrofluorocarbons
HSLA	High-strength Low Alloy
IC	Integrated circuit
IEA	International Energy Agency
IIASA	International Institute for Applied Systems Analysis
IK	Indigenous knowledge
IMF	International Monetary Fund
IMPRA	Improved pedal cycle rickshaw
IPCC	Intergovernmental Panel on Climate Change
IPP	Imperfect production process
IPP	Integrated product policy
IPRs	Intellectual property rights
IRP	Integrated resource planning
ISEW	Index of Sustainable Economic Welfare
ITDG	Intermediate technology development group
ITK	Indigenous technological knowledge
JIT	Just-in-time
KTN	Kowledge transfer network
LCA	Life cycle assessment
LCI	Life cycle inventory
LDCs	Least developed countries
LNWT	Low and non-waste technology
LSMS	Living Standards Measuring Study
MAPRA	Motor-assisted pedal cycle rickshaw
MEAs	Multilateral environmental agreements
MNCs	Multinational corporations
MNT	Micro- and nanotechnology
MSW	Municipal solid waste
MSWM	Municipal solid waste management
MTBE	Methyl tertiary butyl ether
NARI	Nimbkar Agricultural Research Institute
NEOP	Non-end-of-pipe
NPP	Net Primary Productivity
NTFPs	Non-timber forest products

NWPPC	Northwest Power Planning Council
PAHs	Polycyclic aromatic hydrocarbons
PAN	Peroxyacetyl nitrate
PAR	Participatory action research
PASIR	Pressure–State–Activity–Impact–Response
PCBs	Polychrorinated biphenyls
PEM	Polymer electrolyte membrane
PIC	Prior informed consent
PLS	Pregnant leach solution
PMDC	Permanent magnet DC
PME	Participatory monitoring and evaluation
POPs	Persistent Organic Pollutants
PPP	Polluter Pays Principle
PPPs	Public private partnerships
PPR	Primary production requirement
PRA	Participatory rural appraisal
PRTRs	Pollutant release and transfer registers
PSS	Product service system
PTD	Participatory technology development
PVC	Polyvinyl chloride
QOL	Quality of life
RFID	Radio frequency identification
SANet	Sustainable Alternatives Networks
SCP	Sustainable Cities Programme
SEA	Strategic Environmental Assessment
SI	Suitability index
SIT	Sterile insect technique
SMEs	Small and medium-sized enterprises
SRB	Socially Responsible Business
SWM	Solid waste management
SXEW	Solvent extraction and electrowinning
TMBT	Tailor-made Biotechnologies
TNCs	Transnational corporations
TPA	Tonnes per annum
TPD	Tonnes per day
TRI	Toxics Release Inventory
TRIP	Transformation-induced plasticity
UNCHS	United Nations Centre for Human Settlements
UNDP	United Nations Development Programme
VOC	Volatile organic compounds
WCED	World Commission on Environment and Development
WEEE	Waste Electrical and Electronic Equipment

WEHAB	Water, Energy, Health, Agriculture and Biodiversity
WIPO	World Intellectual Property Organization
WKS	Western knowledge systems
WSSD	World Summit on Sustainable Development
WTO	World Trade Organization
ZET	Zero Emissions Technology
ZVI	Zerovalent Iron

1
Cleaner Production

Since the Rio Summit in 1992, United Nations Environment Programme (UNEP) has been monitoring global progress on cleaner production and similar approaches such as eco-efficiency and green productivity. This monitoring has shown that the environmental gains achieved by such programmes are being offset by trends on the demand side—population growth, rising living standards, increasing demand for products and services. Since 1992, the world population has increased nearly by 800 million. Fifty years ago, population of Africa was one-third that of Europe. Now, the case is just opposite. Countries with high-income are consuming bulk of the planet's resources, even as consumption in low-income countries is increasing. This "rebound effect" makes it even more urgent to switch to sustainable consumption in addition to cleaner production.

If the overall aim of cleaner production is to minimize the environmental impact of a product's manufacture, sustainable consumption means satisfying a maximum of consumer needs and wants, while at the same time cutting down environmental impacts of products and services.

Only by taking a preventive environmental management approach throughout the product's life cycle—from design and manufacture through use and disposal—can we hope to establish a framework for action in which producers and consumers can move together towards suitable development.

What we need to see is that "life cycle thinking" and related approaches succeed through cooperation and collaboration by private enterprise. Some specific efforts required to meet this challenge include:

- Integrating environmental costs into prices and stimulating new technology
- Managing the growing demand for water, partly through cleaner production
- Cooperating with private business
- Integrating financial institutions into the process of change
- Using eco-labelling to inform consumers about products' life cycles
- Initiating take-back systems for cars and other products
- Working with the media to help change consumption patterns
- Involving young people

Sustainable development strives to create a balance between the ideals of humanism and nature protection, preference for a long-term perspective over short-term gain, and humility and respect for everything that has been created in nature.

Today, more than ever, there is need for a strong sense of collective responsibility for the survival of humankind. There is need for people to apply integrated preventive techniques to processes, products and services with a view to increase overall efficiency and reduce the risks to environment and human health. The world community must ensure that services and products respond to basic needs of present and future generations and help to improve the quality of life (QOL) by minimizing use of natural resources and toxic materials (as well as waste generation and polluting emissions) over the life cycle. The ultimate goal of sustainable development requires adoption of sustainable consumption and production practices.

Cleaner production involves striving for a fairer society by defending consumer rights and promoting responsible, sustainable consumption by everyone. Meeting consumer needs and desires, while promoting cleaner production and sustainable consumption, is a serious challenge today. Both alleviation of poverty and environmental degradation will require certain changes in how goods are produced, distributed and consumed. Also, conservation and more efficient use of resources such as energy is essential.

Consumers can play a vital role in pushing societies everywhere towards socio-economic justice, sustainable development, prosperity and environmental quality. They also have a right to expect business operations (including all stages of production, distribution and marketing) that do not comprise consumer interests or harm the environment. Since many resources are finite, any strategy focused on their efficient use (which is what cleaner production is all about) should be promoted.

The term cleaner production is defined as the continuous application of an integrated preventive environmental strategy to processes, products and services to increase overall efficiency, and reduce risks to humans and environment—and as applicable to the processes used in any industry to products themselves and to various services provided in society. Instead of managing outputs of emissions and waste, producers should rather improve management of raw materials and other inputs, such as energy and water, from the moment a product or a process is conceived.

One obstacle in adopting prevention-based approaches is resistance to change. Another involves preconceived ideas about the amount of investment and possible unknown risks. Fortunately, despite these and other challenges, cleaner production is making headway. Its benefits are clear—not only do producers save money on the end-of-process treatment, they also save on raw materials at the beginning of the chain. Cleaner production effectively reconciles economic growth and environmental protection.

The economic benefits are even greater when the 'polluter pays principle' is applied, so that the environmental and other real costs of production are fully taken into account (Larderel, 2002). The most pressing need today is integrating cleaner production and sustainable consumption.

Some tangible progress worldwide with respect to cleaner production has already been made and includes:

- A network of over 100 cleaner production centres, is operating in all regions to deliver technical assistance, training and information, and other services at the local and national levels
- Meetings in Africa, the Asia-Pacific region, Europe and the Americas have facilitated information dissemination and exchange of experience between and across the regions
- Many educational institutions offer courses on cleaner production, educating students as well as in-job professionals
- Over 1000 demonstration projects in various countries, provide proof of the enormous scope for reducing material and energy intensity in production processes, and hence reducing waste and pollution
- The establishment of institutional mechanisms for transfer and adoption of cleaner technologies has contributed to greater uptake of such technologies
- Cleaner production financing programmes and related technical assistance are enabling practical application of cleaner production measures and installation of safer and cleaner technologies by many companies

There exists considerable scope to further strengthen and integrate cleaner production. Some strategies that have been proposed include the following:

- An approach that covers the entire life cycle of a product or service, expanding the horizon from production facilities to product use and disposal
- 'Mainstreaming' cleaner production into the national and local development planning processes
- Linking related issues; implementation of multilateral environmental agreements (MEAs), energy efficiency, health and safety, and environmental management systems
- Increasing outreach to small and medium-sized enterprises (SMEs) to help them implement cleaner production measures

Seventh International Seminar on Cleaner Production (7CP) held in 2002 in Prague, Czech Republic, made these recommendations for achieving cleaner production:

1. Further strengthen government policies and strategies to build institutions for mainstreaming cleaner production.
2. Expand the scope of cleaner production to address sustainable consumption, with particular attention to the rebound effects of unsustainable consumption.
3. Continue development of policies, planning and strategies oriented towards cleaner production.
4. Develop synergy between the cleaner production and the multilateral environmental agreements.
5. Promote cleaner production in investments and obtain the commitment of the private financial sector.
6. Promote application of cleaner production in sectors such as services and infrastructure, using complementary approaches including energy efficiency, safer production and resource protection.

7. Increase trade links and business-to-business interactions through networks, such as the Sustainable Alternative Networks (SANets), initiated by UNEP and the Global Environment Facility.
8. Increase demand for cleaner production-related information by moving beyond information networking to knowledge management and counselling.
9. Promote innovative partnerships, focusing on those involving the private sector.
10. Emphasize and integrate workplace related health and safety issues, gender issues and labour rights in the application of cleaner production.
11. Continuous efforts to promote cleaner production in SMEs.
12. Continuous efforts towards capacity building in cleaner production.

Sustainable Consumption

The consumption patterns throughout the world are threatening sustainable development. There are increasing disparities between rich and poor countries' consumption levels and consumption levels within these developing countries. Total growth in use of such resources as water, food and energy in developed countries is offsetting technologically engendered efficiency improvements.

We must immediately ensure that tangible progress towards sustainable consumption occurs in industrialized countries, which are the source of the world's dominant consumption models and aspirations. To break with current conceptions and ensure that aspirations for sustainable prosperity become the global pattern, these aspirations first need to be widely embraced within developed countries.

The high rate of growth of both population and consumption in low-income countries underscores the urgency of sustainable consumption. It is important that we should very carefully think of the final phase of the life cycle before we manufacture products. Such thinking leads to new kind of products and is conducive to more efficient use of resources and lower environmental burden.

Governments, businesses and consumers must adopt more environment-friendly policies, practices and lifestyles. Active collaboration by private enterprise is essential, if life cycle thinking and acting are to materialize.

Although industries in many countries have made impressive environmental improvements, these improvements are often neutralized as consumption increases. As protecting the environment is costly, the key message to be disseminated is that prevention makes good business sense. Preventive approaches yield rich environmental, economic and social dividends, their application in cleaner production significantly enhances implementation of multilateral environmental agreements. Energy efficiency considerations must form part of cleaner production.

Some global and regional trends outlined in Tomorrow's Markets: Global Trends and Their Implications for Business, a joint publication of the World Resources Institute, United Nations Environment Programme and the World Business Council for Sustainable Development are:

- Population growth in developing regions will mean large markets dominated by the young
- With economies are becoming more service-based, women's role in the formal labour force is growing
- Rising consumption and energy demand and continuing pollution, underscore the need for innovation that produces more value with less environmental impact
- Survival depends on preserving natural capital—the resource base
- Business in future will be conducted in an increasingly networked world
- While the spread of democracy improves conditions for market-based economies, it also increases demand for greater accountability from government and business, business must earn the licence to operate

In this context, some notable challenges that face environmental agencies and cleaner production proponents are to:

- Go beyond production processes and introduce a life cycle believing that it includes addressing consumption patterns. (Cleaner production and sustainable consumption are the two sides of the same coin. We need to increase demand and supply for cleaner products.)
- Forge new partnerships and strengthen existing ones
- Add cleaner production and sustainable consumption to the agenda of trade organizations, facilitate increased financing for application of cleaner production
- Improve availability of information to agents of change

Table 1. Issues and Approaches in Cleaner Production and Sustainable Consumption (After 7CP, UNEP Industry and Environment, July–December 2002)

Approach	Tools/Techniques
Integration of issues	Cleaner and safer production
	Cleaner production and eco-efficiency integration
	Cleaner production and environmental convention integration
	Life cycle approaches
Cleaner production in development planning	International declaration on cleaner production to secure commitment
	Policy frameworks conducive to cleaner production
Communication and information networking	Efficient entrepreneur calendar
	Publications and databases
	Dissemination via the media
Partnerships and capacity building	Sustainable alternatives networks (SANets)
	Cleaner production in educational curricula
Technology development and finance	UNEP finance initiatives
	Environmental technology assessment
	Financing cleaner production

Transforming Traditional Production to Cleaner Production

Developing countries should make use of opportunities to leapfrog directly from traditional production to cleaner production and environmentally sustainable growth, while giving due consideration to the social issues involved. According to Claude Fussler [Director, World Summit on Sustainable Development (WSSD) Preparations, World Business Council for Sustainable Development, Switzerland], the right market framework for fostering sustainable consumption requires:

- Sustainable convergence criteria
- Shared targets and performance assessment processes involving governments, companies, communities, even households
- Negotiated transitions
- Removal of perverse subsidies
- Economic instruments to steer change

There is also a strong need to humanize cleaner production and sustainable consumption. The best place to do it is the workplace. Workers are both producers and consumers. Associating cleaner production and sustainable consumption in the workplace through training and education helps achieving sustainability.

According to Rajeswari Kanniah, (Regional Office for Asia and the Pacific, Consumers International, Malaysia), in some European countries, Japan and the United States, total waste generation has been increasing despite eco-efficiency initiatives, because not enough has been done to clean up production, and life cycle thinking has not been sufficiently integrated into cleaner production. Multinational corporations or transnational corporations (MNCs or TNCs) are largely a rule unto themselves in the global economy. In fact, they are larger and more powerful than the governments of many developing countries. Most pollution comes from TNCs' activities. Environmental regulations are lax in developing countries, and hazardous waste from some advanced nations has been exported to developing countries which lack fair access to cleaner technologies.

Since little progress has been recorded in curbing wasteful lifestyles, consumption patterns and the development dimension should be integrated into cleaner production or it will be ineffective. Challenges that need to be met, if consumption patterns are to be changed and cleaner production achieved, include the following:

- TNCs must clean up pollution they are responsible for in developing countries
- International environmental regulations should be made more equitable, to protect weaker parties and place more responsibility on larger ones, environmental regulations must make TNCs accountable
- Material flow via industrial economies must be tracked for measuring progress
- Consumers should be offered incentives to buy environment-friendly products, and systems of extended producer responsibility and product take-back need to be set up

- Banks should impose environmental conditions on loans to TNCs, as is done with governments of developing countries

Changing Production Patterns

Positive changes in production patterns do not necessarily lead to positive changes in consumption patterns or vice versa. In some cases, the concept of sustainable consumption can embrace notions of no consumption or of radically modified consumption. Economic development in today's world is directly and intimately connected to both increased production and consumption. Such development relies upon MNCs, producing and selling more and more of their products. A healthy debate is going on about how to delink economic development from resource use. This debate has highlighted need for much greater efficiencies and waste reduction, as exemplified in the "factor 4" and "factor 10" approaches, and should therefore be welcomed and encouraged (Green, 2002). Efficiency increase will continue to be very important in the foreseeable future, but we should also consider the possible limits to production (however efficient) in the long run.

Challenges of Sustainable Production and Consumption

Modification of production and consumption patterns to increase their long-term sustainability is a daunting task for economic growth *per se* and also for the distributional aspects of such growth. Cleaner production and sustainable consumption can not remain insulated from the many other pressing economic and social realities. Modified production and consumption patterns will largely be determined by needs (poverty reduction, employment generation and maintenance, resource availability) and policy responses (multilateral environmental agreement, taxation, investment and public spending) (Green, 2002).

Attempts to modify currently unsustainable production and consumption patterns should address the respective responsibilities of both producers and consumers. In a market economy, one expects progress in cleaner production to be linked, at least to some extent, to consumer demand. The experience of the organic food movement is instructive in this regard. The developed world in particular needs to do much to get the sustainable consumption message across its citizens.

Consumers in the highly developed countries have become accustomed to the increased availability of goods and services at prices that have declined over time compared to average income. Many consumer durables have become cheaper in the developed countries in comparison to average wages. These consumer benefits have, however, come at a cost. Most of the "externalities" of producing goods and services being consumed (e.g., depleted resources, pollution, loss of biodiversity, undesirable impact on the developing world) are now manifesting as the unpaid costs of largely unchecked "consumerism". One important lesson is that, if producers (industry and business) are not the whole of the problem, they cannot be expected to provide the whole of the solution (Green, 2002).

Unfortunately, it is easier and politically more expedient to target business and industry than to remind consumers of their responsibilities and downside of their consumer choices. For most complex problems, there is usually no simple solution. A much better understanding of the nature of the obstacles that stand in the way of more sustainable production and consumption is required. However, this does not mean that simply because a challenge is difficult, it can or should be ignored—the challenge of climate change is a good example.

Both in short and medium terms, production and consumption patterns that are more sustainable need to be developed in the context of stronger poverty alleviation and increased economic growth. Poverty and unemployment, wherever they occur, act as strong barrier to sustainable production and consumption patterns; but the negative effects that affluence also have had particularly on unsustainable consumption patterns must not be underestimated.

There is little doubt that cleaner production should form the core element of corporate social responsibility. But sustainable consumption also requires shifts in perception and behaviour among consumers, especially those in the developed countries. Indeed, such a shift is now occurring (Green, 2002).

In market economies, particularly in the developed countries, there has been a tendency over the last two decades for governments to take a less pro-active approach than before. However, the free market is good at delivering certain things and also at times incapable of delivering others. To make production and consumption patterns more sustainable, governments will have to address the serious problem of frequent and "perverse" subsidies that promise unsustainable production and consumption patterns. There is emerging evidence of increasing support from the private sector for an enhanced governmental role, notably in the form of large and MNCs seeking market stability and a level playing field as a basic prerequisite for doing business.

Cleaner production objectives needs incorporation in the main stream of all governmental, industrial and fiscal policies. The environmental regulatory regime also needs greater strengthening. Industry challenge programmes, educational initiatives and public-private partnerships should play more important roles. Fiscal policies need to be reformed so that market prices incorporate full environmental costs. It is high time that we moved beyond a focus on merely reducing waste and emissions associated with industrial processes. Carefully focusing on the technical aspects of cleaner production technologies enhances efficiency, functional optimization and waste avoidance in industries. Current challenges confronting sustainable production and consumption systems warrant meaningful integration of broader social and work quality values in the present day cleaner production concept. To make sustainability possible, cleaner production and life cycle approaches must be integrated in emerging production technologies together with occupational safety, environmental and social responsibility concerns.

We will have to make distinctions between macro-economic and micro-economic impacts. It is easy for analysts to say that the net effect of change will be economically, socially or environmentally positive "on average", but one might also argue that someone who sleeps with his head in a refrigerator and his feet in an oven will "on average" have a comfortable body temperature! Managing change and dealing fairly with those most adversely affected will be crucial to the rate, the extent and indeed the very success of such change.

Workers are both producers and consumers. They are eminently suited to influence future production and consumption patterns positively. The number of those who once thought that sustainable production and consumption were someone else's problem are declining. There is no top-down solution to the problems thrown up by current production and consumption patterns, and also there is no critical mass of bottom-up understanding about or support for sustainable production and consumption. The workplace can be a good location for the development of a mutually beneficial and reinforcing approach between employers and workers, upon whom success largely depends. A joint employer/union approach to more sustainable production and consumption issues prove highly beneficial to both employers and workers (Green, 2002).

Clean Development Mechanism (CDM)

Under the UNEP umbrella, one of the component elements is the World Bank's Community Development Carbon Fund (CDCF). A Dutch-funded, technical assistance and CDM project aims at capacity development in 12 developing countries, with the ultimate objective of enabling the target countries to actively participate in global carbon market, thus achieve both local and global environmental improvements.

Another project Carbon Finance for Sustainable Energy in Africa (CF-SEA) in a joint effort with the World Bank's CDCF has the general objective of assisting select Sub-Saharan African countries to fully engage in the global carbon market through providing institutional and project development support to specific public and private entities in the project countries.

Carbon Finance for Sustainable Energy

Capacity building may be used as a tool for CDM project identification and development. To build capacities of local consultants in the project countries, UNEP and World Bank's CDCF have requested the contracted firms implementing the project in selected countries to include in their team a local institution or consultancy firm as a partner. CDM projects designed and formulated by local partners are considered by CDCF for potential procurement of emissions reductions. Several 'virgin' projects are likely to be started in a few existing industrial complexes especially in hydrofluorocarbons (HFC) and methane abatement.

Analytical work can assist developing countries participating in the global carbon market to better understand the market dynamics and how they could maximize their benefit from the market. Several CDM projects have already led to certified emission reductions (CERs) (Table 1.2).

This table shows that eight HFC and N_2O projects gain 52 per cent of all the current CERs or more CERs than the other 460 CDM projects together. The poverty alleviation or sustainability content of these projects is, however, debatable.

Table 1.2 Sectoral Distribution of the CDM Projects (After Fenhann, 2005)

Type	Number	Percentage	CERs/Year (000)	Percentage
Biomass energy	111	24	5,227	6
Hydro	76	16	3,954	5
Agriculture	55	12	3,948	5
EE Industry	56	12	3,161	4
Wind	53	11	4,124	5
Landfill gas	39	8	10,194	12
Fossil fuel switch	18	4	1,007	1
Biogas	20	4	1,028	1
Cement	14	3	2,064	2
HFCs	6	1	28,281	34
Geothermal	4	1	853	1
EE Households	3	1	42	0
Solar	3	1	42	0
N_2O	2	0	15,112	18
Fugitive	4	1	3,532	4
Tidal	1	0	311	0
EE Service	1	0	3	0
Transport	1	0	7	0
Energy distribution	1	0	15	0
Total	**468**	**100**	**82,936**	**100**
Renewables	268	57	15,571	19
Energy efficiency	62	13	3,227	4
Fuel switch	18	4	1,007	1
CH_4 reduction and Cement	112	24	19,738	24
HFC and N_2O reduction	8	2	43,394	52

Many renewable energy projects have entered the pipeline recently; most of these are biomass projects (111) and run-of-river hydropower projects (76). Wind is catching up with 53 projects (Fenhann, 2005).

The small-scale CDM "window" is providing its justification with 47 per cent of the projects in the pipeline being small scale. The smallest so far is the "E7 Bhutan 70 kW micro hydropower project" reducing only 524 tonne of CO_2 annually.

The total annual number of CERs created by the 468 projects is 83 $MtCO_2$. The total number of CERs expected to be generated by these projects from the start of their crediting periods until the end of 2012 is 605 $MtCO_2$.

The geographical distribution picture of CDM among developing countries is not promising. Most of the CDM projects are being implemented in only two countries: India (182 projects) and Brazil (92 projects). There are only 17 projects from China in the pipeline at present. Countries such as Chile, Honduras, Mexico and the Philippines have about 10–20 projects. Africa and the Middle East/North Africa have only a limited number of projects.

Clean Production and Sustainable Development

The Brundtland Commission (WCED, 1987) stated that "Humanity has the ability to make development sustainable to ensure that it meets the needs of the present without compromising the ability of future generations to meet their own needs". Through this statement, it posed a challenge—economic development everywhere had failed to take sufficient account of the natural environment. The degradation of the natural environment not only undermines the ability of future generations to meet their needs but also threatens the health and stability of the global ecosystems, the life-support mechanism on which the survival of both present and future generations depend. This underscores the urgent need to define and initiate an approach to development that does not conflict with the health and stability of the environment—a development i.e., truly sustainable. The challenge is how to articulate and implement sustainable development.

At the core of the issue of sustainable development lies the need to define a framework within which both products and processes will remain compatible with environmental health. Broadly speaking, this goal has been captured by the phrase clean (sometimes cleaner) production (Baas et. al., 1990). Clean production essentially strives to achieve sustainable development, production processes, product cycles and consumption patterns, which allow for human development, and the provision of basic needs without degrading and disrupting the ecosystems in which human development must operate (Jackson, 1992).

What exactly is clean production? The term 'clean' has usually been used to refer to various technological processes including process-integrated preventive measures, end-of-pipe (EOP) abatement measures (Van den Akker, 1990), and remediation or clean-up measures (Newell et. al., 1990). However, the goal-oriented idea of clean production does not offer clear prescriptive indicators with which to guide technological choice. Jackson attempted to look for such indicators, emphasizing the importance of precaution, prevention and integration. He discussed the role of ecology and thermodynamics in identifying principles for cleaner production. The chief aim is to find answers to the following questions: Can certain principles and concepts be formulated with which to guide technological choices about production processes, product cycles and consumption patterns? What is the nature of these principles? Can they help us in designing a comprehensive framework for technological choice?

The emerging central tenets of this approach are that measures should be preventive and integrative.

The preventive character of the cleaner production methodology is crucial. The precautionary principle has highlighted the complexity of ecosystems and the limits of scientific certainty. As EOP approaches to pollution control have been costly and usually quite ineffectual, increasing emphasis is laid on an approach in which hazard is avoided by preventing or eliminating the generation of hazardous waste at the source. Some ways of achieving this, as listed by Jackson (1992) include:

1. **Good Housekeeping** The elimination and prevention of leaks, improved management and documentation of stocks and flows, etc.
2. **On-site Closed Loop Recycling** The closure of material cycles, particularly for hazardous materials in the plant.
3. **Input Substitution** Substitution of hazardous materials by non-hazardous ones in the plant: e.g., the substitution of water-based cleaning methods for chlorinated organic solvents.
4. **Process Modification** Modification of the process in such a way as to reduce emissions of hazardous wastes.
5. **Clean Production Technologies** New technologies, specifically designed, low impact technologies and processes, with low hazardous waste usage and high material efficiency.
6. **Product Reformulation** Reformulation or redesign of products to reduce hazardous waste generation both within the process and within the product.

Three Dimensions of Sustainable Development

Sustainable development has three dimensions—environmental, economic and social. Cleaner production has to be assessed with respect to all the three dimensions. But the difficulty is to measure these parameters.

Environmental Measurements

Sustainable development cannot be achieved without making fundamental changes in the ways societies produce and consume. Several approaches have been developed (e.g., cleaner production, pollution prevention, factor 4/factor 10, linking economic growth from environmental impacts) to determine their success or failure. We need to have appropriate measurements (Kanniah, 2002).

The study of materials flow exemplifies one such concrete measurement. The World Resources Institute (WRI) conducted a study of five industrial economies (Austria, Germany, Japan, the Netherlands and the United States) in 2000. Total output of wastes and pollutants in these countries rose by 28 per cent since 1975, despite more efficient natural resources use. Between one-half and three-quarters of the resource inputs used in the five countries are returned to the environment as waste within a year, this is attributed to "the tremendous scale of economic growth and consumer choices that favour energy and material intensive lifestyles" (WRI, 2000). Similarly, according to UNECE (2001), although progress has been made in improving eco-efficiency in the European region, these gains have been offset by overall increases in consumption.

It is not enough to clean up production. It is equally important to consider the extraction and disposal phases of the materials cycle and also increasing consumption levels. Much attention has been given to clean up the production phase. In contrast, the extraction, disposal and consumption phases have not been adequately addressed. Cleaner production and the life cycle approach usually do not begin at the factory where a product is being manufactured, but at the point where raw materials are extracted. They continue right from the use and disposal of the finished product (Kanniah, 2002).

The challenge to measure environmental impacts from raw materials extraction through consumption and disposal is complex. The main actors here are TNCs, which accounts for the largest share of global economic activity and are mainly responsible for global environmental impacts (Kanniah, 2002). The post-Rio and post-Uruguay Round era has witnessed TNCs acquiring greater economic clout, more economic space and less regulatory constraints on their operations. Not only has there been a failure to monitor and regulate TNCs internationally, there has also been a significant increase in their rights and global access through WTO agreements.

According to Singh (2001), out of the world's 100 largest economic entities in 2000, 51 were TNCs and only 49 were governments. By 2001, 54 were corporations and 46 were governments. Based on these statistics, Walmart is bigger than Indonesia and General Motors is roughly the same size as Ireland, New Zealand and Hungary combined. Three-quarters of all TNCs are based in North America, western Europe and Japan, 99 of the 100 largest TNCs are based in industrialized countries (Corpwatch, 2001).

Kanniah (2002) drew up this environmental balance sheet of TNC activities:

- One hundred and twenty-two TNCs account for 80 per cent of all CO_2 emissions. The oil produced by five private global corporations (ExxonMobil, BP Amoco, Shell, Chevron and Texaco) contributes some 10 per cent of the world's carbon emissions. Greenhouse gas emissions from the fuel they produce exceed total GHG emissions from Central America, South America and Africa combined (Bruno et. al., 1999)
- The key mining industries as also production and use of ozone-destroying CFCs and related compounds are virtually exclusively controlled by TNCs
- Eighty per cent of land worldwide is cultivated for export crops by TNCs
- Most of the world's chlorine (the basis of some of the most toxic chemicals, including PCBs, DDT and dioxins) is manufactured by TNCs
- The main transmitters of environmentally unsound production systems, hazardous materials and products to the third world are TNCs

- TNCs dominate the trade in (and in many cases also the extraction or exploitation of) natural resources and commodities that contribute to depletion or degradation of forests, water and marine resources, toxic waste and unsafe products
- TNCs through aggressive advertising and product promotion, promote the culture of unsustainable consumption

The largest oil companies whose new explorations and oil or gas pipelines threaten the survival of indigenous people in the Amazon basin, Southeast Asia, North America and elsewhere, have not facilitated the development of renewable energy. In 1973, geothermal, wind and solar accounted for 0.1 per cent of world energy supply. In 1996, renewables accounted for a mere 0.4 per cent. During the same period, oil declined in terms of dominance of fuel supply, from 44.9 per cent to 35.3 per cent, though it remained the biggest source. This decline was largely offset by use of natural gas, which contributes equally to global warming, and nuclear power (Kanniah, 2002).

Economic Measurements

Post Rio, financial flows to developing countries have been declining. The UN members agreed that industrialized countries should contribute 0.7 per cent of their GNP to Official Development Assistance (ODA). In reality, since the Earth Summit, most of these countries fell farther and farther behind. Only Denmark, Luxembourg, the Netherlands, Norway and Sweden met or exceeded the 0.7 per cent aid target in 2000. Most of the least developed countries (LDCs) suffered a decline of ODA by at least 25 per cent. The share of ODA targeted for sustainable development of oceans and seas, protection of the atmosphere, sustainable agriculture and combating deforestation fell from 25 per cent in 1996 to 17 per cent in 1999 (UNESCO, 2001).

Since it came into existence in 1995, the WTO has ruled that every environmental policy it has reviewed is an illegal trade barrier which must be eliminated or changed. It has also ruled against many health or food safety laws. Countries whose laws have been declared trade barriers, or which merely threatens WTO action, have changed or dropped their policies to meet WTO requirements.

There has been no significant improvement in technology and harmful production methods have not changed. Indeed, according to TWN (1997), in the South, liberalization took a different form. It was liberalization of mining laws, derestriction and deregulation. The common trend in many Third World countries is the removal of most barriers and instruments previously used by governments in the preservation, development and utilization of their mineral resources. Many countries in Latin America, Africa and Asia Pacific are now liberalizing their mining laws and deregulating land rights and mineral rights, taxation, and environmental protection, with a view to attracting foreign mining investors (TWN, 1997).

Far from effecting the promised technology transfer to the South, new obstacles have emerged, e.g., enhanced intellectual property rights (IPR) protection (WRI, 2002). The IPR regime can keep developing countries from having effective access to Environmentally Sound Technology (EST). Harmful technologies continue to be exported to the South. Waste in the guise of recyclable material from the North has been transported to the South.

Small and medium-sized industries in the South face strong challenges to their survival, let alone their ability to implement cleaner production policies, when pitted against the combined might of the Northern countries, their TNCs, and biased implementation of the economic policies of the WTO (Kanniah, 2002).

Social Measurements

Poverty continues to be a major problem in developing countries, and the development dimension has not been properly integrated in cleaner production. Consumption levels constitute a good way to measure progress in natural resource savings. Household consumption worldwide increased by 68 per cent between 1980 and 1998. The working age population in developing countries will increase from three billion in 2000 to four billion in 2025 (WRI, 2002). These figures point to the potential for an explosion in consumption in the North and by elites in the South. In the affluent North, increase inputs and consumption of large amount of commodities whose production is the most damaging to the Earth (energy, chemicals, metals and paper) are continuing unchecked.

Cleaner production and the life cycle approach in themselves are not the solution. The unsustainable consumption patterns of the wealthy and the middle class will also have to be reduced. A global survey by UNEP and Consumers International recorded fairly slow progress by governments in implementing the sustainable consumption provisions of the UN Guidelines for Consumer Protection, 38 per cent of the governments responding were not aware of the Guidelines' existence. Some of the largest resource consuming countries (including the US which ought to shoulder the greatest responsibility) did not respond at all (UNEP, 2002).

Accountability of TNCs

TNCs dominate and use the lions' share of the earth's resources and enjoy the spoils of their power, it is only fair that they should accept the greatest share of responsibility by sustainably promoting development that meets basic human needs. Self-regulation has not worked and may not work in future. Therefore, international regulatory agencies should keep track of and exercise a check on their activities. Today, MEAs bind only governments. They should also hold TNCs accountable for their activities at home and abroad. Legislations should be enacted to impose obligations on TNCs to implement cleaner production and promote sustainable consumption.

Tracking of Materials Flow

No satisfactory systems are in place to track down flows of natural resources from extraction, production, use and recycling to final disposal. Materials flow can measure the impact of industrial activities on the environment. Flows of natural resources, goods, pollutants and wastes generated by an industrial economy could provide a new way to measure countries' environmental performance. There is an urgent need to develop databases and indicators that document materials flows through industrial economies and to produce a global report card of their environmental performance.

Reducing Wasteful Consumption

It should be the joint responsibility of government, industry and civil society to educate and impress upon consumers to change their consumption patterns. A start in this direction should be made by curbing, advertising of harmful and unhealthy products. Consumers should be given incentives to choose environment-friendly products, produce less household waste, and actively participate in "reuse, reduce and recycle" campaigns.

As living standards improve and expectations grow in both developed and developing countries, earliest efforts to find a sustainable development path is increasing. Achieving sustainability requires basic change in production and in consumption-related activities. Finding ways to deliver better performance using less energy and raw materials, and creating less waste contributes to the betterment of living standards worldwide. During the last decade, many businesses have begun to adopt a more responsible attitude towards sustainability, e.g., in areas of eco-efficiency, social dialogue with stakeholders and corporate social responsibility. Companies are recognizing that they must cooperate with a wide range of partners and stakeholders to become more sustainable in the marketplace.

Though the world scenario has changed since 1992 when Agenda 21 was adopted at Rio, the basic problem of unsustainable development remains almost the same. Today it is more urgent than ever to embark on a more sustainable path. While much remains to be accomplished in tackling global environmental problems, a shift towards the social issues of sustainability is an urgent priority (Kornevall, 2002). It is not fair to continue to deprive a majority of the world's population of the benefits of our common development. Poor countries need to be a part of the global market on much better terms than before. Business should cooperate with governments and civil society to create a global market, which could benefit everybody.

More than ever, transparency and ethics need to receive emphasis in business practices. At the same time, business needs to address specific demands of other stakeholders. "Triple bottom line" reporting is becoming the business response to stakeholders' requests. A survey by Environics International, reported at the last World Economic Forum, indicated that the general public has relatively little trust in global companies (Kornevall, 2002). Even this level of trust fell sharply following some major accounting frauds (leading to the bankruptcy of major companies). There is a feeling that business is not doing enough to protect the environment. According to many, business is responsible for some of the adverse effects of the present development path.

Far from narrowing, global inequalities are in fact increasing. According to WRI/ UNEP (2002) publication *Tomorrows' Markets: Global Trends and Their Implications for Business*, 78 per cent of the world's population is poor, 11 per cent is rich. More and more people regard this situation as unfair and are demanding for a new business approach that goes far beyond self-interest, thus making a greater contribution to an increase in the quality of life of all people (Kornevall, 2002).

The present generation's ecological footprint is too large. It is estimated that the world's average ecological footprint exceeds available bio-capacity by about 20 per cent, and this overdraft is being contained by destroying the Earth's capital stocks of fertile land, forests and fisheries.

The CO_2 level in the atmosphere is increasing, causing the earth's temperature to rise and hence contributing to the melting of polar glaciers. The frequency of forest fires is increasing. Rivers are drying up. In 1997, the Yellow River in China did not reach the sea for 226 days. Plants and animals are facing the brunt, desperately trying to adapt, but many will not make it. There is a dramatic increase in coral bleaching. Seventy per cent of marine fisheries are either fished to capacity or overfished. And the increase in destructive weather events is known to everybody.

There are also striking social inequalities with 20 per cent of the world population accounting for over 80 per cent of total consumption. Nearly half the world population lives on less than two dollars a day. Without access to simple products that could help them meet basic needs, these marginalized people are not part of the global marketplace. A World Bank's Living Standards Measuring Study (LSMS) revealed that the poor lack basic infrastructure services. There are few exceptions in urban areas. If the QOL of all these poor people is to be improved, they will have to be incorporated into the marketplace.

Global development in coming years will generate several business opportunities by producing new and affordable products and basic services for poor people. Consumption by the poor is likely to increase. Business will have to incorporate local markets that serve the poor into the future global marketplace (Kornevall, 2002).

Production and Lifestyles

Sustainability is intimately connected to production and consumption related activities. Pressures to find a sustainable development path arise from the way we live, how we produce and consume. These pressures are growing, as living standards and expectations increase everywhere. The world population will grow rapidly (by about 80 million a year) in the decades to come. We may have over nine billion people around 2050.

The current world production system is unsustainable due to the constant increase in resources used and waste produced. Industry must see to it that the present modernization and globalization of activities bring production and use of products within the ambit of sustainability. Growth needs to be decoupled from materials and energy. We need to accommodate more growth while using less materials and energy. This can be done by increasing our efficiency, adopting new technologies more rapidly, and stimulating radical innovations.

The market may be the only system that can take us in the right direction provided, that prices are not distorted by perverse subsidies. We need realistic prices to transform technologies towards the reduction of pollution and resource consumption. Governments need to support full-cost pricing.

Sustainability is best served by open and competitive markets. The developed world must open up for basic products coming from the developing world. In turn, the developing world must open up for trade by liberalizing internal markets and introducing the necessary infrastructure reforms to allow international trade to flourish (Kornevall, 2002).

Technology assumes a role in ensuring that sustainable production systems remain competitive in the marketplace. Our current unsustainable culture of consumption is greatly influenced by technologies that support modern communications, advertising, media and fashion. It is spreading rapidly to even middle class citizens of developing countries.

Recently, many business houses have begun to adopt a more responsible attitude towards sustainability, especially in regard to eco-efficiency, social dialogue with stakeholders, and corporate social responsibility agendas. In the environmental field, the adoption of EOP and compliance approach by business leaders preceded their adoption of cleaner production practices, which are more precautionary and cover not only manufacturing processes but also products and services.

Clean Heating

Two major sources of air pollution in many countries are home heating (particularly wood burners and open fires) and transportation involved vehicles. Air pollution impairs health and several nations are finding creative means to clean up their air by enacting legislation and rules with a view to facilitating the installation of clean heating in newly purchased homes. Also, people are encouraged to replace their wood burners with a clean heat system or approved burners to improve air quality. Several transport measures can be adopted. This includes introduction of cleaner fuels and reducing the harmful emissions from buses, trucks or other vehicles.

Poor air quality causes countless premature deaths each year. The air quality can be improved by banning open fires in urban areas as well as by phasing out old enclosed burners in a city.

Cleaner and Sustainable Product Design

The dead bodies of the Hindus are traditionally cremated (burnt). Most other religions prescribe burial, i.e., placing the dead body in a coffin and burying the same in a grave. These coffins can have some environmental impacts.

Plastic, synthetic linings and glue containing formaldehyde are used in many coffins. With more and more people becoming aware of the impact of such coffins on the environment, the demand for natural burials and eco-friendly coffins has been growing. This prompted the "Return to Sender" eco-coffin, designed by Greg Holdsworth from Holdsworth Design, in New Zealand. It uses a minimum of materials which are also bio-degradable and non-toxic (Enviro NZ, New Zealand, pp 12–13 (Nov 2007).

The stylish, unique design of this coffin appeals to many people besides 'green' consumers. It exemplifies how good product design can go hand-in-hand with sustainable principles. Products need to be designed in such a manner that consumers feel assured that the product of their choice is sustainably sound.

It is well-known that about 70 per cent of the environmental impacts of any product are determined at design stage; thinking about sustainability at the drawing board can effectively improve a product's green credentials. Besides the design world, awareness is also growing in the packaging industry.

An example of good sustainable design is a kiwifruit export tray launched in New Zealand. The tray, developed by Maniaia Mist Paper Solutions, incorporates environment-friendly principles throughout its life cycle—from design, to production and disposal (EnviroNZ, Nov 2007). The export tray is made of 65 per cent waste kiwifruit pulp and 35 per cent unbleached wood pulp. It is well-suited for use in organic export markets because no artificial additives or chemicals are used in the production process and the trays are biodegradable, compostable and recyclable.

Another merit is that the kiwifruit plants are not sprayed with a weed killer because vine trimmings are used to make pulp. This prevents growers from mulching into soil under vines.

Furthermore, fairly sustainable practices are used in the tray's production. During the pulp making operation, water is recycled and energy is conserved by using energy efficient light bulbs and time switches are used on machinery to avoid wasteful usage of electricity.

Indeed, the packaging industry can increasingly adopt sustainable practices, by relying on the principle that all players in the life cycle of a product assume responsibility for its environmental impacts. In this context, there is an urgent need to bring together any country's packaging manufacturers, brand owners, retailers and recycling operators, besides the central and state governments. Launching a variety of initiatives across the packaging life cycle, from design to disposal, can help divert a substantial fraction of packaging from landfill.

Product Stewardship

Product stewardship represents a 'cradle to grave' tool that encourages producers, brand owners, importers, retailers, consumers and other parties to assume responsibility for the environmental effects of their products throughout the product life cycle. It is especially useful for waste streams such as old computers, tyres, used oil, and unwanted agrochemicals, which have a negative impact on the environment. Some examples of product stewardship schemes include paint and packaging take-back, collection of used agricultural chemical containers, Vodafone's Telecom's cell phone take-back, refrigerant recovery, Tyre Track for used tyres, and some used oil collection programmes, launched in New Zealand.

Clean and Green Chemistry

That modern life strongly depends on the petrochemical industry and is borne out by the fact that most drugs, paints and plastics are made from oil. Unfortunately, current processes for making chemical products are not at all sustainable in terms of resources and environmental impact. Recent progress in green chemistry is now helping companies to tackle this problem (Poliakoff and Licence, 2007).

There are two reasons that make chemical manufacture unsustainable. Firstly, that most chemical products such as perfumes, plastics and pharmaceuticals are based on carbon that is supplied by Earth's limited petroleum feedstocks. There are alternative carbon sources—coal used to be the basic feedstock for chemical production, even before oil, and it could be used again. The problem is that readily accessible coal is in limited supply and its conversion into fine chemicals requires catalysts based on metals that are also becoming scarce. And secondly, industrial chemical processes generate large amounts of waste whose safe disposal burdens the environment.

Unfortunately, we cannot deal with these problems by using existing technology. Finite natural resources will always constrain our ability to manufacture chemical products for the growing world population. The industry may have to struggle hard even to supply existing consumers. The challenge of green chemistry for industrialists is to devise sustainable strategies that can meet the escalating demand for chemical products.

Green chemistry addresses all aspects of manufacturing. The first aim of an industrial process is to identify suitable renewable feedstocks. Choice feedstocks are non-food plants; for these, effective ways of converting the whole plant into useful products need to be found. The processes and reactions involved in making chemical products are then devised to minimize environmental impact. Most traditional catalysts contain toxic or scarce metals. We need to develop metallic catalysts based on organic compounds (organocatalysts) or use enzymes, which have been suitably modified to drive useful reactions. Industrial processes and reactors must be engineered to maximize efficiency and reduce waste. We also need improved analytical techniques to monitor the fate of potentially harmful chemicals in the environment. The impact of chemicals on the environment may possibly be reduced by finding replacements with reduced toxicity and increased biodegradability as compared with existing mass-produced compounds.

Some principles can guide in determining whether or not a chemical process is green. These address the amount of waste produced, the number of sequential chemical steps (the fewer the better), the use of catalysts (to be encouraged, because catalysts are needed only in small amounts and they reduce the quantities of reagents used), and the toxicity of the products (Fig. 1.1).

- **Prevent Wastes**
- **Renewable Materials**
- **Omit Derivatization Steps**
- **Degradable Chemical Products**
- **Use Safe Synthetic Methods**
- **Catalytic Reagents**
- **Temperature, Pressure Ambient is Maintained**
- **In-process Monitoring**
- **Very Few Auxiliary Substances**
- **E-factor, Maximize Feed in Product**
- **Low Toxicity of Chemical Products**
- **Yes, It is Safe**

Source: Tang et. al., 2005

Fig. 1.1 A mnemonic to illustrate 12 principles of green chemistry. Catalytic reagents reduce the amount of chemicals needed in a reaction; in-process monitoring allows harmful substances to be detected and eliminated, auxiliary substances are those that do not take part in the chemical reaction such as solvents or separating agents and the E-factor is the mass of waste generated in a process divided by the mass of product.

By measuring the amount of waste produced, it is possible to quantify how green a process is. From the balanced chemical equation for some process, the theoretical quantity of waste is calculated per unit mass of starting material, assuming that the yield of product is 100 per cent. In reality, most reactions give lower yields and the actual amount of waste is greater than the theoretical value. To deal with this matter, processes can be assessed by using their 'E-factor'—the ratio of the mass of waste to that of the product. All processes should aim for the lowest possible E-factor. Truly green processes have a zero E-factor.

Of course, some waste is unavoidable and energy is required to break the bonds in the starting materials of a reaction. Usually, the energy input is not balanced by the energy generated from bonds forming in the product, so the extra bonds must be created, usually in a by-product. Although some by-products can be used as feedstocks for further reactions, by and large most by-products are either not reactive enough or are too diluted to be recycled economically. In such a case, the wisest treatment for organic waste is careful incineration so that at least its energy content can be exploited.

As the bulk of waste is usually constituted by solvents, these solvents attract top priority. Many solvents are flammable or toxic and most of them are volatile organic compounds that cause atmospheric pollution. Solvents are needed for most reactions because they aid mixing, transfer heat and sometimes control the reactivity of reagents. But very large amounts of solvents are spent in the isolation, separation and purification of materials. Optimizing reactions to prevent the formation of byproducts would eliminate or minimize the need for purification processes and reduce the volumes of solvents required to a great extent.

Engineering of chemical processes is extremely important. Green chemistry brings chemists and chemical engineers together. Green solvents have provided novel design options for reactors, and the need for quantitative data on reactions in these media has renewed interest in physical organic chemistry.

Many industrialists are interested in green chemistry. Green processes can usually be more profitable than traditional ones. Enzymatic reactions have already displaced conventional catalysis as a low cost option in the manufacture of several generic pharmaceuticals. Some industrial process chemists have been successful in significantly reducing the volume of toxic solvents used in pharmaceutical manufacture by careful identification of less harmful replacements (Wasserscheid and Welton, 2007; Poliakoff and Licence, 2007).

Urban Design

A large number of people live in towns and cities where urban areas have impacts on their health, local economy and sustainability.

One important aspect of urban design is the public space between buildings such as parks and streetscapes and the principles used in creating them. There is need to design towns with local shops and amenities and interconnected streets that encourage people to walk and exercise.

Dumb growth such as car-oriented suburbs, with limited connection in streets and where people have to move away from those communities to get any services or facilities, is undesirable.

Formulating a good Urban Design Protocol facilitates creation of a network for people to share information. Signatories to the protocol can be from big or small organizations, and each signatory can present an action plan as an urban design champion. By signing such a protocol, design professionals, government agencies, developers and many others can encourage innovation, make good connections, recognize the character of places, and ensure diversity and environment-friendly design. These principles cannot only be applied to a metropolitan region but also to a street or a building.

Many people need a regular prompt to think about what they buy, what they use, what they throw away and how they travel. Many also want not only advice on what they can do but also on some easy ways to get started. Many work programmes deal with issues such as climate change, air quality, fresh water, urban design and sustainable business. They all are fundamentally about a nation's sustainability. Similarly, some other programmes significantly help in moving a country towards sustainability, and say are exemplified by, tougher insulation requirements for new homes, the Choke, the Smoke and Low Carbon Diet campaigns, Walking School Buses, and the Energy Wise programmes, launched in New Zealand.

Safer Production: The Concept of Inherent Safety

The approach of inherent safety involves the use of processes and materials with little or no toxicity, flammability or instability. It is an important concept in the design of chemical plants. It has become well-known among chemical engineers as a sound set of principles for the design of new facilities and has been developed into a vital part of the curricula of engineering colleges in many countries. Inherent safety is seldom used to improve existing plants and plays a small role (if any) in the currently popular approaches to safety management (Zwetsloot and Ashford, 2002). But the traditional notion of safety management entails identification of hazards of the existing situation in existing production processes, assessment of the associated risks and minimization of these risks. The inherently safer production approach helps in the identification of hazards and risks, search and evaluation of alternative technological options, and elimination or reduction of hazards by implementing inherently safer technological options. In both approaches, organizational and human aspects are as important as technological factors. However, the inherently safer production approach is more future-oriented and is more proactive with technological options, while traditional safety management focusses on management of the present technology (Zwetsloot and Ashford, 2002). Inspired by the successful development of cleaner production, Zwetsloot and Ashford conducted a feasibility study for a similar development towards inherently safer production in 1999. In four pilot projects carried out in 1997-98, a methodology to generate inherently safer technological options was developed and tested. It emerged that many options had payback times of less than two years, and that inherently safer production was a feasible concept with great potential for simultaneous improvement of safety and economic performance and for integration into cleaner production programmes (Ashford and Zwetsloot, 2000; Kletz, 1998).

Biodigesters for Cleaner Farming Systems

Biodigesters have been usually viewed as a means to generate combustible gas from waste organic matter. Increasing emphasis on the sustainable use of natural resources

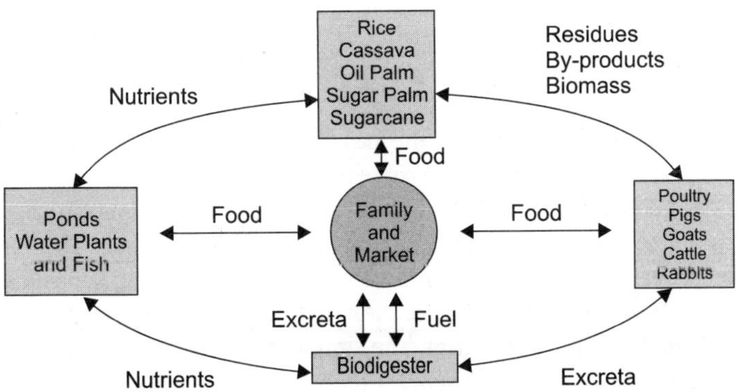

Fig. 1.2 An integrated farming system (After Preston, 2005)

in farming systems has led to biodigesters being considered specifically for their potential role in the recycling of plant nutrients. This not only reduces dependence on inorganic fertilizers but also makes it easier to grow organically (Preston, 2005).

The introduction of a low cost plastic biodigester made from tubular polythene film has brought the technology within reach of many end users. As its installation process is quite simple, farmer-to-farmer extension of the technology has been facilitated. Integration of the biodigester within the farming system has shown that the biodigestion process produces substantial improvements in the value of the livestock manure as fertilizer for crops as well as for water plants or fish cultivation in ponds. Sustainability of farming systems necessitates an intimate relationship among the various interacting components for the conversion of solar energy and soil nutrients into food of animal and plant origin (Fig. 1.2). If properly integrated into the farming system, a biodigester can:

- Provide a source of fuel for cooking and lighting and reduce the need for fuelwood and the work of collecting it. Cooking with biogas leaves cooking utensils much cleaner, and the absence of smoke improves the health of women and children who spend much of their time in the kitchen and often suffer from respiratory problems and eye irritations
- Improve the quality of the manure put into the biodigester and yield high-quality fertilizer for crops as well as plants or fish raised in ponds
- Substantially improve the sanitary conditions and hygiene in the farmyard and reduce the spread of parasites and potentially harmful bacteria by eliminating and de-contaminating manure and organic waste from the farmyard
- Improve the environment by decreasing dependence on fuelwood. Use of biogas also reduces the emission of methane (a greenhouse gas contributing to global warming) into the atmosphere

Design and Construction

Many biodigesters have been engineered with a focus on maximizing gas production and efficiency. There has been little change in the basic design of the floating canopy system developed in India or the liquid displacement system developed in China (Preston, 2005). Unfortunately, these systems are costly. Further, their construction can only be done by skilled artisans, this has limited their wide adoption.

Recently developed polythene tubular biodigester technology (Bui et. al., 1997) is an inexpensive, simple way to produce gas by small-scale farmers (Fig. 1.3). It can be used in rural or urban areas, and low or hilly lands. There are more than 30,000 users of this technology in Vietnam (Preston, 2005). Subsidies are not needed for the purchase of the construction materials, which can be found in most of the towns in developing countries. The simplicity of the installation process has promoted farmer-to-farmer extension.

An essential component of the tubular plastic system is the installation of a reservoir for the gas, preferably in the roof space in the kitchen, as close as possible

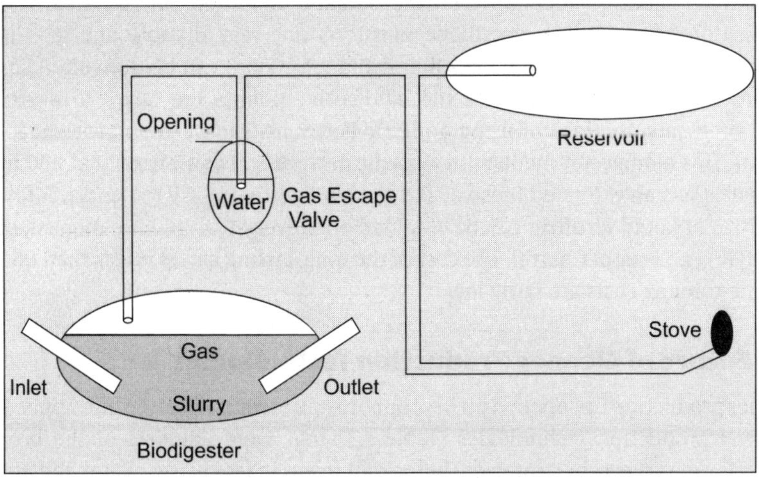

Fig. 1.3 Schematic drawing of biodigester (After Preston, 2005)

to the stove where the gas is to be used. The gas pressure in the biodigester is quite low, so if the biodigester were placed some distance away from the kitchen, the flow rate along the gas line will be too slow to maintain the flame in the stove. Having the reservoir close to the point of usage ensures that friction losses in the short distance from the reservoir to the stove remain minimal and it is easy to pass a string around the reservoir to increase the pressure (Preston, 2005).

On the negative side, there is relatively fragile nature of the polythene film and the inefficient mode of operation as compared with more sophisticated biodigesters. But the construction cost of the plastic biodigester is very low as are the demands on skills for construction. The cost of the double-layer polythene film is only around US $ 10.00 and replacement takes about three to four hours. All the other components can be used again when the polythene is changed (Preston, 2005).

Biodigesters for Producing High Quality Fertilizer

One simple biodigester can be made from a tubular polythene sheet. This sheet, with a minimum length of five metres, is placed on a flat surface. The two ends are closed around two PVC pipes (40 cm long, with a diameter of 10 cm) with rubber strings made of an old bicycle tube. A plastic soda bottle (1.5 litres) is then cut in half and each of the halves are inserted and glued into the respective PVC pipes, closing one and leaving a small opening in the other. Before closing the biodigester, farmers fill it with equal amounts of water and manure from cattle or other ruminants. It is then closed and allowed to ferment for two to three months. The gas produced during fermentation can be released by opening the screw lid of the top half bottle. The cost of this "stomach" model varies between US $16-25, depending on the quality of the polythene sheet used. It produces as much as 200 litres of liquid fertilizer once every three months, depending on the climatic conditions in the area (Osorio, 2005). Unfortunately, the polythene plastic is not very durable and it is often damaged by animals. Its handling (filling and emptying) can be difficult. Also, the discarded plastic materials from the biodigester pollute the farm. To overcome these problems, the idea of using a plastic barrel instead of the plastic sheet was floated. This biodigester made with a plastic barrel also has a capacity of 200 litres. The barrel has an extended lifespan and the biodigester is easy to handle. A total of 100 litres of liquid fertilizer can be obtained once every two to three months, or up to 400 litres a year per barrel. The cost of the long-lasting barrel is less than US $35, and the running costs are fairly low.

The Future of Cleaner Production Technologies

Cleaner production has opened up new opportunities for innovation and application of novel production technologies (Table 1.3) that were adjuncts of the broader search for management strategies that would result in less waste, water and energy consumption, and less use of hazardous chemicals (Freeman, 1995; OECD, 1995).

A clear focus on the technical aspects of cleaner production technologies promotes efficiencies, functional optimization and waste avoidance in industries and government facilities. However, it is usually the management and use of production technologies that is a central objective in striving towards environmentally superior performance. Cleaner production means much more than changing the materials and equipment of production, and no effective integration of broader social and work quality values into our conception of cleaner production has so far been achieved (OECD, 1995; Geiser, 2002).

The recent technology advances recorded in adopting cleaner production have been incremental and cautious. Yet the larger marketing opportunities generated by cleaner production initiatives have also catalysed some technology innovation. Thus, powder coatings, aqueous cleaning systems, fluxless soldering, counter-current rinsing, mechanical paint stripping and water-based inks have all been developed and promoted as cleaner alternatives to conventional process technologies (Geiser and Griener, 2001; Geiser, 2002). Many of these innovations have come from innovators in the production industries themselves or from undercapitalized entrepreneurs.

Table 1.4 lists some rapidly developing current areas of technology that offer opportunities for cleaner production (Jaworski and Minns, 2001). One rapidly developing area with a focus on environmental performance is green chemistry (or sustainable chemistry). It is defined as the utilization of principles that reduce or avoid the use or formation of hazardous substances in the design, manufacture and application of chemical products (Anastas and Warner, 1998). Green chemistry offers many new directions for chemical synthesis, catalysis, reactions and degradation. Since it directly addresses the chemistry of materials and production processes, it offers valuable opportunities to advance cleaner production.

Table 1.3 Conventional Cleaner Production Technologies (After Geiser, 2002)

Waste Reduction Technologies Involve various operation improvement technologies that reduce likelihood of spoils, leaks, accidents, contamination and unwanted volatilization. These technologies range from simple devices such as lids and covers to more complex couplings, connectors and valves and to sophisticated single-vat batch processing equipment.
Energy Efficiency Technologies Include energy-efficient pumps, fans and blowers, reduced friction surfaces, energy-conserving conveyors and materials transport vehicles, and energy-efficient heating and cooling systems.
Processing Efficiency Technologies Involve various physical, electrical or chemical sensors and process control devices that permit more effective monitoring and process management.
Cleaner Material Technologies Chemical substitutions may include simple "drop-in" replacements or more complex toxic substance replacements involving alternative catalysts and reagents, as well as conversions from liquid to solid material processing and solvent-base to water-based cleaning or processing.
Recycling and Loop-closing Process Technologies Employ separation technologies that permit materials to be cleaned or treated so as to permit recycling and reuse. For example, distillation, filtration and extraction technologies.
Cleaner Products Longer life, adaptable, materials and energy-conserving, easily recycled, and non-hazardous products reduce waste and environmental burdens throughout a product's life cycle.
Cleaner Product Management Technologies Materials separation technologies enhance product recycling. Returnable packaging, containers and shipping cartons permit product take-back and reuse or re-manufacturing.

Table 1.4 Developing Technologies Providing Cleaner Production Opportunities (After Jaworski and Minns, 2001; Geiser, 2002)

Sustainable Energy Technologies New technologies provide opportunities for processing at ambient temperatures and pressures, reducing the need for heating and cooling, and increasing the options for renewable and self-generating energy sources. Photovoltaic and wind energies are developing rapidly, so are fuel cells and hydrogen-based sources.
Chemical Processing Technologies Innovations in chemical synthesis and processing technologies involve new (non-metallic) catalysts and reagents that process in supercritical fluids, new means of enhancing selectivity and new "zero-waste" processes that close water and materials cycles so as to reduce or eliminate wastes and material inputs.
Information Technologies Advanced information technologies provide new opportunities for monitoring, measuring, managing data and communicating information that can improve processing technologies performance. New information technologies also offer new directions for reducing product consumption and increasing service substitution and servicing.
Biotechnologies The life sciences offer many new opportunities for the use of renewable materials and for bio-processing and biodegradation. Enzyme-catalysed reactions and harvesting materials from microbial processes offer new routes to chemical synthesis, particularly in the production of acids, bases and polymers.
Nanotechnologies Recent advances in nano-scale technologies offer opportunities for more selective, finer scale and more tailored production with the potential for low and no waste processes.

2

Business Imperatives and Retail Trade

Retail trade is the selling of individual units or small lots directly to multiple customers (usually the ultimate consumers of the goods) by businesses. Global retailing has grown into a huge industry with annual sales of roughly US $ 7 trillion (Fig. 2.1). The world GDP is around US $ 30 trillion.

Wal-Mart is the world's largest retailer, with over 1.3 million employees' worldwide (255,000 of them outside the United States) and turnover of US $ 218 billion in 2001. The sector also includes major manufacturers who sell directly to end-customers via retail outlets (often franchised, like car dealerships) and over Internet. This type of sales shows a growing trend. Retailers are also selling services such as dry cleaning or manicures.

The world's 200 largest retailers account for 30 per cent of worldwide demand. With regard to the three main aspects of sustainability, department stores, discount stores, supermarkets and hypermarkets, convenience stores, etc., account for most of the industry's economic and environmental impact.

Retailing is a highly competitive sector. Besides prices, competition is in terms of location, selection of merchandise, how the merchandise is displayed, attractiveness of the store or other outlet and intangibles such as reputation.

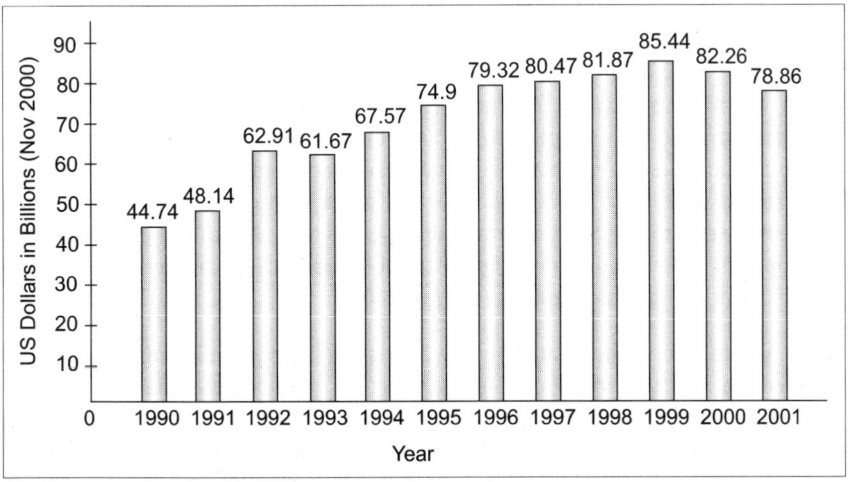

Source: World Federation of Direct Selling Association

Fig. 2.1 Global retail sales 1990–2001

Many retailers voluntarily report on their economic, environmental and social policies, practices and performance. The challenge of sustainable retailing is to ensure that internal operations are sustainable and to motivate suppliers to produce sustainably and customers to consume sustainably.

The UNDP Human Development Report of 1998 pointed out that global spending on advertising (even in developing countries) has been growing more rapidly than the world economy, and that the retail sector plays a major role in the development process.

The main role of retailers is to respond to consumer demand and to offer them a variety of different products. Being the link between manufacturers and consumers, retailers communicate consumer demand upstream to suppliers and deliver products and services downstream to their customers. They influence changes in production processes and consumption patterns, and can pressurize producers to adopt more sustainable consumer choices. Many retailers understand the importance of sustainable development strategies and can drive demand for "green" products. One instrument supporting sustainable development strategies is corporate social responsibility (CSR). The CSR concept promotes company actions beyond basic legislative requirements (Durieu, 2003).

Lessons can be learnt from the different initiatives undertaken in the retail sector to support sustainable consumption and production patterns:

1. There is a latent demand for ethical and green products, which is not always reflected in consumers' purchasing decisions. Producers and retailers should satisfy this emerging demand when it becomes more concrete. The role of the retail sector is primarily to offer educated consumers a choice.
2. Retailers can propose or even influence consumer choices in favour of greener products, but success can come only through educated consumer demand.
3. With a view to enable consumer choice, retailers should insist on open and continuous information from manufacturers on production processes with respect to energy consumption, use of raw materials and pollution. Some retailers who buy chiefly from manufacturers show a commitment to sustainable development. New supplier codes have been drawn up, setting out processes and product requirements to help manufacturers to minimize impacts through product's life cycle. Some supermarkets refuse to stock products which they feel are environmentally unacceptable. Others have launched their own brand range of more environmentally sustainable products to capture a niche in an increasingly saturated market (Durieu, 2003).

Coop (a consumers' cooperative) is Switzerland's biggest seller of environment friendly and fair trade products (Zogg, 2003). Its sustainable retailing efforts are focused on four "ecological flagship" labels covering organic and free-range food, organic textiles and cosmetics, fair trade goods, and other products. The success of these products largely depends on close cooperation with suppliers. As the guarantor of product quality, Coop makes use of guidelines, codes of conduct, certification and independent monitoring to ensure that products are up to the standard. In case of organic cotton textiles, Coop has helped farmers in developing countries to make the transition from conventional methods to organic ones.

Green Business

Business people, traders and consumers are increasingly becoming aware of the unsustainability of producing the goods we use everyday. Such concerns have prompted earnest efforts to develop green businesses that produce products which are environmentally and socially sound. Many environmentally conscious or "green" companies have demonstrated that adopting and implementing the principles of sustainable development and environmental protection are not only good for public relations and employee morale but also sales (Table 2.1).

Table 2.1 Desirable Goals for an Eco-efficient Economy

Avoid introduction of hazardous materials into air, water or soil
Measure prosperity by natural capital accrued by productive means
Measure productivity by how many people can be gainfully and meaningfully employed
Measure progress by buildings that are free from smokestacks or dangerous effluents
Declare the countless complex governmental rules which now regulate toxic or hazardous materials, as being unnecessary
Do not produce anything requiring constant vigilance from future generations
Marvel at the abundance of biological and cultural diversity
Try to live on renewable solar income rather than on fossil fuels

Green business flourishes because consumers are concerned about the ecological consequences of their purchases. There has been an explosive growth of green commercial products. *The National Green Pages,* published by Coop America, lists more than 2,000 green companies, including eco-travel agencies, telephone companies that donate profits to environmental groups, entrepreneurs selling organic foods, shade-grown coffee, straw-bale houses, paint thinners made from orange peels, sandals made from recycled auto tires, and a variety of hemp products, including burgers, ale, clothing, shoes, rugs and shampoo. Organic food marketing has now grown to a US $ 7 billion market segment. In the USA, natural-care health and beauty products earned US $ 2.8 billion in sales in 1999 out of a US $ 33 billion industry.

Corporations that swear by eco-efficiency and cleaner production include such reputed giants as Monsanto, 3M, DuPont and Duracell. By gainfully and judiciously applying the concept of three Rs' (reduce, reuse, recycle), these and other companies have saved a lot of money and also gained welcome publicity.

Japan, a world leader in environmental technology, has long recognized the tremendous economic potential of green business. It sells some US $ 10-12 billion worth of equipment and services annually, marketing advanced waste incinerators, pollution-control equipments, alternative energy sources and water-treatment systems. The highly efficient "hybrid" gas-electric cars which have recently been introduced in the US market became available in Japan much earlier.

Fair and Green Trade

Over the last two decades, "fairly traded" products have become widely available and quite popular. Prompted by the realization that consumers' buying power can mean much. Several groups have launched fair trade schemes whereby farm produce (initially coffee), was bought directly from farmers. Farmers get a better price and a guaranteed market, and consumers can buy fairly traded products. The international market for 'fair and green' products has been growing stronger and stronger and now ranges from coffee, tea, chocolate, fruits and spices to textiles and several other bulk commodities. Its mainstreaming is happening at the consumers' end.

Quality control is a critical issue with organic, green and fair trade products. Certification is necessary but is expensive for small-scale producers. There is need to find solutions to address financial obstacles and to make certification procedures more strict. Community guarantee schemes and possible 'alternative' certification mechanisms may be worth exploring in this context. Another important issue relates to short supply chains, where (groups of) consumers buy directly from (groups of) producers. There is a real need to document examples of the benefits of fair trade and disadvantages or difficulties encountered, if any. As green and fair trade initiatives take off around the world, it will become important to weigh the pros and cons and critically examine local, regional and global opportunities.

Responsible Consumerism

Responsible consumerism can promote green business if everybody practises the things listed below with a view to reducing humanity's ecological impacts:

- Live simple life. Analyse if we really need material goods to make life happy
- Rent, borrow or barter whenever possible. Reduce the amount of stuff consumed. Instead of buying rent certain machines and equipment rarely used.
- Recycle or reuse building materials such as doors, windows, cabinets or appliances. Shop at salvage yards or thrift stores
- Cultivate the habit of buying green products as far as possible. Look for efficient and durable materials produced in environment-friendly manner. Subscribe to any available clean energy programmes
- Buy locally grown products made under humane conditions
- Think about the total life cycle cost of the things we buy, especially big purchases like cars. Try to account for environmental impacts, energy use, disposal costs and initial purchase price
- Invest in socially and environmentally responsible companies, funds or green businesses where we can spare some money for investment

Role of the Retail Sector

At the World Summit on Sustainable Development (WSSD) held at Johannesburg in 2002, many governments stressed the need to work actively to speed up the shift to sustainable production and consumption. While all countries must be involved in this effort, the developed countries ought to lead the way. UNEP has also emphasized the need to strengthen work on sustainable consumption, promote design of sustainable products and services, reinforce voluntary work with business sectors, increase support for awareness raising campaigns, enhance the image of green lifestyles and increase the availability and impact of information in this area. With a view to promoting more sustainable production and consumption, UNEP accords high priority to its activities with the retail sector, which can help in changing consumption patterns. The importance of the retail sector can be exemplified by some of our simple retail transactions, e.g., involving a cotton shirt or a packet of ground coffee or a major purchase such as a leather and wood armchair or a refrigerator-freezer. Even these ordinary transactions can exert several environmental and social effects for instance:

1. **Resource Use** From metal extraction to consumption of water and wood (the latter may often involve unsustainable forestry)
2. **Energy Use** By a car, if one drives to the store where the purchase was made, by the store itself, any vehicles involved in delivering products to the store, by wholesalers, and by the furniture assembler, leather producer, animal breeder, woodcutter, fabric mill, coffee packager and so on. And we should not forget the CO2 emissions resulting from energy consumption
3. **Waste Generation** Any packaging that is thrown away when the buyer gets home represents just one end of a long stream that begins in the mine, the coffee grove, the farmyard or the forest
4. **Adverse Land Use Effects** For example, damage to the landscape from big stores and surface sealing by their huge parking lots in many developed countries
5. **Risk of Health Effects** For consumers as well as store and supplier employees, if the use of hazardous substances (e.g., arsenic in wood treatment, heavy metals in appliance manufacture) is involved

In the recent years, some companies in retail sector have willingly started to green their operations. They play an important role in global efforts to make consumption and production patterns more sustainable. This can be done by developing logistical strategies for transport, making life cycle assessments (LCAs) of packaging, adopting Environmental Management Systems (EMS), marketing green products, making sure that sustainability is duly respected in supply chain management, drawing up codes of conduct for suppliers, carrying out consumer and employee awareness-raising campaigns, demanding innovation in building design and energy systems. Most companies have found that such efforts prove beneficial.

Indeed, some big retailers encourage and participate in the development of robust and widely applicable indicators of corporate responsibility and accountability.

Changing Unsustainable Consumption Patterns & Production

It is not possible to achieve global sustainable development without making fundamental changes to the way societies produce and consume. While nations should promote sustainable consumption and production patterns, the developed countries must take the lead. In fact, all countries can benefit from this process, if they take into account the Rio principles, including *inter alia*, the principle of common but differentiated responsibilities as set out in Principle 7 of the Rio Declaration on Environment and Development. Unsustainable consumption and production patterns must be changed. This would require the actions set out below.

A 10-year framework of programmes should be encouraged and promoted in support of regional and national initiatives to speed up the change towards sustainable consumption and production. It promotes social and economic development within the carrying capacity of ecosystems. This is done by addressing where appropriate, delinking economic growth and environmental degradation through improving efficiency and sustainability in the use of resources and production processes, and reducing resource degradation, pollution and waste. All countries should take action (but developed countries must take the lead). They should take due cognizance of the development needs and capabilities of developing countries, through mobilization of financial and technical assistance and capacity-building for developing countries. This would require actions at all levels to:

1. Identify specific activities, tools, policies, measures and monitoring and assessment mechanisms, including where appropriate, life cycle analysis and national indicators for measuring progress. It should be kept in mind that standards fixed by some countries may be inappropriate and entail unwarranted economic and social cost to developing countries.
2. Adopt and implement policies and measures aimed at promoting sustainable patterns of production and consumption, applying, *inter alia*, the Polluter Pays Principle (PPP) as described in Principle 16 of the Rio Declaration on Environment and Development.
3. Develop production and consumption policies to improve the products and services provided, while reducing environmental and health impacts, using where appropriate, life cycle analysis.
4. Develop and adopt, where appropriate, on a voluntary basis, effective, transparent, verifiable, non-misleading and non-discriminatory consumer information tools to provide information relating to sustainable consumption and production, including human health and safety aspects. These tools should not be used as disguised trade barriers.
5. Increase eco-efficiency, with financial support from all sources, where mutually agreed, for capacity-building, technology transfer and exchange of technology

with developing countries and countries with economies in transition, in cooperation with relevant international organizations (UNDESA, 2003).

Much greater investment in cleaner production and eco-efficiency is needed in all countries through, *inter alia*, incentives and support schemes and policies directed at establishing appropriate regulatory, financial and legal frameworks. This may include actions at all levels to:

1. Establish and support cleaner production programmes and centres and more efficient production methods by providing, *inter alia*, incentives and capacity-building to assist small and medium-sized enterprises, particularly in developing countries, in improving productivity and sustainable development.
2. Collect and disseminate information on cost-effective examples in cleaner production, eco-efficiency and environmental management and promote the exchange of best practices and know-how on environmentally sound technologies between public and private institutions.

The issue of production and consumption patterns should be properly integrated into sustainable development policies, programmes and strategies, including where applicable, into poverty reduction strategies.

Industry should be encouraged to improve social and environmental performance through voluntary initiatives, including EMS, codes of conduct, certification and public reporting on environmental and social issues, duly considering International Organization for Standardization Standards and Global Reporting Initiative guidelines on sustainability reporting, bearing in mind Principle 11 of the Rio Declaration. Also, workplace-based partnerships and programmes, including training and education programmes, should be developed.

There is an urgent need on the part of the governments, regional and international organizations and other relevant stakeholders to implement the relevant recommendations and conclusions adopted by the Commission on Sustainable Development concerning energy for sustainable development, including the issues and options listed below, bearing in mind that in view of the different contributions to global environmental degradation, states have common but differentiated responsibilities. This would include actions at all levels to:

1. Mobilize provision of financial resources, technology transfer, capacity-building and diffusion of environmentally sound technologies according to the recommendations and conclusions of the Commission on Sustainable Development.
2. Integrate energy considerations, including efficiency, affordability and accessibility, into socio-economic programmes, especially into policies of major energy consuming sectors, and into the planning, operation and maintenance of long-lived energy consuming infrastructures such as public sector transport, industry, agriculture, urban land use, tourism and construction sectors.
3. Develop and disseminate alternative energy technologies with the aim of giving a greater share of the energy mix to renewable energies, improving energy

efficiency and greater reliance on advanced energy technologies, including cleaner fossil fuel technologies.

4. Combine judiciously more efficient and renewable energy resources, greater dependence on advanced energy technologies, including advanced and cleaner fossil fuel technologies, with the sustainable use of traditional energy resources, which could meet the growing need for energy services in the long term to achieve sustainable development.
5. Diversify energy supply needs by developing advanced, cleaner, more efficient, affordable and cost-effective energy technologies, including fossil fuel and renewable energy technologies (hydro included), and their transfer to developing countries on concessional terms. The global share of renewable energy sources should be substantially increased with the objective of increasing its contribution to total energy supply, recognizing the role of various targets as well as initiatives. It should be ensured that energy policies are supportive to developing countries' efforts in poverty eradication.
6. Reduce flaring and venting of gas associated with crude oil production in developing countries. Indigenous energy sources and infrastructures should be developed and utilized for local usage. Rural community participation, including local Agenda 21 groups, should be promoted with the support of the international community, in developing and utilizing renewable energy technologies to meet their daily energy needs to find simple and local solutions.
7. Speed up development, dissemination and deployment of affordable and cleaner energy efficiency and energy conservation technologies and the transfer of such technologies, in particular to developing countries, on favourable terms.
8. Phase out any subsidies that inhibit sustainable development.
9. Promote an integrated approach to policy-making at national, regional and local levels for transport services and systems in promoting sustainable development, including policies and planning for land use, infrastructure, public transport systems and goods delivery networks.

This should be done with a view to providing safe, affordable and efficient transportation, increasing energy efficiency, reducing pollution, congestion and adverse health effects and limiting urban sprawl, taking into account national priorities and circumstances. This include the actions listed below:

1. Implement transport strategies for sustainable development, reflecting specific regional, and national and local conditions to improve the affordability, efficiency and convenience of transportation as well as urban air quality and health, and reduce greenhouse gas emissions, including development of better vehicle technologies that are more environmentally sound, affordable and socially acceptable.
2. Develop sustainable, energy efficient multi-modal transportation systems, including public mass transportation systems and better transportation systems both in rural and urban areas, with technical and financial assistance for

developing countries and countries with economies in transition. The quality of roads will need to be improved greatly to make this possible.

Prevent and minimize waste and maximize reuse, recycling and use of environment-friendly alternative materials with a view to minimizing adverse effects on the environment and improve resource efficiency. This could include actions at all levels to:

1. Develop effective waste management systems, with the highest priority placed on waste prevention and minimization, reuse and recycling, and environmentally sound disposal facilities, including technology to recapture the energy contained in waste, and encourage small-scale waste-recycling initiatives that support urban and rural waste management and provide income-generating opportunities, with international support for developing countries.
2. Promote waste prevention and minimization by encouraging production of reusable consumer goods and biodegradable products and developing the required infrastructure.

As proclaimed in Agenda 21, top priority must be assigned to sound management of chemicals throughout their life cycle and of hazardous wastes for sustainable development as well as for the protection of human health and the used and produced ways that lead to the minimization of significant adverse effects on human health and the environment, using transparent scientific assessment procedures and science-based risk management procedures, taking into account the precautionary approach. Developing countries should be supported to strengthen their capacity for the sound management of chemicals and hazardous wastes by providing technical and financial assistance.

India is now making world-class high quality cars, scooters and motorcycles. It can perform well not only in foreign lands but also within the different states of the country itself.

Countries should be encouraged to implement the new globally harmonized system for the classification and labelling of chemicals at the earliest so as to have the system fully operational by 2008. Earnest efforts should be made to prevent illegal international trafficking of hazardous chemicals and wastes and to prevent damage resulting from the trans-boundary movement and disposal of hazardous wastes in a manner consistent with obligations under relevant international instruments such as the Basel Convention on the Control of Trans-boundary Movements of Hazardous Wastes and their Disposal. There is need to promote reduction of the risks posed by heavy metals that are harmful to human health and the environment, including a review of relevant studies such as the United Nations Environment Programme (UNDP) global assessment of mercury and its compounds.

Production Inventory Model

A production process sometimes deteriorates due to ageing or other factors that make units defective during a production run. Lin and Lin (2007) proposed a

production-inventory model for a manufacturing process used to produce a single product in batches to meet a deterministic demand. While the process may be in-control at the start of a production run, it sometimes shifts to an out-of-control state at a random point in time, and a fixed portion of items produced is defective. These defective items cannot be repaired or reworked and must be scrapped with an additional cost. However, it is often possible to repair, rework, or scrap these defective units depending on the characteristics of product and process.
Lin and Lin (2007) considered the impact of an imperfect production process (IPP) on the classical Economic Manufacturing Quantity (EMQ) model (Erlenkotter, 1989) in which the defective units have to be scrapped with an additional cost. This model is the most commonly applied inventory control model in industry. Rosenbaltt and Lee (1986) studied an EMQ model with an assumption that after the process shifts from an in-control state to an out-of-control state, a fixed percentage of items produced will be defective until entire lot is completed (Silver et. al., 1998).

Lin and Lin (2007) describe models to deal with issues of whether and when a screening process is implemented with a view to determining an optimal production run time that minimizes expected (long-run) average cost per unit of time, including setup, production, inventory holding, screening and defective costs. They developed a numerical approach to seek an optimal solution and derived a closed-form solution based on an approximation to an exponential function. What Lin and Lin considered is an EMQ model for an imperfect production process in a single-machine single-product system subject to scraps.

At the start of each production run, the process is assumed to be in controlled state due to some maintenance that forms part of the set up process. In course of time, the process may shift to an out-of-control state at some random point. Consequently, a fixed percentage of items produced when the process goes out of control will be defective. The elapse time from the beginning of a production until a shift occurs (time-to-shift) is assumed to be a random variable with a known exponential distribution (Kim and Hong, 1999; Lin et. al., 2003).

In one model, a defective item is detected at the demand point and there is no screening during a production cycle. In a second model, a screening process is implemented immediately after the end of a production run. The screening rate is greater than the production rate. All the defective items that are detected are scrapped as a batch and with an additional cost at the end of the screening process. In the last model, all the items produced are effectively screened. The defective items are scrapped in a batch at the end of a production run. The objective for each model is to minimize the expected (long-run) average cost per unit of time including setup, production, inventory holding, screening and defective costs. The object function follows a pseudoconvex relation of the production run time. Possible extensions of these models include allowing shortages to occur, considering a general distribution of the time-to-shift random variable, conducting inspection schedules to reduce the number of defective units, and incorporating the random machine breakdowns in the model (Lin and Lin, 2007).

Product Stewardship

Product stewardship (also known as 'extended producer responsibility') involves producers, brand owners, importers, consumers and all those who handle products, helping to manage the environmental effects of products throughout their life cycle. While this can significantly change the way some industries manage products, it can also introduce incentives to make products less harmful and less wasteful.

Some products cause environmental problems when disposed of. For example:

- Vehicles, computers, cell phones and agricultural chemicals containing hazardous chemicals which damage the environment
- Tyres that are bulky and hard to manage in landfills, if disposed of whole
- Waste packaging that forms a major fraction of the total waste to landfill but contains materials that can be recycled

Numerous industries are willingly adopting the philosophy of taking a "cradle to grave" responsibility for what they produce. Some countries have voluntary programmes based on product stewardship principles that include:

- Use of oil recovery programmes offered by large oil companies to their commercial and industrial customers
- Programme for the management of end-of-life tyres
- Schemes for the collection of old mobile phones and batteries
- Attempts at reducing packaging waste in the packaging sector
- Recovery of old paints by some manufacturers

The water efficiency labelling standards need to be fixed. Registration and labelling for washing machines, dishwashers, taps, toilets, showerheads and urinals deserve urgent consideration. Labelling of such products can allow consumers to know how water-efficient a product is, and thereby contribute to the improvement in water management programmes.

The economics of sustainability appears to be far more complex than the neoclassical (Newtonian) economic approach to economic efficiency. Forest resources provide a good starting point for the economic analysis of sustainability. Kant and Munk (2005) have given a useful critique of neoclassical economic approaches and their limitations with respect to sustainability. Leading economists from different streams of economics have discussed key economic aspects of sustainability and sustainable forest management including complexity, ethical issues, consumer choice theory, inter-generational equity, non-convexities and multiple equilibria. This monograph integrates different streams of economics complexity theory, behavioural economics, post-Keynesian consumer choice theory, social choice theory and non-convexities, suggesting the main features of post-Newtonian economics.

There is need for a new economic theory, rather than a new public policy based on an old theory, to orient humanity towards sustainability. Institutions make up a critical dimension of sustainability and sustainable forest management. Economic analysis of institutional dimension requires an inclusionist rather than an exclusionist approach. Kant and Munk have provided a good critique of neoclassical economic approaches and their limitations with respect to sustainability. Leading institutional economists discuss theoretical perspectives about appropriate institutions for sustainable forest management, markets for environmental services, deforestation and specialization, and some country experiences about Kyoto Protocol, international trade, biodiversity conservation, and sustainable forest management in general. This monograph includes the ideas from old as well as a new institutional economics and discusses the main features of post-Newtonian economics.

Designing Product Service System

The following approaches help in addressing environmental issues and opportunities holistically, and to evaluate or design product service system for reducing potential environmental impacts over the entire life cycle.

1. **Life cycle assessment** Evaluating the environmental burdens associated with a product, process or activity by identifying the energy and materials used and wastes released to the environment, to make environmental improvements.
2. **Life cycle management** An integrated structure of concepts, techniques and procedures to address environmental, economic, technological and social aspects of products and organizations, to achieve continuous environmental improvement from a life cycle perspective.
3. **Design for environment (Ecodesign)** Effective integration of environmental and social issues into product and process design.
4. **Product service systems** A marketable mix of products and services that can fulfil client needs with less environmental impact.
5. **Integrated product policy** To stimulate each phase of a product's or service's life cycle to enhance its environmental performance ranging from natural resources extraction through design, manufacture, assembly, marketing, distribution, sale and use, and onto eventual disposal as waste.

The life cycle approach not only benefits the environment, but also provides new business and employment opportunities that can help alleviate poverty and improve the living conditions of the poor in the developing world.

Today's waste management issues are associated with products. Wastes and pollution from end-of-life products attract greater attention than production wastes and pollution. An example might be end-of-life vehicles and electro-scrap where an enormous increase in amounts of waste is directly linked to the increase in consumption and shortening of the product's cycle.

Primarily, the issue is one of changing the consumption formula that would lead to sustainable development. A product that retains its environmental friendliness throughout its whole life cycle needs to meet consumer requirements. It must not lose its quality and utility and must be safe. Experiences and methodological procedures of cleaner production projects related to production can also be used for product change.

The road from political consensus to day-to-day reality can sometimes be long and complex. The same is also true for the preventive approach to environmental protection. Cleaner production should logically be perceived as a natural and obvious first step towards adopting the proposed measures. It should form a part of other projects and programmes for regional and territorial economic development.

In the course of transition to market economy, certain time lines required by companies/enterprises and their management to acquire economic stability have to be considered. As soon as they achieve this and plan their development, at least on the medium-term horizon, they should start considering options for environmental protection solutions (resulting especially from new legislation and control of its compliance) using voluntary activities. While a stabilized company can identify the advantages of a preventive approach and make the most of it, it has the ability to estimate the benefits of a cleaner production project and accept the implementation of EMS.

In economically unstable companies with obsolete technologies, where a cleaner production project could bring the greatest benefits, the cleaner production strategy is perceived as an unnecessary burden that can wait for sometime. Such companies will not implement cleaner production without support, or may not implement cleaner production without support, or may not finish the project. At the same time, support can be counterproductive, in view of the low standard of management or various other problems, it fails to reduce the environmental load and only postpones the trouble. The knowledge and approaches acquired by employees in the course of cleaner production training can go a long way in minimizing social instability.

Small and Medium Enterprises

In many countries, small and medium-sized enterprises (SMEs) are the fastest-growing part of the economy, so they account for major shares of exports and many new jobs. SMEs have for long accounted for the great majority by number of businesses and at least for half of all jobs. Most SMEs are in the service sector and about one-quarter are engaged in manufacturing produce and constitute a good share of industrial wastes. SMEs are especially strong in sectors characterized by high intensity of resource use and by polluting emissions.

Very often SMEs do much less than large businesses to address their adverse environmental impacts. This may be because many SMEs happen to be micro enterprises; many of them in developing countries suffer from inadequate training, know-how, technology and money. In some countries, SMEs are not even covered by occupational health and safety laws.

All over the world, many SMEs lie into the gray area termed the "informal sector", and are usually run by women. With regard to the sustainability of their operations, SMEs are under less pressure from consumers or NGOs than are big firms. For many SME managers, upgrading technology, management and marketing to meet stiff price competition attracts the highest priority.

SMEs can play a substantial role in providing products and services that require smaller amounts of materials and energy. In this way, they help in changing the way consumer needs are met. Some SMEs may even be better than large companies in this context. This is particularly true for the most innovative businesses in chemical management, energy efficiency services and renewable energy supply.

Many tools and approaches can be environmentally and economically beneficial to businesses, including SMEs, provided that SMEs can be persuaded to adopt them. SMEs must increasingly cope with sustainability demands from large companies whose supply chains they feed.

Not only government and businesses but also financial institutions and business development services should actively provide SMEs with triple-bottom-line tools and approaches. SMEs need not always be required to file full-scale sustainability reports, with comprehensive coverage of environmental matters, e.g., including impacts on biodiversity, these requirements may be much more relevant to large companies or businesses. Most SMEs may not be capable of complying with such complex systems as ISO 14001. However, "SME-friendly" EMS should be developed to help in the introduction of SMEs to integrated management systems and certification schemes.

If big business forms the "backbone" of national economies, SMEs make up the flesh and sinews. While the social and environmental impacts of the largest companies have aroused serious concerns in many countries, the cumulative impacts of SMEs are just as high, if not higher.

The term "SMEs" is usually restricted to non-primary enterprises and does not include farming, fishery or the extractive industries. Nevertheless, small-scale fishery and mining operations, for instance, are very important economically in many countries, especially the developing ones. The European Union categorizes SMEs as "micro" (one to nine employees), "small" (up to 49) and "medium-sized" (up to 249). For the OECD, companies with up to 19 employees are "very small", those with up to 99 are "small" and those with 100 to 499 are "medium".

In Canada, the United States and Mexico, definitions of "small businesses" vary from sector to sector and are based on the number of employees (a maximum of 500 employees bing the commonest cut-off point) or annual gross income. Brazil defines a "micro enterprise" as having up to 19 employees and a "small enterprise" as one having between 20 and 99, with a gross annual income under 1.5 million Reals in each case. In India, a "small enterprise" is one whose total investment in plant and machinery is not more than 7.5 million Rupees.

In Europe and many other nations, most SMEs are micro in size and fall in the tertiary sector. A 2001 Survey of EU member states; Iceland, Liechtenstein, Norway and Switzerland showed that 25 per cent of SMEs were involved in manufacturing and construction and the remaining were engaged in wholesale and retail commerce, transport and communications, and business and personal services.

The Triple Impact

About 90 per cent of all the businesses in the world are SMEs and are responsible for 50-60 per cent of total employment. In OECD countries, 95 per cent of businesses are SMEs with 60-70 per cent of jobs in these businesses. In 1998, 66 per cent of European jobs and 46 per cent of those in the US were in SMEs. OECD figures show that SMEs create the largest number of jobs in the rich world. SMEs account for over half of India's GDP. Around 51 per cent of shipped manufactured goods in Japan are produced by SMEs.

Besides their growing economic significance, the environmental impacts of SMEs are also growing. In India, SMEs produce over 65 per cent of industrial waste. According to the Foundation for International Training in Canada, a recent survey of 116,300 SMEs in China's Jiangsu Province found 67.7 per cent to be causing serious pollution and 28.5 per cent moderate pollution. Only four per cent appeared to be pollution free (Anonymous, 2003).

SMEs prevail in industries with relatively high resource and emission intensity (e.g., metal finishing, leather tanning, dry cleaning, printing, dyeing, brewing, food processing, fish farming, textile making and chemicals (Hillary, 2000). Many companies in the "sustainability sector" (e.g., eco-services, eco-tourism, triple-bottom-line consulting) are SMEs.

Social Impact

The SMEs sector has registered good growth worldwide due to the following reasons:

- Regional shifts in employment location, sometimes associated with "downsizing" related to globalization or with the dismantling of large state-run entities in the transition economies and China, which may prompt mid-career employees to create businesses of their own
- Growth in franchising
- Subcontracting and outsourcing by large companies

In some countries, environmental health and safety inspections of SMEs are either not required or are quite lax or loose. Both SMEs and the informal sector encounter similar barriers to the adoption and practice of environmental and social responsibility (UNIDO, 2002), some of which are:

- Insufficient technology, expertise, training and capital
- Lack of initiatives suitable for small companies
- Inadequate understanding of what the business case is for SME environmental and social responsibility
- The need to deal with more pressing matters such as upgrading the quality of technology, management and marketing
- Price competition
- Limited consumer pressure

In general, environmental activities are more difficult for SMEs to carry out than those concerned with social responsibility, probably because many SMEs are intimately integrated into the social fabric. Relationships with the local community and with employees and their families mean much to them while environmental issues seem less urgent and unnecessarily expensive (Anonymous, 2003).

The strongest influence on SMEs is that from multinational corporations (MNCs), which motivate their suppliers to meet social and environmental standards as a precondition for doing business. Such standards may be presented either as codes of conduct for individual supply chains or as certification systems for the entire sector.

In a globalizing economy, liberalization, deregulation and privatization not only redraw the lines between state and market, but also change the basis on which private enterprise may contribute to public wealth. As a result of the growing legal, ethical, social and environmental expectations of various stakeholders, demand for corporate environmental and social responsibility (CESR) has been increasing. Because of growing pressure from governments, consumers, NGOs, research institutions and financial markets, some companies have started implementing CESR or Socially Responsible Business (SRB) processes such as public commitment to standards, community investment, continuous improvement, stakeholder engagement, and corporate reporting on social and environmental performance (Kuhndt et. al., 2003).

CESR refers to business decision-making linked to ethical values, compliance with legal requirements, and respect for people, especially workers, employees, local communities and the environment. IT industry encourages business to operate in such a manner that it can meet or exceed the ethical, legal, commercial, public and environmental expectations of society.

Debates and responses concerning CSR's objectives chiefly focus on large transnational corporations (TNCs) serving northern markets but operating in developing countries. Mega companies have developed and implemented various tools and instruments like codes of conduct, EMS and sustainability reports. Application of CESR issues has a positive impact on business's financial performance.

Like MNCs, SMEs are increasingly expected to take responsibility for their own environmental and social impacts to understand different stakeholders' interests and demands, and to demonstrate responsible behaviour through greater transparency. Several factors can either hinder or promote adoption by smaller companies of strategies promoting CESR. To overcome barriers for adoption of such strategies, available tools need to be adaptable to small and medium companies' requirements. Promising initiatives have been launched in some areas, with TNCs being a key stakeholder group (Kuhndt et. al., 2003).

SMEs make up the backbone of many supply chains and are crucial in enabling these chains to meet future standards. The global trend of larger enterprises to reorganize, downsize and outsource, and increase in franchising and self-employment is very likely to increase the number of SMEs in the future. Also, many TNCs are becoming more and more interested in having reliable, flexible and innovative partners that make high quality, environmentally sound products that meet social standards (Kuhndt et al., 2003).

In general, SMEs are mostly focused on internal issues such as staffing, employee skill development, team building and motivation within the organization. Usually, community and environmental initiatives are designed to impact on employees. Internal benefits appear to be the most distinctive feature of SMEs involvement in CESR activities. Many SMEs are traditionally well integrated in the community through their employees and their limited spatial mobility. However, with regard to strategic actions, SMEs do not address local civil and cultural issues as systematically as the TNCs do (UNIDO, 2002).

One general management problem relating to CESR improvement strategies is that improvement opportunities are viewed as only process-related. Product-oriented CESR strategies, e.g., upgrading the quality of technology, management and marketing are very often not brought within the scope of SMEs. The financial benefits of product management beyond the factory gate are not quite apparent for many SMEs and CESR may mainly be perceived as a cost factor (Kuhndt et. al., 2003).

Often, it is possible to engage SMEs in CESR by providing suitable tools and improved communication and cooperation with relevant stakeholders. In this context, the suitable tools are those that can reflect their specific needs and enhance information base cost effectively. Economic performance measures/indicators are being widely accepted as management tools and are being used throughout business. Considerable effort has been made recently to develop CESR indicators for use by large companies. Regrettably, appropriate indicators for SMEs have not been the primary focus of any research. This gap needs to be bridged. There is an urgent need to strengthen the role of SMEs as a source of innovation towards sustainable development (Kuhndt et. al., 2003).

Chemical Industry Initiatives for Environmental Health Protection in SMEs

BASF, a German chemical company, has taken commendable initiatives for its products. It insists on compliance with its high standards among suppliers, which are usually SMEs (Kranz and Sagasser, 2003). BASF manufactures and sells over 8,000 products worldwide to customers in 170 countries. Its product range includes chemicals, plastics, coating systems, dispersions, agricultural products and fine chemicals, and crude oil and natural gas. To reduce the impacts on humans and environment from production, storage, transportation and distribution, use and disposal of these products, globally valid standards have been adopted and implemented. This has been done along with an environmental management system that applies even beyond the factory gates. The company expects its suppliers also to comply with these standards. BASF joined the global chemical industry's initiative over 10 years ago and is committed to its goals and principles, including continuous improvement in environmental protection, product stewardship, occupational safety, occupational health, process safety, emergency response, distribution safety and dialogue.

BASF have installed wastewater plants and filter systems to reduce environmental emissions. It builds highly efficient power plants that help conserve natural resources and reduce CO_2 emissions. It has adopted occupational safety programmes to further reduce accident rates and to promote workplace safety.

High safety standards are maintained for transportation of BASF products. The company's logistics partners are assessed by independent third parties using standardized assessment criteria. It is only after BASF has ensured that carriers meet their safety requirements that it entrusts them with their products.

A bonus system for safe working practices has been established for contractors involved in repair work, transportation or installation. To enhance occupational safety among contract staff, bonuses are awarded for safe working practices. If an employee of a contract company breaches BASF's safety regulations, the bonus will fall by a certain predetermined percentage. Forgetting to wear safety gloves, for example, costs 2.5 per cent of the contractual sum. A lost-time accident exceeding three days lowers the bonus by 30 per cent and the sum is credited to BASF. The higher the contractors' safety levels, the more bonus is collected by the employees/ contractors at the end of the project. This new system may help BASF to achieve the target of zero accidents by 2010, while enhancing the safety and health awareness of the contract partners (Kranz and Sagasser, 2003).

In 2002, BASF bought more than 10,000 different raw materials from some 5,000 different suppliers worldwide. The share of raw materials coming from non-OECD countries has been increasing in keeping with rising economic growth in Asia.

Besides price, quality and supply security, compliance with specific environmental, safety and health standards is a precondition for business partnerships with raw materials suppliers. BASF purchasers not only negotiate terms, but also evaluate the risk associated with each product and supplier. For this purpose, a safety matrix (Fig. 2.2) has been developed.

According to this matrix, all the raw materials purchased are classified into one of the three hazard categories according to their environmental, toxicological and safety properties, i.e., A (safe), B (harmful) and C (e.g., toxic). Sodium chloride would

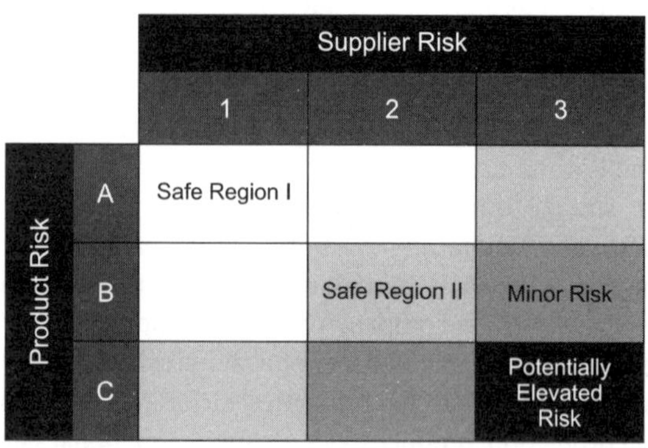

Fig. 2.2 Safety matrix for raw materials purchased (After Kranz and Sagasser, 2003)

come in category A. Ethanol is classified as highly flammable and would therefore be in category B. Methanol, a highly toxic alcohol, would be in category C. Suppliers and potential suppliers are at first classified according to their location in OECD or non-OECD countries. As a first approach, the risk of non-compliance with environmental and safety standards may be higher in non-OECD countries.

Products/producers assigned a C3 rating are potentially high-risk and therefore subject to extra careful scrutiny. In this case, BASF officers, along with environmental health and safety (EHS) experts, visit the supplier and carry out an EHS access-stipulated standards (e.g., regarding wastewater treatment, maintenance, safety equipment and quality control).

If a potential supplier's facilities meet the BASF requirements, the product/producer is upgraded to a C2 rating, and regular purchasing of raw materials from this supplier begins. If certain suppliers do not meet the EHS requirements, BASF encourages and helps them in solving the problems by developing a joint action plan. Once the improvements called for in the action plan have been put into practice, regular purchasing of raw materials can commence.

Some typical measures implemented by suppliers are:

- Installation of emergency showers (body or eye showers)
- Installation of sprinkler systems
- Usage of personal protection equipment (e.g., hard hats, safety glasses, appropriate boots, gloves, masks, respirators with external oxygen tanks)
- Implementation of action plan in case of an emergency

In some countries, e.g., Hungary, SMEs' overall environmental performance is now improving with growing awareness on the importance of environmental management among the environmental authorities and other businesses (e.g., important customers). However, there are a number of barriers to the implementation of environmental management systems by SMEs, and many of these companies still give low priority to environmental issues. There is no doubt that cleaner production and other preventive approaches have several advantages over end-of-pipe approaches.

Nanotechnology and the Expanding Supply Chains

A recent inventory has identified over 500 nano-enabled consumer products. This may be an underestimate – there are many products that are not readily identifiable as nano-enabled but use materials or structures at the nanoscale. These products are finding their way into a wide range of markets ranging from electronics to paints, cosmetics and medicines.

In the UK, 23 national nanocentres have been established in the key areas of nano-micro fabrication, nanomaterials, nanometrology and nanobio. The micro and nanotechnology (MNT) network is focusing on building capability and promoting networking across the supply side. The MNT network is currently transitioning into a knowledge transfer network (KTN). The challenge of the new nanotechnology KTN is to stimulate the user side and link the supply and demand sides together. Besides, these initiatives the department for trade and industry has intensified interest in nanotechnology (Pitkethly, 2007).

The number of companies engaged in nanotechnology is growing substantially as they incorporate nanotechnology into their products. Furthermore, more and more new start-ups are coming up.

Because the UK has a robust presence in almost every market sector, the potential for using nanotechnology as a driver for growth is considerable. The European Commission's Seventh Framework Programme has a significantly enhanced budget for nanotechnology. SMEs can now claim up to 75 per cent of eligible costs so that this will become an attractive source of development funding. The new nanocentres, and also recent investment in university equipment and infrastructure, have produced a welcome facilities base. The new KTN is committed to support the exploitation and commercialization of MNT through informing linking, and facilitating innovation and collaborations between suppliers and users with the aim of building a vigorous MNT community. What matters most is that everyone involved in nanotechnology recognizes that what the UK has in place now is the platform to accelerate growth but that this will need support and encouragement not only from government departments, regional development agencies and the finance houses, but also from the various companies through their expanding supply chains (Pitkethly, 2007).

Industry Perspectives in Sustainable Production and Consumption

Special challenges confront developing countries in promoting cleaner production and sustainable consumption. Environmental degradation is an issue around the world but has more severe impacts in developing countries. While MNCs operating in the developing world may use cleaner practices, local SMEs cannot. Consumption patterns imported from the developed world have a substantial impact on lifestyles and the environment in developing countries.

To create the right conditions for industry to promote sustainability, governments must prioritize local and regional action programmes, emphasize cost-effective approaches to pollution and waste treatment, and introduce market-based economic instruments. Ultimately, it is the market that will drive industrial behaviour in developing countries. Besides data collection, the case for sustainable development will need to be couched in concrete business language.

L'Oréal, a leading manufacturer of cosmetics, has banned the use of heavy metals and pesticides throughout its products' life cycles. The alternatives cost more, but consumers are willing to pay more because they like L'Oréal products. Doing a good business and environmental responsibility need not be mutually exclusive. Good business and environmental responsibility go hand in hand.

Cleaner production professionals should share the various success stories relating to environmental and cleaner production with businesses, particularly

SMEs, in the countries where they operate. There is need to discuss about tools and outcomes in a language that can motivate business. The way to meet the challenge of promoting cleaner production to SMEs is to provide affordable access to pollution prevention technology. Also, involving workers in cleaner production is crucial.

Governments can play an important role in enabling small companies to make their consumption and production patterns more sustainable. The Netherlands government has adopted a new sustainable consumption and production agenda for the near future. Although it does not differentiate between small and large companies, many issues addressed in the Dutch debate on corporate responsibility concern SMEs. An important element of Dutch policy is the categorization of companies according to their readiness to use sustainability approaches. The primary focus is on encouraging voluntary approaches. Further regulation is not seen as a solution. Companies are responsible for their own progress (Blaauwbroek, 2003).

In the Netherlands, companies have been classified according to their environmental and social outlook (Fig. 2.3).

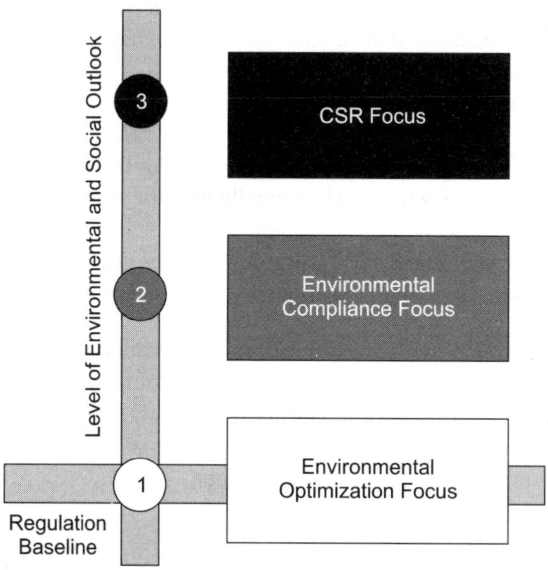

Fig. 2.3 Company classification

Environmental Compliance Focus

The group includes companies that focus on compliance with regulations. It includes those that fall below current regulatory standards and those that comply, often reactively. For these companies, a combination of permitting, reporting, inspection and enforcement is the most practical approach.

Environmental Optimization Focus

Businesses in this group work proactively to meet their legal obligations or even perform beyond them. They actively seek ways to improve their environmental strategies. Many of these companies voluntarily sign sector-level agreements called "environmental covenants"; each covenant rests on a framework and a jointly developed action plan for meeting environmental targets. The covenant obliges companies to produce an annual environmental report (Blaauwbroek, 2003). Covenants now exist in the following 11 industrial sectors: basic metals and chemicals, dairy, metal products and electronics, textiles and carpets, paper and cardboard, printing, concrete and cement products, abattoirs and meat products, rubber and plastics, and oil and gas.

These sectors cover over 20,739 enterprises, which account for 90 per cent of all industrial pollution in the Netherlands. Among the tools included in the covenants are EMS. Covenants can help increase uptake of EMS by SMEs. The existing covenants have been developed as follows:

- Each sector specifies its integrated environmental targets for 2000 and 2010
- The regional licensing authorities and the sector sign an agreement representing the sector-wise plan
- A consultative committee made up of representatives from industry and/or trade associations, the licensing authorities and concerned ministries, provides workbooks on Best Available Technology (BAT) for the sector, coordinates and reviews implementation, reports annually on progress, and acts as a solution provider
- In consultation with the licensing authorities, each company draws a four-year company environmental plan incorporating the sector's BAT targets

Covenants attract much feedback from users, with industry generally being very supportive of the agreements. The participating companies benefit financially through incentives or rebates. A company that buys new machinery with substantially low energy consumption, or with the latest technology for emission reduction, is entitled to extra tax reductions on the investment.

CSR Focus

Companies under this category are concerned not only with their environmental impact, but also with their societal impact and their "licence to operate", which means that they must get the support of stakeholders. Without such support, they lose the credibility to produce and sell. There is a strong connection with reputation management and they look for possibilities to improve the whole system.

VROM is a group of ministries (Development Cooperation, Housing, Spatial Planning and Environment). It works mainly with or on behalf of the first two groups. Many SMEs come in the first group. There are rather fewer in the second group and a very few in the third.

The Netherlands strongly implements environmental policy to reach its sustainable development goals. It has four paths for transitions, towards sustainable biodiversity, sustainable energy supply, sustainable agriculture and sustainable mobility. Focus on CSR does not mean less concentration on the first two groups. It rather means that CSR is considered as a top level, difficult process of managing transitions. At this top level, it is impossible to regulate or even foresee the business practices to be promoted.

Environmental Management in Micro and Small Enterprises

Many micro and small enterprises find it difficult to deal with environmental issues because they lack adequate financial, technical and human resources to implement environmental control measures. Although they often realize the importance of environmental issues, they usually have little knowledge or experience of environmental management. Furthermore, public opinion gives much less attention to the environmental, health and safety issues of micro and small enterprises than to those of larger companies. Many small SMEs do not consider their environmental impacts very significant as compared to those of bigger companies.

Small Businesses: Triple Bottom Line Performance

Although SMEs must increase their efficiency to sustain their market position, they often lack the time, money and information to critically evaluate their own activities, set targets. Thus, continuously improve products and services, economically, socially and environmentally. Existing international environmental management schemes are too complex to be used by SMEs. This means that in order to move towards sustainable development, business must recast their behaviour. In this case, companies start from various stages of development and corporate culture with respect to environmental and social issues (Fig. 2.4). The following phases may be distinguished (Klinkers et. al., 1999; Geibler and Kuhndt, 2002).

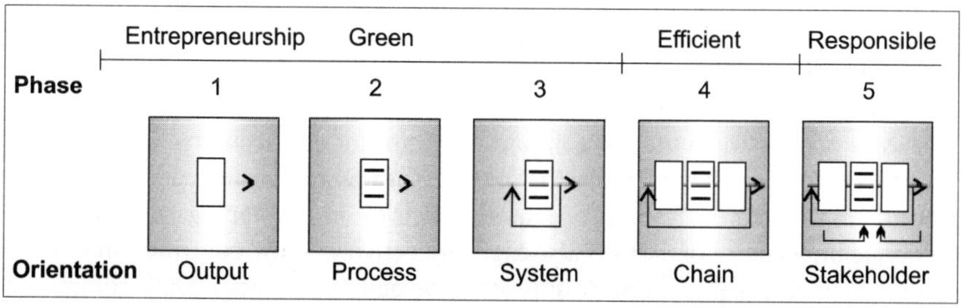

Fig. 2.4 Phases of sustainable business development (After Klinkers et. al., 1999, and Geibler & Kuhndt, 2002)

1. **Phase 1 (Output-oriented)** Errors can be detected after they have been made, companies may be labelled reactive with respective to the environment
2. **Phase 2 (Process-oriented)** Focus is on the production process and its management and major mistakes can be corrected
3. **Phase 3 (System-oriented)** The entire organization, including support processes and their management, are the focus of performance improvement measures and a system is created to control production processes that aims at preventative measures, including corrective actions if mistakes occur
4. **Phase 4 (Chain-oriented)** In contrast to the previous phases, which are focused internally, the emphasis is on external effects within the market and companies relate their whole organization to other parties in the product system; in a cooperative manner, win-win situations are created for the entire chain
5. **Phase 5 (Stakeholder-oriented)** Companies base their vision and policy on stakeholder expectations, and show a commitment of responsibility towards society (Geibler and Kuhndt, 2002)

The sequence of the different phases, from green to eco-efficient and then to responsible entrepreneurship is usually the route taken by most of the companies aiming towards sustainable development. At first, they address internal environmental issues. Then they look beyond their companies' boundaries to address environmental issues in the product chain and still, further along, to include stakeholders such as the community and NGOs (Geibler and Kuhndt, 2002). Sometimes, it is not necessary to focus first on internal environmental management before moving along the chain. Companies can occasionally start directly with, for example, Phase 3 or 4.

Many SMEs remain at an early stage of environmental management but due to increased pressure from public procurement agencies, central wholesale organizations or industrial companies within the product chain and authorities, environmental and social concern is now gradually increasing. In business-to-business customer relationships, information demand regarding general environmental and social management, use of environmentally and socially sound technologies, and products' environmental and social impacts during their life cycle is greater than ever before. Assisting SMEs in improving their economic, environmental and social (triple bottom line or TBL) performance is the major and challenging task of information providers on the international, national, regional and especially local level (Geibler and Kuhndt, 2002).

SMEs happen to be the most important sector for any economy. Their work is strongly customer-oriented. In the EU, about 90 per cent of all enterprises are SMEs that account for 70 per cent of economic activities. In developing countries, the economic importance of SMEs is also high. Collectively, SMEs' contribution to total industrial environmental impacts appears to be quite substantial. SMEs commonly dominate such resource and emission intensive sectors as metal finishing, leather tanning, dry cleaning, printing and dyeing, brewing, food processing, fish farming, textile manufacturing and chemical production (Hillary, 2000). The majority of

SMEs in developing countries and countries in transition still lack awareness of their own environmental and social impacts and those of their lax management of such issues. But they are certainly essential for realizing policy targets like "Factor 4/10" (Weizsäcker et. al., 1997). Being mobile, flexible and innovative, they have a crucial role in the implementation of cleaner products and services.

SMEs are very important in defining product chains for future demands and making high quality, environmentally sound products. An integrated management system including TBL performance measures should help improve business-to-business customer relationships along the chain, reduce risks resulting from external effects and inefficiencies, and reduce costs (Geibler and Kuhndt, 2002). Most SMEs view environmental improvement as a costly burden. Being primarily concerned with short-term economic survival, they seldom seek environmental information or support (UNEP-DTIE, 1997).

According to Geibler and Kuhndt, the following measures could be taken by larger companies to promote environmental improvements in SMEs:

- Incremental approach to implementation, with potential rewards
- Incremental certification, with certificates issued at every step
- Joint EMS and group certifications
- Mentoring by larger companies

Sustainable development broadly depends upon cooperation within a dynamic SME sector that is environmentally and socially aware. The information and tools provided to SMEs need to be designed specifically to meet their needs. The nature and extent of the TBL performance information required by SMEs depends on their level of interest and the strategic level of the decision. Broad distinctions can be made by considering the following:

- Compliance with legislation and agreement made between parties (environmental legislation, covenants, international treaties)
- Market-oriented considerations (competitive advantage, pressure from customers)
- Pro-active economic considerations (waste reduction, cost-effectiveness, anticipation of future policy measures, environmental liability)
- Ecologically/societal considerations (aiming at sustainable development) (Geibler and Kuhndt, 2002)

Eco-efficiency, Innovation and Beyond

The World Business Council for Sustainable Development (WBCSD) has stimulated further progress by promoting the eco-efficiency concept, which has the following six aspects:

- Reduce the material intensity and the energy intensity of goods and services
- Reduce toxic dispersion

- Enhance material recyclability
- Maximize sustainable use of renewables
- Enhance material durability
- Increase the service intensity of goods and services

Manufacturing industry welcomed the concept of eco-efficiency because by adopting an eco-efficient strategy in the production process companies improve their economic bottom line. Progressive companies introduced eco-design into products to further reduce material and energy use in production processes. This promoted recycling and re-manufacturing possibilities. In future, many business houses plan to introduce information technology and advanced command and control systems ("industrial IT") across the whole industrial process so as to radically change the environment of factory floors in a manner akin to that in which Microsoft has transformed the office environment. This will make production processes more cost-efficient and prove conducive to optimal use of resources while minimizing waste. Processes will be remotely controlled. Employees will no longer need to remain close to the process, thereby eliminating occupational health and safety concerns along the supply chain (Kornevall, 2002).

The top priority for industry should be to find new ways to perform better while using less energy and raw materials and creating less waste. Continuous improvement in these areas can limit the size of the environmental footprint while raising the living standards. The major challenge is to delink environmental degradation from increased production and economic growth through addressing both supply and demand. Such delinking can be achieved by decreasing the growth rate of environmental degradation to a level that is less than the economic growth rate (as it happened in the case of SO_2 emissions). Delinking requires integration of the economic, social and environmental aspects of sustainability and vice versa. It implies adjusting to changes in the quality of economic growth, as well as changes in existing consumption patterns and the lifestyles of developed countries. When well managed, this neither pose a threat to jobs nor means deterioration of life quality. It may actually promote economic growth, the creation of new business opportunities and promotion of human well-being everywhere.

We need to develop new technologies that not only reduce environmental impact but also improve existing products' environmental performance—products that show high economic performance over their complete life cycle. Only if they save time, labour and capital can these products replace traditional and less eco-efficient counterparts (Kornevall, 2002). To be eco-efficient, the entire industrial process from product design and material selection through manufacturing and distribution to waste management should be considered holistically. A life cycle approach can reduce environmental impact, save energy and resources, and reduce waste.

For the industrial sector in general, the greatest environmental impact (99% or more) usually occurs during the useful life of the product, especially for electrical products. Much energy can be saved if product performance increases. Industry uses 50 per cent of all electricity, of which 65 per cent is for electric motors. Conventional motors always run at maximum capacity. Up to 70 per cent of their energy could be saved by varying motor speed according to actual need for energy. Only about five per cent of the world's motors are currently fitted with energy-saving drives (Kornevall, 2002).

Environmental Management Systems

An outstanding advance has been the introduction of EMS: ISO 14001 and European Eco-Management and Audit Scheme (EMAS). An EMS allows a company to integrate environmental improvements into day-to-day work at production sites. It ensures that production sites comply with environmental laws and regulations, and helps in continuously improving environmental performance through concrete actions.

By April 2002, registration of ISO 14001 certifications had reached a level of about 38,000 companies worldwide. Japanese industry is in the lead, followed by companies from the UK, Germany, Sweden and the US. German companies account for 65 per cent of all EMAS certifications. At least 100,000 companies have implemented an EMS without external certification (Kornevall, 2002).

Environmental Product Degradations

These inform customers of a product's total environmental impact. Environmental Product Degradations (EPDs) are based on LCAs, which measure products' environmental impacts over their entire life cycle. These impacts can be measured by analysing material and energy use, as well as emissions and waste, taking all phases of the product's life cycle into consideration.

"Catch 22" – The Rebound Effect

The total impact of many products is determined by their usage. However, manufacturing products that only deliver more per unit of input, with less environmental impact throughout their life cycle, is not enough. They must also pass the market test by being competitive and meeting customer requirements.

According to Kornevall, in view of the "rebound effect", modernization of production, eco-efficiency and the introduction of EMS are not sufficient to achieve sustainability. With higher productivity and less use of material and energy, the prices of products can be reduced and consumers are enabled to purchase more products. Despite taking the right steps during the production phase and providing cleaner and more efficient products, the gain for the environment may be neutralized or reduced by increased consumption—resulting in a net increase in the size of the ecological footprint (Greening et. al., 2000; Pearce, 1998).

This makes it unwise to consider only the production side in measuring sustainability. Consumption and lifestyles need to be included as well. To attain sustainability, new ways should be found to produce products and services which meet our needs while limiting the ecological footprint. To find new sustainable solutions, consumption and production will have to be integrated. While efficiency strategies involve linear thinking about lowering inputs for a given activity, sustainability strategies are concerned with finding new ways to meet human needs, focusing on the idea of product service systems required to meet these needs and on the performance required of products. A few examples of these new ways as compared with traditional practices are selling flooring services rather than carpets, clean clothes rather than washing machines, mobility rather than cars, and building systems rather than cement, etc. Creativity will become more important in the coming years.

Eco-efficiency and Innovation

To make development sustainable, we need to design a robust and durable economy that works for everybody. Business can contribute innovation to this common undertaking. Innovations in technology, consumer behaviour, social relations and policy frameworks will have to be combined to ensure success.

Very often our current patterns of development use up more natural resources and create more waste than they should. The Western economy, on the supply side, involves using natural resources to create infrastructure, consumer goods and wastes. On the demand side, these goods are used by consumers, who accumulate or dispose them. Consumers also need energy, water and natural space. This physical process goes hand in hand with a financial process worth trillions of dollars in added value (1998 World GNP)—producers stretch the natural inputs to create value that is reinvested in more productive capacity for payment of taxes levied by the state, and for distribution to consumers. This process remains hooked on growth for three main reasons:

- Increasing world population
- Increasing need for financial security, in view of greater longevity, with a larger proportion of time being spent on education or retirement plans
- Growing aspirations to a better quality of life (QOL), chiefly expressed through shopping, giving and collecting material goods

Tomorrow's Markets

Some key statistics will help assess the direction taken by this process. The World Business Council for Sustainable Development, the World Resources Institute and UNEP selected 19 key trends that will shape the global business environment (WRI, 2001), some of which are summarized below (Fussler, 2002):

- World average life expectancy increased from 47 years in 1950 to 66 years in 2000 and will be around 70 years in 2010
- Rich countries will have a bulge of people aged 50–90 in 2020. In developing countries, the working age population will reach 5.2 billion in 2020

- Seventy-eight per cent of the world population lives below the poverty threshold and the richest one per cent receives as much income as the entire bottom 57 per cent
- World economic output has averaged 2.9 per cent per year since 1975. At this rate it more than doubles every 25 years
- World energy production rose by an average of two per cent per year from 1980–2000. At this rate it would only double in every 35 years
- Water consumption will increase twice as fast as population growth. About 2.3 billion people are now exposed to water stress affecting sanitation, agriculture and freshwater fishing
- In the last decade, there was a loss of two per cent of the world forested area
- Total material throughput of various economies point to efficiency gains in North America and Europe, while most other economies become more material intense to meet the needs of a growing population

In absolute terms, most environmental impacts are growing in the richest countries, but for rest of the world and majority of its population, things are worsening. Consumption and demographics increase the pressure on water and forest resources, yet many continue to remain below the poverty line.

According to the World Wide Fund for Nature's Living Planet Report 2000 (*www.panda.org*), we had already crossed the threshold of available biocapacity in the 1970s. The human ecological footprint now exceeds the capacity of natural systems to regenerate resources at the rate we use them and to absorb wastes at the rate they are generated. And we are going further away from the equilibrium.

What we need is some more change to maintain conditions that might be improving. To achieve another doubling of economic output will also depend on a doubling of efficiency in resources use. But that would leave pollution at existing levels. We also need another fairly substantial efficiency gain to bring down a current overshoot of our biocapacity. However, this would still leave over 75 per cent of the population in poverty. To raise the world's population into a similar QOL range would require a Factor 5 boost to physical efficiency. Whether one prefers Factor 10 or 2 is debatable and will depend on our vision of the world in the next generation, but it seems certain that innovation will form the core of most of the strategies adopted to cope with the trends outlined above, and incremental change alone will not take us where we should be in 2025 (Fussler, 2002).

Eco-efficiency aims at providing affordable products and services for the expanding unsatisfied wants of the global population while reducing environmental impacts. Successful business innovation rests on four pillars:

- Creative people
- A stimulating work environment
- Competence to deliver cost-efficient solutions that exceed customers' expectations and competitors' solutions
- A compelling purpose or vision (Fussler, 2002)

Two good examples of reputed companies that adopted eco-efficiency and turned out important innovations are: Toyota's hybrid technology engines for the Prius, a car that doubled energy efficiency in just three years from concept to commercial launch, and Aventis Pasteur which creates affordable vaccines for immunization in poor countries (Holliday et. al., 2002). Innovative corporate practices in the area of the environment usually increase international competitiveness, and innovative products that prove useful under conditions of environment scarcities are sure to have a tremendous market potential. In this context, we may safely bet on dematerialization, energy and fresh water conservation, safe and healthy food, also on meeting the needs of the billion poor people for sanitation, health and housing. We may bet on mobility with little or no carbon combustion, on agriculture without nitrates run off, on knowledge, skills and new partnerships rather than mines, oil fields or ore smelters (Fussler, 2002).

Although energy is expensive, its high price only is not enough to tilt consumers greatly towards technologies that would save them costs and energy. Hybrid powered cars or compact fluorescent light bulbs have a price premium that is soon recovered after a few months of use. At the current price level of energy or road and parking access (if any), most consumers lack an incentive for change. In most cases eco-efficient products and services meet an early-adopters and fringe market situation rather than flooding the market to establish dominant eco-efficient consumption patterns.

Beyond Eco-efficiency

While eco-efficiency gains are critical to sustainable development, they are not sufficient; they must also affect the behaviour of many producers and consumers. For this they will have to outcompete less efficient solutions in the marketplace. But being human arrangements, markets reflect human conventions and preferences. For millennia, societies have been ignoring the value of water, forest and clean air. Rather, state subsidies were granted for using fossil fuels, agriculture and transport intensity. Myers and Kent (2001) estimated the world's total subsidies towards unsustainable practices to be approximately US $ 1,900 million, with the lion's share going to road transport; our market signals and subsidies nourish the belief that we can afford to overuse water, energy or natural space! While the disastrous economic consequences of pollution and the mountains of wastes are underestimated, dissociated or delinked from those who generate them; clean air, stable climate, fresh water security, abundant fish stocks and marine life, pollinating insects or the stratospheric ozone shield convey no direct price signals and hence their value is not noticed in monetary terms. Meanwhile, consumers and suppliers continue to misuse common goods without an economic penalty. In a "free" albeit distorted market, if governments can provide a competitive premium for eco-efficient solutions, it would certainly change the status quo for the better (Fussler, 2002; Von Weizsäcker et. al., 2003).

"Core and Shell" Approach to Building Projects

Some principles of eco-efficient construction can be applied in many building projects. The real estate's entire life cycle is carefully considered, from site acquisition to a building's anticipated demolition. The "core and shell" concept separates business buildings into the shell (the real estate itself) and the adaptable core (the business operations), which differ with respect to their expected life cycle (Kuisma, 2003). Some important factors are the versatility of the shell and the adaptability of the systems inside. The objective to minimize energy changes and other costs in the building's life cycle for environmental and economic reasons. When energy consumption and premises' adaptability are managed and controlled throughout the life cycle, the premises' operating expenses can be kept low while the tenants' competitiveness is increased.

Careful planning can minimize environmental impacts. Eco-efficient construction requires simplification, keeping to the basics, identifying what is essential and appraising possible alternative uses during the life cycle at an early planning stage. Cooperation with various parties and experts will create business premises with a reasonable investment and less than normal costs throughout the life cycle (Kuisma, 2003).

Promoting Socially Responsible Business in Developing Countries

Many large corporations now claim to be taking steps to improve their environmental and social performance through the use of voluntary initiatives such as codes of conduct, environmental certification and reporting, social audits, fair trading schemes and social investment programmes. There is much debate about the potential and limits of voluntary initiatives for improving the social and environmental record of big business companies, as well as their role in developing countries, where companies may not be subjected to the same types of pressures and market opportunities that encourage responsible business in the richer industrialized countries.

One of the most controversial topics in the field of economic development is the regulation of international firms. The process of developing a multilateral framework for regulation has been slow and lopsided. While some steps taken in areas of investment, taxation and competition strengthen the rights of TNCs, there has been no attempt to develop a regime that balances property rights with obligations linked to labour and environmental issues. What is needed is a more balanced global social contract, particularly in view of the limits of both voluntary approaches and regulatory regimes based exclusively on domestic legislation.

In Singapore, a fairly high degree of corporate environmental responsibility has been achieved, due as much to the relatively strong capacity of the government to enforce legislation as to purely voluntary initiatives. Nevertheless, low levels of community awareness of environmental issues and a weak environmental movement have mitigated the pressures on corporations to adopt voluntary initiatives. These pressures have been more apparent in Malaysia where corporate environmental responsibility has tended to be limited by weak enforcement of legislation. In Singapore, compliance with environmental legislation is relatively high. In Malaysia, however, the adoption of EMS has stimulated improvements, in the absence of resources to ensure regulatory compliance.

Ecology of Overshooting Human Economy

Sustainability requires living within the regenerative capacity of the biosphere. One way to measure the extent to which humanity actually satisfies this requirement is to translate human demand on the environment on the basis of existing data, into the area required for the production of food and other goods, together with the absorption of wastes. Wackernagel et. al., (2002) adopted this approach. Their findings indicate that human demand may well have exceeded the biosphere's regenerative capacity since the 1980s. According to this preliminary and exploratory assessment, humanity's load corresponded to 70 per cent of the capacity of the global biosphere in 1961, and grew to 120 per cent in 1999.

Humanity's Use of the Global Biosphere

The human economy depends on the earth's natural capital, consisting of ecological services and natural resources. When the natural capital is extracted beyond its regenerative capacity, it depletes. This depletion may be detected through comprehensive resource accounting that compares human demand to the biological capacity of the globe.

By using consumption estimates to calculate humanity's appropriation of the biosphere's Net Primary Productivity (NPP), Vitousek et. al., (1986) concluded that the human economy co-opted organic material equivalent to 40 per cent of the NPP of terrestrial ecosystems in 1980. Fischer-Kowalski and Hüttler (1998) developed the concept of "societal metabolism" by using material flow analysis as a macro indicator for the environmental performance of societies. Although UNEP (1999) and WRI (2000) described human impacts on various ecosytem types in detail, both reports lack an aggregated summary of the impacts. Others have focussed on certain subcomponents of the biosphere, such as carbon cycles, freshwater use and the nitrogen cycle, or assigned approximate monetary values to the ecological services that humanity depends on (Costanza et. al., 1997). Wackernagel et. al., (2002) identified a wide variety of human uses of nature measured, and expressed in units that allow comparison of human demands with nature's supply of ecological services.

These global accounts extend assessments of the "ecological footprint" of humanity (Wackernagel et. al., 1999; 1999a) are based on following six assumptions:

1. It is possible to keep track of most of the resources humanity consumes and of the wastes it generates.

2. Many of these resources and waste flows can be measured in terms of the biologically productive area needed to maintain these flows (resource and waste flows that cannot are excluded from the assessment).
3. By weighing each area in proportion to its usable (i.e., of economic interest) biomass productivity, the different areas can be expressed in standardized hectares. These standardized hectares, termed "global hectares," represent hectares with biomass productivity equal to the world average productivity that year.
4. Because these areas stand for mutually exclusive uses, and each global hectare represents the same amount of usable biomass production for a given year, they can be added up to a total representing the aggregate human demand.
5. Nature's supply of ecological services may also be expressed in global hectares of biologically productive space.
6. Area demand can exceed area supply. For instance, a forest harvested at twice its regeneration rate appears in the accounts at twice its area. This phenomenon is called "ecological overshoot" (Catton 1980; Odum, 1997: Wackernagel et. al., 2002).

The above approach allows measuring the ecological impact of humanity as the area of biologically productive land and water required to produce the resources consumed and to assimilate the wastes generated by humanity, under the predominant management and production practices in any given year. Human demand on nature, as also nature's supply, changes over time because of innovations in technology and resource management, changes in land use, and cumulative damage of past impacts (Wackernagel et. al., 2002).

Wackernagel et. al., considered the following six human activities that require biologically productive space:

- Growing crops for food, animal feed, fibre, oil and rubber
- Grazing animals for meat, hides, wool and milk
- Harvesting timber for wood, fibre and fuel
- Marine and freshwater fishing
- Accommodating infrastructure for housing, transportation, industrial production, and hydro-electric power
- Burning fossil fuel

In each category and every year for a 40-year time series, they calculated both human demand and existing capacity, relying on publicly available government data sources, and using conservative estimates where uncertainties exist. Their findings are summarized below:

1. Growing crops require the most productive land of all. According to FAO (1999), about 0.5 billion hectares of cropland exist worldwide—1.3 billion hectares of cultivated crops and 0.2 billion hectares of unharvested land that supports temporary pastures and fallow land, failed plantings and shoulders, shelterbelts, and other uncultivated patches.

2. Grazing animals require pasture. A permanent pasture (3.5 billion hectares currently) is "land used permanently (five years or more) for herbaceous forage crops, either cultivated or growing wild (wild prairie or grazing land)" (FAO, 1999). The demand for pasture for each year was calculated by estimating the metabolic requirement of populations of five major classes of livestock—cattle, sheep, goats, equines and camels, and then subtracting dietary needs met from cultivated feeds and crop residues from the total dietary requirement to obtain the amount supplied from grazing.
3. Timber is harvested from natural forests or plantations. According to the FAO's Forest Resource Assessment (FRA) 2000, there exist 3.8 billion hectares of such forest worldwide, which suffered an annual deforestation rate of 0.2 per cent between 1990 and 2000 (FAO, 2000).
4. Fishing requires productive fishing grounds. Of the total ocean area, six per cent is concentrated along the world's continental shelves and provides over 95 per cent of the marine catch (Pauly and Christensen, 1995), roughly translating into 2.0 billion biologically productive hectares of the earth's 36.3 billion hectares of ocean area. Inland waters make up an additional 0.3 billion hectares. Wackernagel et. al., (2002) used FAO fish catch figures including by-catch, and compared them to FAO's "maximum sustainable yield" figure of 93 million tonnes/year (FAO, 1996; 2000). The 93 million tonnes were then expressed as their primary production requirement (PPR) per hectare, according to the 1996 mean trophic level and by-catch composition of 25 categories of fish, mollusks, crustaceans, and other aquatic animals. Annual Landings were calculated by deducting aquaculture from production in these 35 categories, yielding the wild harvest. The harvest was also converted into a PPR and compared with the sustainable PPR, documenting the effect of fishing down food webs, as described by Pauly et. al., (1998).
5. Creating infrastructure for housing, transportation, industry and hydroelectric power results in built-up land whose area is very difficult to track by satellite imagery. So, an estimate of 0.3 billion hectares, a minimum estimate of the extent of infrastructure worldwide today, was used and it was assumed that built-up land replaces arable land. Built-up area was estimated by consulting data from SEI (1998) and EC (2000).
6. Burning fossil fuel enriches the atmosphere with CO_2. The area requirement was calculated by estimating the biologically productive area needed to sequester enough carbon emissions to avoid an increase in atmospheric CO_2. Because the world's oceans absorb about 35 per cent of the CO_2 emissions from fossil fuel combustion (IPCC, 2001), Wackernagel et. al., and accounted only for the remaining 65 per cent, based on each year's capacity of world-average forests to sequester carbon. This capacity was estimated by taking a weighted average across 26 forest biomes as per reports by the IPCC and the FAO. The sequestration capacity will change in the future. Some sequestration and oceanic absorption may even be reversed. Also, sequestration rates may decrease as more and more

forest ecosystems reach maturity. Eventually, afforestation will saturate so that the net rate of CO_2 uptake becomes zero (Wackernagel et. al., 2002).

Aggregating Impacts

Wackernagel et. al., aggregated the impact components by adjusting the land and sea areas according to their bioproductivities and multiplying each land use category by an "equivalence" factor. These factors scale the area of each category of space in proportion to its maximum potential crop yields as estimated in the Global Agro-Ecological Zones (GAEZ) of the FAO and the International Institute for Applied Systems Analysis (IIASA, 2000). The GAEZ was used to determine the agricultural suitability index (SI) of each major land area. In the case of fisheries, an SI was created by comparing the ability of fishing grounds to provide animal protein with that of pasture. For each year, the equivalence factor of each of the area types was determined by dividing its SI by the global average SI (Wackernaget et. al., 2002) The global average area (of a given year) was assigned the equivalence factor of 1. The actual area of bioproductive space and those adjusted with the equivalence factors add up to the same global total. Once the human impacts are expressed in such "global hectares," they are aggregated into one number: the biologically productive space required by a given human population (Table 2.2).

Table 2.2 Summary of Equivalence Factors, Humanity's Area Demands, and Earth's Biological Capacity in 1999 (per capita) (After Wackernagel et. al., 2002)

Area	*Equivalence Factor (gha/ha)	Average Global Area Demand (per capita)		Existing Global Biocapacity (per capita)	
		Total Demand, ha (per capita)	Equivalent Total, gha (per capita)	World Area, ha (per capita)	Equivalent Total, gha (per capita)
Growing Crops	2.1	0.25	0.53	0.25	0.53
Grazing Animals	0.5	0.21	0.10	0.58	0.27
Harvesting Timber	1.3	0.22	0.29	0.65	0.87
Fishing	0.4	0.40	0.14	0.39	0.14
Accommodating Infrastructure	2.2	0.05	0.10	0.05	0.10
Fossil Fuel and Nuclear Energy	1.3	0.86	1.16	0.00	0.00
Total			**2.33**	**1.91**	**1.91**

Since 1961, Wackernagel et. al., annually compared humanity's demand for natural capital to the earth's biological productivity, and showed that human activities have exceeded the biosphere's capacity since the 1980s. This overshoot is expressed as the extent to which human area demand exceeds nature's supply whereas humanity's load corresponded to 70 per cent of the biosphere's capacity in 1961, this percentage grew to 120 per cent by 1999. In other words, 20 per cent overshoot means that it would require 1.2 earths, or one earth for 1.2 years, to regenerate what humanity used in 1999.

Aggregate biophysical indicators can gainfully complement an economic perspective. Today, only dominant economic worldview provides valid guidance if one assumes that all individual actors in the market are well informed, but this is not always the case. Farmers can make mistakes, for example, when they only focus on economic aspects of their activity and are unaware of the factors that influence soil erosion or its consequences. The environmental assessment proposed by Wackernagel et. al., could possibly provide a biophysical indicator of sustainability that is easy to determine and may help inform production choices.

Also, the standard economic model of resource use over time is based on the assumption that economic actors are informed of the total availability of a resource to be used overtime, i.e., whether the resource will run out when the price of the resource rises to that of a substitute resource or technology. Biophysical data are not only needed for individual production to be efficient, but also to keep the market itself on an efficient path over time.

Economic theory admits that market prices do not reflect all costs which need to be adjusted by the costs borne by the third parties (the social costs) including costs to future generations, adjustments referred to as "shadow prices." To make such adjustments in market prices, economists need biophysical data. Achieving sustainability is not just a matter of including third party effects but of seeing that future generations have sufficient resource rights. According to Wackernagel et al., the decisions concerning the distribution of rights to resource access should be made on the basis of biophysical data and ethical criteria, not economic values for values derive from the distribution, and not vice versa. Aggregate indicators given by Wackernagel et. al., point to the consequences of the current distribution of resource access within and between generations from which, along with ethical criteria, new distributions of rights might possibly be made.

Eco-procurement

Eco-procurement refers to basing all purchasing decisions and allocation of contracts on environmental criteria, as well as on price and quality, creating a powerful market demand for green production while positively affecting the environment. The concept of eco-procurement and green purchasing attracts considerable interest today. The concerned authorities at all levels should promote public procurement policies that encourage development and diffusion of environmentally sound goods and services.

In fact, public authorities are very influential regulators and market actors. Nevertheless, the tendency of international (trade) agreements to restrict opportunities for local policy makers still exists and needs to be strongly questioned.

Today, markets, products, capital exchange, food, technology, standards and communication networks have become increasingly globalized. Countries rich in products, markets, technologies and capital are progressing rapidly as new opportunities emerge. For developing nations, the economic scenario resulting from the globalization drive has generated some problems as their internal markets are suddenly exposed to international competition. Ziman (1999) studied cultural artefacts and showed that technological evolution is a socio-cultural process. Institutions play an important role in directing technological changes. Developing nations need to evolve the socio-cultural platforms essential for the conceptualization, propagation, and diffusion of innovation. Globalization often exerts novel pressures on developing countries which can lead to unwelcome outcomes. The effects of globalization on less developed countries have in general been adverse because these countries lack strong technological capabilities.

Eco-efficiency in Industry and Science

Eco-efficiency is one of the buzzwords of our time. The term reflects the paradigm shift that has taken place since the 1980s. Rather than regarding ecology and economy as mutually opposing entities, it is now generally agreed that eco-efficient production provides a good opportunity to enhance a company's competitive position in the market. Correspondingly, the general view of industry's role in the sustainable development debate has also changed – rather than being identified as a part of the problem, business is perceived increasingly as a part of the solution. Industry faces a new range of opportunities and challenges in product design, material and supplier choice, producer responsibility for the waste stage, and product image.

Ever since the 1992 Rio summit, corporate environmental responsibility has gone beyond mere complying by increasingly stringent environmental regulation and taking up proactive initiatives. The business and financial performance of companies is seen to depend on being socially and environmentally responsible. Customers do not distinguish between a company and its suppliers. This makes greening the supply chain an innovative idea that is attracting much current attention (Sarkis, 2006).

Integration or collaborative use, of computer technologies across different disciplines through interdisciplinary research and development can go a long way in enhancing an understanding of a variety of specialty areas of forestry, including inventory, remote sensing, information management, modelling and visualization, biometrics, forest and harvest planning, bioeconomics and marketing, and decision science for management. Shao and Reynolds (2006) have provided new insights on how to continue advancing computational technologies in forest management to achieve better the basic goal of sustainable forest management.

A major shift is now taking place towards uneven-aged forest management based on the notion that such stands increase or at least maintain soil fertility, increase biodiversity and improve stand resilience. This tilt in forest management practice renders existing yield tables increasingly unreliable. Among potential alternatives are tree growth models, because they predict the growth of each tree within a forest stand (Hasenauer, 2006).

Plants play a crucial role in purifying the biosphere of the toxic effects of industrial activity. Systematic application of the results of investigations into the metabolism of xenobiotics in plants can make a substantial contribution to planetary well-being. Deep physiological knowledge gained from an accumulation of experimental data enables the sharp differences between the detoxifying abilities of various plants for compounds of different chemical nature to be optimally exploited. Hence, planting could be much more systematically adapted to actual environmental needs than is the case at present.

Current research in tropical forestry faces the challenge of finding strategies to alleviate pressure on remaining forests, and techniques that can enhance forest regeneration and restore abandoned lands, by using productive alternatives that can be useful to local human populations. In addition, sustainable forestry in tropical countries needs to be supported by effective policies to promote and maintain specific activities at local and regional scales.

3

Trade, Globalization and the Century of the Environment

The 20th Century saw a galloping production and extravagant use of energy to meet the ambitious demands of people in advanced countries. A similar trend has caught up in many developing countries as well. Industrial wastes and indiscriminate use of diverse chemicals have played havoc to the environment in the industrialized countries. It is increasing population, poverty, water-borne diseases and nutritional deficiencies and disorders that have negatively impacted the environment in the developing countries. As the large-scale damage to the global environment has crossed acceptable level, it is true mankind changes its wasteful and luxurious lifestyle to a sustainable form otherwise our children may not be able to live on this planet half a century from now. Human activities must be tuned for sustainable, environment-friendly development. The use of non-renewable resources at the present rate must be checked in the advanced countries, and the current rates of environmental pollution in the developing nations must be brought down (Kumar, 2001).

The economy is not an independent system, but an integral part of the earth's natural balance. It has its limitations. Man as an economic agent dealing with his resources, and through his interventions, has transformed the ecosystem structure of nature into utility ecosystems, which may be of four types, all interdependent. Thus, an agricultural ecosystem is just as dependent on industrial urban ecosystems (markets, machines, fertilizers and pesticides, energy supply, agricultural management, capital) due to diverse input relations. Conversely, the urban ecosystems (food and water supply, disposal services) are dependent on the agricultural ecosystems. Local natural ecosystems are overtopped by regional, sometimes global, 'artificial' systems, and so are interdependent. Economic behaviour has to be oriented toward the vitality and productive force of ecosystems.

The economic agents of any given region (or of the world) should only consume as many renewable natural resources as will 'grow back' in nature. Likewise, only the same amount of emissions may be released into nature as it can tolerate, without losing its future processing capacity. Another good way to define sustainable economic growth is the increase in real gross national product (GNP) per capita over time, the increase not being threatened by 'feedback' from either biophysical impacts (pollution, resource problems) or from any social disruption. People should willingly accept some losses or sacrifices in income and affluence, in favour of long-term advantages.

Over the last five decades while global GDP rose by a factor of six, there was a 14-fold increase in trade. The world economy has become more integrated. The growth of world merchandise trade has exceeded the growth of merchandise output almost every year. Figure 3.1 shows the volume of world trade in goods growing by an average seven per cent per year in the 1990s, reaching US $ 6.2 trillion in 2001. This growth was accompanied by international economic integration and by marked changes in the composition and geographical distribution of economic activities (McInnes, 2002).

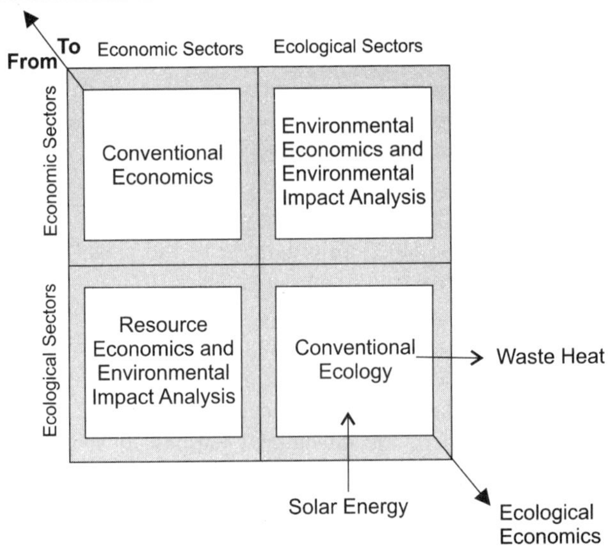

Fig. 3.1 Ecological economics involving interactions between economics and ecological sectors. The overall system is driven by sun and dissipates waste heat (After Costanza, 1991)

Globalization of manufacturing witnessed a particularly strong growth of intra-industry trade, illustrating two key aspects of globalization–specialization and exchange based on product differentiation and economies of scale and production chains extending across national borders.

The enormous increase in world trade was facilitated by marked advances in transport, communication and information technologies that substantially reduced the transaction cost of international commerce, stimulating trade directly (by allowing countries to specialize in production) and indirectly (by allowing production processes to be located in specialized units around the world). The political will to reduce trade barriers has been clear at all levels: at national level, with an explosion of unilateral trade liberalization (often as part of a shift from import substitution to export promotion), at regional level with some 114 regional trade agreements, and internationally through the multilateral trade system, the complex set of trade agreements now being looked after by the World Trade Organization (WTO).

According to McInnes, many environmental consequences of trade result from a growth of world economic output (scale effects), a reallocation of production and consumption worldwide and between sectors (structural effects), and technological development and diffusion (technology effect). Each economic activity is influenced by a combination of these sometimes conflicting effects.

The links between trade and the environment are complex. The positive and negative environmental effects of economic globalization and trade liberalization have strong implications for both trade and environmental policies.

One notable structural effect of trade is that it promotes specialization. Trade usually allows countries to specialize in the goods and services they produce most efficiently. While the economic benefits of trade specialization through increased efficiencies and economies of scale are widely acknowledged, the environmental benefits are highly uncertain.

Even if we assume that allocative efficiency is optimized, the net effect of trade specialization on the local environment can be positive only if expanding export sectors are less polluting than contracting import sectors. In a regional or global environmental context, positive structural effects emanate from maximizing allocative efficiency among nations according to environmental carrying capacities and the efficient use of natural resources. For trade specialization to move towards environmental sustainability, environmental assets should be correctly valued and internalized into market prices. Otherwise, consumers are attracted to underpriced, environmentally harmful products. The companies that specialize in polluting, resource intensive activities will flourish with increasing profits (Nordstrom and Vaughan, 1999; McInnes, 2002).

A recent WTO study (Nordstrom and Vaughan, 1999; McInnes, 2002) found no indication of differences in environmental standards affecting global trade patterns, though capital, labour and natural resource endowments were major factors. Likewise in 1999, the World Bank found that contrary to common perception, developing countries do not specialize in highly polluting industries. They import more pollution-intensive goods than they produce, while the opposite is true for developed countries. Data for the 1980s and 1990s suggests that pollution-intensive industrial activity is increasingly located in countries with more stringent environmental regulations. This points to the classic comparative advantage factors predominating over the differential environmental standards, probably because polluting industries, e.g., refining, chemical industries, and primary metals industries) often are capital intensive, and abatement costs, even in countries with the most stringent regulations, make up only a small percentage of production costs.

Ecological Economics

Historically, both ecology and economics have been viewed as distinct disciplines. While each borrowed some theoretical concepts from the other, they addressed separate issues, utilized different assumptions to reach answers, and supported different interests in the policy process. Ecological economics provides an

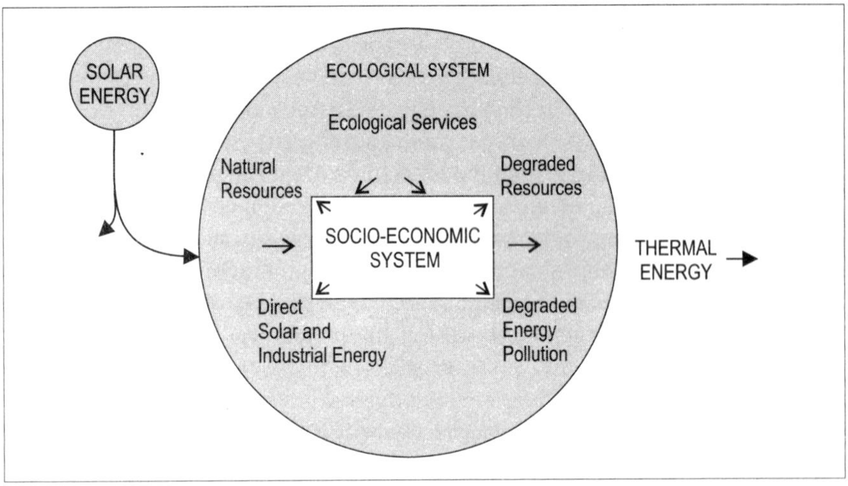

Fig. 3.2 Dependence of economy as part of its life-supporting environment on energy and natural resource inputs for production and consumption and various services generated by ecosystems. Being parts of ecosystems, species sustain those crucial services. If human societies do not recognize their place in the overall system, their activities will continue to cause biodiversity loss, reducing environmental support on which human welfare depends (After Perrings et. al., 1992)

opportunity for economists and ecologists to interact with each other to formulate and implement new economic and environmental policies. Figure 3.1 illustrates the linkages between ecology and economics. Ecological economics has evolved as a transdisciplinary exercise concerned with the sustainable management of the interconnected ecological and economic systems. It is founded on the fact that humanity is very much a part of nature. Keeping the development of socio-economic activities within the resilience of their ecological resource base—locally, regionally and globally—poses a strong challenge for sustainability. Any loss of resilience means that limits for socio-economic development are approached more rapidly. Because limits are not static, human behaviour in tune with the resource base, instead of working to degrade it, will not face limits as rapidly and so keep more options open for development (Kumar, 2001). As per the new economic view, the environment is finite and the economy is a subsystem of the environment (Fig. 3.2).

The Century of the Environment

The large magnitude of human impact on the ecological systems of the planet has brought out clearly that there are intimate connections between these systems and human health, the economy, social justice and national security. Even the concept of what constitutes "the environment" has changed. The urgency of unprecedented environmental and social changes challenges scientists to define a new social contract that can represent a commitment on the part of all scientists to devote their energies and talents to the most pressing problems of today in proportion to their importance, in exchange for public funding (Lubchenko, 1998). Several new and unsatisfied needs of society include more comprehensive information, understanding and technologies for society to move toward a more sustainable biosphere that is ecologically sound, economically feasible and socially just. New basic research, faster, more effective dissemination of new and existing knowledge to policy makers and to the public will be required to meet this challenge.

Space exploration has not only enhanced our understanding of the cosmos, but also given a new sense of our world and ourselves. Scientific research has been advancing explosively on all fronts. And yet, the immediate and real challenges facing us have neither been fully appreciated nor properly acknowledged by scientists. Several striking and specific, identifiable changes are occurring in natural and social worlds around us. The vastness, pervasiveness and importance of these is so great that they require our immediate attention with a view to generating new technologies.

Global Changes and their Causes

One important way in which the world is changing is that we now live on a human-dominated planet. The growth of the human population and the runaway growth in mount of resources used have been altering the earth in unprecedented ways. Through agriculture, fisheries, industry, recreation and international commerce, humans cause three categories of change as they enterprise in:

1. Transforming land and sea—through land clearing, forestry, grazing, urbanization, mining, trawling, dredging, etc.
2. Altering the major biogeochemical cycles
3. Adding or removing species and genetically distinct populations—through habitat alteration or loss, hunting, fishing and introductions and invasions of species (Vitousek et. al., 1997)

Vitousek et. al., (1997), Kates et. al., (1990), Schimel et. al., (1995), Postel et. al., (1996) and Olson (1989) summarized the extent of human domination of the earth in the following six conclusions:

1. More than half of the land surface has been transformed by human actions
2. The carbon dioxide concentration in the atmosphere has increased by nearly 30 per cent since the beginning of the Industrial Revolution
3. More atmospheric nitrogen is fixed by humanity than by all natural terrestrial sources combined
4. More than half of all accessible surface fresh water is put to use by humanity
5. About one-quarter of the bird species on the earth have been driven to extinction
6. Approximately two-thirds of major marine fisheries are fully exploited, overexploited or depleted (Vitousek et. al., 1997)

Far-reaching changes in land use have accompanied industrialization in the past two centuries. One good example is the development and spread of agricultural activities. Important developments include extensive changes in river flow regimes that accompany these activities, as also the accelerating growth of large urban centres (especially in Asia). There is mounting evidence, from both modelling and observational efforts, that such changes exert marked effects on the climate system.

The rates and spatial scales of most of these changes (some new) are on the rise. Novel chemical compounds like chlorofluorocarbons (CFCs) and persistent organic compounds (DOT and PCBs) are being synthesized and released. Very few of the innumerable new chemicals released each year are monitored; the biological effects of most are not known (Postel, 1987).

Many of the above physical, chemical and biological changes lead to further changes in the functioning of the earth system causing:

1. Disruptions to the global climate
2. Depletion of stratospheric ozone
3. Irreversible losses of biological diversity
4. Changes in the structure and functioning of ecosystems around the world (Lawton and May, 1995)

We are modifying physical, chemical and biological systems in new ways, at faster rates, and over larger spatial scales than ever before. Humans have unwittingly started a grand experiment with the planet which may have profound implications for all forms of life on earth. Environmental problems resulting from human activities are threatening the sustainability of the earth's life support systems; some of the gravest challenges facing humanity are the conservation, restoration and wise management of the earth's resources (Lubchenco, 1998).

Nature's "Free" Services

Contrary to conventional economic wisdom, most of the value in the world economy does not come from pulling things out of nature—rather; it comes from the normal functioning of healthy rivers, forests and fields. Fires have been intentionally set in the Amazon Basin in Brazil and in the forests of Sumatra, Borneo, Indonesia and other countries by commercial outfits every now and then, leading to criminal immolation of some of the world's most valuable natural assets. In 1997, a large part of the Amazon Basin in Brazil was blanketed by fire and smoke, over 50 per cent more forest being destroyed that year than in 1996, which in turn had recorded five times fire during a single six-week period in 1995.

For the timber and plantation barons of Indonesia, as for the cattle ranchers and frontier farmers of Amazonia, setting fires to clear forests has become standard practice. To them, the natural rainforests are an obstruction that must be sold or burned to make way for their profitable pulp and palm oil plantations. Yet, these are the same forests that for many others serve as both homes and livelihoods. For the hundreds of millions who live in Indonesia and in the neighbouring countries (Malaysia, Singapore, Brunei, Thailand and the Philippines), it has emerged that without healthy forests, it is difficult for people to remain healthy.

When the smoke finally clears, Southeast Asia and the world has to bear the cost, of impaired health and sometimes death, from both lung diseases and accidents caused by poor visibility. Productivity is lost as factories, schools, roads, docks and airports are shut down (over 1,000 flights in and out of Malaysia were cancelled in September 1997 alone). Crop yields too falls as haze keeps the region in daylong twilight, and the harvests of forest products are wiped out. Timbers (some of the most valuable species in the world) are devoured by flames. Over three-fourths of the world's remaining wild orangutans live on the fire-ravaged provinces of Sumatra and Kalimantan. Some of them, caught fleeing the flames, often become part of the illegal trade. Because of their location, the Indonesian fires, like those in the Amazon, have dealt a heavy blow to the biodiversity of the earth as a whole.

Likewise in the United States, more than 50 per cent of all honeybee colonies have disappeared in the last 50 years, with half the loss occurring in just the past few years. Similar losses have been observed in Europe. Thirteen of the 19 native bumblebee species in the United Kingdom are now extinct. These bees are just two of the many kinds of pollinators and their decline is costing farmers, fruit growers and beekeepers millions of pounds in losses every year.

Both the ravaged Indonesian forests and disappearing bees share a commonality—they are both examples of "free services" that are provided by nature and consumed by the human economy—services that have immense economic value, but that go largely unrecognized and uncounted until they are lost. Many of those services are indispensable to the people who exploit them, yet are not counted as real benefits or as a part of GNP (Abramovitz, 1998).

The "free" services provided by the natural world form the invisible foundation that supports all societies and economies. The oceans provide abundant fish, forests give wood and medicines, insects and other creatures pollinate crops, birds and frogs keep pests in check, and forests and rivers supply clean water. When we need timber, we can cut trees; when we need water we can find a spring or drill a well. It is assumed that clean air will blow the smog out of our cities, that the climate will be stable and predictable, and that the ever-increasing quantity of waste we generate will continue to disappear, if we just take precaution. Nature's services have always been taken for granted. Our economies have relied on the premise that they always will be available for free. We are no different from small children who think that food comes from the refrigerator, and do not realize that what seems free is in reality not so.

By grossly undervaluing natural services, economies provide incentives to misuse and destroy the very systems that produce those services. Rather than protecting their assets, they squander them away. Nature, in turn, becomes increasingly less able to supply the vast range of services that the earth's expanding population and economy demand. The continued erosion of natural systems threatens not only the continuing viability of today's human enterprise, but also the prospects for our continued existence. Sadly, much of the human economy is based on practices that convert natural systems into something simpler, either for ease of management or to maximize the production of a desired commodity. But simplified systems lack the resilience that allows them to survive short-term shocks such as outbreaks of diseases or pests, or forest fires, or even such long-term stresses.

Resilience is destroyed by fragmentation and simplification. Healthy rainforests seldom suffer from fire, as by nature they are too wet to burn. But as they are opened up and fragmented by roads, for instance, they become drier and prone to fire. When fire strikes forests, it is extremely destructive. The fires in Southeast Asia's peat swamp rainforests bring further disruption by releasing long-sequestered carbon into the atmosphere.

Today, the United States and Europe are left with less than five per cent of the original forest area. One-third of Asia's forest has been lost since 1960, and half of what remains is threatened by the same industrial forest activities responsible for the Indonesian fires. In the Amazon, 13 per cent of the natural cover has already been cleared, mostly for cattle pasture. As the natural ecosystems disappear, so do many of the goods and services they provide. Governments and business owners typically feel that the way they can make profit from an ecosystem is to maximize its production of a single commodity e.g., timber from a forest. For the community (or society) as a whole, however, that is often the least profitable or sustainable use. The economic value of other uses, and the number of people who benefit added up can be truly enormous. A forest on the one hand, if not cut down to make space for a one-commodity plantation, can produce a rich variety of non-timber forest products (NTFPs) while providing essential watershed protection and climate regulation, on the other. These uses not only have more immediate economic value but can also be sustained over a longer period of time and benefit more people (Abramovitz, 1998).

Non-timber commodities form only a part of the loss when a forest is converted to a one-commodity industry. There exists a nexus between the two catastrophes of the Indonesian fires and the American and European bee declines since forests provide habitat for bees and other pollinators. They also provide habitat for birds that control disease-carrying and agricultural pests. Their canopies break the force of the winds and reduce rainfall impact on the ground, thereby reducing soil erosion. Their roots hold soil in place, further preventing erosion. In monetary terms, a forest's capacity to protect a watershed alone often exceeds the value of its timber. Forests also act as effective water-pumping and recycling machinery, helping to stabilize local climate. And, through photosynthesis, they generate enough of the planet's oxygen, while absorbing and storing so much of its carbon (in living trees and plants), that they are essential to the stability of climate worldwide (Abramovitz, 1998).

Mangrove forests and coastal wetlands link land and sea. They buffer coasts from storms and erosion, cycle nutrients, serve as nurseries for coastal and marine fisheries, and supply critical resources to local communities. For flood control alone, the value of mangroves has been calculated at $ 300,000 per kilometre of coastline in Malaysia, which is the cost of the rock walls that would be needed to replace them. One force responsible for the recent accelerated loss of many mangroves has been the enormous growth of intensive commercial aquaculture, especially for shrimp export.

The value of a forested watershed emanates from its power to absorb and cleanse water, recycle excess nutrients, hold soil in place, and prevent flooding. When plant cover is removed or disturbed, water and wind not only run across the land, but carry valuable top soil along with them.

Bees

We are not only blind to the value of free products we take from nature, but also overlook the value of those products which are not harvested directly and without which our economies would stop functioning. Among these less conspicuous assets are the innumerable creatures that keep potentially harmful organisms in check, build and maintain soils and decompose dead matter so that it may be used to build new life and also those that help in pollination. These birds, insects, worms and microorganisms demonstrate that small things can have greatly disproportionate value. Unfortunately, their services are becoming increasingly scarce because pesticides, pollutants, disease, hunting and habitat fragmentation or destruction have greatly reduced their numbers and ability to function. Nature's most productive workers are slowly being put out of business.

For example, take the case of pollinators who have enormous value for agriculture and the functioning of natural ecosystems. Without them, plants cannot produce seeds that ensure not only their own survival but also ours. The highly evolved plants are those that use flowers, scents, oils, pollens and nectar to attract and reward animals to do the job of pollination (Kumar, 2000). More than 90 per cent of the world's flowering plant species are animal-pollinated.

Developing a mutually beneficial relationship with a pollinator effectively enables a plant to ensure reproductive success. Spending energy producing nectars and extra pollen is a small price to pay to guarantee reproduction. Performing this service are many thousands of animal species, including bees, beetles, butterflies, moths, ants and flies, along with over 1,000 species of vertebrates such as birds, bats, opossums, lemurs, and others. Many of these pollinator species are threatened with extinction.

Eighty per cent of the world's 1,330 cultivated crop species (including fruits, vegetables, beans and legumes, coffee and tea, cocoa and spices) are pollinated by wild and semi-wild pollinators. In monetary terms, honeybee pollination services are 60–100 times more valuable than the honey they produce. The value of wild blueberry bees is so great, with each bee pollinating 15–19 litres (about 40 pints) of blueberries in its life, that they are viewed by farmers as "flying $ 50 notes" (Abramovitz, 1998). In Europe, the contribution of honey bee pollination to agriculture has been estimated to be worth about $ 100 billion in 1990. The most pervasive threats to pollinators include habitat fragmentation and disturbance, loss of nesting and over-wintering sites, intense exposure of pollinators to pesticides and of nectar plants to herbicides, breakdown of "nectar corridors" that provide food sources to pollinators during migration, new diseases, competition from alien species and excessive hunting.

Ironically, several modern agricultural practices actually limit the productivity of crops by reducing pollination. The high levels of pesticides used on cotton reduce annual yield significantly by killing bees and other insect pollinators. One-fifth of all honeybee losses involve pesticide exposure and may cost agriculture millions of dollars every year.

Many plants have developed interdependence on particular species of pollinators (Kumar, 2000). In peninsular Malaysia, the bat *Eonycteris spelaea* is thought to be the exclusive pollinator of the durian, a large spiny fruit that is highly valued in Southeast Asia. The bats' primary food supply is a coastal mangrove that flowers continuously throughout the year. The bats routinely fly several kilometres from their roost sites to the mangrove stands, pollinating durian trees along the way. However, many mangrove stands like inland forests are under siege. Without both, bats are unlikely to survive.

Pollinators that migrate long distances (e.g., bats, monarch butterflies and hummingbirds) need to follow routes that offer a reliable supply of nectar providing plants for the entire journey. However, such nectar corridors are breaking.

Many of the disturbances are also hurting creatures that provide other beneficial services such as biological control of pests and disease. Much of the habitat inhabited by beneficial predators such as birds has been wiped out. The "pest control services" that nature provides are incalculable and do not suffer from the ill-effects of chemical pesticides (which kill beneficial insects along with the pests). Individual bat colonies in Texas can eat 250 tonnes of insects every night. Worldwide, about 25 per cent of bat species are threatened with extinction. Without birds, leaf-eating insects become more abundant and affect the growth of trees or damage crops.

The necessary protection to these essential service providers can be provided by using no-till farming that reduces soil erosion, allowing nature's underground economy to flourish. This can also be done by cutting back on the use of toxic agricultural chemicals and protecting migratory routes and nectar corridors, thereby ensuring the survival of wild pollinators and pest control agents.

There is no doubt that buffer areas of native vegetation and trees can have many beneficial effects. They act as havens for resident and migratory insects and animals that pollinate crops and control pests. They help reduce wind erosion, and absorb nutrient pollution that leaks from agricultural fields. The "sacred groves" in South Asian and African villages are natural areas intentionally left undeveloped, and they still provide such havens.

Pollinators can be encouraged by providing them their nesting sites such as hollow logs or by ensuring that pollinators have the native plants they need during the "off-season" when they are not working on the agricultural crops. Some wild pollinators may be domesticated. The bumblebee, for example, has been domesticated and is now a pollinator of valuable greenhouse grown crops.

Macroeconomics and Environment

Costanza et. al., (1997) attempted to price the services that the world's ecosystems provide to humans (Table 3.1). The price was estimated as $ 33 trillion per annum, with a confidence interval of $ 16–54 trillion. Given that the combined GNP of all the countries in the world was about $ 28 trillion in 1995, ecosystems would appear to be providing 1.2 times as much economic value as people are creating. There are valid

Table 3.1 Estimates of Annual Global Value of Ecosystem Services (After Costanza et. al., 1997 and Pearce, 1998)

Service	Trillion $ (as in 1994)
By Biome	
Marine	
Open Ocean	8.4
Coastal Areas	12.6
Total Marine	**21.0**
Service	**Trillion $ (as in 1994)**
Terrestrial	
Forests	4.7
Grass- and Rangelands	0.9
Wetlands	4.9
Lakes and Rivers	1.7
Croplands	12.3
Total Terrestrial	**12.3**
Total	**33.3**
By Ecosystem	
Gas Regulation*	1.3
Disturbance Regulation**	1.8
Water Regulation	1.1
Water Supply	1.7
Nutrient Cycling	17.1
Waste Treatment	2.3
Food Production	1.4
Cultural Services	3.6
Other***	3.6
Total	**33.3**

* Regulation of the chemical composition of the atmosphere

** Mitigation of environmental fluctuations such as storms and floods

*** Includes climate regulation, erosion control and sediment retention, soil formation, pollination, biological control, provision of habitat, raw materials, genetic resources and recreation.

reasons for assigning monetary value to ecosystem functions. The environmental rationale arises from the widespread concern about loss of habitats and species and the continuing depletion of natural resources. The concern has not translated into any significant progress in conservation because modern environmentalism has failed to address the underlying economic causes of environmental degradation (Pearce, 1998). The benefits and gains from any conservation effort appear to be significantly smaller than the economic returns to society from converting natural assets into commercial ones. Hotels and tourism replace pristine coastlines, tropical forests are burned to create new pasture, and croplands and roads are built through ecologically valuable landscapes. The motive is to belief that people would be better off by giving up a natural asset.

The erroneous belief comes from the fact that the services provided by ecological systems are not traded in markets and thus have no ready perceived value. Because we do not buy and sell clean air, nutrient cycling or carbon storage, the value of such services is erroneously perceived to be zero. Governments make the odds against conservation and even worse by subsidizing irrigation water, energy, fertilizer, pesticides, agricultural output, fishing and transport. Hardly any country subsidizes conservation. All this favours economic development. It needs to be widely realized that ecosystems have economic value. Also, we must find a way to 'capture' the non-market values of ecosystems and turn them into real benefits for those who practice conservation. Conservation should be a paying venture either by selling ecological services to tourists, getting conservationists to buy land and preserve it or paying forest dwellers for storing carbon. According to Daily (1997), economic markets have a major role in patterns of human behaviour.

Natural Services

Natural services have been greatly undervalued by regarding the natural world as an inexhaustible resource and sink. The tools used to measure the economic health and progress of a nation have reinforced and encouraged these attitudes. The gross domestic product (GDP), for example, supposedly measures the value of the goods and services produced in a nation. But the most valuable goods and services—the ones provided by nature—are measured poorly or not at all. As ecologist Norman Myers put it, "Our tools of economic analysis are far from able to apprehend, let alone comprehend, the entire range of values implicit in forests."

Economic calculations grossly underestimate the current and future value of nature. Nature's services are not counted at all. When the goods are considered free and therefore valued at zero, the market sends signals that they are only economically valuable when converted into something else. For example, the profit from deforesting land is counted as an addition on a nation's balance sheet because trees have been converted in to saleable lumber or pulp, but the depletions of the timber stock, watershed and fisheries are not subtracted.

The loss of ecosystem services can have severe economic, social and ecological costs even though we can measure only a fraction of these. The loss of timber and lives in the Indonesian fires and the lower production of fruits and vegetables from inadequate pollination are only the tip of the iceberg. The loss of individual species and habitat, and degradation and simplification of ecosystems impair nature's ability to provide the services we need. Many of these changes are irreversible, and much of what is lost is simply irreplaceable. Almost half of the forests that once covered the earth are now gone, and much of what remains is in fragmented patches.

Consumers must realize that it is possible to reduce and reverse the destructive impact of our activities by consuming less and placing fewer demands on those services we have erroneously taken to be free. We need to reduce the high levels of waste and over-consumption of timber and paper. We must increase the efficiency of water and energy use. In agricultural fields, we can leave hedgerows and unplowed areas that serve as nesting and feeding sites for pollinators. We can reduce reliance on agricultural chemicals and improve the timings of their application to avoid killing pollinators (Abramovitz, 1998).

Ecosystem Services

Many environmental changes have strong consequences for humanity. Climatic disruption, increased ultraviolet (UV-B) radiation or insufficient drinking water exemplify undesirable outcomes. Many serious consequences are less obvious and mediated through the functioning of ecological systems. Humans and their social and economic systems depend strongly upon the ecological systems now undergoing rapid changes (Kennedy, 1993; IUCN, 1997).

Wetlands, forests, coral reefs, tundra, grasslands, estuaries, open ocean and other natural ecosystems provide a broad range of essential goods and services to the humanity. In fact, they are the lifeline for all life on the earth. Human well-being and prosperity greatly depend upon diverse functioning ecological systems in ways that are beginning to be appreciated. It is well-known that humans extract goods from nature, for example, seafood, fodder, fuelwood, timber, pharmaceutical products, and they buy, sell and trade these goods. But little attention was paid to another benefit provided by natural ecological systems, viz., the fundamental life-support services without which human civilization would cease to thrive (Daily, 1997). These "ecosystem services" include the purification of air and water, mitigation of floods and droughts, detoxification and decomposition of wastes, generation and renewal of soil and soil fertility, pollination of crops and natural vegetation, control of many agricultural pests, dispersal of seeds, maintenance of biodiversity from which humanity has extracted key elements of its agricultural, medicinal and industrial enterprise, partial stabilization of climate, and moderation of temperature extremes and the force of winds and waves (Daily, 1997; Lubchenco, 1998).

All these services are essential to human societies. Their continued existence cannot be taken for granted. As these services are not traded in economic markets, the society has no feedback mechanisms to signal changes in their supply or in deterioration of underlying ecological systems that generate them. When land is transformed globally or when biogeochemical cycles are modified on a grand scale or when genetic, population, species and ecosystem diversity is lost, the functioning of ecological systems becomes disrupted and the continued provision of ecosystem services is threatened (Mooney et. al., 1996). Primary threats to ecosystem services include habitat degradation or loss, changes in biodiversity and synergistic interactions between these factors and rapid climate change, release of toxic substances and depletion of stratospheric ozone (Lubchenco, 1998).

Redefining the Environment

When E O Wilson realized the significance of the above global environmental changes, he suggested that humanity would soon enter the century of the environment. The intimate manner in which we humans depend on the ecological systems of the planet, makes it increasingly obvious that many issues that we previously considered to be independent of the environment are in fact intimately related to it. Whether that be human health, economy, social justice or national security, all have important environmental dimensions. Human health has very strong environmental components such as good air quality, clean drinking water, clean food and minimal exposure to toxic chemicals and UV-B radiation; less apparent examples are the impact of land-use practices, climatic change and population density on emergence and transmission of diseases (e.g., Lederberg et. al., 1992). Bad roads and the accompanying ditches and canals of stagnant water provide suitable conditions for the numerical increase and spatial expansion of population of mosquito vectors for the malarial parasite.

Global climatic change has both direct and indirect effects on human health. Direct effects include increase in heat stress, decrease in cold-related mortality and increase in air pollution-related pulmonary and allergic complications. Indirect effects, some of which are mediated through interactions with land-use practices, include increase in the geographic distribution of various diseases such as malaria, dengue, fever and yellow fever (McMichael et. al., 1996).

The economy is strongly interlinked with the environment. It is often mistakenly claimed that society must choose between the economy and the environment. In fact, according to Lubchenco, this "jobs versus the environment" choice is a false dichotomy; the real choice should be between short and long-term gain and sustained prosperity (PCSO, 1996). Economic development and prosperity flow from maintaining an adequate supply of essential services provided by natural ecosystems. When humans fill in wetlands, clear-cut forests, drive natural populations and species to extinction, they can disrupt the functioning of the systems or lose the ecosystem entirely.

Besides the above, national security, social justice, economy and human health are environmental issues because each depends on the structure, functioning, and resilience of ecological systems. Linkages among the social, political, economic, physical, biological, chemical and geological systems offer novel challenges that may sometimes be met by scientists.

The wide range of ongoing biological, physical, chemical, social and economic changes reveal many ways in which society's needs for scientific knowledge are changing. Many of the studies on environmental challenges all point to:

1. Need for improved understanding, monitoring and evaluation to protect, manage and restore the environment
2. More effective communication of existing knowledge to the public and the policy makers
3. Desirability of developing new technologies to minimize the ecological footprints of human activities
4. Better guidance about decision making in the face of uncertainty (Dooge et. al., 1992; Kendall et. al., 1995; Lubchenco, 1998)

While science alone cannot suffice to achieve the objective of greater sustainability, scientific wisdom can help in making decisions that will enable society to move toward that end. A sustainable biosphere should be ecologically sound, economically feasible and socially just. Scientific understanding can help in developing new technologies. There is a strong need for innovative mechanisms that can facilitate the study of complex, interdisciplinary problems spanning multiple spatial and temporal scales, encouraging international cooperation on societal problems and building effective bridges between policy, management and science, as well as between the public and private sectors (COER, 1993; Lubchenco, 1998).

The New Wave

Environmentalists certainly have scored several major triumphs such as achieving significantly cleaner air and water in some parts of the world. The USA has enacted impressive environmental laws and enforced them. Far-reaching international agreements watch over the ozone layer, climate change and biodiversity. These and other environmental successes justifiably make us feel proud, but they also warrant that we should not take them for granted. In general, the news which people most vividly remember, is more about the problems and the moments of peril than about increments of progress. Easterbrook (1995) rightly chastised environmentalists for overlooking problems of developing nations such as drinkable water, clean air, food supply and disease control.

A new environmental wave has been emerging during the past few years. Its main characteristic is a swing back toward the grass roots and one that will encompass some fundamental value shifts.

Biodiversity for Plant Protection

Of the total area planted to genetically modified (GM) crops worldwide in the year 2000, 19 per cent represents insect-resistant crops and seven per cent covers crops combining both herbicide and insect resistance.

Research on genetic modification is underway, predominantly focusing on plant health: herbicide-tolerant cotton and soya, resistance to lepidopterons in cotton, resistance to nematodes in potatoes and resistance to white leaf in rice (Osorio, 2001).

Agriculture demands continuous fight against harmful organisms. It is therefore necessary to develop appropriate technologies to regulate and control pests. Environment-friendly biological options that do not make use of genetic modification do exist. These options are based on natural crop protection approaches that make use of the diversity found in nature itself. Several institutions are promoting these non-chemical and non-GM options, providing excellent and competitive alternatives for pest management.

The challenge in natural crop protection is to have simple and low cost technologies that can regulate pests and diseases and reduce or eliminate the problem of contamination by agrochemicals. One such natural crop protection approach is based on the use of plants with biological control properties. Plant types with insecticidal properties that can be used as curatives are equally important.

Plants that protect other plants

Within the framework of ecological pest management, an important and promising bunch of technologies makes use of plants as biological control agents. An inventory made in Peru indicated the existence of over 300 plant species—both native and imported—that are useful for controlling population of harmful insects. Several possible applications emerge from this inventory, the most important ones being insecticide, repellent, nematicide and fungicide. This indicates that ecological pest management has a great potential for further development (Osorio, 2001).

Extract from a wild forest plant, *Argemone sufusiformis*, has proved to be an effective regulator of the larvae of *Spodoptera frugiperda* (armyworm). *Vallesia glabra* and *Nerium oleander* are efficient fungicides, especially to control *Fusarium solani* and *Rhizoctonia solani*. *Equisetum* spp. are being used to control infection of *Phytophthora infestans* in potatoes.

Similarly, research is being done on the identification of plants with properties for controlling nematodes such as *Crotalaria* spp. Furthermore, the oil of various plants helps to fight pests that cause damage to grain in storage.

Neem *(Azadirachta indica)*

The neem tree (Meliaceae family) originated in Southeast Asia and has become well-known worldwide because of its biological control properties. It is cultivated in many parts of the world now because it adapts very well to the soils and semi-arid climates in tropical and sub-tropical countries. It shows good tolerance to dry conditions and soil salinity. Its medicinal properties have the potential for treating animals and humans.

The active substances of the neem seed (azadirachtin, salanin, nimbin, nimbidin, meliantrol, etc.) have repellent effects. Upon ingestion, they strongly affect the metamorphosis of insects, preventing their growth and development. These substances are not toxic to human beings, mammals, birds, reptiles and fish. Applied in the indicated concentrations they do not affect the beneficial flora or fauna in the cultivated fields.

Insect Outbreaks

Insects have been widely viewed as pests. A different perception emerged from Schowalter (2000) who concluded that insect outbreaks are simply ecosystem regulators that are good for stability. Several decades ago, DDT and aerosol insecticides were widely used to keep away various insects. Even today, insects are feared, mismanaged and generally viewed as pests, but cute 'bugs' have been enjoying an incredible increase in popularity among the general public. Despite the relative popularity and importance of insects, insect ecologists are unable to give answers to basic questions: How do insects defend themselves against different types of natural enemies? What are the effects of insects on plant diversity in terrestrial communities? What are the regulatory roles of insects in natural ecosystems? Schowalter discussed many of these issues, particularly the last question. How insects respond to environmental gradients? There is, no doubt, that insects have strong effects on ecosystems.

Schowalter postulated the idea of ecosystems as cybernetic systems and developed the concept by providing a strong case for why insect ecologists should test the regulatory role of insects in ecosystems.

Insect detritivores, pollinators, seed dispersers and phytophagous insects profoundly influence key ecosystem processes and they could also have some regulatory role. If insects are regulators of ecosystems, there are important implications for applied issues and integration of ecosystems ecology with insect management strategies. These goals need to be integrated (Dyer, 2000).

Non-target Effects of Biological Control

Several examples of conflicts of interest in biological control are known where an organism targeted by biocontrol was classified as a pest by one group but was considered useful by another. There has also been concern that introduction of exotic organisms for 'classical' biological control may produce adverse effects on the native biota. Despite some early examples of the invasion of native systems on a regional scale, the potential for biocontrol agents to damage native systems was dismissed throughout most of the 20th Century. Even in the 1970s and 80s, a popular belief was that there was no evidence that an insect introduced for biocontrol had ever caused significant damage to any natural system (vertebrates excluded). With the emergence of conservation biology, a challenge to this viewpoint was inevitable, and based on the increasing rate of publications on this topic, this challenge is now rapidly gaining momentum. Biological control now confronts a new conflict of interest, contrasting the need to solve pest problems economically and permanently and the need to protect native ecosystems from yet another potential source of contamination by exotic organisms (Follett and Duan, 2000).

Most people realize that it is virtually impossible to predict exactly an insect's host range based on laboratory studies, or to guarantee that any biocontrol agent will not attack a non-target species in the future. A weevil (beetle from Curculionoidea superfamily) introduced into North America for the control of exotic thistles shifted onto native thistle species over 20 years after its introduction. It reminded that insects can evolve fairly quickly and that predictions of future host ranges are tenuous. If predicting future host ranges is imperfect for insects, it is an even more serious problem for pathogens. Studies on the host ranges of entomopathogenic fungi and nematodes bring out how little we know about the host ranges of these organisms and how much more information is needed before we could generate any informed opinions about potential nontarget effects (Follett and Duan, 2000).

Some Challenges of Industrial Development

In Africa, during the past two decades, there has been negative economic growth largely due to poor performance in the manufacturing sector (UNECA, 1999). The manufacturing sector's contribution to sustainable development in Africa has been minimal. From 1980–2002, Africa's industrial sector neither recorded meaningful growth nor significant structural change. The average share of manufacturing value added (MVA) in GDP fell from 13.4 per cent in 1985 to 12.9 per cent in 1998 (Mebratu, 2000, 2002). When we consider the trend in low-income countries, the share of MVA in GDP increased from 16.4 per cent in 1985 to 20.3 per cent in 1998 (Table 3.2). In the case of high-income countries, the share of MVA in GDP declined from 22.5 per cent in 1985 to 21.2 per cent in 1998, largely by a shift in the industrial structure from manufacturing to services usually observed at the later stage of the industrialization process (Mebratu, 2000, 2002).

Table 3.2 Average Share of MVA in GDP (Economic Groupings in Africa) (After UNIDO, 1999, 2001)

Developing Countries	1985	1990	1995	1996	1997	1998
Low Income	16.4	18.6	20.4	20.7	20.7	20.3
Middle Income	20.2	22.1	22.8	23.0	23.5	22.9
High Income	22.5	21.8	21.0	21.1	21.2	21.2
Africa	13.2	13.4	12.7	12.5	12.8	12.9

In the past few decades African governments recognized industrialization as the logical, preferred road to self-sufficiency and self-sustained growth, and most development strategies that influenced national industrial development policies were promoted by various international agencies such as the United Nations and the World Bank. These initiatives only had some limited success in terms of promoting industrial development in the region, but they did provide important lessons (Mebratu, 2000):

1. **Limitation of supply-driven initiatives** Development and promotion of "supply-driven" and "top-heavy" regional initiatives in the absence of the appropriate mechanisms, infrastructural foundations and sense of ownership at the national level limits success.

2. **Transformational rather than transplanting processes** Attempting industrial development by promoting economic reform packages under a "one-size-fits-all" model limits success.
3. **Complementary roles of the market and governments** Successful industrialization in other regions over the last few decades indicate that government intervention supportive of market trends and competitive forces strongly promotes early stage industrial development.
4. **Industrial competitiveness** Good economic development depends on a country's ability to break into the vicious circle of investment-economic growth-competitiveness-investment (Mebratu, 2002).

Several constraints and challenges confront sustainable industrial development in Africa. Some are related to global socio-economic trends whereas others relate to regional socio-economic dynamics. The impact of globalization as an important challenge has created a divergence in living standards of developed countries and the fast-growing industrialising countries of East and Southeast Asia. Africa has failed to penetrate international markets for manufactured goods largely because of globalization. Existing manufacturing industries are going out of business even in the domestic market due to their inability to compete with imported industrial products from other countries through the liberalized trade regimes. Globalization in the form of trade and investment liberalization, without commensurate enhancement of domestic manufacturing capacity has led to marginalization.

Judicious development of industrial skills and technological capability is extremely important for developing countries to advance their industries on a sustainable basis and participate effectively in the global economy. The transfer of environmentally sound technologies to the developing world is a major item of the global agenda for the 21st Century.

According to Mebratu, progress towards sustainable production and consumption will involve redefinition of the linkages between trade, environment and development. The redefinition process is primarily driven by industrialized countries' consumer preferences and has commenced. The shift towards sustainable production and consumption leads to multiple socio-economic and socio-ecological benefits.

Impact of Trade-induced Economic Growth

Assuming that increased trade enhances economic growth, the scale effect of trade on the environment generates the concern that these increasing outputs may exacerbate environmental problems. This is the reason why environmental NGOs oppose economic globalization. Both in post-war industrialization in OECD countries, as well as more recent export-led economic growth in Southeast Asia, trade-induced growth took place without proper environmental management because environmental regulation and enforcement were lax, monitoring inadequate and infrastructure (notably waste and water treatment) virtually non-existent.

Many indicators of environmental quality deteriorate with growth at lower levels of income and then improve; usually the most localized environmental effects (local water and air pollution) show the most evident "inverted U" relationship, and others that are more diffuse (e.g., CO_2 emissions do not exhibit such a relationship at all. The more positive effects of income growth on environmental quality are weaker, the more "public" is the environmental good.

A study of 145 countries by Dasgupta et. al., (1995) revealed that at the starting lowest level of development, economic development increases environmental policy capacity, the typical progression being from natural resource protection through to the regulation of water and air pollution. However, though there is evidence that as incomes rise, economic growth provides financial resources and willingness to pay for a cleaner environment, this positive effect is often not strong enough to counterbalance the adverse environmental impact of trade induced economic growth. Controlling economic growth need not, however, be a requirement for a sustainable society. There exists much scope for decoupling the relationship between economic growth and environmental impacts through the implementation of sustainable development policies (McInnes, 2002).

Equilibrium Effect: The Complexity of Trade-environment Links

A sector-by-sector analysis of the environmental impact of trade can overlook significant interactions between the different economic sectors and countries, so-called "equilibrium effects". The overall environmental impact of increased trade is the sum of structural, scale, product and technology effects. General equilibrium modelling work has led to the conclusion that trade will mitigate local pollution problems in countries with a comparative advantage in cleaner industries and magnify the problems elsewhere. Global environmental conditions will deteriorate if differences in environmental standards dominate over classical factors of comparative advantage (capital abundance in developed countries, labour abundance in developing countries) (McInnes, 2002).

Trade Liberalization and Environmental Policies

The impact of trade liberalization on environmental policies is the key question underlying much of the trade and environment debate. There is some evidence that environmental regulations are not of primary importance for competitiveness or location decisions. Nevertheless, there is public concern that trade liberalization may reduce efforts to protect the environment because of the "regulatory chill" effect, clear instances of how new environmental regulations are defeated by the political leaders on the grounds that they would harm national competitiveness.

Evidence of positive effect of environmental regulations on international competitiveness has emerged recently. Such regulations are conducive to innovation and adaptation to deal with the cost implications of regulations. No doubt, this adaptation is sometimes costly initially, but the firms that make this investment profit from introduced new technologies at an early stage, the so-called "Porter hypothesis" that is best exemplified by DuPont's strategy to be a world leader in the development of CFC substitutes (which later gave the company an advantage over its competitors).

Trade liberalization can be beneficial by correcting trade policy intervention failures, notably by removing trade distorting policies which exacerbate environmental problems as well as adverse effects related to trade expansion in the absence of environmental protection measures. These protection measures sometime lead to environmental degradation. The environmental value may not be fully reflected in the price of traded goods, appropriate pollution control policies or sustainable management practices may not be in place, and environmental and economic policies may be weakly integrated, if at all (McInnes, 2002). For instance, agricultural trade liberalization should benefit the environment to the extent that it removes production supports, export subsidies and quantitative restrictions that have contributed to over-specialization, intensive farming operations and poor land use practices. On the other hand, the expansion of agricultural export markets sometime leads to greater specialization with environmentally damaging consequences, while increased competition favours intensive farming operations.

Trade liberalization often harms the local environment in countries with a comparative advantage in polluting industries, while it improves the local environment elsewhere. The income gains of trade could, in principle, pay for additional abatement costs so as to counter adverse environmental effects and still leave a surplus. By combining trade and environment reforms, incomes could rise without compromising environmental quality. There is no inherent conflict between trade and the environment; rather, it arises from a failure to tackle global environmental problems.

Over the last decade, several environment-related trade disputes have focussed on the often conflicting relationship between free trade and environmental protection (Sampson, 2000). Nevertheless, the list of WTO members reflects that of the signatories of a range of multilateral environmental agreements (Table 3.3). The dismantling of economic borders reinforces the need to cooperate on environmental protection and adopt common approaches and instruments, particularly in the case

Table 3.3 Some Major Multilateral Environmental Agreements (MEAs) incorporating Trade Measures (After McInnes, 2002)

Year	MEA
1973	Convention on International Trade in Endangered Species
1987	Montreal Protocol on ozone-depleting substances
1989	Basel Convention on hazardous waste
1997	Kyoto Protocol on climate change
1998	Rotterdam Convention on the prior informed consent procedure for certain hazardous chemicals and pesticides in international trade
2001	Stockholm Convention on persistent organic pollutants (POPs)

of transboundary concerns. Some 200 MEAs already have been signed out of which about 20 incorporate trade measures. Among the most important ones, the Montreal Protocol permits parties to ban imports of CFCs from non-parties which breaches the "most favoured nation" and "national treatment" clauses of GATT. The inclusion of this measure in the Protocol has contributed significantly to its success. The future MEAs may likewise benefit from similar inclusion of certain trade restrictions.

There is now a general consensus among both proponents and opponents of economic globalization that the integration of trade and environmental policies is largely the responsibility of national governments rather than of supranational organizations. It is widely agreed on the need for further knowledge and understanding of the linkages between trade and environment to ensure that trade rules remain sustainable in the long term (McInnes, 2002).

Environmental Safety Evaluations

Safety issues in biotechnology have aroused much controversy. Public concern is focused in particular on the degree of uncertainty associated with inadvertent and unforeseeable impacts of the deliberate or accidental release of genetically engineered organisms into the environment. There is a factual and scientific basis to environmental safety issues. With this real basis, case-specific hazards requiring serious consideration by scientists, regulatory agencies and public can be distinguished from conjectural hazards and naturally occurring background processes (Kappeli and Auberson, 1997).

Although the principles of biotechnology have been unknowingly followed for centuries (e.g., during the selection of higher-yielding plants, microorganisms and animals by breeding for particular phenotypic characteristics), the general public has never raised any safety concern for these traditional activities. The methods traditionally used to obtain the desired phenotype relied on the same biological mechanisms, which are now being exploited with the tools of modern genetic engineering, enabling new variants of microorganisms and plants to be produced swiftly. The differences lies in the fact that genotypes and phenotypes can potentially extend outside the range of traditional genetics and conventional plant breeding. Modern molecular biological techniques have raised potential for making of important medical and agricultural products.

In the pharmaceutical industry, the production of proteins such as monoclonal antibodies and interferonexploits genetically engineered mammalian cell lines and the production of antibiotics and antiviral vaccines relies greatly on recombinant DNA technology for the selection of appropriate microbial strains. Outside the laboratory and the contained industrial production units, genetically engineered organisms are being released into the environment for pollution control and agricultural applications.

Public concerns about environmental biotechnology applications come from the ever-increasing number of modified organisms whose long-term fate in the environment cannot be judged. However, before the environmental release of any genetically modified organisms (GMOs), safety evaluations are carried out so as to seek the approval of regulatory bodies and general public. The existing safety guidelines ensure that an organism is environmentally safe. But safety cannot be expressed in absolute terms, it is a relative concept more adequately defined in terms of tolerance and acceptability limits. Yet, a rational and analytical approach towards environmental safety is possible and could provide the necessary foundation for constructive discussions on the real issues of interest to scientists, regulatory communities and the general public.

The analytical rationale of safety assessments can also be useful in evaluating the impacts associated with the release of naturally occurring microorganisms. The most emerging infections are caused by pathogens that are normally present in the environment. These pathogens may become serious health threats when ecological or environmental conditions encourage pathogen multiplication and spread. Consequently, the incidence of emerging infectious disease increases suddenly, possibly extending to other geographical areas. Safety assessments may be invaluable in uncovering the underlying factors of epidemic diseases such as population shifts, changing human behaviour, changing agricultural and food practices or changing ecology and climate.

Technology Phases

Technology developments may be considered to have taken place in three phases. The first generation of environmental technologies usually involved additions to existing production systems that treated waste. Generally, the pollution burden was transferred from one location or medium to another. This incurred additional treatment costs but did not reduce waste generation or raw material and energy consumption.

The second phase involved cleaner production systems emphasizing pollution prevention through reduced consumption of raw materials and energy and reduced waste generation, thereby increasing productivity and accruing environmental, financial and other benefits to the enterprise and the community.

The third (current) generation of technologies and systems integrates environmental performance considerations with economic and other operational issues so that the system as a whole becomes sustainable. Sustainable production and consumption requires planning, design and management practices that facilitate innovative approaches to reuse, remanufacture and recycle the limited amounts of "waste" that cannot be avoided (Hay, 2002).

Hay (2002) provided a valuable overview of decision support tools that can facilitate uptake of cleaner production systems at the national to enterprise level. It is useful in addressing the challenge of how to reach and equip individuals participating in cleaner production education and outreach programmes, while providing relevant content and learning opportunities that reflect each individual's capacity, capabilities and context. Electronic learning systems can greatly enhance access to existing information.

Technology assessment attempts to understand the likely impacts of the use of new or upgraded processes and technologies by an industry, municipality, country or society.

Environmentally Focused Technology Assessment (EnTA)

It cuts or reduces the need for detailed technical data but facilitates multi-stakeholder dialogues, leading to consensus decision-making related to selecting a technology that will be the most environmentally sound, socially acceptable and economically viable. It overcomes some shortcomings of environmental impact assessment (EIA). By early recognition of key issues, alternatives, solutions and areas of consensus, EnTA focusses on points of major conflicts and dispute (Hay, 2002).

EnTA focusses on characterizing the potential impacts associated with the various outcome categories as follows:

- Human health impacts
- Local natural environment impacts
- Social and cultural impacts
- Global impacts
- Resource sustainability
- Economic viability

The performance of each technology option can be judged by using these mentioned broad categories.

Strategic Environmental Assessment

It is designed to ensure that the environmental consequences of policies, plans, programmes or proposals are considered early in the decision-making process and are properly addressed along with economic and social considerations.

Cleaner production being an important element of environmentally sound design, use of Strategic Environmental Assessment (SEA) at the policy, planning and initial design stage can facilitate identification of processes that minimize environmental degradation and contribute to sustainability.

Life cycle assessment (LCA) is used to strengthen an EnTA through a more formalized analysis of the technology investment over its entire life cycle. Both tools complement the SEA. This ensures that decisions made at the pre-investment stage of the technology intervention will enable identification of technology options that minimize environmental degradation and contribute to sustainability (Hay, 2002).

Environmental Impact Assessment

This is a decision support tool that helps ensure that development and investment proposals, activities, projects and programmes are environmentally sound and sustainable. It allows identification, analysis and evaluation of the significance of potential environmental impacts, and the identification and elaboration of measures that will avoid, give remedy or mitigate any adverse impacts. It helps in creating a monitoring and environmental management regime for implementing mitigation measures, monitoring impacts for compliance and ascertaining if impacts are as predicted.

Environmental Management System (EMS)

An EMS can go a long way to maintain environmentally sound operations by ensuring that environmental issues are managed consistently and systematically. It sets out environmental policies, objectives and targets for an organization, with predetermined indicators that provide measurable goals and serves as a tool for determining if the performance level has been reached.

For organizations, an EMS can be an excellent mechanism for effecting positive change such as increased uptake and continuing effective implementation of cleaner production systems. Successful implementation of an EMS increases environmental awareness, and continuous improvement, adoption and use of environmentally sound technologies (Hay, 2002).

Need for Change

International Food Policy Research Institute and International Water Management Institute, Washington DC, (Report released on World Food Day, 16 October, 2002), stated that if current trends in water policy and water investment continue to remain the same, or worsen, the world will soon suffer increased environmental damage, threats to global food supply and enhancement of health risks for the many millions of people who lack access to clean water.

Unless policies and priorities are amended suitably, in two decades there wil not be enough water for cities, households, the environment or for growing food. Water is not like oil. It has no substitute. Should we go on taking it for granted, much of the earth is going to run short of water or food or both. Rosegrant (2002), citing rapid population increase and urbanization in developing countries, predicted that water use by households, industry and agriculture will increase by at least 50 per cent in the coming decades. Rising water competition would severely limit its availability for irrigation, which in turn would bring down food production.

Lack of clean water and sanitation happens to be a primary cause of disease and child mortality. While world leaders recently agreed at the World Summit on Sustainable Development (WSSD) to cut in half the number of people without access to clean water by 2015, this goal cannot be achieved unless governments recast their water policies to meet the needs of poor people.

Rosegrant recommends pricing water to reflect its cost and value, and increasing investment in crop research, technology and rural infrastructure to boost water productivity investment that would concomitantly increase crop yields from rain-fed farming, which is likely to account for half the increase in food production between 1995 and 2025.

If countries fail to create strong institutions and adopt sensible policies supporting water governance and approaches that provide greater access to water in poor communities, the crop yield will decline. There is also need to invest in water conservation. This can be done by using innovative low-cost, small-scale irrigation technologies such as drip kit or manually operated treadle pumps that allow smallholder farmers to irrigate crops by using less water.

World Summit on Sustainable Development

Sustainable development rests on the three pillars, namely, economy, society and environment. Each of these pillars is essential for achieving the goal of sustainable development. The environmental pillar promotes sustainability by ensuring that negative effects of resource use are avoided, remediated or mitigated. It imposes limits on the use of public resources such as air, water and coastal space to avoid overexploitation and enable fair and reasonable access for people and communities.

Sustainable management can certainly be a useful concept for designing or guiding appropriate legislation for fisheries, indigenous forestry, transport, electricity and local governments, adopting sustainability as the core theme.

Some notable initiatives that can help a country in realizing the economic opportunities as well as environmental benefits can be achieved by shifting towards greater sustainability. These are usually aimed at promoting sustainability in business, households and public services. Hence, it reduces waste and improves certification of environment friendly products and services.

The WSSD held in Johannesburg in August 2002, ended with some sensible agreements. This summit may put us on a path that reduces poverty while protecting the environment. Governments agreed at this summit on certain concrete commitments and actions that should make a real difference for world community.

The major agreement ensuing from WSSD–the Plan of Implementation–lays down several targets and timetables on various issues. A few of these are as follows:

1. Halving the proportion of people who lack access to clean water or proper sanitation by 2015
2. Restoring depleted fisheries by 2015
3. Reducing biodiversity loss by 2010
4. Using and producing chemicals in ways that do not harm human health and the environment by 2020
5. Adopting a new international approach to chemical management and the harmonization of labelling and classification of chemicals by 2008 (Falt, 2002).

Many countries pledged to increase the use of renewable energy. The summit also forged partnerships by and between governments, citizen groups and businesses, in corporate responsibility and environmental standards. A ten-year programme was developed for sustainable consumption and production patterns, on science-based approaches and life cycle analysis. A new initiative was taken to encourage industry for improving its social and environmental performance, taking into account ISO standards and the Global Reporting Initiative.

Management of Industrial Accidents

The risks of technology have an inevitable institutional dimension. All technologies are essentially "socio-technical" systems and many hazardous technologies pose significant challenges to the limits in our organizational capacities in identifying problems and clearly analysing them. It is usually impossible to preclude failure by technological design alone.

Beamish (2002) explored the factors involved in the largest oil spill in American history up to 20 million gallons of oil and chemical "diluent" at the Unocal Corporation's oil field in Guadalupe Dunes, California, 170 miles north of Los Angeles. Production at the Guadalupe Dunes oil field began in 1948, peaked in 1988, and ended in 1990. To enhance the recovery of the field's extremely viscous crude oil, petroleum thinners (diluent) were injected into well bores. The California Coastal Commission estimates that spillage of diluent has contaminated 60 per cent of the field's 3,000 acres. According to Beamish, such common excuses as greed, avarice, deception and dereliction of duty are offered for events such as the Guadalupe spill. But these events cannot explain decades of serious leaks that many individuals and organizations, with divergent interests, have known about.

With a view to understanding the dimension of "crescive" event in Guadalupe spill, Beamish postulated the new accident analysis. Falling between crisis and the laissez-faire routine of things, the spill eluded the crisis-oriented attention until it reached such large proportions that it could no longer permit clear regulatory jurisdiction (Turner, 1978; Perrow, 1999) and an agreed upon remedial approach. "Like the proverbial frog in the frying pan, such slow motion problems do not offer clear thresholds or tripping points that activate detection and response. These events may well escape our current efforts at environmental regulation and management" (Schulman, 2002).

Disaster Management

Disasters are usually regarded as sudden, unexpected events that unfold over much longer period of time. Evolving human societies encounter or generate new and unanticipated vulnerabilities including marked instabilities of the ecosystems in which they live. Globally, interdependency across long distances interact with previously unnecessary rigidities of scheduling, and hence these vulnerabilities have become more and more complex and unpredictable. Consequently, disasters grow in the scale of their effects and become more frequent, threatening to match efforts to develop new technological means of managing them (Hoffman and Oliver-Smith, 2002; Adams, 2002). Most disasters involve unexpected combinations of properties and consequences, at several levels of aggregation. In responding to them a holistic approach that embraces the social as well as the natural setting proves beneficial.

Anthropologists have a responsibility for active roles in disaster anticipation, management, reconstruction or rehabilitation. Like the processes leading to disasters, responses to catastrophes extend over time and are shaped by complex interactions among individuals, groups and organizations having disparate needs and interests. Adjustment and recovery require observations of the victims and discussions with them. To understand disasters, Hoffman and Oliver–Smith advocate a coupling of multisite ethnography and quantitative methods capable of accessing greater levels of aggregation. Some disasters are so strong that the victims form a view of nature as a benevolent mother wounded by human abuse or even as a vengeful monster (Adams, 2002).

Sometimes the narrow frame of most media stories around motive precludes the search for causes of disasters in broader social patterns. One fairly common oversight is to rely on only official or professional sources, while failing to record the voices of the victims. Another is preoccupation with the ecological impacts but very little follow-up on the complex and long-continuing losses of local communities. Sometimes, the legal system can deny or delay justice so much that the victims of the event are pushed beyond the recoverable state of cultural and spiritual despair.

Just as disasters are subject to multiple constructions, so are perceptions of hazard, danger and risk—and for that matter—normalcy (Adams, 2002).

Using the Bhopal gas tragedy of 1984 as an example, Ravi Rajan points to the frequent deficiencies of bureaucracies in meeting the challenges of disasters—lack of contingent expertise, no effective warning systems, evacuation procedures, means to mobilize medical facilities and overcome paralysing medical rivalries, or mitigation programmes for victims and their families. Equally absent was the conceptual expertise required to design, implement and troubleshoot long-term rehabilitation strategies (Hoffman and Oliver–Smith, 2002).

In the case of Bhopal gas tragedy, anthropologists from the University of Delhi played a welcome role in opening up civic space in which activist groups could operate. Providing political cover for grass root mobilizations and protests, they also helped to frame the public discourse on its meaning. This prompts the questions: What should be the role of anthropologists in crises? Should they work largely outside of and in opposition to the establishment? Or are there greater benefits to be gained from some trained social scientists, if not anthropologists, serving inside institutions as active participants in amelioration and reconstruction? (Adams, 2002).

Globalization

Advocates of economic globalization consider globalization as an inevitable process and outcome of uncontrollable economic and technological forces that have evolved over centuries to their present form. They feel that nothing can be done to control them. However, while it is true that global trade has existed for centuries in various forms, the earlier versions differed sharply from the modern version in scale, speed, form and impact. The modern version of economic globalization was intentionally created by some people with a specific goal i.e., to give high priority to economic or corporate values and to aggressively propagate and implement those values globally. The modern form of globalization integrates and merges the world's economic activity within a single homogenized model of development.

This model mainly serves the interest of the largest corporations by allowing them to duplicate their production and marketing efforts on more and more territory. Special emphasis is placed on economic hypergrowth and is driven by a continuing search for access to new and cheaper labour sources and new markets. Such instruments of globalization as the WTO, the World Bank and the International Monetary Fund (IMF) support these processes by framing rules that require nations to conform to these principles, while removing impediments within individual nations that might restrict corporate access to markets, labour and resources. In fact, most such impediments are laws enacted by governments, which are considered as "non-tariff barriers to trade" by free traders and are subject to WTO challenges.

Some advocates of economic globalization have suggested that it stimulates long-term environmental protection. As the countries globalize, often by exploiting forests, minerals, fisheries, wildlife and water, their increased wealth enables them to save more patches of nature from their ravages. This means that after reaping profits, these countries could introduce technical devices to mitigate the adverse environmental impacts of the increased production. However, the past experiences show that most of the benefit actually accrues to global corporations, who have no incentive to invest their profits into environmental improvements.

Industrial Agriculture and Ecological Destruction

Industrial agriculture is often claimed to be efficient and to produce cheaper food. But there is no warrant for these claims since the efficiency ignores the costs of air, water and soil pollution. For instance, consider the toxic rivers that lead to the death of fishes, loss of topsoil due to heavy pesticide usage and machine-intensive production, and the growing use of fossil fuels. Nearly one-half of the world's population comprise the small farmers who have intimate knowledge of local crops, soils and climate.

These farmers know how to minimize insect outbreaks and keep soil productive, feed their families, communities and local and regional markets. However through the new industrial agriculture system those are usually run by TNCs, farms are bought up and consolidated into huge ones. They discourage diverse cropping and prefer single crop monocultures for the export market. The net effect is that sooner or later the farmers and their families flee to crowded urban slums where they compete for rare and poorly paid urban jobs. The poor becomes poorer and the rich becomes richer. The world has already lost up to 75 per cent of its crop diversity because of the globalization of industrialized agriculture.

Globalization and Poverty

In recent years, the World Bank, the IMF and the WTO have repeatedly proclaimed that their primary purpose in stimulating economic globalization is to help the world's poor. Their contention is that removing barriers to corporate trade and financial investments is the best route to growth, which offers the best chance to lift the poor from poverty. Sadly, the evidence from around 1970-2000, the period of economic globalization's most rapid ascendancy, shows that exactly the opposite is happening. Poverty and inequality have rapidly increased everywhere on the earth. Inequalities between the rich and the poor, within and among the countries, are expanding. Global trading and finance system is one of the primary causes for this increase in poverty and inequality.

The new rules of globalization and the players framing them focus on integrating global markets, neglecting those needs of people that markets cannot meet. The process is concentrating power and marginalizing the poor, both countries and people. The debate about globalization often neglects such serious human concerns as persistent global poverty, growing inequality within and between countries, exclusion of poor people and countries, and persistent human rights abuses. While the rising tide of the global economy may create many economic winners, it cannot satisfy everyone. Rather it may generate conflicts at home and abroad, creating an even wider gap between regional winners and losers than exists today. Globalization's evolution can be rocky, marked by chronic financial volatility and lengthening of the economic divide. Those regions, countries and groups which are left behind can face deepening economic stagnation, political instability and cultural alienation. They can foster political, ethnic, ideological and religious extremism, along with the violence that often accompanies it.

Robert Wade of the London School of Economics wrote in *The Economist* (2001), "Global inequality is worsening rapidly. Technological change and financial liberalization result in a disproportionately fast increase in the number of households at the extreme rich end, without shrinking the distribution at the poor end.... From 1988 to 1993, the share of the world income going to the poorest 10 per cent of the world's population fell by over a quarter, whereas the share of the richest 10 per cent rose by eight per cent."

Although economic globalization has succeeded in making global corporations and a few elites immensely wealthy, its ideologies and rules, including free trade, deregulation, privatization and structural adjustment, have destroyed the livelihood of millions of people and have left many of them homeless, landless and hungry, while removing their access to even the most basic public services such as health and medical care, education, sanitation, freshwater and public transport. Economic globalization tends to make things worse for the poor, not better (Mander, 2001).

Contrary to its claims, wealth generated by globalization often fails to trickle down and gets locked up at the top. This removes the very tools needed by the governments and the communities to redistribute wealth, protect domestic industries, workers, social services and environment, and sustainable livelihood. No doubt in a few isolated instances, some improvement could be achieved among the Third World countries over short periods. The proponents of globalization widely boast about these examples even though in reality the benefits of this "growth" are ephemeral and nearly all the benefits have accrued to the elites in these countries, not the common people.

Creation of Poverty

Economic globalization policies as enforced by the World Bank, IMF and the WTO actually do more to create poverty rather than remove it. Free trade necessarily requires all countries to adopt the same economic model and so eliminates any variations that might slow down the smooth global operations of major corporations as they seek new resources, markets and cheap labour.

According to the free market ideology, the best way to fight global hunger and improve the economic situation of farmers in developing countries is through liberalization of trade and investment, production for export, and cuts in domestic support. However, these policy changes have severely undermined food security and the livelihood of marginal farmers in developing countries (Kumar, 2003).

The specific role of the WTO is to fix homogenized global rules for all countries and to challenge those national environmental and social laws that are perceived to hinder corporate free trade. By enjoying draconian enforcement powers, the WTO can impose harsh punishments on those democratic nations which deviate from its rules.

Export-oriented Agriculture

Probably, the most painful impacts of globalization policies—both in terms of poverty creation and environmental devastation—have come with the forced shift of local economies away from the small-scale diversified agricultural models to the industrial export model, directed by global corporations. According to Mander (2001), about one-half of the world population lives directly on the land and grows food for their families and communities. They usually grow staples and a mix of diverse crops, and they replant with indigenous seed varieties that their communities developed over millennia. They have perfected their own fertilizers, crop rotations and pesticide management. Their communities share all elements of the local commons, including seeds, water and labour. Such systems have nurtured millions of people since time immemorial. In a global economic system, corporate profits primarily come from increased processing activity and global trading. This is why several large corporation now spend millions of dollars in public relations and advertising campaigns arguing that small farmers are not productive enough to feed the hungry world. Global corporations replace local, diverse farming for self-reliance with monocultures (Kumar, 2003).

An export-oriented system of agriculture favours high priced, high margin luxury export items such as flowers, potted plants, shrimp, cotton, coffee, exotic vegetables which are then exported to the already overfed countries. The people who used to live on the lands, growing their own foods for their communities and for local markets, are driven off their lands. Many people who once fed themselves have become landless, jobless, cashless, homeless, dependent and hungry. While dependency and starvation has replaced self-sufficiency of the nations, the global corporations have become rich by exporting luxury foods to other countries.

Market Fundamentalism

The IMF, the World Bank and the WTO have been pursuing an ideological commitment to two basically false principles:

1. Economic growth and increased trade achieved through deregulation and privatization automatically increases the wealth of communities and humanity, and contributes toward a better future for all. In other words, what benefits corporations benefits all.
2. Increased foreign investment in the Third World countries increases productive capacities and development and also contributes to the well-being of the poor.

Neither of these has proved true. What is true is that the system has added to the well-being of the corporations that have perpetuated it.

Most measures of "economic growth" such as GDP and GNP only measure the increases in the market value of economic production, i.e., the rate at which resources are converted to commodities, and other paid services and activities are undertaken. By such standards, expansion of military hardware, wars, crime, clear cutting of forests or building of toxic dumpsites are all made to seem positive since they increase GNP and GDP. Meanwhile, the unpaid household labour care for the sick and elderly and self-sufficient food growing and distribution are not deemed positive results because they do not get counted (Mander, 2001).

Such standards also contribute to the depletion of social and natural capital (nature) which is the foundation of all real wealth. In fact, export-driven globalization may well be the greatest single contributor to the massive ecological crises of our time. Its emphasis on exponentially increased trade and transport activity necessitates corresponding expansion of airports, seaports, roads, rail lines, pipelines, dams and electric grids; many of these are in pristine places, often on indigenous lands. Increased transport also uses drastically increased fossil fuels and so aggravates the problems of climate change, ozone depletion, and oceanic and air pollution. And an ever expanding economy requires the depletion of the last resources on the planet; under free trade these are usually located in the global South. Southern countries are net resource exporters to the already rich northern states.

Indeed, ecological degradation of forests, rivers and biodiversity has the most devastating impact on the poor, and resource depletion reduces livelihood and creates poverty. So economic growth is certainly not a measure that benefits the poorest parts of the world. In any case, depleting nature does not serve anyone for long, not even the rich (Kumar, 2003).

Is Globalization Inevitable

An arrogant, foolish proposition and omnipotent illusion has been floating around that the aim and the final destiny of humans is to manage the planet earth. Management concerns planning, organizing, directing and controlling. The earth harbours millions of species and hundreds of billions of individuals and the number of possible relationships among them is far greater. To imagine that we humans can manage life on the earth is absurd. The volume of information to accomplish this impossible task would be enormous. This is best exemplified by a map store in Yarmouth, Maine, which has built a scale model of the earth, 42 feet in diameter, with the printed data on the three-storey model rotating in the lobby of the store being equivalent to 214 CD-ROMs. Considering that an average person can read one CD-ROM worth of text in a lifetime (Berryman, 2000); it would thus take about 200 lives just to read the information on this image of the earth (DPC, 1998). And this is only a scale model, without all the essentials: lives, waters, minerals, soils, air, relationships, etc. It is time that we abandon the crazy idea. Berry (1992) rightly wrote, "The abstractions of sustainability can ruin the world just as surely as the abstractions of industrial economics. Local life may be as much endangered by those who would "save the planet" as by those who would "conquer the world. For "saving the planet" calls for abstract purposes and central powers that cannot know and thus will destroy the integrity of local nature and the local community."

Likewise, Orr (1994) highlighted the vital importance of local place in the following words, "We are inescapably place-centric creatures shaped in important ways by the localities of our birth and upbringing that environmental movement has grown out of the efforts of courageous people to preserve and protect particular places... problems that occur all over the world are not necessarily global problems, and some truly global problems may be solvable only by lots of local solutions...a purely global focus tends to reduce the earth to a set of abstractions that blur what happens to real people in specific settings...we have not succeeded in making a global economy ecologically sustainable, and I doubt that we will ever be smart enough or wise enough to do it on a global scale."

Globalization, Textiles and the Environment

Clothing is one of the three basic requirements of humans, the other two being food and shelter. The making, the use and the disposal of textiles exert considerable environmental impacts. Usually, the textile chain begins and ends in some developing country but quite often the intensive value-added phases in between are located in an industrialized country.

The clothing industry has become markedly globalized. A garment may travel thousands of kilometres along its international production route to some place in the West to be sold. This journey usually leaves a trail of environmental pollution and health problems for people.

Transformation of crops into textile fabrics involves many stages of processing, usually in different countries. For instance, organic cotton does not necessarily produce an ecologically sound final product, since the processing of fibre into fabric requires chemical substances as well as huge amount of water, energy and waste. It is not enough to produce crops naturally, followed by their processing in a conventional and polluting system. In this context, healthy shift in textile production toward cleaner and greener clothes is taking place in some countries where reforms in all the links in the chain from the field to the fashion shop are being attempted. Under the umbrella of sustainability, the concept covers organic cultivation, sound production methods, safe treatments and dyes, fairer wages as well as long-life healthy garments. While these eco-textiles make up less than 10 per cent of the global textile market, their share is increasing. Today it an important new market for producers in the South.

Cotton Processing

The product life cycle covers all activities from raw material cultivation, processing, transportation, distribution and use to final disposal. Each stage of the cotton textile life cycle has environmental impacts which vary according to the way the fibre is cultivated, the fabric is made and how the fabric is used.

Clothing textiles have much higher environmental costs in the consumer 'use' stage than furnishing textiles, as they are washed more frequently. The main environmental impacts for furnishing fabrics come from fibre cultivation and processing, and for carpets, from processing and disposal. Synthetic fibres use more energy in their initial extraction than natural fibres, but less energy in later processing. Although not biodegradable, synthetic fibres can usually be recycled. A shift in consumer demands, design specifications or structural relationships can minimize environmental costs of textile production. It is quite possible to produce and design textiles that are durable. The scale and degree of mechanization as also the environmental impacts of cotton processing can vary greatly. Processing may be carried out in a small locally based unit or in a large modern mill.

The chain from cotton fibre to textile fabric processing encompasses yarn manufacture, fabric manufacture and fabric finishing. Fabric processing involves ginning (separation of the cotton fibre from the seed), conversion of the raw fibre into yarn and spinning of the yarn. Two common methods of processing cotton yarn into fabric are weaving and knitting. Like yarn manufacture, fabric making also is dominated by mechanical processing, and the major environmental burdens are related to energy use, waste production and the generation of dust and noise.

The last stage in fabric processing covers preparation of the fabric to be dyed or printed, fabric colouration itself and the application of any specialist fabric finishes such as water repellents or those used to resist creasing (Fig. 3.3). It is this stage that exerts major environmental impacts e.g., the use of large volumes of water, energy and chemicals and the production of large volumes of effluents. Effluents from the textile processing chain usually are grey in colour, have high polluting load of heavy metals, high solids content and high temperature.

Because many of the processes in fabric finishing cannot be avoided, the emphasis should be on energy efficiency, waste minimization and effluent treatment.

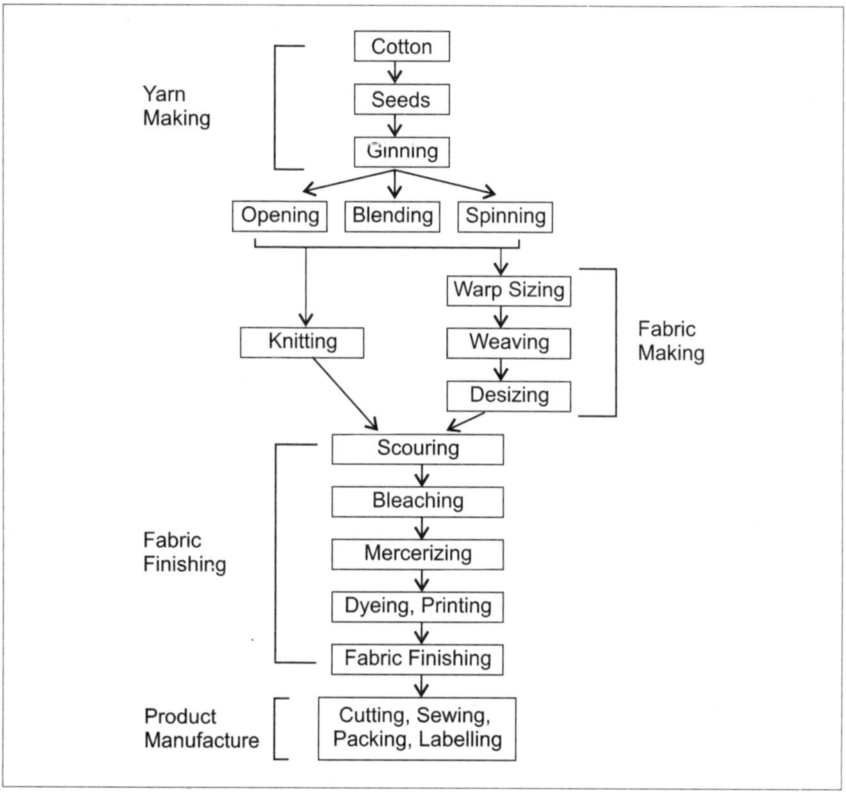

Source: Intermed. Technol. Prod., London, 1999

Fig. 3.3 Different stages in the cotton chain
(After ITP, Organic Cotton: From Field to Final Product)

A standard sequence of treatment for woven and knit fabric finishing includes screening (removal of fibrous waste from the effluent), equalization (mixing waste so as to achieve a standard effluent for downstream processing) and biological treatment (decreasing the effluent's polluting power).

Dyeing and Printing

Textiles can be dyed as fibres, yarn or fabric. Fibres show affinity for different dyes.

The colouration process is highly resource intensive in terms of water, energy and chemicals. It generates a highly coloured but rarely toxic effluent. In developing countries where environmental protection measures are lax, dyeing and printing can pose serious threat to humans.

Cotton has an affinity for various natural, reactive, sulphur, direct or vat dyes. While the yarns pose no particular hazard, most low-cost synthetic dyes are extremely toxic in the long term. If used carelessly, these dyes can cause ailments ranging from skin rash to cancer. If waste synthetic dye water is released to the environment without proper treatment, it can contaminate soils. Some dye components can enter the food chain, posing further environmental and health threats. For these reasons, many Western countries have not only banned the most toxic kind of dyes, but also imports of textiles using such dyes. A marked preference for natural and harmless dyes is growing.

Textile Industry and Environmental Pollution

The textile industry is one of the world's biggest polluters. Chemical fertilizers, pesticides, herbicides and defolinants are widely applied or sprayed on cotton and flax. Eighteen per cent of all pesticide used in the world is sprayed on cotton alone. From the harvest onward, every successive step involves various chemical treatments ranging from fungicides, whiteners, softners, moth-proofers through to toxic dyes. Around six tonnes of chemicals are used to make 10 tonnes of clothing. Besides people at large, it is textile workers whose health suffers greatly. Some people suffer skin irritation and allergies from conventional textiles. Some 25 per cent of children in Germany suffer textile-related allergies triggered by dyes, especially dispersion dyes so often found in cheap synthetic garments. Garments also occasionally contain carcinogenic substances.

But in recent years, the attitudes have undergone change. Many consumers in Europe are willing to pay more for healthy and environmentally sound clothes. Many manufacturers also are willing to undertake eco-audits and consider more informative labelling. Some 2,000 European companies are now working with a certification scheme which guarantees the non-toxicity of garments. The specifications involve parameters that can be tested by analysing products rather than monitoring production processes.

Global Environmental Citizenship

Environmental citizenship or global environmental citizenship aims at creating environmentally responsible citizens, through creating awareness and knowledge of the environment and of environmental problems leading to environmentally responsible attitudes and actions (Palmer et. al., 1995). These being central themes in environmental citizenship, the discipline uses almost the same goals and objectives as those for traditional environmental education. But there are subtle differences in emphasis as the global environmental citizenship approach is more informal and chiefly targets the out-of-school, using partners to assess the needs of certain groups in society and develop custom-made information strategies with specific environmental citizenship messages. Environmental citizenship also overlaps with the philosophy and goals of traditional environmental education.

Sustainability and Global Change

Global environmental problems need to be viewed in a perspective of "sustainable development" defined as the development that meets the needs of the present without compromising the ability of future generations to meet their own needs. While this definition sets a lofty objective, it also raises questions concerning:

1. The extent to which the long-term impact of human action can be assessed
2. The extent to which irreversible changes of ecological system can be avoided
3. The importance assigned to enhanced quality of life (QOL) in balance with nature for both present and future generations
4. The scope, the content and the reach of a precautionary strategy

We must realize that we can never carry the world on our shoulders, the earth carries us. Global sustainable development appears to rest on certain contradictory qualities, e.g., fear of the actual world and strong belief that we can build a better one to suit our fancies and desires.

The more we attempt to manage nature, the more it can erupt. Consider for example a dammed river where drainage has been controlled and where people have settled in the flood plain. If the control mechanisms fail to order nature, the resulting disorder can have a much greater impact on the settlements along the river. As Livingston (1986) puts it, it is not the environment that needs to be managed and controlled but our uses and abuses of it.

A sustainable society will be a society in which all the aspects of civil and personal life will be compatible with sustainable development and where all the services of the state at all levels will work together for the progress of that society (UNESCO, 1997a, pp 27). UNESCO affirmed, "Reorienting all of education in the direction of sustainability concerns all the levels of formal and non-formal education in all countries" (UNESCO, 1997b, pp 2).

These strong words smack of extreme intolerance or totalinariasm. We should not forget that there are many other different ways of looking at the nature, the world and our situation. Sustainable development is but one aspect; it cannot possibly cover all the various possible environmental visions.

According to Postman (1995), the most important new gods to have failed are "Economic Utility, Consumership, Technology and Multiculturalism" some of the gods of globalization and partly the gods of education for sustainable development. Postman mentioned some ideologies that may serve us better in the long run collectively by caring about our locality, humility, openness and questioning attitude accompanied by a willingness to argue, diversity and finally learning "how humans use language to transform the world and then, in turn, are transformed by their own invention."

This signpost seems to be far more promising than the map of education for a sustainable development (Berryman, 2000). Of course, some radical changes are warranted in order that diverse human communities can thrive in a thriving world. These changes are called for particularly in the Western capitalist-urban-techno-culture since that is the source of most of the damage. We must think twice before extrapolating solutions of Western problems to a global scale.

Ecopsychology and Global Environmental Change

Processes such as global warming, ozone depletion, loss of biodiversity and species extinction happen at the same time to be ubiquitous and invisible. These global environmental changes appear elusive and intangible because they take place at ecological scales that are difficult to perceive.

Thomashow (2000) explored how the emerging field of ecopsychology could contribute to a greater awareness of the deep ecological and spiritual issues intrinsic to global environmental change. He proposed, "ecopsychology cultivate a place-based perceptual ecology as a bridge to connect psyche and ecosystem, and that this whole terrain becomes the home and the heart of learning how to contemplate spatial and temporal scale—local and global, human and more than human, civilized and the wild."

According to him, ecopsychology must pay attention to natural history and local ecology as primary sources of wisdom for healing and collective responsibility. Only then can a deeper global perspective emerge. Ecopsychology should simultaneously explore the implications of global environmental change, while remaining firmly grounded in the local landscape.

Global environmental change poses the challenge of scale, demanding imaginative juxtapositions of place and time. From the spatial perspective, what is the relationship between different regions in the world? How, for instance, do changes in the tropical rain forest impact coastal bird migrations? From the temporal perspective, what is the relationship between the past, the present and the future? How does the 20th Century industrialization promote rising sea levels in the present century? What is the geological significance of a three degree temperature rise in a single century? (Thomashow, 2000).

Changes sometime involve contradictions. How, for instance, do we reconcile the unprecedented affluence of the global growth economy with the widespread environmental damages that accompany it? Or how do we reconcile the material benefits of natural resource extraction with the displacement of indigenous cultures and species? (Thomashow, 2000).

Global environmental change is fraught with some ambiguity and has both ecological and existential dimension. The full global significance of such change cannot be apprehended without considering the specific local and ecological consequences of what happens to the place where we live. Along with the beauty and grace we discover while observing the natural world, the loss and the pain of habitat destruction or potential extinctions, or the disruptions that human communities experience. It is these contradictory feelings that constitute the core of the ecopsychology agenda. Ecopsychology aspires to integrate the ecological and existential, psyche and ecosystem, individual and community, local and global (Thomashow, 2000).

Ecopsychology emerges as a response to diffuse the anxiety of ecological alienation—dislocation, stress, deprivation and fragmentation that accompanies human separation from habitat and landscape. Abram (1996) described the perceptual dimensions of this separation, e.g., how text and screen replace land and sky, or how the alarm clock drowns out the early morning wake-up call of the cock (rooster). Roszak et. al., (1995) integrated several disparate dimensions of everyday life, implying that there is no effective psychology without an ecological context and the separation of psyche from ecosystem has profound spiritual consequences, contributing a pathological dimension to human/nature relationships. In fact, many of the emerging healing practices of ecopsychology have this earth-body-mind integration as their foundation. In recent years, ecopsychology has invented, resurrected, borrowed and translated catalogues of such practices, attempting to integrate the ecological, spiritual and perceptual dimensions of human awareness (Thomashow, 1995, 2000).

One's intimate familiarity with a landscape can provide the basis for the disposition to affiliate with flora, fauna and ecosystem.

The great American environmental archetypes (Henry David Thoreau, John Muir, Rachel Carson) had explored the full dimensions of psyche and ecosystem. They realized how crucial it is to practise the wild, to delight in the intricacies of habitat and landscape. They knew about the profound connection between the health of an ecosystem, the community life and the personal well-being. Their greatness stems not only from what they contributed to environmental thought but also through their close involvement in and knowledge of natural history. It is this foundation of environmental studies that leads to ecological identity, ecological citizenship and ecological spirituality (Thomashow, 2000).

Ecopsychology has a collective intuition for urgent challenges of global environmental change such as ozone depletion, global warming and habitat loss arouse a vague foreboding, the elusive shadow of industrial affluence. Within the penumbra of the shadow lurks the complex and ubiquitous anxiety of uncertain futures, ecological alienation and cultural displacement. The unique, substantive integration of ecology and psychology has the emergent properties to discern the shadows, reveal their contents and use them for ecopsychological restoration (Thomashow, 2000).

A conceptual connection links students of the psyche and observers of ecosystems; both appreciate the significance of scale and perception. The psychologist knows that neuroses often reflect the inappropriate interpretation of scale. One's world may become either too big or too small, and a feeling of self-aggrandizement or lack of self-esteem can result. Likewise, the naturalist pays close attention to the various scales and perceptual worlds that bind populations, communities and ecosystems. It is not possible to determine causation for any ecological situation without carefully defining the spatial and temporal dimensions of the situation in question (Allen and Hoekstra, 1993).

In both cases, for the psychologist and the naturalist, there is a basic similarity. The more we can judge the scale and consequences of our actions the better we shall understand the responses to those actions. The lack of due consideration of appropriate scale and perceptual context, lie at the heart of both psychological and ecological dysfunctional behaviour (Thomashow, 2000).

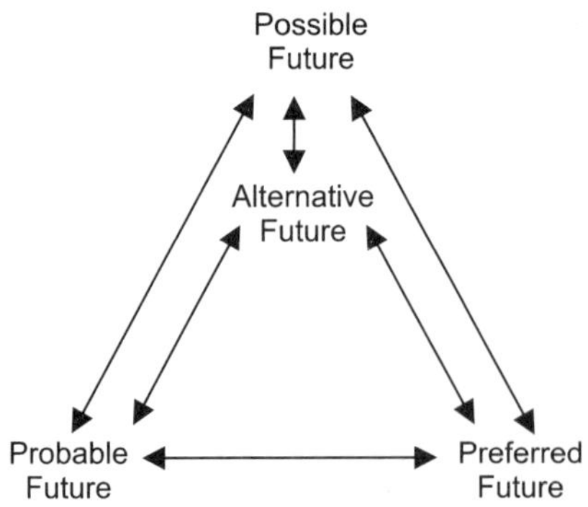

Fig. 3.4 The temporal dimension of global education (After Selby, 2000)

Education for sustainable development, education for sustainability and education for sustainable futures are all future-oriented, each being imbued with notions of intergenerational accountability and intergenerational justice. Each avoids compromising the ability of future generations to meet their own needs. Selby (2000) discussed a model whose temporal dimension is a triad of probable, possible and preferred futures, with interplay between the three bands (Fig. 3.4) that enhance understanding of the merits and demerits of the fullest range of options.

Environmental Education and Sustainability

Many environmental problems have reached unprecedented levels by now—problems as diverse as global warming, deforestation, desertification and threats to biodiversity, population-resource imbalances, poverty and pollution. The field of environmental education that saw considerable progress and development over the past few decades has been closely associated with growing awareness on global socio-ecological crisis. More recently, emphasis shifted on sustainability as a focus for environmental education. Sustainability now dominates in most national and international discussions, policies, and intergovernmental conventions concerned with the environment. The virtues of sustainable development are highlighted and communities are urged to live more sustainably. Education has been assigned a role to bring about a change towards more sustainable societies and sustainable living patterns (Tilbury, 1995). Sustainability has emerged as a focus for environmental education. This focus is quite understandable in the light of a deepening global socio-ecological crisis, usually attributed to the apparently unsustainable character of human society.

Enhanced understanding of environmental education as a process of social change towards healthier environments has led to wide acceptance of education for sustainability.

Modern civilized society often views education as a panacea. Faced with crisis, society regularly turns to education to address societal ills as if education were not a part of the problem. As aptly pointed out by Orr (1992), the decisions or actions wreaking havoc on the planet are often those of supposedly well-educated people. This may be ascribed to what Schreuder (1995) termed "miseducation" – education that serves to reproduce the values of the dominant social paradigm based on economic growth, production, consumption and development.

It appears that sutainability has often been interpreted from an overwhelmingly anthropocentric position (Sauvé, 1999). She also pointed out that with its focus on the future, education for sustainability may have a limited appeal to the younger generation. Indeed, sustainability is currently a controversial concept (Jickling, 1992). It means different things to different people.

Sustainability—Anthropocentric or Holistic

The anthropocentric view of sustainability has generated many controversies. The proposed principles of ecological sustainability (e.g., Fien, 1993), have decidedly anthropocentric leanings. Another example is that of biodiversity–widely accepted as one of the core principles of ecological sustainability. Biodiversity is often regarded as "...a living bank account, providing the capital that underlies all human enterprise and prosperity" (WWF, 1997, pp 1). Under the anthropocentric perspective, natural resources are managed sustainably for the benefit and future of humans, not for the intrinsic worth of nature itself. The contributions of living organisms towards making the earth and its atmosphere livable are viewed as "ecological services" (to humans). Such approaches reinforce and perpetuate modernist views of the earth and natural resources exclusively for human use. In contrast to this, Schreuder et. al., (1995) argued for a more holistic view of sustainability–integrated natural and social systems. This approach allows us to draw on examples of seemingly sustainable processes in natural systems, which can serve to guide more sustainable human living.

The images of sustainability as gleaned from natural systems may be gainfully used as metaphors for more sustainable human lifestyles.

The Planetary Green Plan

The first International Conference on the Human Environment, held in Stockholm in 1971 two years after the first celebration of Earth Day in the United States and Nature Conservation Year in Europe, brought out the global scope of environmental degradation. It highlighted the alarming diagnosis of the impact of human activity on the environment. Misdevelopment and urban expansion were identified as the primary causes of the degradation of life support conditions, particularly air and water pollution, and soil erosion. Growing social imbalances and inequalities were also highlighted.

This United Nations Declaration later catalysed a long-term approach involving economic growth and development as subjects for critical analysis. This led to the development of the concept which takes into consideration the satisfaction of the needs and aspirations of all the citizens of the globe, the pluralism of societies, equilibrium and harmony between humanity and the environment. It was felt that Environmental Education (EE) should consider in its totality the natural environment and the man-made, ecological, political, economic, technological, social, legislative, cultural and aesthetic environment. The environment mostly appears as a set of problems to be solved and prevented. To better understand the complexity of environmental situations, the need to adopt a more global outlook based on an interdisciplinary approach was appreciated. Education emerged as a tool for change conducive to the creation of new relationships between humans and their environment (Orellana and Fauteux, 2000). In the context of a world crisis, environmental education is a key element in the creation of a new development ethic, a universal ethic of individuals and societies corresponding to humanity's place in the biosphere, an ethic which recognizes and actively feels the complex interrelationships, in continual evolution, of humans with their own kind and with nature.

Continuing discussions about the relationships between environment and development emphasized the need to promote a type of development which respected the biosphere's capacity for assimilation and regeneration, based on a new ethic which went beyond strictly economic and growth principles (often confused with development and progress).

The World Conservation Strategy *Union Internationale de Conservation de la Nature* (IUCN), 1981 generated a world conservation strategy. Presented as one of the strategies required for human survival and prosperity, it postulated the conservationist concept of sustainable development. The focus on the impact of human activity on the environment was now on its destructive dimensions combined with the poverty of the majority of the world population in contrast to the wealth of a highly consumer-oriented minority. At this meeting, the fundamental relationship between humanity and biosphere was viewed as an economic relationship, with the environment being seen as a resource to be used, even though this resource was seriously affected by human activities (Orellana and Fauteux, 2000).

Conservation was defined as a type of management that generates maximum benefits from living resources in order to continue to harvest them in the future. The conservation and protection of the biosphere were viewed through a change in people's consumer habits. Three specific objectives included the maintenance of the ecological systems which support life, the preservation of biodiversity and the sustainable use of species and ecosystems. These objectives could be met through environmental education and the active participation of the general public—these were indispensable to the achievement of change in the behaviour of individuals and societies with regard to the biosphere. The need was felt to establish a new world economic order, since the strategy to achieve it was sustainable development based on conservation. Development was defined as the modification of the biosphere and the use of animate and inanimate human and financial resources to satisfy the needs of mankind and to improve the QOL (meeting current needs without restricting the satisfaction of the needs of future generations). Social, ecological and economic factors have also to be considered. The conservation strategy was associated with the UN's strategy for international development, whose purpose is to minimize inequalities in the relationship between rich and poor countries.

The work of the International Commission on the Environment and Development was published in 1988 as the Brundtland Commission Report. This report highlighted the connection between the dominant style of social development, the under-development of so-called "Third World" societies, and existing social and environmental problems. The Brundtland Report was the first comprehensive survey of the planet's health. The problems of atmospheric pollution, desertification, overpopulation, overconsumption, water shortages, poverty and underdevelopment pointed to a gloomy picture of the impact of human activity on the living environment. Even 15 years after the Stockholm conference, the inability of the international community to deal with environmental problems could be seen clearly.

The International Commission proposed the concept of sustainable development, with a view to achieving a convergence between the social players and to reconcile the interests of both parties in order to stop the destruction of the planet caused by human activity. The foundations of sustainable development refer to responsible development, which implies the use of less polluting technologies and the elimination of the enormous inequities which hamper the development of the peoples of the third world (Orellana and Fauteux, 2000).

Agenda 21, Planetary Green Plan *United Nations Commission for the Environment and Development*, 1992, Rio de Janeiro. This conference formulated conservation strategies for building a sustainable future. Chapter 36 of the action plan adopted by the Conference, Agenda 21, focused on public education, awareness and training.

Education for sustainable development adopts a behavioural concept based on knowledge transmission and question. It does not concern itself with generating critical knowledge, but rather with changing values and lifestyles (consumption, production, etc.,) disseminating knowledge to allow the emergence of a culture of change conducive to sustainable development, and informing people that they are in a position to support these changes and promoting them. International Conference on Environmental and Development Education and Communication, ECO-ED, 1992, Toronto, deliberated on adopting the principles of sustainable development as conceived from an economic standpoint. It affirmed that in future governments and their citizens should together work hard to reconcile the concepts of economic and social development with the long-term preservation of natural resources (UN, 1992).

Development occurs in a perspective of growth, in which nature is capital to be managed by reducing, in particular, the impact of harvesting activities on the environment. In this context, the environment may be regarded as a resource to be exploited and environmental education is an instrument of sustainable development. Sustainable development was seen as a compromise, as a result of which too great a turnabout from the predominant order of things could be avoided. The objective is to use all forms of capital, especially human, to achieve rapid and more equitable economic growth while reducing the impact on the environment.

An awareness was growing that population, the environment and development are issues so inextricably linked that none of them can be contemplated in isolation (UNESCO/UNEP, 1994).

It was realized that although humanity has the knowledge and technologies required for sustained economic growth and development, the imbalanced distribution of resources, overexploitation of environmental resources and unrestricted population growth are detrimental to socially equitable and ecologically rational development. The problems linked to population growth strongly impact both the QOL and the environment. The role of women was seen as decisive in solving population and environmental problems.

The balance between population, the environment and development required sustainable development. An appeal was launched to intensify efforts to stabilize the world population. In this context, environmental education plays a vital role as the necessary utopia which can guide us and bring the world to converge in mutual understanding, the development of a sense of responsibility and solidarity, to learn to live together for a better world with respect for spiritual and cultural differences (Sauve, 1996). This utopia should catalyse evolution of societies in a situation characterized by technological and scientific advances on the one hand and by disenchantment with the harmful effects of misdevelopment on the other. Both the individuals and the societies need to move toward the ideals of peace, freedom and social justice. They must learn to know, to do and to live together.

We should strive toward achieving an integral human development that goes beyond economic growth. A patient quest for strategies to deal with the various issues facing contemporary societies led to the identification of three interrelated imbalances: between North and South, between rich and poor, and between humans and the natural environment. These imbalances are intimately associated with the crisis in relations between societies, humans, and humanities and the environment. What is needed is a responsible world that is based on solidarity.

Montreal Declaration on Environmental Education at the Planet' ERE Forum
Quebec Association for the Promotion of Environmental Education Quebec, Montreal (1997).

The new concept of a "viable future" emerged from this meeting. Education is a factor in well-being and has a crucial role in giving means to individuals for becoming productive and responsible members of society. This involves a process of transmitting knowledge so that humans can accomplish their productive role and act responsibly in society.

The phrase "viable future" is a redefinition of the concept of sustainable development, which is itself associated with the concept of viability. The Montreal Declaration called for a commitment to incorporate environmental education in a more comprehensive and global process, one which links environment and development. It includes the dimensions of education for peace, justice and democracy.

At the Montreal meeting, the values of solidarity, sharing, respect for diversity and traditional knowledge, as well as the responsibility of all the players in society, were considered necessary to meet the challenges in order to achieve a harmonization of relations between people, societies and the environment as a function of sustainable development for a viable future. The concept of viability embraces not only environmental issues but also those of poverty, population, health, food security, democracy, human rights and peace. Viability is an ethical and moral imperative which implies respect for cultural diversity and traditional knowledge.

The idea of sustainable development inspired social scientists to suggest new political agendas related to equity not only between generations but also between genders, ages, cultures, North/South and more. It also aroused some tension between conservationists and developers. Some examples of these and other tensions are those between:

- Environmental conservationists and social reformers, the resource system and the consumer system
- Environmentalists who are issue-based with priorities for quick changes in people's behaviour, and educators who are people-based, with longer-term priorities and whose focus is on the development of competence
- Policy makers and educationists reluctant to be told what to do by amateurs, however well-intentioned
- Advocates for change and the vested interests of established academic disciplines and professional institutions
- Need for educational change and the stressful impacts of change on a complex system—ironic because it was the damaging effects of stress on the human-environment system which gave rise to the concern in the first place (Smyth, 2002).

According to Smyth, the following are some constructive steps which might be taken to relieve the above tensions:

Polarization in education between natural and social scientists, the latter usually with more political power, is being resisted but already some fragmentation of effort has occurred as, for example, when natural scientists retreat to the leafier refuges of biodiversity education with no provision to reconvene with sustainable development educators to bring their findings together. The unifying concept of the World Conservation Strategy must not be allowed to fade away.

Educationists should come together into a common front, which may include those involved in education consistent with sustainable development.

Environmental educators are very often not social scientists. They need to develop a wider awareness of social justice and economic contexts in order to be able to meet, and deliver on the challenge of education for sustainability. The achievement of sustainability and sustainable development demands an understanding of the social sciences, of power structures, of social justice and equality and the like. Happily some convergence is taking place between the natural and social sciences around the overarching public policy goal of sustainable development. The achievement of sustainable development is exerting a unifying cooperative bond among educators, engineers, planners and conservationists along routes that allow substantial sharing of common aims and objectives and common goals.

One major problem of environmental education is the demands made on people untrained in the handling of large complex systems when they are invited to deal with issues involving geomorphological, climatic, ecological, social, cultural, economic, political and ethical aspects or more, in complex interaction. Traditionally, our educational system has been founded on a reductionist approach to complexity. This approach is not quite appropriate for systems which are significantly greater than the sum of their parts. The resulting deficiencies manifest themselves when e.g., local officials assess an environmental impact statement, or members of a community try to agree on a local service (Smyth, 2002; Blackmore and Smyth, 1998).

Accelerating change is a hallmark of today's world. We are in an age of change which usually stresses both ecological and human systems (Smyth and Stapp, 1983). "Complex structures and processes in systems breakdown, long-term specialized functions, storage and other forms of future provision, information content, stratification and the like, give way to simpler relationships, short-term outlooks, opportunistic policies, competitiveness and intolerance. The systems are too complex for these generalizations to be taken very far but educators function in a state of affairs beyond their ability to control" (Smyth, 2002).

A Cleaner Environment

The United States may be credited to have pioneered development of pollutant release and transfer registers (PRTRs) in the world when it launched its Toxics Release Inventory (TRI) in the 1980s. This TRI was continuously upgraded and exemplified how information on pollutants could be made accessible to the public. Indeed, it has served as the model for all national and regional PRTRs developed thereafter. The first experiences with the TRI also motivated several governments to establish emission inventories in the Rio Declaration in 1992.

The transparency of environmental information has been a major asset in the Western societies. It seems paradoxical, therefore, that the United States should now lag behind other countries by not requiring facility-based reporting of greenhouse gas emissions, it is surprising that it is not following the underlying "right-to-know" principles in this context (Mehlhorn, 2007).

This paradox has already had some international implications: The United States, unlike 36 other countries and the European Community, did not sign the United Nations Economic Commission for Europe PRTR Protocol in 2003, largely because of its reluctance to report greenhouse gases on a facility basis, which is required by the protocol.

According to Mehlhorn (2007), in spite of the advantages of greater transparency, even with regard to emission reductions, high priority needs to be given to directly reducing greenhouse gas emissions, for instance, by implementing a cap and trade approach at the earliest.

Environmental Care for Sustainable Development

Physical and social environmental care is an essential component of integral and sustainable development. Bauer (1988) proposed a methodology identified as environmental management of development (EMD) which involves the three aspects of management, viz., planning, execution and control, in a continuous and interactive process whose instruments and characteristics are enunciated by stressing their environmental aims. EMD can be applied within a region and specific questions addressed about regional management oriented to water resources development. The water basin can be adopted as the regional unit for efficient management.

The evolution of human societies in the past few decades has clearly demonstrated that, besides strong scientific-technological and economic-financial support, development also requires social, cultural and environmental support. If this support is not available, development could fail for two main reasons:

1. The development is not comprehensive enough and does not satisfy the spiritual, affective, aesthetic, ethical and religious aspirations of human beings.
2. It is unstable and short-term (i.e., unsustainable) because it does not have the background of political, social and individual understanding, motivation and/or capacity and lacks the necessary physical support due to the impairment, spoilage or exhaustion of the latter. In keeping with reasoning, the term 'environment'

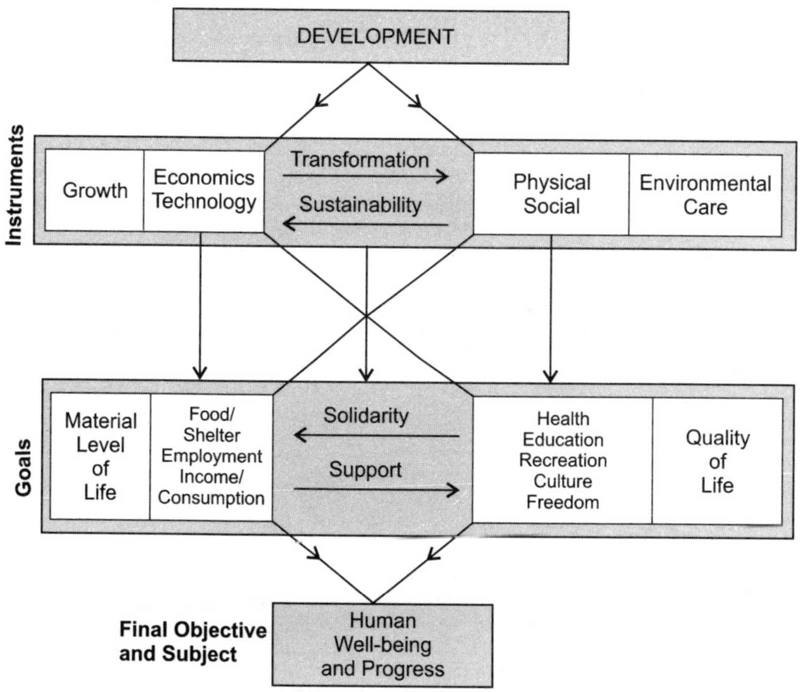

Fig. 3.5 Development and well-being (After Bauer, 1988)

encompasses concepts related to the physical world and ecology, to human beings themselves, and to their social and cultural circumstances, all of which influence the QOL (Fig. 3.5).

Environmental Considerations in the Management of Regional Development

Development, while necessary, is only acceptable and fruitful when it is adapted to the reality within which it occurs, when it serves the population and is in harmony with nature and the general environment. To achieve this kind of development, one essential requirement is to integrate environmental considerations into planning, execution and control of development. At the regional level, apart from the external influences mentioned above, there are three special and complementary factors to be considered such as organization of teams, involvement and participation of the public, and continuing consideration of environmental parameters.

An interdisciplinary team must participate from the very beginning in the organization of regional planning, no matter how small the team, it should include people educated in the natural, social and human sciences, engineering, technology, environmental economics. Management teams must be properly trained, beyond their environmental responsibilities, to improve their skill and creativity for coping with their duties and to interact effectively with the various social groups (Fig. 3.6).

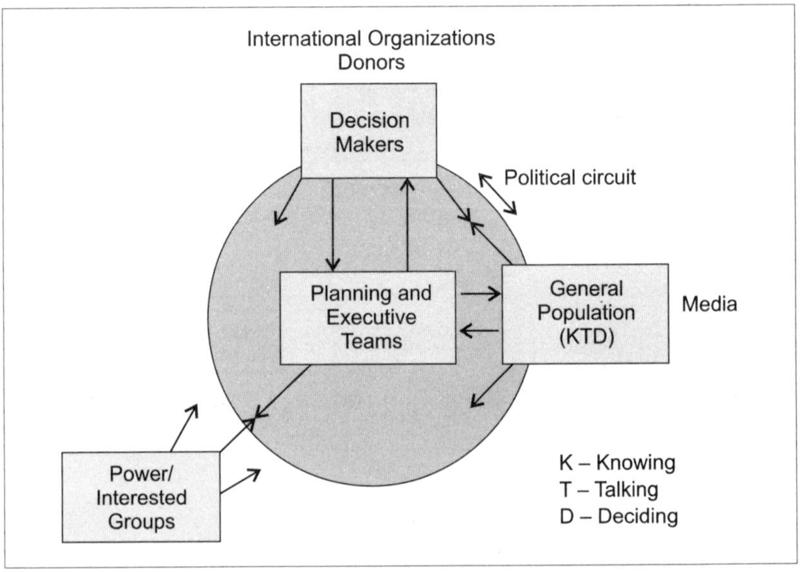

Fig. 3.6 Management relationships (After Bauer, 1988)

Ecological Restoration

The field of ecological restoration demonstrates the importance of interdisciplinary approaches to real-world problems. It draws on ecology, other life sciences, physical and social sciences, and the humanities (Hall, 2005). Much practical experience over past several decades in treating degraded landscapes has generated and nourished the field of ecological restoration with its focus on returning biological potential and ecological integrity to damaged land (Bradshaw and Chadwick, 1980; SER, 2002). It attracts active interdisciplinary participation from land managers, policy-makers, scientists and educators (Gold et. al., 2006).

Three major goals of ecological restoration projects are maintaining biodiversity, controlling erosion and enhancing sustainability.

4
Wastes and Toxic Substances

The industrial economy is virtually linear (Pearce and Turner, 1990) the flow of resources is linear and unidirectional and economic wealth is created as a result of this unidirectional flow. Waste accrues (Fig. 4.1) from every stage of the linear economy (Jackson, 1992). Two factors which explicitly show the linearity of the human economy are resource depletion on the one hand and environmental degradation on the other.

Many of the resource input (R) to the linear model are exhaustible. After extraction and passage through the economy, they cannot be used again. Resource depletion points to the generally unidirectional flow of resources through the economy.

A major concern that points to the linearity of the economy is the effect of waste on the environment. The discarded material throughput of the industrial economy creates various environmental problems in the atmosphere, in water supplies, in oceans and on land. The dispersal of industrial and domestic wastes into air, water, earth and oceans can cause much damage to the environment, disturbing ecological balances and harming the stability of entire ecosystems. Such environmental problems as acid rain, greenhouse effect, eutrophication of water supplies and

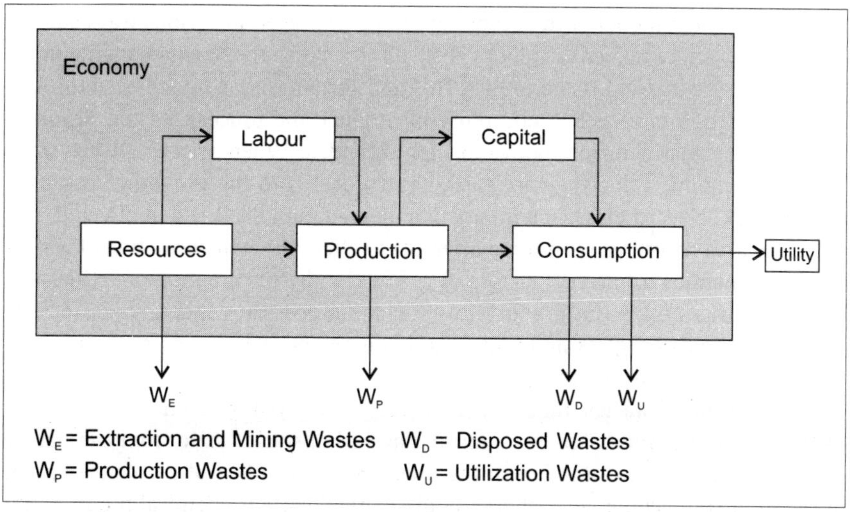

Source: Stockholm Environment Institute, Stockholm

Fig. 4.1 Waste in linear economy (After Jackson, 1992)

marine environment, dispersal of toxic chemicals throughout the environment, toxic leachates from waste sites into groundwater supplies, dioxins from incineration, Polychrorinated biphenyls (PCBs) and DDTs in marine life, Chlorofluorocarbons (CFCs) in the ozone layer, volatile organic compounds in working environments and a wide range of atmospheric pollutants including carbon monoxide and lead from vehicle exhausts all testify to the crisis. In fact, in many cases, the sheer volume of waste emissions has increased greatly in recent years.

Furthermore, the extent of the impact on the environment depends not just on annual waste generation but also on the cumulative load sustained by the environment as a result of continued emissions over several years. Also, it appears that some of the increase in environmental damage, and the increase in danger to human health is a result of changes in the structure of the economy and the nature of industrial production. This is best exemplified by the growth in chemical production in the second half of the 20th Century.

So waste is an important factor of production in the economy, and needs to be recognized as such. Environmental problems caused by waste emissions not only directly affect the economic and industrial infrastructure but also exert considerable indirect economic effects as a result of the physical, social and political disruption and instability that can be caused by environmental degradation (Jackson, 1992).

There seems to be little doubt that the linear economy is on the verge of foundering, in view of its failure to include the fourth factor of production ("waste") in its deliberations. Besides the economic impacts of this failure, in the process untold damage can be caused to the ecological system in which the economic system is embedded.

Improvements

The simple linear model of the economy can be improved in various ways such as including a variety of feedback loops that can transform the linear economy into a circular one (Pearce and Turner, 1990). This transformation can be achieved through the introduction of recycling and reuse of product and process wastes. Resource scarcity has been a major motivation for this idea. When wastes attract some positive economic value they are easily drawn back into the economy, distorting its linearity. Nevertheless, environmental degradation has also motivated this move towards recycling, with some attempts to effect the transformation of wastes from externalities to internal factors of production by the creation of artificial or "shadow" prices on waste products to provide an economic incentive to recycle. Deposit schemes on glass and aluminium containers or batteries exemplify this (Lindhqvist and Christiansen, 1990).

Significant obstacles hinder the success of recycling. Some of these are physical whereas others are economical. Physical obstacles arise from the nature of production and consumption in the linear economy. Most of the consumption in the industrial economy is inherently dissipative. Various chemical products are dissipated as fertilizers, pesticides and pharmaceutical products such as detergents,

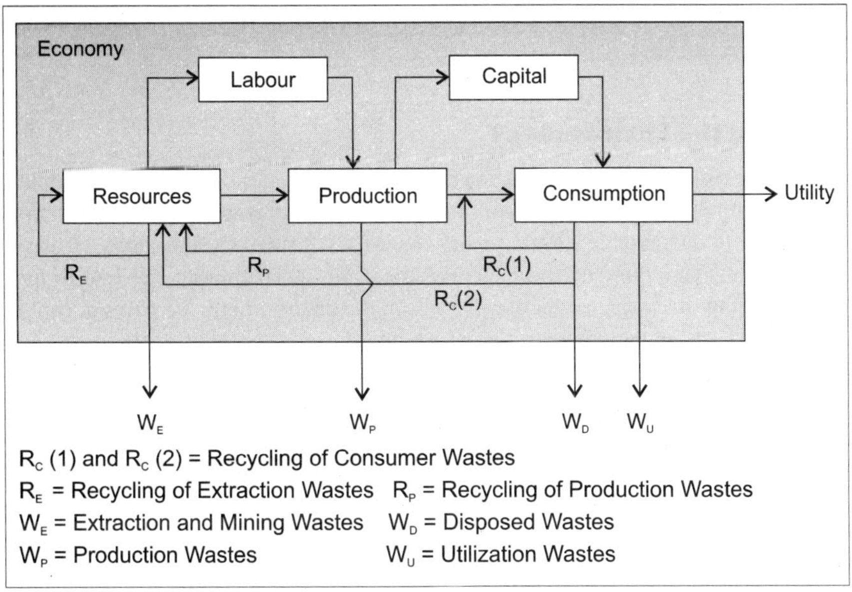

Source: Stockholm Environment Institute, Stockholm

Fig. 4.2 Recycling of waste in linear economy (After Jackson, 1992)

or disinfectants, which are not conducive to their recovery. Lead from car emissions exemplifies an inherently dissipative source of metal pollution. Non-point source pollution has become the most significant source of pollution. The single biggest source of marine pollution is from non-point sources through atmospheric deposition and run off (Jackson, 1990). Eutrophication of water sources mainly occurs from the non-point source pollution by pesticides and fertilizers. This precludes implementation of a recycling loop for many waste streams within the industrial economy. This is why in Fig. 4.2, no recycling is shown for utilization wastes which pose intractable waste problem, in particular.

Besides these physical obstacles, short-term economic assessments have often suggested against the economic feasibility of recycling. Whereas transport and collection costs can be high, land and sea disposal costs have traditionally been fairly low (Long, 1990).

No doubt, that due attention must be paid within the linear economy to material efficiency. But, there are also limitations to the material efficiency of the economy. Therefore beyond material efficiency, the real need is to distinguish among material throughput on the basis of hazard. Material efficiency is often limited, but efficiency of hazardous material usage need not be so. This important distinction warrants critical consideration of the issue of which wastes are hazardous and non-hazardous to human health and the environment. Also, it strikes an appropriate balance in the trade-offs between hazard in the environment and utility in the economy revealed by this distinction. It is these kind of problems that lie at the core of the challenge of cleaner production.

Waste in the Environment

The question of waste is crucial in any discussion on cleaner production. Our ability to make suitable technological and social choices that lead to clean production and hence to sustainable development is severely limited by the kinds of waste streams being generated by these technological and social choices. The importance of considering the ways in which waste acts in the environment, it creates or causes hazard, and the extent to which it can enter the environment without causing ecological damage or hazard to human health, cannot be overemphasized.

There are essentially only four ways of dealing with waste matter. It may be redirected and treated to reduce hazard or it isolated or sequestered to prevent environmental damage (Jackson, 1992). For the first option all kinds of wastes have been emitted to the atmosphere, discharged into rivers or dumped into oceans and landfills, and are simply left there. The rationale for this approach is that wastes disperse and dilute and in this process lose their potential for hazard.

The second strategy typified the first tier of responses to environmental pollution and the initial efforts at protection of human health and the environment. One good example refers to the problems caused by sewage in Britain in the 17th and 18th Centuries that were later addressed in the 19th Century by creating extensive sewage systems that carried sewage away from domestic areas and deposited it elsewhere, usually in rivers or oceans. A more recent example is the response to atmospheric pollution from unrestrained emissions of particulates into the atmosphere. During the middle part of the 20th Century, this problem became so acute that most industrial countries enacted laws to limit and regulate the particulate content of flue gases. Various abatement strategies were implemented. In the so-called 'end-of-pipe abatement', particulate pollution is filtered out from flue gases generally by electrostatic precipitation. The particulates are then deposited as fly ash and disposed of on land. These strategies in fact only redirect the waste from the atmosphere to the land.

The third option is exemplified by the incineration of wastes. Incineration partly involves waste treatment as combustion and thermal treatment change the nature and composition of some wastes. It also involves disposal. Combustion products are either disposed of into the atmosphere (through flue gases) or on landfill as fly ash and bottom ash.

The fourth approach to waste management is the isolation or sequestration of wastes from the environment. In some cases, it is merely an extreme example of the previous approaches. Capping of contaminated dredged material in ocean disposal sites with clean material exemplifies this (Morton and Polermo, 1989) and also the disposal of radioactive wastes in deep geological formations or mineshafts (NEA, 1988). Another example is the deep sea disposal of packaged radioactive wastes.

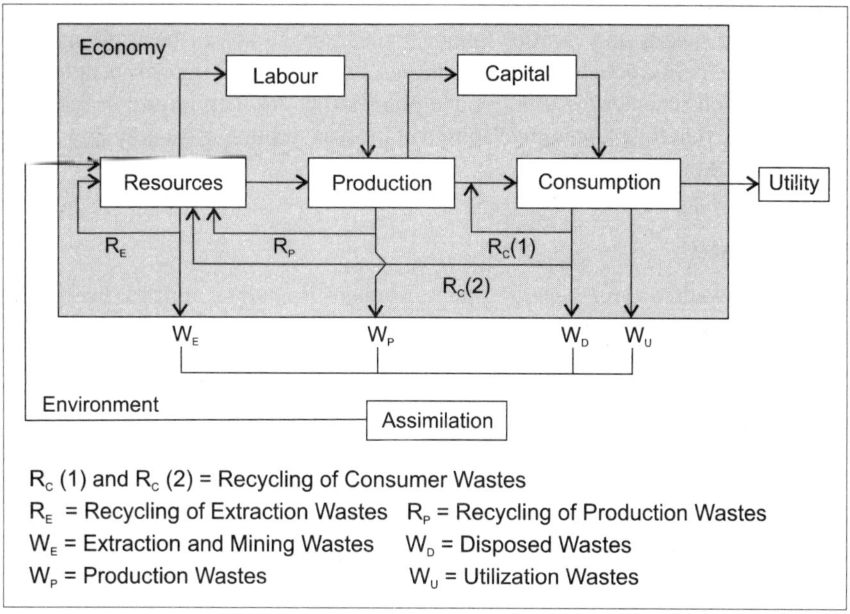

Source: Stockholm Environment Institute, Stockholm

Fig. 4.3 Assimilation of wastes: The circular economy (After Jackson, 1992)

All the four approaches outlined here rest on the basic assumption that in certain quantities and concentrations, over certain time periods, the environment can assimilate our wastes without causing harm either to the ecosystem or to human health. It is this assumption that has inspired the rationalization of the linear economy, and its transformation to a supposedly circular one (Fig. 4.3). In this latter view, assimilative capacity acts as a natural "recycling loop" to complement the recycling loops in the industrial economy.

E-waste

Computers, mobile phones and digital music players are some of the electronic devices being used everyday for work and entertainment. These devices have also created a new type of waste.

Waste Electrical and Electronic Equipment (WEEE), also known as 'e-waste', contains several toxic heavy metals such as lead, cadmium and mercury. This e-waste is now attracting much interest in view of its potential risk to the environment and human health. Some companies are already taking back and recycling their products. For example, Hewlett Packard, Dell and IBM have agreed to take back unwanted IT equipment from corporate customers.

Valuable resources like copper is lost when waste electrical and electronic equipment is sent to landfill rather than recycled. Reusing and recycling electrical and electronic equipment is better for people's health and for the environment because the metals and plastics found in these products can be used again to manufacture new products. In some countries, Vodafone and Telecom are operating free collection schemes for used mobile phones that are then reused or recycled. This ensures that the phones are disposed of in an environment-friendly way and at no cost to the owner (user).

Tyre Waste

Old and unwanted tyres have become a problem in many countries. Every year several millions of tyres require disposal or recycling.

Tyr-mesh NZ Ltd., New Zealand, has developed a simple and innovative tool that quickly, safely and efficiently processes tyres to a state that makes recycling and reuse a viable economic option.

Whole tyres cause problems in landfills because they are bulky, trap air and move around. The Tyr-mesh system significantly reduces the size of old tyres, making them easier to transport and store. The Tyr-mesh cutter attached to a standard tyre changing machine cuts up old tyres, reducing their volume and making them easier to transport.

Approximately, 70 whole tyres fit in a standard, 7.5 m rubbish skip. Using the Tyr-mesh system, this number increases to 350. This substantially reduces the volume of the tyre waste and saves money in transportation costs.

Tyre waste created by the Tyr-mesh system can be used in many different ways such as a rubber 'hardstand'. This is an underground rubber mat made from old tyres which provides a stable platform to reduce bogging at farm troughs and gateways.

Pesticides

Within two decades of Rachel Carson's 1962 publication of *Silent Spring*, it was established that pesticides poison people, degrade the environment, create resistant "superpests" and destabilize agricultural systems. Pesticide proliferation and abuse were recognized as symptoms of the growing power of transnational corporations (TNCs), and a key component of industrialized monocrop agriculture in the North and the Green Revolution in the South that pushed many small farmers in debt, forced people off the land, and weakened communities' abilities to shape their livelihood and future.

Still later, as a result of several international agreements, standards and treaties, global trend today is shifting from synthetic chemicals toward agro-ecological approaches that value human labour, farmers' experience, and the rights of communities and countries to genuine food security.

The concept of "prior informed consent" (PIC) emerged in the 1980s to empower nations to resist pesticide dumping. PIC became international law in the 1998 Rotterdam Convention, which has been ratified by 33 countries to date (50 are needed to make it enforceable). And seven pesticides out of the so-called 'Dirty

Dozen', including dieldrin, chlordane and the infamous DDT, have since been banned globally under the new Persistent Organic Pollutants (POPs) treaty. The new PIC and POPs treaties can potentially accelerate pesticide bans around the planet in the next decade. Many countries have started implementing the PIC treaty even before it enters into force (Scholl-Buchwald, 2002).

This commendable move threatens the agrochemical and crop biotechnology industry.

Pesticide Use in Developing Countries

Pesticide use in developing countries has steadily increased in the last 20 years. International pressures, especially the trend towards trade liberalization, have been responsible for much of the increase. Since the early 1980s, the World Bank and the International Monetary Fund (IMF) have insisted that developing countries implement structural adjustment programmes as a condition of aid, investment and debt relief and the cultivation of export crops forms part of the bargain. Export crops produced in monoculture systems such as bananas and cotton normally require much greater applications of pesticides than food crops for domestic use.

The growth in pesticide use also poses other hazards for poor people. According to the International Labour Organization (ILO), in the year 1994, estimates indicate two to five million annual occupational cases of pesticide poisoning and 40,000 fatalities (ILO, 1994). In some countries, pesticides cause 14 per cent of all occupational injuries and 10 per cent of fatalities in agriculture (ILO, 1996).

Many governments are unable to legislate and monitor the use of pesticides. Water supplies and land are both at risk.

Threat from Pharmaceuticals

In recent times, most research on the impact of chemical pollution has focused on the conventional 'priority' pollutants i.e., POPs (Birkett and Lester, 2002). In fact, these pollutants are not very relevant today, especially in many first world countries because emissions have been substantially reduced by adopting appropriate legal measures and by the elimination of many of the dominant pollution sources. In advanced countries, the focus has shifted to compounds present in low concentrations but which nevertheless might be able to do harm (Larsen et. al., 2004). One interesting aspect of many such chemicals is that they do not need to be persistent in the environment to cause adverse effects, because their high transformation and removal rates can be offset by their continuous introduction into the environment, often through sewage treatment works (Suter and Giger, 2001; Ayscough et. al., 2000).

Pharmaceuticals have attracted much interest in this context, in view of their potential to enter potable supplies. Drinking water can be a direct route into the body for any drugs that might be present. Although many countries employ advanced treatments such as granular activated carbon, membrane technologies, ozonation and ultraviolet radiation for treating water intended for human consumption, some compounds remain unaffected by these treatments.

To date, most of the published research work on pharmaceuticals (and their metabolites) in the aquatic environment has been on the occurrence of drugs in sewage effluent and receiving waters. The risks of exposure to drugs are perhaps most significant with regard to the natural environment, but the general public is more interested in human exposure. This is especially pertinent in areas where water reuse is mostly indirect, where sewage effluent is discharged into streams and rivers which are in turn used as a source of raw water for the production of potable supplies for communities living downstream (Van Dijk-Looijaard and Van Genderen, 2000). There is an acute paucity of data on the occurrence of pharmaceutical products in point-of-use (i.e., tap water at the sink) drinking waters. This is partly related to the misconception that modern treatment processes can remove pharmaceutical compounds from potable supplies (Jones et. al., 2005). In fact, some endocrine disruptors, pharmaceutical residues and the drug compounds are resistant to water treatment processes. Examples include the antiepileptic drugs carbamazepine and primidone, and the lipid regulators clofibric acid and gemfibrozil (Heberer and Stan, 1997; Heberer, 2002; Tauber, 2003).

In many countries, for example in the UK, there is no regulatory requirement for the monitoring of pharmaceuticals in drinking water. Table 4.1 lists the concentrations of various drugs in finished drinking water supplies. Human pharmaceuticals are generally found in a very low amount in drinking water, with concentrations generally being in the ng/l range. Most research in this area has been done in Germany and the UK.

Table 4.1 Concentration of Drug Compounds Reported in Finished Drinking Water Worldwide (After Jones et. al., 2005)

Compound	Theraputic Group	Maximum Concentration detected (ng/l)	Country
Bezafibrate	Lipid regulator	27	Germany
Bleomycin	Antineoplastic	13	UK
Clofibric acid	Lipid regulator	70–270 5.3	Germany Italy
Carbamazepine	Antiepileptic	24 258	Canada USA
Diazepam	Psychiatric drug	10	UK
Ibuprofen, Diclofenac	Analgesic and antipyretic	3–6	Germany
Gemfibrozil	Lipid regulator	70	Canada
Phenazone	Analgesic and antipyretic	250–450	Germany
Propylphenazone	Analgesic and antipyretic	80–120	Germany
Tylosin	Macrolide antibiotic	1.7	Italy

Even advanced water treatment does not always remove all drugs. Tauber (2003) detected both carbamazepine and gemfibrozil in four out of the 10 Canadian cities tested that all used advanced water treatment such as ozone *(CTV: Quantitative Analysis of Pharmaceuticals in Drinking Water From Ten Canadian Cities; http://www.ctv.ca/servlet/ArticleNews/story/CTVNews/1044053088271 39462288/?hub = SciTech).*

Although only three of the 440 analyte-sample combinations showed detectable levels for carbamazepine, and only one had detectable level for gemfibrozil, a clear possibility emerges that drug compounds can pass through even modern, advanced water treatment facilities (Jones et. al., 2003).

Significant amount of drugs are being released from sewage treatment plants to the environment. This generates a risk that humans could be exposed to drugs through potable water from contaminated supplies. Today, this risk may be fairly low (in advanced countries, at least) but the rapidly escalating demands on the freshwater supplies of the world could lead to greater incidences of indirect and direct water reuse situations as the spatial and temporal distances between wastewater and drinking water shorten. The potential for adverse effects must not be ignored especially because nothing is known regarding the environmental or human health hazards that might be posed by chronic, sub-therapeutic levels of pharmaceutical substances or their transformation products.

Further, regardless of the absence of any proven risks, drinking water will always be a primary focus of consumer concern as it constitutes a direct path to the human body for any drug compound that might be present (Webb et. al., 2003). Other (indirect) routes can be bathing or showering in water containing effluent, or consuming crops irrigated with effluent or grown on sewage-sludge-amended soil. The presence of pharmaceuticals in drinking water, however small, will increase the public's already negative attitude to water reuse (Bridgeman, 2004).

However, it appears that the likelihood of any form of short-term human health risk originating from the presence of low concentration of pharmaceuticals in drinking water is extremely low (Webb et. al., 2003). Still, there is a possibility that mixtures of different compounds might act synergistically (Jones et. al., 2004; 2005). Even if concentration of individual substances are low, we do not know what effects, if any, exposure to repeated doses of a mixture of sub-therapeutic amount of drugs and other chemicals (such as endocrine disruptors) could have on human health.

Fortunately, no serious problem exists today. But prudence warrants application of the precautionary principle, and an endeavour to reduce the levels of drugs and their compounds in drinking water before any harm is proved (e.g., Betts, 2002).

Pollution Prevention

Undoubtedly, prevention is the best way to reduce pollution. Several companies have adopted pollution prevention techniques which not only improve efficiency and increase profits but also minimize environmental impacts. This is done by reducing material inputs, re-engineering a process to reuse byproducts, improving management practices and substitution of toxic chemicals.

Some pollution prevention techniques and processes currently used by the nonferrous metal industry are classified as:

1. Process equipment modification
2. Raw materials substitution or elimination
3. Solvent recycling
4. Precious metals recovery

Process equipment modification reduces the amount of waste generated. Some copper, lead and zinc refiners have modified their production processes by installing sulphur fixation equipment which not only captures the sulphur before it enters the atmosphere but also processes it to marketable sulphuric acid (H_2SO_4). Use of pre-baked anodes in primary aluminium refining is another example. Such a use allows closing of the electrolytic cell, thereby increasing the efficiency of the collection of fluoride emissions. New carbon liners have been developed which greatly increase the life of the aluminium reduction cell. This has greatly reduced the amount of spent potliner material (hazardous waste) generated by the aluminium industry.

Raw material substitution or elimination involves the replacement of raw materials with other materials that either produce less waste or a non-toxic waste.

Precious metals recovery involves the modification of a refining process so as to allow the capture of marketable precious metals such as gold and silver. Precious metals recovery is a common way of minimizing waste.

From Pollution to Prevention

The general history of waste management is illustrated in Fig. 4.4. The earliest strategies let waste of all descriptions simply to flow unhindered into the environment. A slightly better approach redirected hazardous wastes from one place to another, more appropriate, disposal or sequestration sites, although this also created environmental degradation requiring post-hoc clean up and remediation.

The third approach involved redirection of wastes by the introduction of end-of-pipe abatement and treatment strategies. A common problem with end-of-pipe treatment methods has been that the redirection of the pollution does not always remove the environmental problem.

While end-of-pipe strategies have certainly produced some limited success, they have also revealed significant disadvantages such as:

a. The tendency to transfer pollution from one medium to another, where it may either cause equally serious environmental problems or even end up as an indirect source of pollution to the same medium.
b. Although not as expensive as remediation of environmental damages, end-of-pipe abatement significantly escalates the costs of production processes and products.

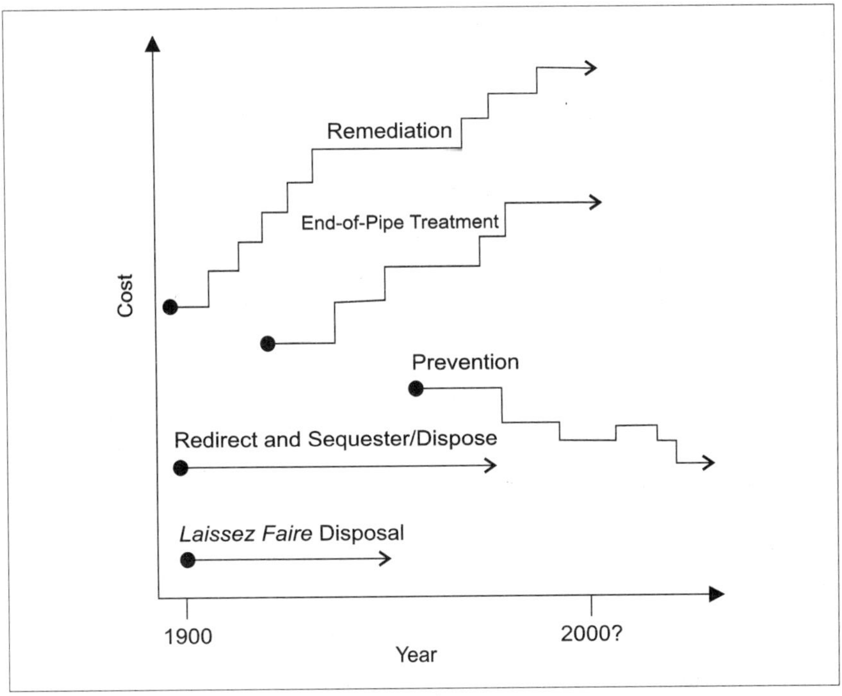

Source: Stockholm Environment Institute, Stockholm

Fig. 4.4 Historical course of waste management strategies (After Jackson, 1992)

c. End-of-pipe abatement of pollution requires regulation through control legislation which is not only costly and cumbersome but also leads to potentially inefficient regulatory structures.
d. Such abatement technology represents a significant technological market with an associated economic inertia that works against the reduction of pollution at the source (Jackson, 1992).

It is now increasingly realized that the only way to achieve the broader objective of multimedia environmental protection warrants a fresh way of thinking about waste management in which the emphasis is not so much on waste disposal or end-of pipe control strategies but on eliminating the need for such management and disposal by reducing or eliminating the generation of hazardous wastes in the first place. This new approach focuses on prevention rather than control and remediation of hazard. Some terms used to describe this shift from control and disposal to prevention include waste reduction, source reduction, pollution prevention, toxics use reduction, best available technologies, clean technology and clean production.

The Paris Commission (PARCOM, 1989) regulating land-based source of pollution of the marine environment in the North Sea and North Atlantic region defined the term Best Available Technology (BAT) as, "The term 'Best Available

Technology' is taken to mean the latest stage of development (state of the art) of processes, of facilities, or of methods which indicate suitability of a particular measure for limiting emissions. It is further stated that in determining whether a technology is the best available, several aspects must be given special consideration, among others the economic feasibility and the precautionary principle."

The US OTA (1986) defined waste reduction as, "In-plant practices that reduce, avoid or eliminate the generation of hazardous waste so as to reduce risks to health and environment."

The term 'source reduction' is generally used synonymously with 'waste reduction'. The term 'pollution prevention' (INFORM, 1990; Pollution Probe, 1982) is sometimes used synonymously with waste reduction but may also be used more broadly to refer to a hierarchical approach to waste management in which waste reduction at source has primacy. The term toxics use reduction (Allen, 1987) has sometimes been employed in the general sense of preventing specific kinds of waste, in particular toxic wastes.

The term "low and non-waste technology" (LNWT) is a concept developed by the United Nations Economic Commission for Europe who described it as "a manufacturing method (process, plant, territorial-industrial complex) where the totality of raw material and energy is used in the most rational and integrated way in the production cycle i.e., raw material resources-production-consumption-secondary material resources to prevent any negative impact on the environment likely to affect its normal functioning" (UNECE, 1984).

The term clean production was coined by experts convened to advise the UNEP Industry and Environment Office on how to proceed with a new global information network on low and non-waste technologies. The idea was to "encompass the broader constellation of conceptual, attitudinal, ethical and procedural, policy and scientific-technical factors that must be addressed to ensure a sustainable human future".

Hazardous Wastes

Hazardous wastes may be liquids, solids or sludges. They may be the byproducts of manufacturing processes, or simply commercial products. For example, household cleaning fluids or discarded battery acid. Whatever their form, however, proper management and disposal of hazardous wastes are essential to protect any country's valuable resources.

A hazardous waste can also be a solid waste such as garbage, refuse or sludge. A solid waste can be solid, semi-solid, liquid or contained gas, and it must meet the criteria where because of its quantity, concentration, or physical, chemical or infectious characteristics, it may cause or significantly contribute to an increase in mortality or an increase in serious or incapacitating illness. Or the criteria where it poses a substantial actual or potential hazard to human health and the environment when improperly treated, stored, transported, disposed of or otherwise managed.

The wastes usually excluded from the definition of hazardous waste are domestic sewage, irrigation waters or certain industrial discharges, certain nuclear materials, household wastes, certain mining wastes and agricultural wastes (excluding some pesticides).

A waste is hazardous, if it shows any of the following properties:

1. **Ignitability** For example, liquids such as solvents that readily catch fire and friction-sensitive substances.
2. **Corrosivity** Acidic wastes and those which are capable of corroding metal (such as tanks, containers, drums and barrels).
3. **Reactivity** Wastes unstable under normal conditions and can create explosions and/or toxic fumes, gases and vapours when mixed with water.
4. **Toxicity** Toxic wastes are harmful or fatal when ingested or absorbed and when disposed of on land, contaminated liquid may drain (leach) from the waste and pollute groundwater.

Some specific wastes are hazardous. These comes under three categories:

1. **Source-specific wastes** Sludges and wastewaters from specific industries such as petroleum refining and wood preserving.
2. **Generic wastes** Wastes from common manufacturing and industrial processes, e.g., solvents that have been used in decreasing operations in any industry.
3. **Commercial chemical products** Such chemical products include creosote and some pesticides.

Table 4.2 lists various types of hazardous wastes being generated by various businesses and industries. It is to be noted that hospitals also generate a variety of wastes. Tables 4.3 and 4.4 show different ways of classifying these wastes.

Table 4.2 Examples of Hazardous Waste Generated by Businesses and Industries

Waste Generators	Waste Types
Chemical manufacturers	Strong acids and bases, spent solvents, reactive wastes
Vehicle maintenance shops	Heavy metal paint wastes, ignitable wastes, used lead acid batteries, spent solvents
Printing industry	Heavy metal solutions, waste inks, spent solvents, spent electroplating wastes
Leather products manufacturing	Waste toluene and benzene
Paper industry	Paint wastes containing heavy metals, ignitable solvents, strong acids and bases.
Construction industry	Ignitable paint wastes, spent solvents, strong acids and bases
Cleaning agents and cosmetics manufacturing	Heavy metal dusts, ignitable wastes, flammable solvents, strong acids and bases

Contd...

Contd...

Waste Generators	Waste Types
Furniture and wood manufacturing and refinishing	Ignitable wastes, spent solvents
Metal manufacturing	Paint wastes containing heavy metals, strong acids and bases, cyanide wastes, sludges containing heavy metals

Table 4.3 Classification of General Wastes

Waste	Content	Composition	Moisture Content (Approx %)
Trash	Highly combustible waste, e.g., paper, wood, plastics	100% trash	5
Rubbish	Combustible waste, e.g., paper, rags, wood, from domestic, commercial and industrial sources	Rubbish : Garbage 80 : 20	27
Refuse	Rubbish and garbage from residential sources	Rubbish : Garbage 50 : 50	50
Garbage	Animal and vegetable matter	Garbage : Rubbish 65 : 35	70
Organic, animal	Carcasses, organs, solid organic wastes	Animal and human tissue 100%	85
Gaseous, liquid or semiliquid	Industrial wastes	Variable	Variable
Semisolid	Combustibles requiring hearth, retort, or other burning equipment	Variable	Variable

Toxic Substances

Earnest efforts are required to prevent or reduce human and ecological exposure to toxic materials such as pesticide residues, PCBs, lead and their adverse consequences.

For toxic materials there is need to focus on improving the characterization and communication of risks, developing cost-effective policies for managing exposures to toxic materials, and developing cost-effective, innovative solutions for pollution avoidance, control and remediation (Kumar, 2003).

Table 4.4 Classification of Hospital Wastes

Waste Type	Liquid Wastes	Treatment/Disposal
Biological	Blood, excrement, body fluid	Sewer
Chemical	Solutions, inorganic salts	Sewer*
Over-date medicines	Unused or over-date drugs	Sewer
Radioactive	Wastes from radiology (iodine 125, iodine 131, etc.)	Sewer
Perforating and cutting	Solid Wastes Needles, syringes, scalpels, blades, broken glass, vials	Container dump
Non-perforating Non-cutting	Wastes from treatment (dressings, stool napkins, plaster casts)	Watertight bag** dump
	Body parts (organs, placentas, tissues)	Cemetery
	Household wastes, other wet and dry wastes	Recycle or dump

*Dilute before flushing, **Autoclave where possible

Until recently, most risk assessment efforts for toxic substances focused on potential causes of cancer. The risks of other human health effects (e.g., neurological, developmental and reproductive) and ecological impacts received much less attention. Comprehensive databases on cancer and noncancer end points are available on very few toxic substances. Differences in individual genetic susceptibilities to the toxic effects from environmental chemicals sometimes produce a wide range of responses.

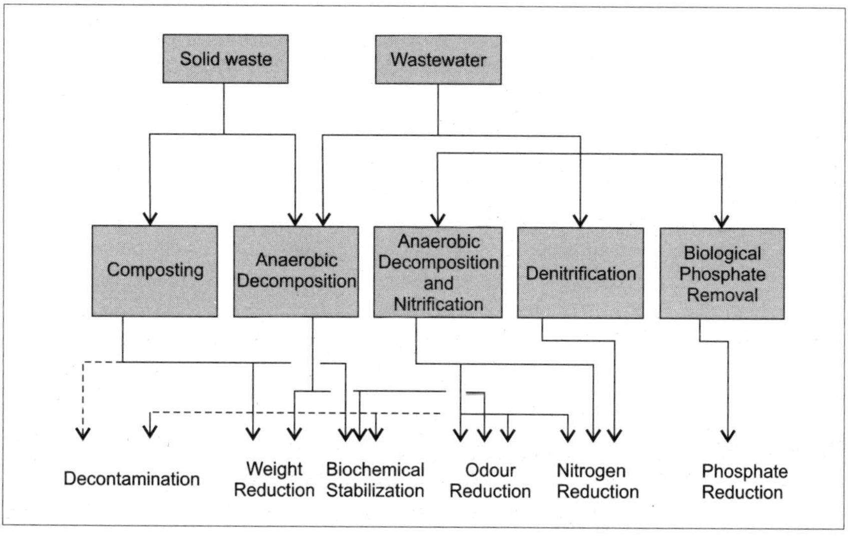

Fig 4.5 Process sequences in anaerobic waste treatment

Past research on risk management has focused heavily on control and remediation technologies and on characterization and monitoring. Emphasis is placed on field evaluation for remediation technologies. More cost-effective approaches are needed for certain toxics or types of contamination. Recent research has begun to emphasize pollution prevention.

Management of Chemicals in Waste Stream

It is necessary to effectively manage toxic chemicals in wastes and also to either completely eliminate them or at least reduce their quantities. The primary and secondary metals industry produce huge quantities of production related wastes, of which a substantial fraction is either transferred off-site or released to the environment. Some of the industry's toxic wastes are managed on-site through recycling, energy recovery or treatment. Much of waste released or transferred off-site may be divided into portions that are recycled off-site or recovered for energy off-site. The remaining portion of the production related wastes is either directly discharged to air, land, water and underground injection, or is disposed off-site.

Summary of Some Pollutants Released

Brief accounts of selected pollutants released by non-ferrous metal industries to the environment are given below:

Chlorine

Breathing small amount of chlorine for short periods of time affects the respiratory system in humans and causes cough and chest pain. It is irritating. Repeated long-term exposures have adverse effects on the blood and respiratory systems. Chlorine is highly toxic to aquatic organisms at low doses. Most of the chlorine released to the environment quickly evaporates.

Copper

Metallic copper is not toxic but copper salts are. Inhalation of copper oxide fumes and dust causes nausea, sneezing, coughing, chills, muscular pain, gastric pain and diarrhoea. Certain nervous system disorders may be due to copper poisoning. Long-term exposure to copper can cause hair, skin and teeth discolouration.

Copper is an essential micronutrient for plants and animals. High concentrations in soil kill some soil microorganisms and disrupt nitrogen and phosphorus cycling in soil.

Hydrochloric Acid

Acid aerosols cause and aggravate respiratory ailments. Accidental releases lower the pH of water and hence affect aquatic life. Releases of hydrochloric acid to surface waters and soils are neutralized to some extent by buffering.

Lead

Short-term poisoning occurs from ingestion of acid soluble lead compounds or inhalation of lead vapours. Symptoms include nausea, abdominal pain, vomiting, diarrhoea or constipation, shock, muscular weakness and kidney damage. Death might occur within two days. Chronic lead poisoning affects gastrointestinal, neuromuscular, blood, kidney and central nervous system. Exposure to lead is also linked to decreased fertility in men. Lead appears to be a human carcinogen.

When released or deposited on soil, lead is retained in the upper 2-5 cm of soil. Normally, neither leaching nor uptake of lead from soil into plants is considered important. Lead enters water from atmospheric fallout, runoff or wastewater and is effectively removed from the water column to the sediment predominantly by adsorption to organic matter and clay minerals. Some lead can re-enter the water through methylation by microorganisms. Lead does not appear to bioconcentrate significantly in fish but does so in some shellfish like mussels.

Zinc

An essential micronutrient, zinc has very low toxicity from ingestion. Swallowing of zinc dust can cause gastritis with vomiting. Short-term exposure can produce lethargy, dizziness, nausea, fever, diarrhoea, and reversible pancreatic and neurological damage. Long-term poisoning causes muscular stiffness and pain, loss of appetite and nausea.

It is relatively stable soft metal, bioconcentrated in aquatic organisms. Significant zinc contamination of soil is only seen in vicinity of industrial point sources.

Heavy Metals: Impact and Remediation

Heavy metals are important environmental pollutants that can be cytotoxic, mutagenic and carcinogenic. Their prominent sources that contaminate soil are geogenic, mining and smelting, disposal of municipal industrial wastes, use of fertilizers, pesticides and automobiles. Natural contamination of soil and groundwater with arsenic, selenium and fluoride in many parts of the world, particularly in the Australasia-Pacific region, is a cause of serious concern to human health. In the context of sustainable agricultural development, soil health is crucial for achieving future food security targets. Environmental monitoring of radio-nuclide contamination in very essential as more and more nuclear power plants are expected to be installed for generation of power in the future. Indiscriminate overuse of garbage as manure in Hyderabad has polluted the natural resources like soil and water. The plant growth has been affected due to the build-up soluble salts, sodium and heavy metals. Higher contents of heavy metals such as Pb, Cd, Ni, Cr and Co have been detected (Joshi and Luthra, 2000) in sewage-irrigated soils of Hyderabad. In Secunderabad, there is the danger of heavy metals build-up in soils irrigated with mixed industrial effluents. Leather tannery effluents are often rich in Cr, Fe, Ni, Mn, Cu, Pb and Zn and these effluents should not be used as manure in agriculture. The status and distribution of Cr in tannery waste contaminated soils of Vellore district, Tamil Nadu, where over 70 per cent of the tannery industries are located, has been assessed: total chromium and Cr (VI) in these soils ranges from 154 to 568 and from 48 to 467 mg/l, respectively.

It has been reported that Vrishabhavati river water, the primary source of land pollution in Bangalore, contains Cu 138, Zn 261, Pb 100, Ni 54 and Cr 34 mg/l and plants grown in such soils absorb enough metals to render their edible tissues unfit for animal/human consumption. Some early warning systems for the detection of copper, mercury, cadmium, lead, chromium, cobalt and aluminium have been made by using biomonitors such as *Poecilia reticulata* (guppy fish), *Aedes aegypti* (mosquito), *Musca domestica* (housefly), *Chironomus* sp. and *Mesocyclops leukrati* (Joshi and Luthra, 2000).

Electroplating industries have been mainly responsible for chromium contamination in groundwater of Ludhiana in Punjab where it ranges from 10–3320 mg/l. Prolonged exposure of dairy animals to toxic levels of fluoride (> 1 mg/l) in drinking water has sometime resulted in anaemia, hepatic, kidney and bone disorders associated with significant alteration in plasma mineral status. More than 100 million people are at risk from groundwater arsenic contamination in Bangladesh and West Bengal. Soil contamination with arsenic can be toxic to vegetation and animals feeding on the latter accumulate arsenic in their bodies, thereby aggravating the problem of arseniosis.

Remediation of metal contaminants is a major focus in the area of environmental biogeotechnology. Allophane-bearing and halloysite-bearing clays serve as more economical materials than the expensive bentonite clays for the removal of Cd from the waste disposal sites. Sphagnum (a moss), crushed limestone, waste wood pulp, fly ash and waste wood felt have been used as substrates to remove heavy metals (Cu, Pb and Zn) from artificial road run-off. Soil amended with calcium carbonate significantly reduces the uptake of Cd in wheat grains. The content of heavy metals declines greatly after 60 days of composting in a vermicompost prepared with Azotobacter, Azospirillum and phosphorus solubilizers. Sewage sludge composted with poultry manure at 1:3 ratio minimizes the heavy metals enrichment and their availability in soil.

Another approach is the use of heavy metal hyperaccumulator plants for remediation of heavy metals. *Brassica juncea* has a good potential for removing Cd from moderately contaminated soil and *Eichhornia crassipes* plants may be used as phytoextractors of Cr from tannery effluents. The *arbuscular mycorrhizal* fungi can potentially play an important role in soil remediation by enhancing growth and biomass of hyperaccumulator plants on contaminated sites. Lime, farmyard manure, tree leaves, zeolites or iron oxides/hydroxides, alum, superphosphate and fly ash have been used for reduction of Cu, Ni, Cd, Zn and Pb in the growth medium. Application of some cow manure reduces the concentration of Cd, Ni and Zn in rice plants grown under both flooded and non-flooded conditions. Possibly sawdust and coir pith may be utilized for removal of Cr from tannery effluents. Some earthworm species are able to solve the problem of tannery sludge disposal.

Microbes for Environmental Cleanup

Few bacteria naturally possess all the enzymes needed to convert chlorinated synthetic chemicals such as polychlorinated biphenyls and dioxins into nontoxic constituents, including cabon dioxide, water and halogen ions. Given enough time, some microbes in chemically contaminated environments do figure out ways to use these substances. However, typically the microorganisms found at such sites do not work efficiently enough to be useful for environmental cleanups. Natural microorganisms do not evolve very efficient degraded pathways since they can feed on natural organic waste materials. By creating conditions where a toxic chemical is the only major food that they have, improved strains can be developed.

For this microbial improvement process to work, microorganism-rich soil sample is placed into a chemostat. Organisms within the chamber are provided no nutrients for growth other than the pollutant desired to be degraded like Agent Orange. In less than a year of continuous exposure to this contaminant, pseudomonads from soil have acquired all the enzymes that they need to break down the contaminant.

Mutations alone can never achieve this rapid adaptation. Besides changes in already present genes, the adaptable bacteria also incorporate DNA from other microorganisms that were present in the soil samples. The acquisition of those genes is very slow in soil but speeds up in the chemostat.

Successful processors of synthetic chemicals pick up all sorts of genes with little regard to the origin of the DNA molecules.

Usually, bacteria that incorporate genetic material from other microorganisms seem to compile the new genes with a transposable promoter into a plasmid. But the microbes in the chemostats contain many small replicons. Moreover, sometimes the genetically modified microorganisms recruit a mere two or three new gene for a job that typically would require a dozen or more genes, if the organism were to build a metabolically complete degradative pathway. We are likely to see chemostats being used increasingly to exert selective pressure on microorganisms in redesigning them to do specific degradative tasks. This approach thus could become part of an emerging set of genetic engineering technologies that may catapult bioremediation into an increasingly important role in cleaning up environmental contaminants (Pennisi, 1995).

Microbial Biosorbents of Heavy Metals

Many water bodies suffer from heavy metal pollution. Existing chemical processes are not economical for treating these polluted water bodies because usually the metal concentrations are fairly low. Microbial biomass is a better option for developing economic and ecofriendly wastewater treatment processes. Non-living and dead microbial biomass can passively sequester metal(s) by biosorption from dilute solutions. This biosorption technology involves low operating cost and is effective in dilute solutions and generates minimum effluent. The dead microbial biomass acts as an ion exchanger by virtue of such reactive groups found on the cell surface as carboxyl, amine, imidazole, phosphate, sulf-hydryl, sulfate and hydroxyl. The process can be made more economical by procuring natural bulk biomass or spent biomass from various fermentation industries. The performance of a biosorbent can be enhanced by various physical and chemical treatments. Certain pretreatments can modify the cell surface either by removing or masking the groups or baring more metal binding sites. Immobilized microbes constitute a continuous sorption/desorption system in a fixed bed reactor. A variety of commercial microbial biosorbents, e.g., AlgaSorb, AMT-Bioclaim and Bio-fix are now available (Gupta et. al., 2000).

The degree of treatment of wastewater can range from a main process for heavily polluted industrial waste to a polishing process for removing the trace concentrations which remain after the main treatment. Some common processes used for effluent treatment are precipitation as hydroxides/sulphides, oxidation/reduction and ion exchange. These processes are quite expensive and have an adverse impact on the environment. They generate some sludge. As a result, an aquatic problem is changed into one of solid disposal. Amongst the chemical adsorbents, ion exchange resins have been considered as the preferred option for remediation with least ecological trouble. But chemical resins are expensive and the increasing demand of ecofriendly technologies has led to the search for low costing and single use alternatives. In this context, biological materials have emerged as an ecofriendly and economic option. Peat is a good biosorbent, but it is not available everywhere. Microbial biomass is therefore better. It can passively bind large amounts of metal(s) by biosorption, so provides a cost-effective solution for industrial wastewater management. On prolonged contact with a metal-bearing solution, living biomass also can sequester metals intracellularly by an active process called 'bioaccumulation'. Biosorption can occur both in living and non-living biomass wheras bioaccumulation occurs only in living biomass. Bioaccumulation is a growth-dependent process in contrast to biosorption which is growth-independent. Thus, microbial biomass can be used and exploited more effectively as biosorbent rather than as bioaccumulant (Gupta et. al., 2000).

A large number of microorganisms belonging to various groups, viz., bacteria, fungi, yeasts, cyanobacteria and algae can bind a variety of heavy metals to different extents (Hodgson, 1987; Gupta et. al., 2000).

Since biosorption involves mainly cell surface sequestration, cell wall modification can greatly alter the binding of metal ions. Various methods can be employed for cell wall modification of microbial cells to enhance the metal binding capacity of biomass and to elucidate the mechanism of biosorption. *Aspergillus niger* biomass grown in the presence of large amounts of potassium hexacyanoferrate from a citric acid fermentation plant shows a high biosorption capacity due to change in cell wall composition. In gram-positive bacteria, Cd^{2+} biosorption increased by about 14 per cent after addition of nutrients in 2 hour of incubation, indicating that some metabolic uptake also occurs besides the passive uptake in these cells. However, in gram-negative bacteria, nutrient addition did not cause any significant increase in Cd^{2+} uptake. In *Phormidium laminosum*, biosorption decreased initially with nitrogen starvation and subsequently increased until it reached the value of nitrogen-sufficient cells. Pregrown biomass could be given several physical and chemical treatments to tailor the metal-binding properties of biomass to specific requirements. Some physical treatments for modifying cell walls include heating/boiling, freezing/thawing, drying and lyophilization. The various chemical treatments used for biomass modification include washing it with detergents, cross-linking with organic solvents and alkali or acid treatment. Certain pretreatments can modify the surface characteristics/groups either by removing or masking the groups or by exposing more metal-binding sites (Gupta et. al., 2000).

Novel Biodegradable Flocculants

Treatment of wastewater and industrial effluents requires both inorganic and organic flocculants (Bratby, 1980; Singh et. al., 2000). In inorganic flocculants, the salts of multivalent metals such as aluminium and iron are mostly used. Among the organic type, polymeric flocculants (synthetic as well as natural) are preferred because of their low dosage, easy handling, resistance to pH changes, production of large cohesive flocs and versatility. Some important examples of synthetic polymers are polyacrylamide, poly(acrylic acid), poly(styrenic sulphonic acid), poly diallyl dimethyl ammonium chloride (DADMAC), etc. Among natural polymers, guar gum, starch and alginic acid are very often used as flocculants and retention aids. The synthetic flocculants are available in all the three forms, i.e., cationic, anionic and nonionic. The rising concern for environmental and ecological issues warrants the use of biodegradable flocculants in wastewater and industrial effluent treatments. Natural polysaccharides such as starch, gums, glues and alginate function as bridging flocculants. It has been established that by grafting polyacrylamide side chains on polysaccharides, the dangling grafted chains become better accessible to the contaminants. As compared to grafted guar gum, xanthan gum, carboxy methyl cellulose and starch, grafted starch flocculates better (Singh et. al., 2000). Starch consists of amylose (a low molecular weight linear polymer) and amylopectin (a high molecular weight, branched polymer). The grafted amylopectin has been found to be a suitable flocculant for various kinds of industrial effluents (Bratby, 1980; Singh et. al., 2000).

Singh et. al., concluded that grafted polysaccharides are shear-stable, efficient flocculating and settling aids for industrial effluent treatment and mineral processing. Of the various grafted polysaccharides, polyacrylamide grafted amylopectin having fewer but longer branches performs best in a variety of synthetic and industrial effluents. As amylopectin itself is branched, its grafted chains are more accessible to contaminants in the effluent (Prasad et. al., 1995).

Exploiting Waste

Livestock produce many million tonnes of collectable faeces every year. Disposing them into watercourses or spreading them on fields can cause nuisance algal blooms and also starve aquatic life of oxygen. On the other hand, if this waste is collected and placed in a sealed, airless biodigester, then microbes within the solids soon turn the slurry into CO_2 and methane.

Digesting just 6.6 tonnes of cowdung can produce enough gas to generate about 180 kWh a day of electricity and 135 kWh a day of heat energy. This can provide steady electricity for 20 homes or heat for at least five homes. This point to the feasibility of popularizing the installation of more and more farm-based biodigesters so as to gainfully utilize animal wastes and generate at least 1.5 TWh of electricity from waste.

In this context, the potential of food waste is also significant. Biodigesting, the millions of tonnes of food waste sent to landfills each year could generate well around 450–760 GWh of electricity every year. This can satisfy the needs of countless households, and lead to saving several million tonnes of CO_2, partly by avoiding methane emissions from the rotting produce.

In the UK, the gas released from landfill and sewage processing sites is being widely used as a renewable source of electricity, but still it is under-exploited. The European Environment Agency in 2006 stated that the UK could produce 85 TWh of heat energy from biodegradable waste and sewage, that would be equivalent to one-eighth of the country's current demand (Hughes and Anslow, 2007).

Faecal Sludge Treatment and Management

Some programmes are underway to establish guidelines for the management and treatment of faecal sludges such as those from on-site sanitation systems (unsewered

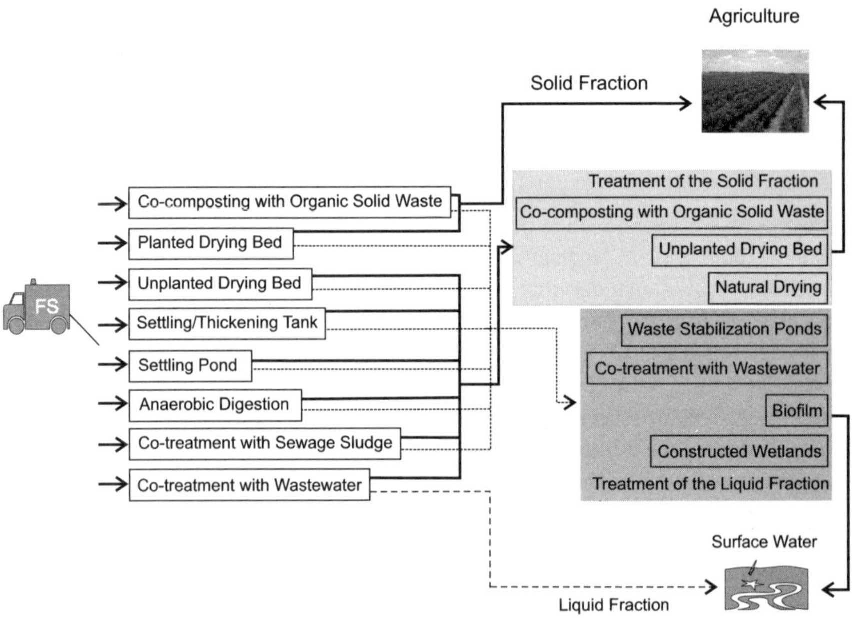

Fig. 4.6 Some treatment options for faecal sludge (After Strauss, 2002)

private and public latrines/toilets, septic tanks) and to strengthen the institutional capacity in this field. Collaborative field research on faecal sludge (FS) management and treatment is currently being done in Argentina, Ghana, West Africa and Thailand. Fig. 4.6 illustrates some treatment options.

Specific treatment options can be selected from several alternatives considered to be suitable for use in developing countries. Two pond-based options, constructed wetlands and co-composting have been investigated, one in Accra (Ghana). This comprises settling/thickening tanks and a series of ponds to treat the separated liquid. The second system in operation in Argentina consists of septage settling/ thickening ponds followed by two lagoons co-treating the septage liquid and municipal wastewater (Strauss, 2002).

Biological Treatment of Municipal Solid Waste

Decentralized Composting of Municipal Solid Waste

In many towns and cities of the developing world, inadequate collection and disposal of waste poses serious health risks to the population and causes environmental degradation. The current solid waste situation may be improved to enhance resource recovery activities. Inorganic material recycling of municipal solid waste is being already practised by the informal sector (Zurbrugg and Drescher, 2002). However, reuse of organic waste material, which often makes up more than 50 per cent of the total waste, continues to be limited. Large centralized and highly mechanized composting plants have very often failed in the past mainly due to high investment and operational costs and limited revenues from product sales (Zurbrugg and Drescher, 2002).

When suitably combined with primary collection services, decentralized schemes can decrease dependency from municipal services, create employment and enhance environmental awareness in a community. Decentralized schemes tend to be more flexible because they adapt rapidly to changes in user needs, thereby allowing close quality surveillance of the service and product by the users. Use of a small-scale, labour-intensive technology in decentralized schemes is very often better suited to the local socio-economic conditions (Zurbrugg and Drescher, 2002).

Principles of Solid Waste Management

Benefit–Cost Analysis (BCA)

The basic principle of rational solid waste management should be Benefit–Cost Analysis. No particular waste management configuration should be chosen unless benefits exceed costs. The optimal scale of activity for any choice would be the point where the difference between benefits and costs is maximized. For any given level of waste the costs of managing that waste should be minimal. Waste may be reduced at source in two ways. The waste from the product may be reduced by concentrating the product, thus reducing the volume and sometime also the weight of product waste. Concentration also reduces the waste from the associated packaging or container.

Polluter Pays Principle (PPP)

Polluter Pays Principle lays down that both producers and consumers should pay the full social costs of their actions (Pearce and Turner, 1991). The full social costs (particularly environmental damage costs) are not currently included in the prices of most products. This means that the receiving capacity of the environment is underpriced. The full costs of waste disposal need to be reflected in product prices.

Municipal Solid Waste (MSW) Disposal

Several methods of Municipal Solid Waste disposal are outlined below:

Sanitary Land Filling

Requires vast areas which are no longer available in metropolitan cities. Useful for reclaiming low-lying areas, but with rising population pressure there might not be enough land available for filling, longer journeys will have to be made daily by trucks for newer out-of-town land filling sites. These dumps contribute to air and water pollution and hence causing health hazards.

Garbage Incineration

Refuse/garbage has high moisture content and low combustible matter. The operation is difficult to control and is expensive due to the need for supplementary fuels to maintain the high temperatures required for combustion. Thus, the method is uneconomical.

Refuse-derived Fuel Pellets

The method produces pellets which while burning, cause secondary air pollution. Also, power inputs are greater than actual power output through burning of pellets.

Aerobic Digestion for Compost

Compost is a good soil conditioner. To avoid haulage, it may be used in nearby areas. Compost is uneconomical for cities, in view of the high transportation costs.

Anaerobic Digestion

Organic matter in the waste is converted to biogas, which is a mixture of methane and carbon dioxide in the proportion of approximately 60/40. Indian waste being richer in organic matter, anaerobic digestion offers a viable process. Besides being hygienic, the method reduces pollution and produces energy in the form of fuel gas/ electricity and organic fertilizer (as dried manure). Also, hot water is produced while cooling the engine when electricity is produced through a dual fuel-fired engine.

Being a source of non-conventional energy, the anaerobic digestion method is eligible for government subsidies and soft loans.

It is estimated that a 200 tonnes per day (TPD) garbage plant, by anaerobic digestion, can produce 20,000 cubic metre per day of fuel gas and 40,000 tonnes per annum (TPA) of organic fertilizer. The gas would contain about 60 per cent of methane. Gas may also be converted to electricity.

Hazardous Waste Cleanup

A genetically modified bacterium that could partially degrade crude oil was first engineered in early 1970s. Researchers then started transferring genes between microbes in the hope of engineering hybrids with a taste for pollution. Naturally-occurring microbes have been tried at some sites with some success. Strains of Pseudomonas have remediated halogenated hydrocarbons like trichloroethylene. It is widely believed that genetically modified microbes should be employed for bioremediation (Zwillich, 2000).

Materials for Sustainable Waste Management

Various materials have helped in cleaning up the environment over the past few decades. Materials scientists have improved the quality of released effluent and exhaust plumes by using catalysts to avoid unwanted byproducts in chemical processes and in the treatment of waste. They have also advanced from solvent-based coatings to powder coatings and biodegradable materials. They are helping to generate cleaner energy by developing photovoltaic materials with improved conversion efficiencies. Here, the materials are used as parts of various types of fuel cell being developed. Materials scientists should also keep in mind the sustainability aspect of the technologies being developed. They need to critically assess the environmental impact and the costing aspect of the materials being designed.

Technology sustainability in terms of energy and environmental impacts is very important. For example, solar cells take up to eight years to pay back their energy costs. Significant energy input comes from the aluminium or steel frames in which the solar cells are placed. Other costs accrue from the manufacture of solar cells, the disassembly and recycling of components, and from certain chemicals that pose occupational health risks to workers but cannot be disposed of. Possibly the energy delivered and the lack of CO_2 produced eventually outweighs these costs. But critical analysis of the life cycle assessment of solar cells can reveal areas of improvement in material and device design to maximize the environmental benefit (Anonymous, 2002).

Metal recycling constitutes an important aspect of sustainability. The mining and processing of aluminium ore releases much CO_2, oxides of sulphur and nitrogen, volatile organic compounds, and waste for disposal in landfill sites. There is need to reduce the mining and production of virgin aluminium.

Industrial companies should address the sustainability of materials and technologies to ensure their long-term survival. The First Materials Science Forum for Sustainable Technologies (MATFORUM) held in 2002 at the University of Augsburg (Germany), brought together and facilitated interactions among some of the world's largest manufacturing companies with members of the World Wide Fund for Nature, the United Nations, the US Environmental Protection Agency and others.

Some strategies are directed towards 'de-materialization' where production and consumption cycles of materials and devices are designed to be closed loops, where the energy content of waste is extracted, the materials are recycled and the reuse and re-integration of components is encouraged.

Researchers must help to ensure that new problems are not generated. The likely long-term commercial success of technologies being conceived in the lab now depends both on their sustainability and functional properties.

Safe Use of Toxic Chemicals

Worldwide, nearly 400 million tonnes of hazardous wastes are produced annually. Thousands of chemicals are used in construction, industry, food production and agriculture; their improper use greatly damages the environment and endangers human health. Safety is critical during manufacture, trade, storage, use and disposal of chemicals. In fact, there are no safe chemicals – there are only safe ways of manufacturing, handling and using them. Some hazards posed by improper use/ handling of chemicals include hazards during use, accidents, pollution from mine wastes, dumping in landfills, exposure at work or home, industrial fires, atmospheric pollution, water pollution, discharge into oceans, pollution from shipwrecks, dumping and spillage at sea, and export to other countries.

The need of the hour is to replace toxic chemicals with less hazardous substances and alternative clean technologies. In agriculture, reliance on pesticides may be greatly reduced by promoting biological methods of insect control. The production and use of internationally prohibited chemicals including asbestos and certain halogen compounds needs to be phased out.

Reduction and Control

Reducing the production of hazardous industrial wastes and improving their safe handling and proper disposal are essential, if human health and the environment are to be protected. The generation, storage, treatment, transportation and disposal of hazardous wastes must be properly controlled and transboundary waste shipments should be banned.

Incentives may be given to prevent or minimize the production of hazardous wastes. Cost-effective, cleaner production methods should be introduced. Biotechnology or other substitutes for hazardous substances should be encouraged.

Techniques need to be developed for recovering useful material from waste products and using it in new ways. Recycling should be promoted. Unavoidable and dangerous industrial waste should be treated at or near its source. Treatment and disposal processes may be combined, wherever possible. Polluters must pay for disposal of wastes and cleanup of contaminated areas.

Cleaning up toxic wastes of chemical manufacture may be controversial, costly and frustrating environmental problem.

Management of Hazardous Wastes

Most human activities generate wastes. Many wastes can be recycled or reduced at source, but some wastes and their residues are inevitable and have to be placed in landfill sites. Up to 80–90 per cent of our refuse has generally been disposed of on the land which is, in many cases, an acceptable receptor for many residues provided that they are properly disposed of and monitored. Of the many types of wastes that end up on the land, several are innocuous. Others can cause problems. Hazardous wastes come from industries, agriculture and other sources. In general, much of a nation's prosperity and economic well-being derive from activities that have produced hazardous wastes. Their proper disposal can be tricky. Big companies have recently adopted a new approach to production based on cleaner technology and recycling by installing huge incinerators to handle the wastes.

Besides gaseous and liquid wastes, humanity piles up mountains of solid refuse. The countries of the European Community (EC) throw away some two billion tonnes of waste every year, ranging from domestic garbage to sewage sludge, mining residues and ash from power stations. Only a small proportion of this waste is 'hazardous'. In mid-eighties, the countries of the OECD generated about 300 million tonnes of hazardous wastes a year, as against 370 million of municipal wastes. Industrialized countries generate over 80 per cent of the world's annual total of some 300–400 million tonnes, mostly from the chemical and petrochemical industries.

In many countries, subsurface emplacement of fluid wastes has been practised. In right conditions, subsurface injection is more protective of public health than certain other (alternative) methods of waste disposal. A properly designed injection well emplaces fluids underneath any underground source of drinking water. But poorly engineered or maintained injection wells can contaminate groundwater.

Recovering, recycling, reusing and repairing are the four 'Rs' that mark the new millennium. While the biosphere is a devoted recycler, humans are habitual waste producers. They transform natural compounds and synthesize novel substances which do not exist in the environment. No animal predator leaves what it cannot eat simply because it does not need it; human beings, on the other hand, do. The squander behind the high consumption levels amongst one-fifth of the population results in heaps of refuse, most of which cannot be reintroduced into nature's biogeochemical cycles. The more advanced the technology and the industrial civilization, the larger the amount of refuse generated per person and the proportion of non-biodegradable refuse. The environment becomes contaminated when materials are not decomposed and recycled. Since producing anything necessarily requires raw materials, water and energy, the production of waste is simply another way of squandering resources. The resources most often used by the consumer society are non-renewable. An analysis of the products used at each step of the manufacturing process, on the basis of their life cycle materials, energy, water and refuse, can show us the path of sustainability in resource use.

Many countries produce prodigious quantities of 'sector-specific' waste, e.g., mining wastes. Household refuse is produced in fairly modest quantity comparatively. Old tips, landfills, slag heaps, contaminated soils and poisoned lake and marine sediments are to be found in many places. A large fraction of the metals being discharged into water come from the tailings and other wastes associated with sulphide ore mines.

Waste Management in Third World Countries

Urban productivity in many developing countries is greatly constrained by deficiencies in infrastructure and weakness of institutional frameworks for waste management. Because of its critical role in protecting the environment and improving productivity, accomplishing effective municipal solid waste management (MSWM) should be a top priority for the third world cities.

As regards solid wastes, open dumping is the commonest disposal arrangement in third world cities. Usually, only five per cent of budget is allocated for the disposal of solid waste management (compared with over 25 per cent in industrialized countries). Due to lax disposal practices, numerous environmental and public health concerns abound in developing countries. For example, municipal solid waste commonly contains excreta because of the lack of sanitation facilities in low income neighbourhood. When refuse is allowed to pile up, disease carrying insects and rodents multiply and transmit diseases. Clogged drains lead to mosquito breeding, flooding and road deterioration. Leachates from dump sites contaminate surface and groundwater resources. Burning of open dumps increases air pollution.

Recommendations on Solid Waste Management

Significant long-term improvements in solid waste management (SWM) may accrue in big cities, if the following recommendations are considered and adopted with or without suitable modifications (Bartone and Bernstein, 1993):

a. Investments ought to include the development of strategic SWM plans addressing the full range of services and related management activities.
b. The investments should support improvements in primary as well as secondary collection operations with vehicle selections based on analyses of solid waste, labour, and other local conditions. Special emphasis is needed for use or development of low-cost community-based technologies within broader solid waste management schemes.

c. All investments in expanding collection capacity must be accompanied by corresponding investments in nonpolluting disposal facilities, and the development of institutional and financial capacity for disposal operations. Where haul distances are longer than 15–20 km or travel times exceed 30 minutes, transfer stations should be established. In most developing countries, most suitable disposal facilities are sanitary landfills.
d. Hazardous wastes should be kept out of the municipal system. Where industrial wastes are collected by the municipality, all potential sources of hazardous waste need to be identified for appropriate management.
e. The root cause of MSWM deficiencies (poor operational performance, environmentally unacceptable disposal practices) is the inefficient institutional arrangements common to municipal governments in the developing countries. Private firms usually prove to be more productive and efficient in carrying out collection and transport operations than municipalities.

The 6 R's of Waste Management are discussed below:

Reduction

Enlightened consumers often reject new or existing products or processes, unless they are environment friendly. Examples include choosing long-lived or durable products or deciding not to buy over-packaged products. Strategies should focus at the beginning of the waste stream so as to minimize waste. This is the most cost-effective strategy for society as a whole and also has the greatest potential for long-term gain, since it is oriented towards anticipation and prevention, it avoids incremental waste generation and greatly reduces site contamination.

Reuse

It emphasizes direct reapplication or repeated use of a product for the same or different purposes in its original form. Reusable containers (e.g., pop bottles) can be returned to the retailer for reuse by the distributor of the product, and office paper printed on one side can be used again (on the other side).

Recycling

It involves collection of post-use materials which are processed for transformation into new products (e.g., old newspapers are collected, deinked, repulped, and then produced as a fully recycled paper or mixed with new fibres).

Recovery

It involves obtaining or reutilizing material or energy from solid or hazardous waste through combustion or other process (e.g., pyrolysis or fermentation). Priority for recovery is given to operations offering maximum reduction of hazardous waste toxicity and volume with an emphasis on operations yielding usable byproducts which may be recycled.

Residual Disposal

Disposal of what is left after the first four R's (reduction, reuse, recycling and recovery) have been taken into account. It ranges from combustion or incineration to chemical and biological transformation, and ultimately disposal which is the last resort.

Remediation

If wastes have been improperly released and pose some risk to human health and/or the environment, there may be a need to rehabilitate or restore the site to an acceptable condition (Kumar, 1998).

Some different types of Hazardous Waste Treatment Technologies are:

1. Biological treatment, using microorganisms to degrade organic compounds in a waste stream.
2. Carbon adsorption, in which substances adhere to the surface of specially treated carbon and particularly effective in removing organic compounds from liquid waste.
3. Dechlorination that removes chlorine from a substance by chemically replacing it with hydrogen or hydroxide ions and used to detoxify chlorinated substances.
4. Incineration, which destroys or renders waste less hazardous through burning and is frequently used to destroy organic wastes.
5. Neutralization, which decreases the acidity or alkalinity of a substance by adding to it alkaline or acidic materials respectively.
6. Oxidation, which detoxifies a waste constituent by combining it with oxygen can treat wastes such as cyanides, phenols and organic sulphur compounds.
7. Precipitation, which removes solids from a liquid waste, so that the hazardous solid portion can be disposed of safely.
8. Solidification and stabilization, which remove wastewater from a waste or change it chemically, thereby making it less permeable and less susceptible to transport by water.

Landfill remains the most widely used method for disposing solid waste. When properly constructed and operated, landfill sites constitute a safe disposal route for municipal solid waste, at much cheaper cost compared to other disposal options. However, uncontrolled dumping of waste into the local environment needs to be replaced by life cycle product management and should be complemented with controlled sanitary landfilling or other treatment and disposal methods. Also efforts should be intensified to compost or digest organic waste and reduce, recycle or reuse as much of other municipal waste as possible. Some different types of land disposal methods are:

Landfills

These are disposal facilities where hazardous waste is placed in or on land. Properly designed and operated landfills are lined to prevent leakage and contain systems to collect potentially contaminated surface water run off. Most landfills isolate wastes in discrete wells or trenches, thereby preventing potential contact of incompatible wastes. In a landfill, hazardous waste is often converted with soil before a cover system is installed.

Surface Impoundments

These are natural or man-made depressions e.g., pit, ponds, lagoons and basins used to treat, store or dispose of hazardous waste.

Underground Injection Wells

These are steel and concrete-encased shafts placed deep in the earth into which hazardous wastes are deposited by force and under pressure. Liquid hazardous wastes are commonly disposed of in underground injection wells.

Waste Piles

These are non-containerized accumulations of solid, non-flowing hazardous waste. While some are used for final disposal, many waste piles are used for temporary storage until the waste is transferred to its final disposal site.

Land Treatment

This is a disposal process in which hazardous waste is applied onto or incorporated into the soil surface. Natural microbial communities break down or immobilize the hazardous constituents. Land treatment facilities are also called 'land application' or 'land farming facilities'.

Waste Reduction

Some approaches to waste reduction are listed below:

1. Source separation (segregation) keeps hazardous waste from contaminating non-hazardous waste through management practices that prevent the wastes from coming into contact. This is the cheapest and easiest method of reducing the volume of hazardous waste to be disposed of, and is widely used by industries. Besides reducing disposal costs, source separation reduces handling and transportation costs.
2. Recycling is widely used by industries. It removes a substance from a waste and returns it to productive use. Solvents, acids and metals are commonly recycled.

3. Substitution of raw materials may offer the greatest opportunity for waste reduction. By replacing a raw material that generates a large amount of hazardous waste with one which generates little or none, manufactures can substantially reduce the waste volume.
4. Manufacturing process changes consists of either eliminating a process that produces a hazardous waste or altering the process, so that it no longer produces the waste.

5

Agro-industrial Economy and Biotechnology

The Rome Summit of 1996, had set a target of reducing the number of persons going to bed hungry to half by 2015. To achieve this, at least 20 million should come out of the hunger trap each year. But the actual rate of decline has hardly been eight million per year since the early 1990s. The availability of abundant food in the market alone cannot solve the problem of poverty-induced hunger. For instance, the Indian Government had a stock of about 60 million tonnes of wheat and rice in December 2001, and yet about 25 per cent of the world's hungry lived in India. A paucity of jobs is contributing to the scarcity of food at the household level.

The Food and Agriculture Organization (FAO), 2001 pointed out the threat posed to global agriculture production (including livestock products) by invasive alien species, introduced through bulk imports of grains, meat and poultry products, and vegetables and fruits. With the abolition of quantitative restrictions and increase in the imports of pulses and oilseeds, novel pests, pathogens and weeds are being introduced.

In India, no adequate or effective steps have been taken since the World Trade Agreement in Agriculture (1994) for strengthening quarantine, sanitary and phytosanitary measures, in relation to the volume of imports often made by commercial interests. They are blissfully ignorant of the damage that can be caused to poor farming families through the introduction of invasive alien species.

The FAO (2001) report analysed the World Trade Agreement in Agriculture, especially the multi-functional role of agriculture that covers environmental concerns from the viewpoint of industrialized nations, and food and livelihood security concerns, from that of developing countries. Worldwide agriculture is evolving in two major directions. In industrialized countries, where hardly three to five per cent of the population is involved in the production phase of agriculture, factory farming or mass production techniques predominate. These require heavy inputs of technology, techno-infrastructure, subsidies and capital. In contrast, the farmer's farming or production-by-masses situation prevails in population-rich but land-hungry countries. Here, agriculture is characterized by weak technological and infrastructure support, coupled with low capital. In these less developed countries, postharvest technologies and opportunities for assured and remunerative marketing are also quite inadequate. Sanitary and phytosanitary measures are virtually non-existent so that the quality of the produce is substandard. In the developed countries, farming is merely a food-producing machine whereas in countries like India, it is the backbone of the livelihood security system. In India, the number of people depending on crop and animal husbandry, forestry, fisheries (inland and marine) and agro-processing has been increasing in absolute terms, although there is a decline in terms of percentage.

While describing agricultural progress in different parts of the world, the FAO report mentions the growing consumer concern about the safety of foods from genetically modified (GM) crops. The European Community (EC), Japan and Switzerland have already introduced labelling requirements for products derived from genetically modified organisms (GMOs).

The FAO's assessment of the long-term outlook for the world's food supply, nutrition and agriculture (Bruinsma, 2003) gave projections of supply and demand for the major agricultural commodities and sectors, including fisheries and forestry. The projections form the basis for a detailed examination of other factors such as nutrition and implications for international trade. The implications of future supply and demand for natural resource base are discussed as also how technology may contribute to more sustainable development. Past experience underscores the useful role of agriculture in the development process, particularly where the majority of the population still depends on this sector for employment and income (Bruinsma, 2003).

Biotechnology has great potential to attract profitable global business everywhere and particularly in India, it has potential usage in the areas of vaccine manufacture, nutraceuticals, traditional or herbal medicines, diagnostics, transgenics in agriculture and environmental biotechnology as applicable to bioremediation or restoration of degraded lands, mangrove afforestation, biosensors, biosurfactants, etc., (Natesh and Govil, 2003). Our major concern should be to address the health and nutritional status of our people.

Table 5.1 Scope of Biotechnology in Industry (After Feddema, 2003)

Sector	Scope
Bio-energy	Biogas, methane, fermentation, ethanol for fuel
Bio-foods	Food additives, functional enzymes, amino acids, biomacromolecules
Bio-medicine	Hormones, vaccines, anticancer drugs, antibiotics
Bio-health	Sanitizing microbes, bioremediation
Life electronics	Biochips, biocomputers, biomecatronics
Life agriculture	GM corns, beans, potatoes
Life information	Bioinformatics

For India and other developing countries, following areas require rapid progress, if globalization of trade is to confer substantial economic and human benefits:

- Productivity per units of land, water and time
- Quality in terms of nutritive, culinary, organoleptic, processing, storage and transportation

- Net income and new employment opportunities
- Innovative management and institutional structures, which can give small producers the benefits of scale, both in the production and postharvest phases of agriculture (FAO, 2001)

Biosciences Industry

The biosciences industry that includes the pharmaceutical, agribusiness, cosmetics and health sectors is engaged in creating novel proprietary products from existing samples of human, plant, animal, fungal and microbial materials by isolating and recombining their genetic fragments in unprecedented ways. These tissue samples, and the genetic material and information that can be obtained from them, are also used to make sophisticated research 'tools' needed for practising molecular science. For meeting this need, several new engineered 'artefacts' such as cell lines, cryogenically stored tissues samples and sequenced DNA are not only being generated from biological materials, but are also being traded internationally as the part of new global resource economy in genetic resources and information (Parry, 2004).

The life sciences industry can revolutionize the ways in which biological materials are industrially used. Various biological resources collected from some locations are transformed into economically valuable commodities. Geographical locations and spatial relations markedly affect generation of new, highly differentiated spaces of commodification for biological materials and derivatives in the 21st Century (Parry, 2006). In fact, the biological materials collected from various sites have since been transformed into tradeable biocommodities. Some institutions have even become focal points for accumulating genetic material and information, with significant implications for 'donor' countries. New regulations introduced at different scales with a view to control the collection and use of genetic resources ensure equitable distribution of monies generated from the commercialization of the collected resources and of this emergent scientific trade in genetic material and information.

Creation of Technoscientific Artefacts

The biotechnological revolution appears to have strongly changed the ways in which biological materials are employed industrially. New biotechnologies make it possible for the component parts of organisms to be engineered on a genetic or molecular level. This, in turn, has transformed approaches to the study of diseases, pharmaceuticasl and crop development. Collcctors actively seek valuable genetic and biochemical information about living organisms and treat them as if it were a commodity.

Till recently, genetic material and information remained firmly embedded within biological organisms. It could not be reproduced or conveyed in isolation from these organisms. But now, this has changed. Increasingly sophisticated biotechnological advances have made it possible to extract genetic material and/or information and to convert it into new artefactual forms. A few examples of these technological artefacts are cryogenically stored tissue samples and cell lines. These artefacts still retain some corporeality, while some others (such as DNA sequences stored in databases) exist in purely informational form.

In a way, these artefacts act as 'proxies' for whole organisms. In a few cases, they can effectively substitute for the organism in its absence. To be sure, they do not always act as effective substitutes for whole organisms, but in many areas of biotechnological research their utility as proxies for whole organisms is fairly well established. For conducting tests of drug efficacy, for instance, cell lines are routinely used as substitutes for whole organisms, including human beings.

With increasing awareness of the extraordinary functional utility of the various new proxies, their demand has tremendously grown. This has catalysed the creation of new commodity markets in these bioinformational proxies.

Trade in Bioinformation

Substantial amount of money is being secured from trading in bioinformation. For instance, the pharmaceutical company Bayer AG paid Millennium Pharmaceuticals a record US $ 465 million in 1999 for accessing the latter's sequence database. Celera Genomics, the bioinformatics industry leader, charges individual pharmaceutical company subscribers in excess of US $ 8 million annually for unlimited access to their proprietary sequence database (Goodman, 2001). According to the industry magazine, *Drug Discovery News*, the value of the European bioinformatics market could well rise to over US $ 700 million per year by 2011, as competition to accelerate the drug discovery process increases *(www.drugdiscoverynews.com/index.php?newsarticle +365).*

However, the translation of commodities into more transmissible forms is not confined to the biotechnological realm. Similar processes are at work in the financial sector, in publishing, and music and film industries. It has become possible to present printed information, music and money in new artefactual forms, as digital MP3 files, as electronic cash or e-journals. New markets have emerged for these and other similar commodities as well.

A striking lesson from recent experience with the new commodities is that the technology has changed the way in which we value commodities or 'works'—that the most valuable entity in a work is not its physical form, but rather its transmissible content. For the life sciences industry, the same is now true for biological material —what is most valuable and most in need of protection is not the biological material *per se*, but the transmissible content of that biological material, i.e., the genetic information embodied in it (Parry, 2005, 2006).

Technology and Development

The technocratic tendency of modern societies reflects one possible path of development, a route that is peculiarly truncated by the demands of power.

Technology has other beneficial potentials that at times emerge along a different developmental path. In subjecting human beings to technical control at the expense of traditional modes of life while sharply restricting participation in design, technocracy perpetuates elite power structures inherited from the past in technically rational forms.

In the process, it mutilates not just human beings and nature, but also technology. A different power structure would innovate a different technology with different consequences (Feenberg, 2005).

Is technology neutral? Neutrality refers to the indifference of a specific means to the range of possible ends it can serve. If we assume that technology as we know it today is indifferent with respect to the human ends in general, then indeed we have neutralized.

Alternatively, technology as such may be neutral with respect to all the ends that can be technically served. But there is no such thing as 'technology as such'. Today, we employ a certain specific technology with limitations that are due not only to the state of our knowledge but also to the power structures that bias this knowledge and its applications. While contemporary technology favours specific ends, it obstructs others.

A full realization of technology is both possible and necessary. We are frequently alerted to this necessity by the threatening side effects of technological advance. The very success of our technology in modifying nature insures that any deferred feedback loop will grow shorter as we disturb nature more and more an attempt to control it. In our society, which is completely organized around technology, the threat to survival is clear. Technological systems impose technical management on human beings. While some manage, others are managed.

We may consider the example of air pollution. So long as those responsible for generating it could escape the health consequences of their actions to green suburbs, leaving poor urban dwellers to breathe filthy air, support for technical solutions to the problem was lacking. Pollution controls were considered to be costly and unproductive by the authorities. Eventually, the spread of the problem and protests by the victims legitimated the externalized interests. Only then did it become possible to make the required reforms. This subject finally forced a redesign of the automobile and other sources of pollution, taking human health into account. This exemplifies a politics of design that can lead ultimately to a more holistic technological system.

An adequate understanding of our daily life processes cannot ignore technology. How we configure and design cities, build roads and transportation systems, communication media, and industrial production is a political matter. We are already making more and more choices about health and knowledge in designing the technologies on which medicine and education increasingly rely. Furthermore, it seems plausible to propose as advances or alternatives to a great extent conditioned by the failures of the existing technologies and the possibilities pointed out by them (Feenberg, 2005).

Effects of High-tech Industrial Operations in Developing Countries

In spite of several voluntary efforts, production and assembly operations of semiconductor companies continue to exert several adverse environmental and social effects in developing countries. This has been recently reported by Nautilus Institute for Security and Sustainable Development (Berkeley, California).

Citing case studies from Taiwan, Malaysia, India, Thailand and Costa Rica, the institute reported that the primary problems were hazardous materials used in production and assembly and contained in the products, high water and energy intensity, weak protection of workers' health and labour rights, and poor oversight by global supply chains. The report focused particularly on overseas operations of California-based high-tech companies. The Nautilus Institute, which aims to use "strategic tools of cooperative engagement to solve fundamental problems undermining global security and sustainability", produced the report as a part of its California Global Corporate Accountability Project *(www.nautilus.org).*

Chronic Disturbance

In all ecosystems, some impact of human activities is being felt, especially in urban landscapes, agricultural fields and tropical forests. Commonly, acute forest disturbance involves logging selectively or clear-cutting. It allows forest to regenerate by natural means. In contrast, chronic disturbance is subtle, slow, equally destructive, but a much less-recognized problem. In the chronic form of disturbance, people remove only a small part of forest biomass at any given time, usually as headloads of firewood, or in the form of fodder, leaf litter and other non-timber forest products (NTFPs). In the chronically disturbed forest, plants or ecosystems are unable to recover adequately in the face of continuing human onslaught even if rates of biomass removal may be within the carrying capacity of the forest (Kumar, 2001). A good analogy is seen in the cumulative effects of low but chronic exposure to air pollution which has generated much concern worldwide. Chronic forest disturbance is analogous to moderate insect herbivory. Fuelwood is a major source of cooking energy in most of the developing countries and is already in short supply for millions of people. It can become more and more scarce in the coming decades with more areas exposed to chronic disturbance in the 21st Century.

Chronic disturbance has also degraded the environment in many developing countries, particularly in such ecosystems as wetlands and croplands where cattle are fed on crop residues, and in grasslands after seasonal harvest. Natives utilize natural biota for subsistence agriculture or for earning some income from NTFPs. Cottage industries based on NTFPs are being encouraged in several developing countries to merge economic growth and biodiversity conservation (Peters, 1994) based on the following assumptions:

1. Harvesting of NTFPs not involving tree cutting so that deforestation is checked
2. NTFPs can be harvested sustainably
3. Sustainability can be estimated at ecosystem level

Fires in the Earth System

In terms of area and variety of biomes affected, fire is the most important disturbance worldwide. Fire affects extensive areas of Savannas (200–400 Mha annually), Circumboreal forest (5–15 Mha annually) and many other ecosystems like woodlands and shrublands of Mediterranean climate regions. Fire and its use by humans as a management tool, now and in the past, has led to dramatic changes in the structure and functioning of ecosystems, and significantly affected the atmospheric composition. Fire regimes and their effects on terrestrial ecosystems are highly sensitive to all global changes,. particularly climate change and land-use change.

Agro-industrial Clean Technologies for Food Production

Regenerative Agriculture

The concept of regenerative agriculture has involved from its predecessor, "alternative agriculture" (Kumar, 1995, 2000, 2003, 2004). Alternative agriculture means a system of food or fibre production that systematically pursues the following goals:

1. Thorough incorporation of natural processes such as nutrient cycles, nitrogen fixation and pest-predator relationships into the agricultural process.
2. Reduction in the use of off-farm inputs with the greatest potential to harm the environment or the health of farmers and consumers.
3. Productive use of biological and genetic potential of plant and animal species.
4. Improvement of the match between cropping patterns and the productive potential as well as physical limitations of agricultural lands to ensure long-term sustainability of current production levels.
5. Profitable and efficient production with emphasis on improved farm management and conservation of soil, water, energy and biological resources (Winter, 1990).

The unifying concept of "sustainable agriculture" has emerged as the most agreed upon term for the varied agricultural practices that began to differ and even challenge more and more conventional concepts of modern agricultural production. It is considered to be ecologically sound, economically viable and socially just and humane (Kumar, 2006). Modern agriculture is a very recent development, not even a century old. However, engineering for input-intensive agriculture versus engineering for sustainability is being challenged. Conventional agriculture systems have been able to sustain growth rates of two to four per cent per annum over some three decades because of their dependence on chemical fertilizers. The following biological considerations are critical for future sustainability:

1. Conservation of genetic resources must be continued and strengthened.
2. Yields per unit area and per unit time must be substantially increased to meet the needs of increasing population.

3. Long-term pest control must be developed through integrated pest management and built-in resistance because intensified production will tend to encourage built-up of pest and to break down the effectiveness of pesticides and host-plant resistance.
4. Improved methods for disease and parasite control will also be important to sustain animal production (Kumar, 2003).
5. A balanced production system involving both crops and livestock will be needed to enhance productivity and avoid overgrazing.

The following physical factors and constraints are deemed to be important:

1. Soil is the most important resource for ensuring sustainability, loss of topsoil through erosion and a reduction in soil fertility by not replacing nutrients both turn a renewable resource into a nonrenewable one.
2. Agriculture is the principal user of water globally. Inefficient use of water and overdrafting of rechargeable aquifers can result in the erosion of another renewable resource (Kumar, 2006).
3. Poor soil and water management in rainfed agriculture can cause severe land degradation.
4. Misuse of agricultural and industrial chemicals can contribute to the accumulation of toxic substances in soil and water.
5. Atmospheric changes brought about by human activities can adversely affect agricultural production.
6. Energy consumption required by high-yielding production systems can probably be justified in the foreseeable future as using a nonrenewable resource (oil) to protect soil from being reduced to a nonrenewable resource (Winter, 1990).

Sustainability is only one of the right questions to ask. What is even more important is the analysis of resource renewability. Many farmers talk less about sustainability, rather they focus on the regenerative nature of all living systems. Many among us are looking at ways and means to mobilize the regenerative tendencies inherent in land and land-based environment. Renewable resources do not renew themselves. Everything regenerates within a very complex environment of a multitude of living systems.

When agricultural land is allowed to rest and regenerate, following six aspects can be observed:

1. Increase in the diversity of plant species
2. Coverage of soil surface with plants leading to decrease in erosion and increase in beneficial microbial populations near the earth's surface
3. More perennial and other plants with vigorous root systems begin to establish and thrive
4. Past patterns of weed and pest interference with growing systems are disrupted

5. Nutrients either tend to move upward in the soil profile or accumulate near the surface thereby becoming more available for use by plants
6. Overall soil structure improves, increasing the water holding capacity

According to Rodale (1988), regenerative agriculture is not organic farming. Unlike organic farmers, regenerative farmers use some herbicides, synthetic pesticides, and artificial fertilizers. These regenerative farmers are not conventional. They strive to use low levels of off-farm inputs and substitute them with internal and regenerative resources available within their farming system. The idea of linking farming to natural land-restoring systems constitutes the core of regenerative methods.

Figure 5.1 brings out several interactions between various inputs in crop agriculture. Reducing soil erosion and promoting a more natural soil structure improves both drainage and water retention. It favours biological and natural techniques of pest and disease control. Certain components of the systems approach involve rotations, innovative cultural techniques, innovative machinery

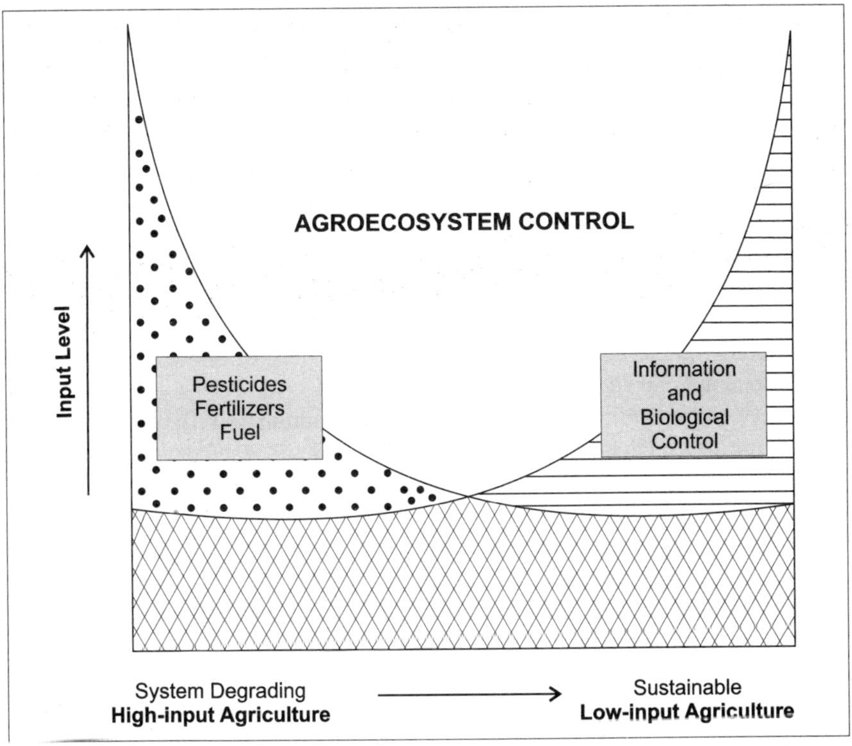

Source: Winter, 1990

Fig. 5.1 Sustainable agricultural systems are shown here as being low in material input—pesticides, inorganic fertilizer and high in information input—applied ecological knowledge of the system. High chemical input practices conceal the importance of ecological processes occurring in agricultural systems

inputs and crop breeding. Regenerative agricultural systems depend upon suitable manipulation of these components. Lower-input agroecosystem is system oriented and consequently, management intensive.

Transition to Sustainable Society

The concepts of industrial ecology and industrial metabolism offer important insights for practical applications. Current approaches do not focus enough on underlying problems at the root of our environmental troubles. Unless some innovative ways are devised that can meet the current challenges, we will lose the battle for the planet (Speth, 1992).

The world population is approaching seven billion. The output of world economy has quadrupled. Economic activity is greater by a factor of four than only a few decades ago. It took a very long time to build a world economy that produced about US $ 600 billion as output at the threshold of 19th Century. Today, the world economy grows by this amount once every two years (Speth, 1992). For over a billion of people in the rich countries, this growth has brought material wealth unimaginable by earlier generations. But it has also brought population, waste and consumption of the planet's resources on an unprecedented scale.

In 1994, the Business Council for a Sustainable Energy Future (BCSEF, Washington, DC) proposed that governments should adopt the following six principles while addressing the global warming issue:

1. Policies for remedying global climate change should, as far as possible, be market-based while taking into account the environmental externalities of energy use. The best policy instruments provide economic incentives to deploy and adopt clean and efficient energy technologies and practices.
2. Clean energy alternatives should receive recognition. Cost-effective technologies and practices for clean energy deserve priority.
3. Energy and environmental planning must be coordinated. The importance of accounting for environmental costs should be shown when developing energy projects. Environmentally sustainable solar-powered photovoltaics hold great promise for cost-effectively meeting a significant portion of energy needs.
4. Progress must be measured and adjustments made. Implementation of global climate change mitigation strategies require good monitoring systems. If strategies for reducing greenhouse gas emissions do not achieve desired results, policies must be modified and results should be monitored.
5. Technology transfer should be encouraged. Popularization of clean-energy technologies throughout the developing world could substantially lower global greenhouse gas emissions while promoting sustainable economic development.
6. Development assistance should support both economic and environmental objectives.

Meanwhile, in poor countries, the number of poor people has swelled dramatically. Over one billion people in the developing world live in hunger and poverty, destroying the fragile base of soils, water, forests and fisheries on which their future depends because no other alternative is open to them. The world's deserts are advancing while its forests with their immense wealth of life forms are in retreat. On average, an acre and a half of tropical forest disappears every second: four species are committed to extinction every hour (Speth, 1992; Kumar, 1999).

For the first time, human numbers and impacts have grown so large that they are eroding on a global scale the natural systems that support life.

These challenges will multiply in the future. World population is projected to double in the lifetime of today's children. World economic activity is projected to be five times that of today in only half a century. If climate-altering gases, industrial waste and other pollutants were to increase proportionately with the five-fold expansion in world economic activity projected for the middle of the 21st Century, it will convert many difficult problems into impossible ones.

Speth (1992) advocated certain transitions in dealing with the root causes of environmental problems with a view to achieve environmental sustainability. These transformations include:

1. A demographic transition
2. A technology transition that includes the "green" automobile
3. An economic transition to one in which prices reflect full environmental costs
4. A transition in social equity
5. An institutional transition to different arrangements among governments, businesses and people

Businessmen and environmentalists are urged to work together to make the environment a personal issue, to call for government action, to recognize the environmental challenges, and to enhance accountability. We must rapidly abandon the 20th Century technologies that have contributed so abundantly to today's problems and replace them with 21st Century technologies designed with environmental sustainability in mind.

The needed fusion of economic and environmental objectives requires technologies that meet two criteria, both linked to the concept of industrial metabolism. First, they must be able to transform industry and transportation from materials-intensive and "high-throughput" processes to systems that use fuel and raw materials more efficiently, rely on inputs with low environmental costs, generate little or no waste, recycle residual products, and release only benign effluents. The need, in short, is for technological systems that are more and more environmentally "closed" i.e., detached as much as possible from natural systems (Speth, 1992).

For any economic system, environmental damage over time is a function of the consumption of inputs from environmentally unsustainable processes, generation of pollution and post-consumption waste and other factors. This damage will not stabilize the pollution per unit of output, and the materials consumption per unit of output should decline rapidly enough to outweigh growth in economic output. Technological transformation for environmental sustainability can reduce environmental damage per unit of output fast enough to greatly outpace production.

Some of the following technologies are possible now:

1. Manufacturing processes and motors that cut energy needs to half.
2. Gas turbines that cogenerate electricity and heat 50 per cent more efficiently than today's power plants.
3. Solar, thermal and wind systems that produce electricity at prices competitive with nuclear power and photovoltaic power that promises to be competitive within a decade.
4. Manufacturing processes that make detoxification possible and waste elimination profitable.
5. New microbial and other bioengineered products that can substitute for chemical pesticides and fertilizers, help treat effluents and other waste, promote vegetation growth on impoverished soils, and increase the potential of biological sources of energy.
6. Miniaturization, microprocessor and computer-aided design and management that greatly improve efficient use of raw materials and reduce both waste and environmental pressures, and other computer and telecommunication applications that can strengthen satellite remote sensing, monitoring instrumentation, and environmental management through artificial intelligence (Speth, 1992).

Some advanced countries are producing and marketing the "green" automobile. There is probably no product that causes so much environmental damage as today's car. Both hydrogen and electric-powered vehicles are possible, and both hydrogen and electricity can be made from renewable energy sources such as photovoltaic and wind power.

Many environmental laws favour old technological processes over new ones and prescribe cumbersome administrative procedures that impede innovation. Relying on "best available technology" standards has tended to entrench existing technologies at the expense of new ones, although that result was certainly not the original intent. Regulations often focus on only one medium (air, water or land) rather than across the whole spectrum and tilt towards "end-of-pipe" pollution controls instead of prevention options.

There is an urgent need to reconcile environmental and economic priorities. Protection of the ecosystems, water, air, land and soils is crucial. But so also is strengthening the national economies. Figures 5.2 and 5.3 illustrate the standard economic vision and the steady-state economic vision, and bring out the linkages between the economy and the environment.

Today, environmental quality and economic growth are no longer seen to be in conflict because:

1. Environment quality is a critical success factor for export of goods and services into the increasingly environment sensitive world markets.
2. Growth of tourism is based on our unique environmental assets.

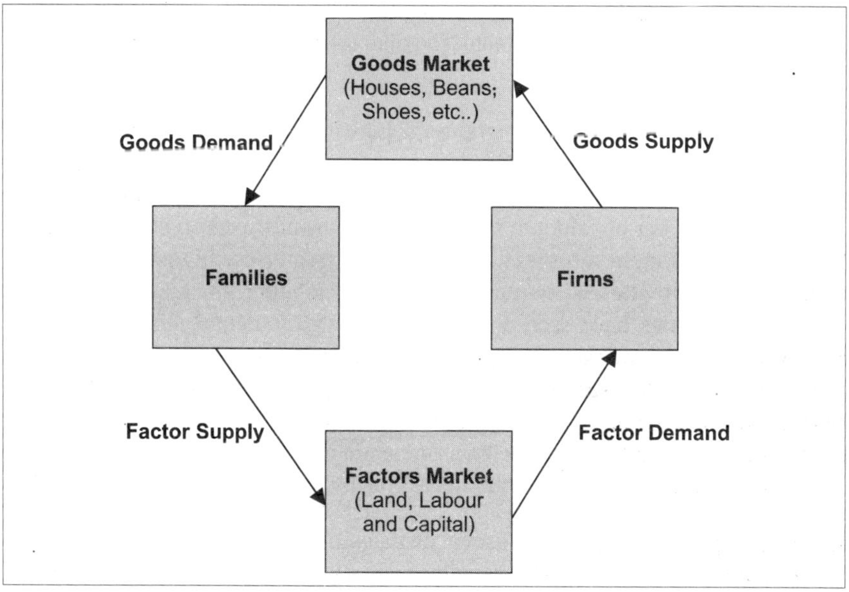

Fig. 5.2 The standard economic vision — Money flows clockwise in payment for real things (After Goodland and Daly, 1990)

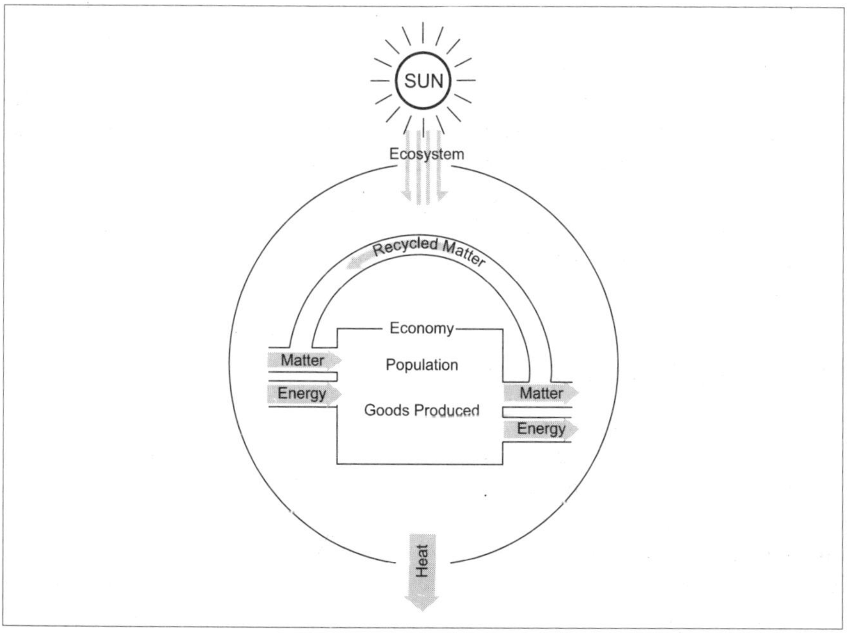

Fig. 5.3 The Steady State Economic Vision. The environment is finite and the economy is a subsystem of the environment (After Goodland and Daly, 1990)

3. Continued growth of farming, horticulture, forestry and fishing depends on access to clean water, sustainable land management and low contamination by industrial pollutants.

A challenge confronting many nations is how to achieve a higher degree of environmental quality during budget stringency. The drive is to find "least cost" policy solutions to meet the desired sustainable environmental standards.

In the US, moves are afoot to shift from burdensome taxes on economic goods (labour and investment returns) towards making greater use of taxes on environmental "bads" (activities like wastage of resources, pollution and congestion).

Many countries have seen a move by the environmental lobby away from an adversarial, anti-market mode to one prepared to work with business and government to achieve sustainable environmental policy. There is need for moving away from the polemic of "environment versus development" to a new sense of cooperation between business and environmental interests.

Thus the trends, nationally and internationally, include moves towards:

1. Less regulation and greater use of financial incentives and disincentives, for example, emission trading and environmental user charges that could have fiscal and environmental benefits.
2. Improved resource use efficiency, this would increase the international competitiveness of Indian businesses and reduce pollution.
3. Minimization of waste at source, some companies which have set targets for reduction of waste at source have achieved substantial savings by reducing material costs and minimizing costly "end of pipe" effluent treatment.
4. Integration of environment and economic policy, for example, through "internalization" of environmental costs in resource prices as advocated by the Rio Declaration on Environment and Development.
5. Environment (natural resource) accounting or "Green GDP" where national accounts include stock of capital assets as well as economic flows as a means of literally "taking the environment into account".
6. Harmonizing international trade and environmental policies.

World Food Summit, Rome

The 1996 Global Plan of Action of the UN Food and Agriculture Organization (FAO) aimed to eliminate world hunger by half (the world population of undernourished people is currently estimated at 815 million) by the year 2015. Realizing that the 1996 aim would not be met, the FAO convened the World Food Summit in Rome from June 8–13, 2002. The primary reasons for the failure to reduce world hunger were probably a lack of political will and commitment of adequate resources by the wealthy nations, unbridled free trade and privatization policies. These may possibly be addressed through true land reform, support for local markets and agro-ecological production practices (Anon, 2002).

Proponents of ecological and organic agriculture were also disappointed by the official summit's emphasis on genetically engineered crops as a means of reducing hunger for people having little or no access to food.

The Three Separations

An intensive bipolar pro-anti debate has been raging between the supporters and opponents of the agro-industrial technological development for several years. Recently, a more promising 'third approach' has emerged as a result of concrete efforts of civil society organizations and research institutions. This approach aims at a re-establishment of new co-creative relations between biotechnological and endogenous developments to reach those people who were bypassed by the industrialization of agriculture and Green Revolution. The chief concern of these multi-stakeholder platforms is to find out, if and how the social/technical potential of modern and traditional biotechnologies can be socially oriented, manipulated and related to food sovereignty, equity and sustainability.

Agro-industrial biotechnology is intimately related to three historical processes of separation, namely:

1. Separation of agriculture from its ecological environment
2. Separation of agriculture and food production
3. Separation of agricultural products from their intrinsic food quality

By supporting these social processes the agro-industrial biotechnology is creating a new global food system where immaterial labour acquires a hegemonic position. The major social process through which the hegemonic position of biotech crops is being established involves the uncoupling of agriculture from its ecological environment.

The genotype and phenotype of a plant is primarily formed during evolution by interaction of the plant with its natural environment. It was through natural selection that plants could internalize the requirements for good growth from their environment into their genotype. On one hand, improved plant breeding techniques 'freed' the agricultural varieties of the limiting characteristics of their natural surroundings. On the other, it made the plants dependent on externalized agricultural research for incorporating specific scientific information into the seeds.

Global food production has long been characterized by two contrasting developments, an increasing regional uniformity of agricultural production by cultivating crops such as wheat, corn and rice, and a regional diversity of techniques to conserve and process the agricultural produce in food products (Perelli et. al., 1984; Ruivenkamp, 2005). It is this diversity of regional methods of preserving and processing the agricultural produce (e.g., milk) that made available to us many regionally different forms of food products. Technical developments in different processing branches catalysed a quantitative change in the processing techniques, from preservation and transformation of agricultural produce towards a splitting up and re-grouping of food components, assembling them together into traditional or new food products to be marketed. An important implication of such a change towards food components aggregating production system, in which food production is delinked from the agricultural produce. Each region is enabled to aggregate its own specific composition from various global/local food components.

As more and more farming products are considered as a sum of biochemical food components, the food industry starts procuring these nutrients from industrial sectors too (e.g., biochemical production of amino acids, fatty acids and proteins). Also, farming products can be used for non-nutritional purposes (e.g., for ethanol production). In this way, the separation between agricultural and food products may be converted into a third process i.e., the separation of agricultural products from their intrinsic nutritional quality. Such a segregation of farming products and their intrinsic quality as food products partly moves the farming sector outside the social organization of the agro-industrial production chain. This implies that the developments in the farming sector will no longer be determined through its relationship to the food industry but by the developments significantly taking place outside the food chain (Ruivenkamp, 2005).

One constructive approach to develop a balanced and dialectical approach towards integrating and indigenizing some biotechnological innovations is to consider whether and how biotechnology, as an exogenous instrument, can be reappropriated by local initiatives and also function as a catalyst for endogenous developments (Ruivenkamp, 2001). The central issue here is whether these platforms can change the scientific information incorporated in the biotech products and challenge the three separation processes on which the hegemonic position of the bio-power system rests. The partners of the international network on Tailor-made Biotechnologies (TMBT) for endogenous developments are devoted to reconnecting agriculture to environment as well as to local food consumption by redesigning traditional and modern biotechnologies (Ruivenkamp, 2005).

Linking Agriculture to Environment

To create a new relationship between agriculture and its environment, crops need to be freed of their relationship with their surroundings on one hand, and on the other, they should be made dependent on externalized agricultural research. Such an uncoupling of the (re) production of seeds from the constraints of the natural environment, and re-coupling it to scientific information constitutes the pillar on which the historical process of separating agriculture from its environment rests and is reinforced by modern developments in plant biotechnology.

Notably a newly developed method of the propagation of neem and teak trees exemplifies a hybrid between modern tissue culture technology and local vegetative propagation techniques (Buijs, 2002). There are also several other examples in which modern and traditional techniques are mixed and hybridized. The science-based tissue culture applications on local tree species in India such as Indian gooseberry (*amla*) and tamarind have been combined with people-based experiences of applying the grafting technique (Buijs, 2002). Another example is the farmers' selection of local strains of *Bacillus thuringiensis (Bt)* and *Rhizobium* for their plant protective and growth stimulating properties. Some Indian farmers can also isolate and ferment the *Bt* material in their fields and distribute end-product pellets to other farmers. The selected strains are claimed to give better results than the commercial *Bt* products delivered by industry because of the very strong regional orientation of the farmers' selection procedure (Ruivenkamp, 2005).

Separation of Economic Growth and Well-being

The ultimate aim of development is to improve the quality of life (QOL) and to equitably distribute it in a given society. This quality is determined by both material factors (such as per capita consumption of food) and non-material factors (such as access to natural beauty in the environment, as shown in Fig. 5.4). Figure 5.5 is a conceptual model of some linkages which exist among population, food and environment. For instance, in any simplified operational model for food, linkages exist between human factors (demography, dietary patterns, technologies) and environmental factors (area of cultivated land and yield per hectare). Demand is generated by a combination of population and dietary patterns. In a given region, the supply of food is met by net imports and agricultural production. Agricultural production in

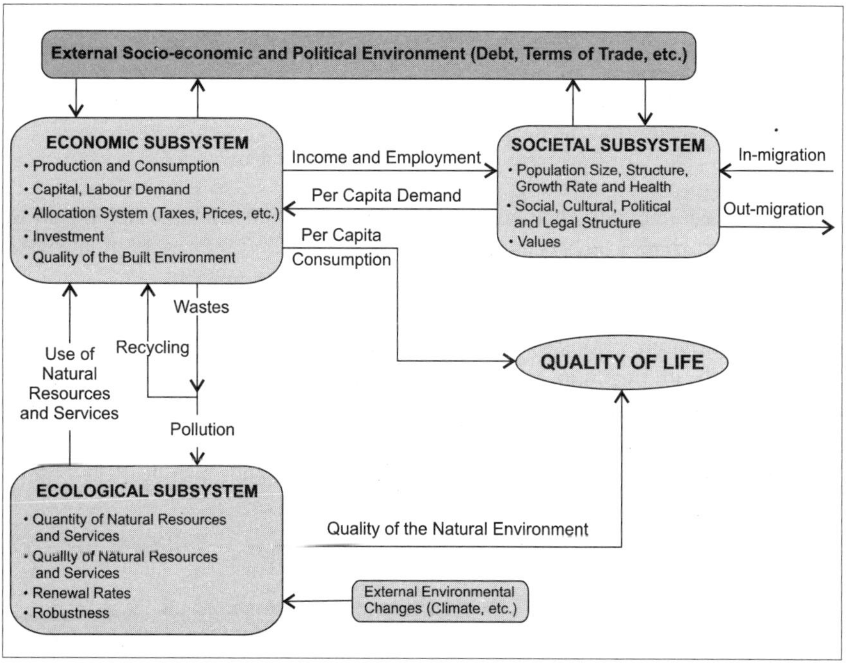

Fig. 5.4 Simplified conceptual model of the socio-ecological system in which we live (After Shaw et. al., 1994)

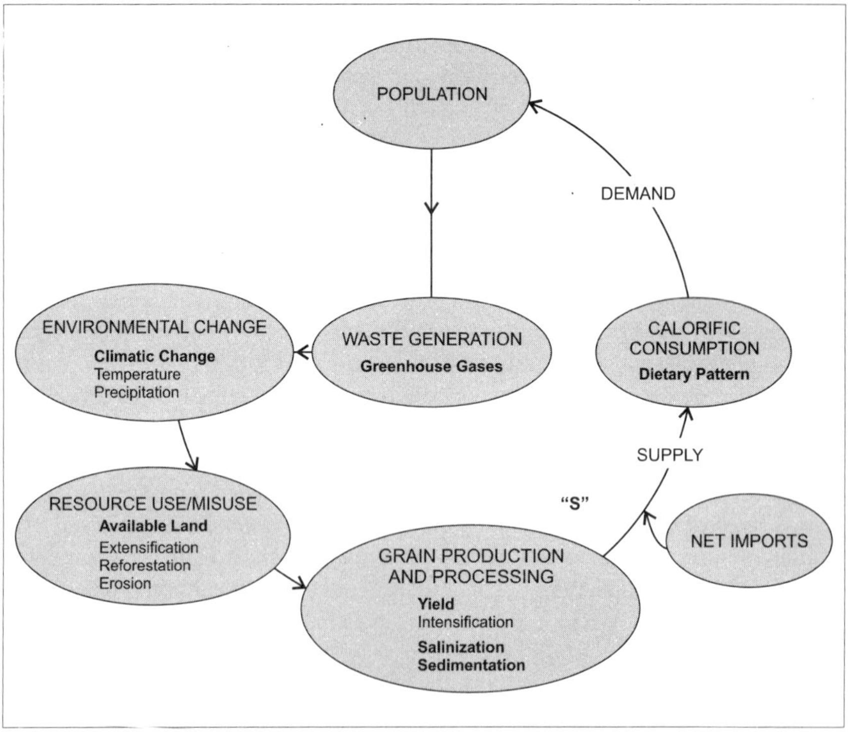

Fig. 5.5 Conceptual model showing some of the linkages among population, food and environmental change (After Shaw et. al., 1994)

a region in turn depends upon land area and yield. Farming area is influenced by environmental factors such as climatic change, erosion and reforestation, likewise, yield is influenced by intensification, salinization and sedimentation.

Food, energy and climatic change are also intimately linked together. Climatic change is intimately connected both to the release of greenhouse gases and our need for energy. In turn, some energy is needed for the production, processing and transport of food, including the use of fertilizers (some of which come from the same fossil hydrocarbons that we use in various ways).

For most small holders (marginal farmers) and poor people, the QOL is determined and/or satisfied by various kinds of needs (Table 5.2).

Table 5.2 Human Needs and their Satisfiers (After Sayre, 1991 and Welbourne, 1992)

Need	Dimension	Satisfiers
A	Subsistence	Food, income, housing, family's physical health, mental health, living environment, ability to work, social setting, ability to procreate, clothing and medicine
B	Participation	Attendance in group work, meetings and the like
C	Leisure	Taking care of farm animals, drinking with peers, going to market, group work and games
D	Creation	Engaging in hobbies and designing new things
E	Protection	Family, regular work, farm and farm animals, children, savings, insurance, social environment, capacity to plan for the future, and capacity to take care of self and others
F	Affection	True friends, family circle, ability to express anger, happiness and love, privacy at home, sense of humour, generosity to others, and ability to respect and appreciate others
G	Identity	Sense of belonging, self-esteem, commitment, ability to decide on important matters, having a religion, a language, a home, and being recognized as a member of the community
H	Freedom	Freedom to dissent, freedom to be different, equal rights and freedom to be open-minded
I	Understanding	Curiosity, availability of books, educators and workgroups
J	Justice	Presence of lawyers and effective local councils

Today a substantial divide separates economic growth and well-being not only in the Third World but also in the industrialized countries. Daly and Cobb (1994) analysed the two curves (of GNP and ISEW or Index of Sustainable Economic Welfare), which were derived by adding certain external costs not normally included in the traditional GNP calculation, and thus closer to a measure of well-being. They found the two curves to run a parallel course until 1975—thereafter GNP continued to grow but ISEW fell sharply. The pertinent issue is that those external costs (the corrective factors of the ISEW) relate mainly to urban, territorial and environmental decay. In fact, this means that we are discussing a new type of poverty and one that pertains to urban, environmental and territorial quality, and that is brought about by models of quantitative growth. This and other analyses demonstrate that the issue of explicitly self-sustainable development warrants a different role of the production of territorial and environmental quality for producing wealth. This need has been felt acutely since the Bruntland Report and differing ways of interpreting sustainability (and in turn, the role of territory and the environment) have emerged (Magnaghi, 2005). Magnaghi mentioned three approaches, termed as functionalist or eco-compatibility approach, environmentalist or biocentric approach and territorialist or anthropo-biocentric approach. Of these, the first interprets the question of sustainable development as an issue of ecocompatibility. Quantitative growth, world market laws and globalization remain unquestioned. The movement from the standardized factory to the virtual company, from salaried work to self-employment, can be interpreted as an evolution of a social-technical system which always goes hand-in-hand with an even further artificialization of the 'second nature'. This process involves the transfer of several activities, production and socialization forms, and community relations into telematic networks and cyberspace, as well as the further severing of nature from culture through genetic manipulation and cloning. Local production is dictated by the laws of the global market, as also are the techniques used. Territory is regarded as a beast of burden—we must not overload it, otherwise it will collapse and will not be able to function. It is this approach which illuminates vividly the divide between the terms 'development' and 'sustainable'. Development is said to be the centre of economic growth, whose laws are dictated by competition among companies, among local and regional systems, and among cities in the world market. In contrast, sustainability is measured against the maximum threshold of degradation and environmental pollution compatible with competition. The threshold is fixed by evaluating environmental impact and defining limits of exploitation and consumption of resources. This kind of weak sustainability concept enables industrialized countries to expand their already huge ecological footprints. The imposition of control mechanisms and the attempts to counterbalance the environmental deterioration (laws, taxes, clean up operations, national parks, protected areas, etc.,) fail to prevent the decay that accumulates exponentially as a function of the economic laws of developing themselves. While fixing these limits and restrictions comes within the purview of local governments, decisions about what, how, where and how much to produce remain in the hands of the world market (Magnaghi, 2005).

According to Magnaghi, the environmentalist and biocentric approach shows sustainability to be a problem of the living mutual interactions between human settlements and the environment. The latter being considered as a natural system (biosphere, geosphere and hydrosphere, with flora, fauna and ecological networks) whose laws of self reproduction need to be respected. A suitable framework for this approach is facilitated by a vision of systems based on high environmental quality and ecological efficiency (not merely the definition of limits to pollution and degradation). Such a positive attitude replaces the functionalist approach characterized as exclusively limiting and regulating to create standards. Certain valuable spin-offs for the economy from the high environmental quality represent the new fixed capital and the structural condition for sustainable development—the environment becomes a valuable resource. While nature suffers some degradation by development patterns determined by the supremacy of economic growth, the ecological approach takes a middle path i.e., protection of the natural environment. The environmentalist approach directs its actions towards safeguarding nature, which entails some risks. It could lead to a rigid determinism in the design of human environments, and also failure to produce a radical critique of the social and economic system causing environmental degradation (by only adopting collateral remedial actions in the face of pre-established laws of growth (Magnaghi, 2005).

Endogenous Development and Diversity

One notable paradox of today's world is the prevalence and co-existence of extreme poverty on the one hand, and many people having food, better health, longer life, more access to education and faster communication. In many rural and even urban areas, education, healthcare and markets function poorly. At global level, the environmental problems have reached alarming proportions, the differences in wealth between countries have increased, social and cultural systems are crumbling, and political and ethnic tensions are growing. These various problems are being tackled through several initiatives and approaches that aim at an economically feasible, socially just, ecologically sound, and culturally acceptable development route. These initiatives are usually carried out by networks working on some particular theme such as poverty reduction, participatory development, natural resources, low external input and sustainable agriculture, energy, biodiversity, indigenous rights or cultural diversity. All these initiatives give much attention to traditional knowledge, particularly the technical part of it. The socio-cultural and spiritual aspects of these knowledge systems usually attract little attention (Haverkort et. al., 2003).

The last few centuries saw a profound dominance of the western culture. Western economic mechanisms, values, science and technology have increasingly replaced traditional cultures and knowledge systems all over the world. The local knowledge systems are further weakened when the younger generation, attracted by the dominant culture, moves away from their cultural background. And yet, because the traditional cultures have considerable resilience, traditional values and practices still play an important role in the decision-making process of rural people in many parts of the world. This includes both the positive and negative aspects of traditional practices. Meanwhile, the limitations of the Western culture and technologies are also manifesting themselves in the persistent problems of industrialized agriculture such as environmental degradation, loss of biodiversity, lack of animal welfare and disintegration of rural communities.

It is now recognized that technologies developed under one set of conditions may not be effective under other economic, ecological and socio-cultural situations. Instead of applying fixed technology packages under all conditions, greater importance is given to the concept of 'diversity' like diversity in values, scientific concepts, technologies, development approaches, farming styles, biological systems, cultural expressions and lifestyles. Diversity undoubtedly holds important keys towards solving major global problems. To base development actions on this concept can lead to a diversity of practices and cultures, which can co-exist and co-evolve. This diversity allows for a variation of options and solutions according to the needs of local situations. Combining the efforts of innovative rural people, development organizations and politicians is badly needed to advance this concept one step further, and to relate it to our increasingly globalizing world (Haverkort et. al., 2003).

Some practices and requirements that enhance endogenous development can include building on local resources and complementing them with appropriate external resources, increasing local control, encouraging local knowledge systems, and retention of benefits in the local areas.

Over the last two centuries, indigenous knowledge systems have often been overtaken or eclipsed by the ongoing globalization which involves the entrenchment of western modern knowledge systems and technologies in many parts of the world. Current education and research systems are mostly based on western knowledge and value systems. Consequently, development activities have generally enhanced technologies with international standards, instead of supporting the needs of specific regions or populations. In agriculture, the use of external inputs has increased due to extension and grant of subsidies. In health, western biomedicine has spread to all part of the world. No doubt these efforts have led to tangible improvements, but awareness about some problems associated with this approach is also increasing. Environmental pollution is a major problem, while privatization and liberalization have pushed health services and agricultural external inputs beyond the reach of many villagers. Many young people from villages are moving to cities. These processes not only strain local economies, but also the social and cultural inheritance of the local communities (Haverkort et. al., 2003).

We can learn much from rural people about their knowledge, practices, traditions, their insights into the local ways of reasoning, methods of experimentation, and systems of learning and communication on which they are based.

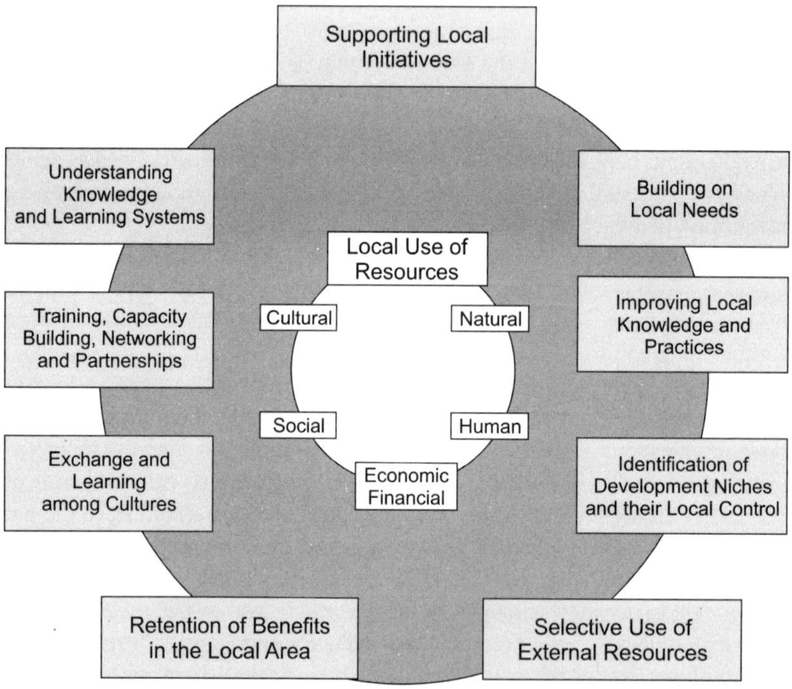

Fig. 5.6 Activities that support endogenous development (After Haverkort et. al., 2003)

Armed with this knowledge, suitable projects can be designed to improve traditional practices and to find innovative development niches for income generation. The use of resources by local people can thus be supported by development agencies and the support activities that can be carried out may be divided into different activities as indicated in Fig. 5.6.

Some indicators for the extent of indigenousness in traditional agriculture are mixed cropping, crop rotation, including long fallows, indigenous methods of crop processing and storage, enterprise diversity and integration of crops, livestock and trees, adherence to accepted seasons and auspicious times for farming activities, minimum tillage, avoiding inversion of surface soil, use of organic manure, labour sharing and village-level cooperation, farm-level breeding and seed improvement, weed control by indigenous methods, harvesting of rainwater or improving rainfall efficiency, applying traditional treatments against plant pests and diseases (Ramprasad et. al., 2003).

Types of Modern Biotechnology

Four major modern biotechnologies are *in vitro* technologies, detection technologies, genomics and genetic modification (Visser, 2001).

In vitro Technologies

In vitro technologies separate parts of living organisms in closed containers to manipulate and maintain this material. Several well-known and relatively older applications belong to this category.

Plant tissue culture involves the maintenance of plant material (complete plants, specific organs or cells) under sterile conditions and in the presence of nutrients. It allows the rapid multiplication of crop plants at a small-scale in comparison to *in vitro* (living) conditions. Supplying starter material for crops in large quantities solves the supply bottlenecks, particularly for farmers who grow vegetatively propagated crops. Plant tissue culture helps multiply starter material. It also allows for the cleaning of virus-infected starter material. Another use of plant tissue culture is to conserve useful crop genetic resources in a less vulnerable environment than in the field. Finally, plant tissue cultured *in vitro* is used to transfer useful traits from wild relatives into crop varieties by crossing sexual barriers that do not take place under normal *(in vivo)* conditions.

Detection Technologies

Technology has been developed to detect the presence or absence of specific traits in individual organisms. A major part of this technology is the use of an array of DNA marker techniques. These make use of patterns of specific DNA sequences that reveal the genetic difference between two individual organisms. This technology has substantially speeded up plant and animal breeding. If DNA marker sequences are linked to specific traits, the sequences can be used to search for the presence of these traits in the offspring of a cross breeding, long before the trait is actually expressed. A major aspect of these techniques is that they do not alter the DNA or the gene rather they just allow a quick appraisal of what can be found in the offspring of a breeding programme.

As compared to *in vitro* technologies, costs in this case are higher and facilities required are more advanced. Until now, the extent to which this technology is applied in plant and animal breeding and its impact has been much larger than that of genetic modification. These techniques are being applied in small-scale agriculture e.g., in maize-breeding projects that aim at increasing the drought tolerance in local maize germplasm in Kenya. Markers have also been used to better understand farmers' selection of local rice varieties in the Philippines and Vietnam, and to more efficiently maintain the genetic diversity in enset, a staple crop of small-scale farmers in Ethiopia (Visser, 2001).

Monoclonal antibodies exemplify another detection technology. Cells from the immune system that produce specific antibodies are maintained and multiplied *in vitro* for making large quantities of antibodies that are used to search for specific material. Besides primary applications in health care, the technology is being used in agriculture to detect pathogens in plants and animals allowing accurate pest and disease management.

These technologies are used to provide the pest/disease free import guarantees on products as required by many countries, facilitating cross-border exchange of plants and animals. The costs for the development of monoclonal cells producing specific antibodies are high and also specialist expertise is needed. But the use of such monoclonal cells and their antibodies is relatively simple and requires only modest facilities.

Genomics

The field of genomics involves the large-scale sequencing of DNA, including entire genomes (all the DNA of a single individual), and the comparative analysis of the resulting sequences across species barriers. Important highlights in this field is not only the sequencing of the total DNA of man, but also substantial number of microorganisms (model organisms, pathogens and organisms used in traditional biotechnology), plants (including rice) and animals.

Genomics produces enormous datasets and a complete new science, bioinformatics, has been developed to handle these databases and to allow retrieval and analysis of the information they contain. The costs of genomics research are so high that only a few specialized institutions located almost exclusively in developed countries can contribute to this newly-evolving science. No immediate spin-off for agricultural applications should be expected in the next few years. But in long run, a detailed knowledge of plant and animal genomes will speed up breeding, also in tropical agriculture.

Genetic Modification

Genetic modification (manipulation) involves the transfer of genetic information in the form of DNA sequences across sexual barriers between species, which under normal conditions would not exchange DNA. The resulting organisms are called GMOs or 'transgenics'. Genetic modification is currently used to introduce either a single new trait, which might be based on the activity of a single gene or a small number of genes. The number of genes with known functions that has been isolated is still too small to allow for more complicated traits or combinations of traits to be introduced by using this method. In agriculture, genetic modification has been applied in several important crops. Most involve the introduction of resistant traits, particularly to herbicides and insects. A few applications involve change in the quality of the resulting product, e.g., the shelf life of tomatoes or the production of alternative sweeteners in sugarbeet. The farmers mainly deal with the former type of agronomic applications, whereas the processing industry and consumers are interested in the latter. Transgenic animals have been produced under laboratory conditions, but so far have not been released for industrial application.

The costs of developing GMOs are high, and the technology requires very expensive facilities and highly skilled experts. In an increasing number of countries, legislation and regulations to contain GMOs and their products during the development and extensive testing phases before release are becoming very strict and costly. Although about 70 transgenic crop varieties were registered for commercial cultivation in 1999, international agricultural biotechnology companies have so far focused on only a few cash earner crops such as cotton, rapeseed, maize, soybean and wheat (Visser, 2001).

Impact on Tropical Agriculture

In advanced countries, agriculture has been highly industrialized and breeding has evolved from a farmer's activity into a specialist's affair. The conditions of the farmers' fields have been adjusted to suit the new breeds (varieties) by extensive application of fertilizers and pesticides. Crops have become increasingly uniform to facilitate mechanized cultivation, harvesting and processing. Because of the more capital-intensive agriculture, the size of an average economically sustainable farm has increased several times over the last century. Agricultural biotechnology will certainly enhance this trend by increasing the dependence of the entire production chain on a very small number of crops and new varieties. Modern agriculture will continue to be high-input dependent and become even more uniform. Genetic modification will allow the production of the same raw materials (e.g., plant oils) in different crops. The negative impact of modern agriculture on agro-biodiversity might be worsened by the large-scale introduction of GM crops and farm animals.

In contrast, tropical agriculture is still dominated by small-scale systems. Often, farmers' access to external inputs is low. International companies developing GM crops do not consider small-scale agriculture as an important market. Besides, these crops would not cater to the diverse agro-ecological conditions encountered in farmers' fields and would not benefit them.

Although GMOs may today have little direct relevance to small-scale tropical agriculture, this reality does not emanate from the biological nature of biotechnological applications. It rather emanates from the socio-economic context in which biotechnological applications are developed. This prompts the question of whether and under what conditions other appropriate biotechnologies for small-scale farmers are feasible.

Biotechnologies for Endogenous Development

More attention in agro and food biotechnological developments has been aimed to establish a new development paradigm involving a marked shift from exogenous to endogenous development and the concomitant changeover from agro-industrial genetechnologies to tailor-made biotechnologies (Ruivenkamp, 2003a).

Adjusting the potential of new food technologies to issues of equity and sustainability is one of the crucial challenges. Modern biotechnology offers several technical possibilities for increasing food security, but doubts persist as to whether biotechnological applications will benefit people bypassed by the Green Revolution. By and large only those biotechnological applications have been pursued, which are related to industrial agriculture. Some social agencies, and public and private organizations have also started linking biotechnologies to sustainable and endogenous development.

Critical reappraisals of the concepts of development, industrialized agriculture and global food chains have generated new possibilities for strengthening the local potentialities of agriculture and food production through a tailored use of new technologies. It has emerged that the industrialization of agriculture, leading to an enormous improvement in productivity and well-being in many areas, has often originated from and facilitated by research institutions external to the producers in the agricultural sector itself. According to Ruivenkamp, the concept of exogenous development refers not only to the external origin of agrarian development, but also means that the industrialization or modernization of agriculture takes place by disconnecting agriculture from those locally specific elements (e.g., local ecosystem, local knowledge, local consumption patterns) that initially introduced specificity and heterogeneity into agriculture. Exogenous agrarian development stresses that the external institutions should apply a concept of modernizing agriculture in which at least some existing practices in farming are discontinued in favour of modern ones. In fact, farmers who adopted the modernization projects are categorized as those that were most 'open' to outside information and innovations. This approach of enhancing agriculture was in keeping with mainstream economics, which regarded agricultural development as essentially an adaptation of farming practices to bring changes in global markets and technologies. Critical analysis of the introduction of biotechnology in the agro-industrial production chain explicitly brought out that biotechnology helps in severing the old links with local farming practices, separating local food consumption from its agricultural produce. It supports the development towards a homogenized agricultural production system with a substantial improvement in productivity and well-being for the progressive farmers and consumers in urban centres. Biotechnology also tends to increase social differentiation in some rural areas. The major drawback or limitation of this model of exogenous development is that it has failed to eliminate poverty and malnutrition as over 800 million people are still chronically undernourished. The primary issue is how to reach them and how to 'go beyond modernization'. The answer may come from pursuing endogenous development where development patterns are founded mainly on locally available resources such as labour force, knowledge and patterns for linking production to consumption. Endogenous developments reinvigorate and dynamize these local resources. In endogenous development, the major part of the total value generated is relocated within the locality itself (Ruivenkamp, 2003).

The need of the hour is to strengthen an international network to exchange information about various attempts being made to tailor-made biotechnologies for endogenous developments.

Biotechnology and Food Security

According to UNDP (1998), by the end of the 20th Century the developing countries had doubled school enrollments, halved infant mortality and adult illiteracy, reduced malnutrition by one-third and extended life expectancy at birth by some two decades. Thanks to the "Green Revolution", food production has outpaced population growth, mainly because of substantially higher yields and increased irrigated land area, food availability per capita grew and prices fell (Serageldin, 1999).

However, poverty continues to limit access to food, leaving many millions of people undernourished in the developing countries. Increased population, income growth and urbanization are greatly stimulating food demand, with a possible doubling of food needs in these countries over the next four decades. Can the world continue to provide the supplies to meet this demand?

In principle, biotechnology has the potential to contribute to food security by helping to promote sustainable agriculture centered on smallholder farmers in the developing countries. Sadly, biotechnology is being showered with brickbats and flowers, with opposing groups making strong claims of peril and promise (Leisinger, 1995; Rifkin, 1998; Serageldin and Collins, 1999).

Today the world is marked by collective affluence, but also by economic uncertainties, poverty, hunger, and violent conflict. Population growth adds some 85 million persons a year, mostly in the poorest countries. Poverty and environmental degradation go hand in hand. Tackling these problems will depend greatly on whether and how to transform agriculture in developing countries (IFPRI, 1999).

Questions are emerging about whether a second, "doubly green revolution" that is both environmentally sustainable and yield-increasing could help meet food needs over the next two decades. Biotechnology will, of course, have a prominent role in making such a revolution successful. To ensure that food production is coupled with both poverty reduction and environmental conservation, increases in cereal and grain yields must occur in the complex smallholder farming systems of the poorest countries (Hazell, 1999). This can be achieved only by promoting agriculture and rural development, an enabling regulatory framework, fair trade, flexible and responsive institutions, increased investments in health and education, especially for women, and good access to credit, roads, marketing and extension. More efficient use of water, energy, and labour is also essential (Serageldin, 1999). Two major shifts in the agricultural research paradigm are needed:

1. To integrate crop-specific research into a broader vision that includes sound management of natural resources, as well as the productivity and profitability of smallholder farming, promoting synergies among livestock, agroforestry, food and cash crop, and aquaculture production, all on a hectare or so, integrated management of soil, water, and nutrients, integrated pest management, and minimizing postharvest losses (Conway, 1998; Hazell, 1999).
2. To harness the genetic revolution. Critical work on genetic mapping, molecular markers and biotechnology needs to be focussed on benefiting poor people and the environment (Serageldin, 1999).

Successes in plant genetic engineering have resulted in production of such useful varieties as *Bt* cotton, *Bt* maize as well as herbicide-tolerant varieties of several crops. James (1999) pointed out the value of these crops in minimum-tillage soil conservation. There have been dramatic increases in the area planted to transgenic crops. The five major transgenic crops were soybean, maize, cotton, rapeseed/canola and potato (James, 1999).

Biotechnology advances are crucial to the problems of food security, poverty reduction and environmental conservation in the developing world. But for many, they raise important issues relating to ethics, intellectual property rights (IPRs) and biosafety. Indeed there have been many protests against the spread of agrobiotechnology. One major fear is that "novel" products may destroy agricultural diversity and change agricultural patterns uncontrollably.

Patenting and IPRs are also arousing concern. It is feared that patenting will lead to monopolization of knowledge, restricted access to germplasm, controls over the research process, selectivity in research focus, and increasing marginalization of the majority of the world's population (Serageldin, 1999). To minimize such fears, e.g., in the context of the so-called 'Terminator Gene' technology, the Consultative Group on International Agricultural Research (CGIAR, 1998) has agreed not to release any germplasm that contains technologies preventing smallholder farmers from holding and replanting seeds. Instead, CGIAR centres prefer the apomictic gene to assist smallholders to replant hybrid varieties. There is need for due caution about the long-term effect of technologies, even if their application is benign.

IPR issues are even more complex. Application of these concepts to agriculture attracts acrimonious debate because technological development in agriculture, particularly in the developing countries, has occurred primarily through public investment and most of the products, including those generated by CGIAR centres, are considered "public goods". The largest germplasm collections of important crops in the developing world are held in trust by these centres and remain in the public domain (Wright, 1996). According to Serageldin (1999), there is need for establishing more precise domains of intellectual property. "Public goods should be left to the public and private goods that stand at the pathway of achieving these public goods and should also be treated differently from private goods that are produced by the private sector in direct relation to the end user."

Certain areas of research with potential benefits to poor people are not being pursued by the private sector. For example, tomatoes with a long shelf life are now available and profitable. Research is desirable on drought-resistant millet, which is not commercially attractive but has a high food security impact among poor Africans. The public sector should be allowed to pursue such researches.

For the developing countries to benefit from biotechnology research, public sector institutions should develop new partnerships with the private sector, advanced research institutions, non-governmental organizations and farmer associations. The Monsanto company has already entered into agreements with Kenyan and Mexican agricultural research institutes on developing virus-resistant crops (Serageldin, 1999).

Biotechnologies for Soil Remediation

Remediation of polluted sites has become a recurring necessity because of increasing concern over pollution, misuse of natural resources and environmental and health effects of various developmental processes. Stringent cleanup standards are being directed to protect the soil vegetation and ecological systems and to prevent contamination of the groundwater with hazardous waste and toxic materials from land spills, leachates from landfills or leakage from underground storage tanks. These measures are strongly influencing the ways in which hazardous compounds are being developed and used.

Various innovative and cost-effective remedial technologies have become available to bring down the high costs associated with conventional technologies and to reduce the time required for cleanups.

Remediation technologies are of two general types—*in situ* i.e., effecting treatment in place or *ex situ i.e.,* treating the contaminant off-site or on-site. Figure 5.7 shows the classification of soil remediation technologies. The specific technology to be used on any site depends chiefly on properties of the contaminant, concentration of the wastes, soil types, governmental regulations and climatic conditions. In general, however, *in situ* techniques are preferable because of reduced cost and hazard-handling resulting from excavation and handling. Those who favour *ex situ* technology argue that *in situ* technologies can prevent reagents, steam or bacteria from reaching all the contaminated material. There is less certainty about the uniformity of treatment because of the inherent variability in soil and aquifer characteristics and also it is difficult to monitor progress. They claim that *ex situ*

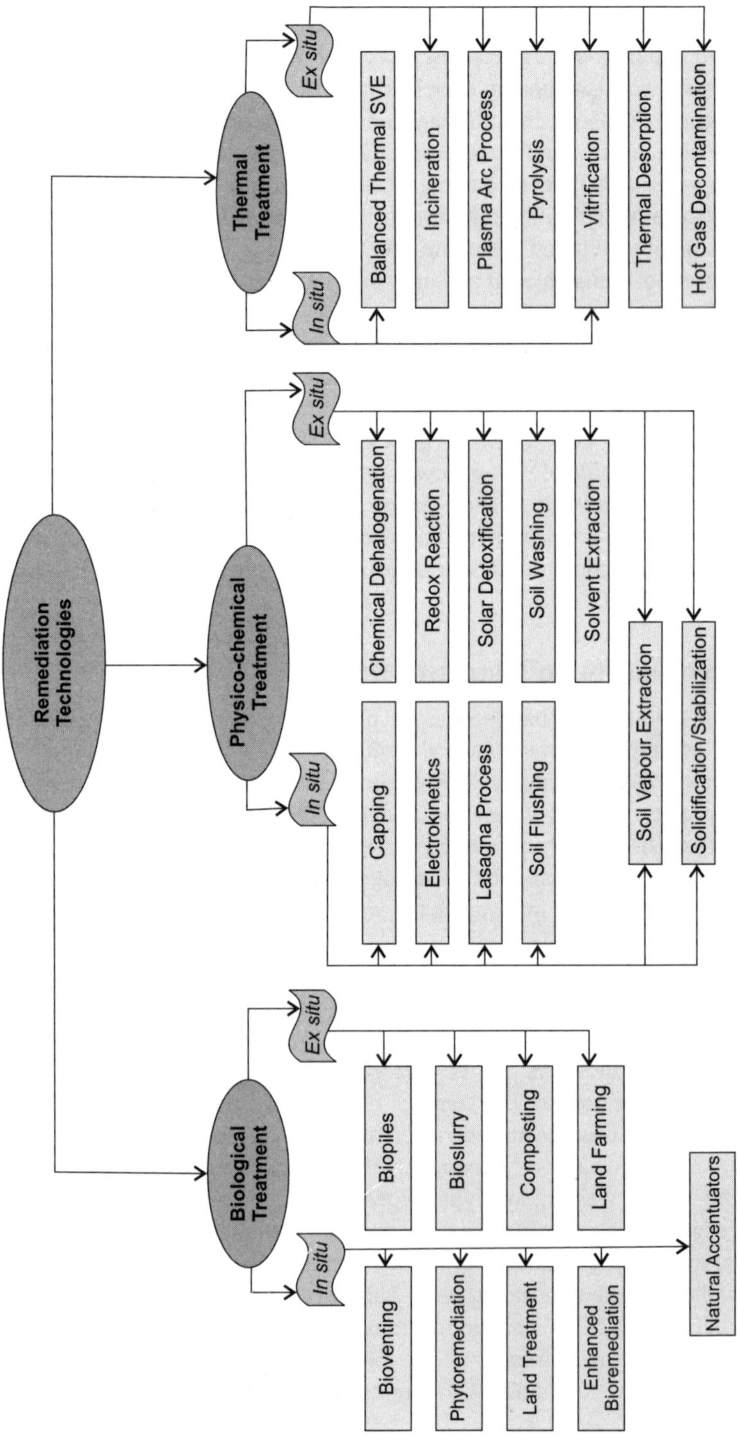

Fig. 5.7 Classification of soil remediation technologies (After Jakpa et al., 1998)

allows homogenization of the contaminated soil ensuring monitoring of the soil cleaning to regulation limits within a relatively short time (Jakpa et al., 1998).

The basis underlying any remediation technology is to reduce or eliminate deleterious effects of pollutants in the environment. Soil is a highly complex matrix and hence its decontamination is difficult. It requires the analysis and control of a large number of variables to ascertain the best choice that would meet regulatory compliance. At certain times, the contaminants may not need any treatment at all, but get naturally degraded in course of time. In other cases, we may have to choose the best technological option from a basket of competing technologies, or a combination of technologies may be needed in curtailing the menace.

Biological, physical, chemical or thermal are the four major types of remediation technologies. Physical and chemical mechanisms are sometime combined into one group (physico-chemical) because they normally occur together and overlap in the treatment process. (Here, only biological treatments are being described).

Biological waste treatment has been known since medieval times. Degradation of many toxic wastes requires some sophisticated engineering techniques to remedy it. One such nature-based engineering technique is called 'bioremediation'. This has been commonly used for the remediation of organic contaminants but is now being applied to metal remediation at the bench and pilot scale. It makes use of natural biological processes that allow certain plants and microorganisms to aid in the remedial action. These processes occur through such mechanisms as adsorption, oxidation and reduction reactions, and methylation (Means and Hinchee, 1994).

In biological treatment, contaminants in soil, sediments, sludge or groundwater are transformed or degraded into innocuous substances such as carbon dioxide, water, fatty acids and biomass through microbial metabolism. It can be used either *in situ* or *ex situ*. Some innovative biological technologies include bioventing, landfarming, composting and enhanced bioremediation. Some limitations are:

- Not too efficient for the cleanup of clayey and other low permeability soils
- May require extended treatment time frames
- Microbes are often sensitive to toxins or high contaminants in the soil
- Possibility of high generation of secondary wastes

Some specific types of biological treatment are outlined below:

1. **Biopile** Biopile is the modification of land farming method of petroleum hydrocarbon decontamination. Biopiles are very advantageous in relatively limited landscape, and in capturing and treating volatile organic compounds. In a full-scale *ex situ* technology, the polluted excavated soils are stockpiled into a heap within the treatment bed to prevent further contamination, and are also mixed with soil amendments and a delivery aeration system. An irrigation/nutrient system is applied to the treatment heap, while a leachate collection system recycles the collected fluid. Moisture, heat, nutrients, oxygen and pH are controlled to enhance biodegradation of the contaminants. This process normally reduces the contaminants to carbon dioxide and water within a few months of operation.

2. **Bioslurry** It is a good option for sites requiring greater process control, more complete degradation or where the cost of importing compost amendments is prohibitive. The contaminated soils are mixed with water to make a slurry to allow contact between the microorganisms and the contaminants. The slurry is fed into a bioreactor where controlled amount of air is used for mixing and aeration, and inoculation made to enhance treatment. Treated slurry is suitable for direct land application. Bioslurry process is ineffective in the removal of metals.

3. **Bioventing** It is a cost-effective innovative approach in which air is supplied through injection wells, and in some cases, existing air is circulated through vacuum extraction. This increases the volatilization of organic contaminants while simultaneously creating conducive conditions for biodegradation of less volatile organics. The basic principle is to deliver low and optimized airflow rates to provide enough oxygen to the zone of contamination, and the addition of nutrients to sustain and promote biological degradation of organic compounds by the naturally occurring soil microorganisms. The process is used for the removal of organic compounds with moderate to low volatility such as petroleum hydrocarbons, oils and lubricants. It cannot be used for the treatment of metal and inorganic contaminants.

4. **Composting** It is an *ex situ* solid remediation technology like land farming but one that requires thermophilic (55–60°C) conditions. Contaminated soil is excavated and mixed with bulking agents and organic amendments (such as wood chips and vegetative waste) to improve soil texture for aeration and drainage. Proper amendment selection ensures adequate porosity and provides a balance of carbon and nitrogen to promote thermophilic microbial activity. Optimization is by maintaining moisture content, pH, temperature and nutrients via irrigation techniques. An organic-rich compost results and is used as a rich fertilizer. Composting process is applicable to soils contaminated with biodegradable organic compounds, heavy oils, polycyclic aromatic hydrocarbons (PAHs) and munitions wastes like 2, 4, 6-trinitrotoluene (TNT).

5. **Enhanced Bioremediation (Biostimulation or Bioaugmentation)** It involves increasing the biodegradation rate of contaminated soil by the addition of nutrients and oxygen. The activity of microflora and fauna is stimulated by circulating aqueous solutions through the contaminated soils and/or addition of indigenous/inoculated micro-organisms, engineered microbial species or seeding with pollutant-degrading bacteria so as to enhance biological degradation of contaminants or immobilization of inorganic contaminants. The process may be used to treat soils contaminated with petroleum hydrocarbons, solvents, pesticides, wood preservatives, nitrotoluenes, etc.

6. **Land farming** It is an *ex situ* solid-phase remediation technology for the treatment of soils contaminated with petroleum hydrocarbons. Land farming is designed to enhance the microbial degradation of contaminants through

periodic tilling to induce aeration, control moisture content and add nutrients such as nitrogen and phosphorus.

7. **Land treatment** It is an *in situ* technology in which the contaminated soils are tilled on site and the combined forces of bulk soil interaction, biological activity and climatic conditions effect cleanup.

8. **Natural attenuation (Intrinsic bioremediation)** It allows contaminants to undergo degradation and mineralization naturally by dilution, diffusion, dispersion, advection, volatilization, microbial degradation, sorption and chemical reactions within an acceptable time frame. Requires virtually no intervention except monitoring of the mineralization process. Contaminants that can be treated using this technology are mostly volatile organic compounds (VOC) and moderately semi-volatile organic compounds.

9. **Phytoremediation** It is an emerging cost-effective remediation technology for *in situ* vegetative treatment of hazardous contaminants in soils, water or air. The technology makes use of certain plants and planting techniques to accelerate the rate of degradation, removal, transformation, stabilization and destruction of targeted soil, waterborne or airborne contaminants. It is best used at sites with shallow contamination scenario of organics and metals. Some practices now use deep-rooted plants such as poplars and alfalfa to attack, mitigate and contain pollutants situated a few metres into the subsurface. The degradative process stimulates microorganisms through the release of carbon-containing nutrients from plant roots (Jakpa et. al., 1998).

Cleaner (Organic) Agriculture

Organic farming is cleaner in the sense that it avoids chemical fertilizers, pesticides and GMOs. It takes the living soil as a basis and employs methods that are compatible with agroecological processes without depleting natural resources. Organic agriculture is founded on the integrity and intrinsic value of the soil, plants, animals and human beings, and is friendly to environment, farm ecology and complexity of nature. The objective of organic plant breeding is to raise plants which enhance the potential of organic farming and biodiversity. Organic plant breeding is a holistic approach that respects natural species crossing barriers. It is based on fertile plants that can establish a viable relationship with the living soil.

Biodiversity is a core feature of any sustainable organic farming system. This is why the organic sector attaches high value to the free exchange of the genepool. Although the rights of breeders are duly respected, patents and techniques to make plants sterile jeopardize and adversely affect the free exchange and consequently, the genetic diversity.

Organic Farming and Biotechnology

Two types of biotechnological techniques being used in modern plant breeding are:

- Those that remain within the realm of life
- Those that go beyond (Table 5.3)

Table 5.3 Biotechnological Techniques Commonly used in Plant Breeding (After Van Bueren and Osman, 2001)

Technique	Use
	At the Cell Level
Embryo culture, Ovary culture, *In-vitro* pollination	Crossing of closely related species. Such crosses occur in nature but do not result in viable seeds as the embryos abort prematurely. When these organs are separated from the plant and grown in test tubes, they can develop into mature plants.
In-vitro selection	Selection of new stress-resistant varieties. Plants are grown in test tubes and exposed to stress like salinity. The survivors are selected.
Anther/Microspore culture	Pollen and anthers are grown *in vitro*. Being haploid, they can be made diploid by treating with chemicals to develop plants that are genetically identical.
Meristem culture, Micropropagation, Somatic embryogenesis	Rapid propagation of genetically identical plant cells are multiplied in test tubes. The cells are regenerated into new plants.
	Below the Cell Level
Genetic modification, Protoplast fusion	Genetic materials of unrelated species are inserted into cells. Protoplast fusion implies the merging of complete cells. In genetic modification, only small pieces of foreign DNA are inserted into the cell.
Cytoplasmic Male Sterility (CMS) without restorer genes	Developing male sterile parent lines for hybrid production. A plant cell is fused with a cytoplast (a plant cell from which the chromosomes have been removed). The cytoplast contains factors which cause male sterility. CMS does occur in nature but is accompanied by factors that neutralize the male sterility. When CMS is transferred from an unrelated species into a crop in the absence of the neutralizing factors (restorer genes), the new male sterile plants cannot be multiplied.
DNA marker assisted selection	Certain sequences of DNA can be associated with certain plant traits. These marker sequences help in selecting plants for traits which are not directly visible in the field like drought tolerance. This technique uses available DNA sequences in the plant cells, but does not change them, and so is compatible organic agriculture. If radiation or GM enzymes are used to detect these markers, then it is not acceptable for organic farming. Detection through fluorescence is acceptable.

The cell being the lowest organized structural entity of life in the eukaryotes (higher organisms), all breeding techniques that intervene below the cell level do not conform to the organic principles. This means that genetic modification (at the DNA level) and protoplast fusion are forbidden for the organic sector, but other cell biological techniques, e.g., embryo rescue and *in vitro* pollination, are acceptable (Van Bueren and Osman, 2001).

Cleaner and Sustainable Crop Production

Sustained growth of crops in the humid tropics can only be maintained at a high productivity level if external resources are used and plant residues are returned to the field. Intensive mineral fertilization in the tropics is often criticized as being an unsustainable practice because strong precipitation can entail nutrient losses through surface runoff and leaching. Losses also result from nitrogen volatilization and phosphorus bonding to aluminium and iron oxides.

In the humid tropics, provision of crops with sufficient plant nutrients may possibly be alleviated by resorting to strip cropping with legumes and hedgerows (alley cropping) that reduces leaching losses, accumulates organic matter, improves nitrogen fixation and enhances buffering capacity. All these augment the nutrient storage capacity of the soil. But sometimes, nitrogen uptake from mulch material and nitrogen export through harvest can be quite low in agroforestry systems.

Most agroforestry systems studied so far, if planted as the sole soil nutrient accumulating measure under conditions typical of permanent cropping in the tropics, cannot prevent the topsoil from impoverishing in important plant nutrients. If it permits a seasonally complementary nutrient uptake, mixed cropping can reduce nutrient losses, especially those through leaching. The amount of nitrogen contributed by tree legumes to the plant–topsoil system can be severely reduced if nitrogen availability in the soil increases as a result of the mineralization processes that operate immediately after clear-cutting or as a result of mineral fertilization. A large part of this nitrogen input can accumulate in the subsoil and escape by volatilization, and so cannot be taken up and exported by the crop plants.

The best way of relieving world hunger and securing the food supply of a growing world population is through self-help, i.e., high genetic yield potentials achieved by plant breeding, which should be exploited by also making use of the available ecological yield potentials. Wherever individual components, e.g., nitrogen, phosphorus or water supply are limiting in the soil, the deficiencies need to be compensated for by biological, chemical or technical measures. Due to their multiple beneficial effects on soil fertility, fodder legumes like lucerne play an important role.

Some measures to preserve soil fertility and health are:

- Suitable sequence of main crops (biological decontamination)
- Suitable sequence of catch crops
- Organic fertilizing (manure, straw, green manuring)

- Technical (goal-directed soil tillage, i.e., erosion protection, increase in turnover, or decreased in turnover)
- Chemical, i.e., mineral fertilizing (calcium, nitrogen, phosphorous, pottassium) and plant protectants (nematicides, herbicides, fungicides, insecticides).

Soil fertility has chemical, physical and biological components. An optimal humus content benefits all three components. Soil tillage enhances the soil's biological activity and decompresses humus. When soil is allowed to rest and sown with grass clover with strong root mass development, there is replenishment of humus in carbon and nitrogen compounds. Increasing the humus content from 1.7–3.4 per cent requires an increase in nitrogen accumulation from 0.1–0.2 per cent (at a C/N ratio of 10 : 1) and hence an increase in nitrogen from 3000–6000 kg/ha. The best way of achieving this is by means of legumes.

The greater the humus (nitrogen) content of the soil, the greater the nitrogen mobilized and the greater is the nitrogen that has to be replaced per hectare to retain a high humus content. Growing clover-grass forage helps preserve and improve soil fertility besides supplying valuable fodder.

Fodder legumes benefit the soil in the following ways:

1. Through humus accumulation (carbon and nitrogen)
2. By rendering the subsoil porous
3. By checking the spread of diseases in cereal crops
4. By weed control as a result of repeated cutting (prevention of seed ripening and dissemination)

By improving the following crop's nitrogen supply, enhancing subsoil rooting and consequently also the water supply, and by reducing stress factors (weeds, disease), the above quadruple benefit leads to considerable yield increases for crops like wheat.

Circular Economy

The Asia–Pacific region that accounts for one-third of the earth's land area harbours about 65 per cent of the world population and 70 per cent of the world's poor people. It shows extreme contrasts in wealth and population, density, terrain and climates. These contrasts are further exacerbated by natural disasters such as earthquakes and tsunami. Economic growth in the region takes place usually at the cost of the environment.

Asia–Pacific poses some formidable environmental challenges to the whole world. How we manage rapid urban development, climate change, water quality and the huge demand on natural resources in the region can define the future status of wealth and health of the planet.

Small island states in the Pacific are highly vulnerable because their survival depends on fragile ecosystems. The activities of the bigger territories literally ripple into these island states, sometimes with profound consequences.

Population density in Asia–Pacific greatly exceeds what the environment can support, and the only way to develop successfully is in an environmentally sustainable way. If we fail in this respect, developing nations could end up worse off than when they started and this will adversely impact the whole planet.

Urbanization is accelerating. About 70 per cent of this construction work takes place in China and India. The energy used and the emissions in constructing and maintaining the various buildings are massive. Mitigating their effects on climate change necessitates encouragement of carbon neutral concepts. The most sensible way to do so is to start with a paradigm of circular economy in which the waste from one area becomes the resource for another.

This concept needs to be adopted in all areas of life, from household to industry and back again. We need to show cause–effect and provide solutions. A circular economy can place sustainability on a firm footing.

In a general model of economic production, unlike land and labour, capital is an input created by the production process itself, and the outputs of produced goods and services are utilized in further production. In familiar physical terms, capital can be viewed as man-made objects such as machines, tools, buildings and factories (all used for making more goods and services). According to traditional capital theory, the cost of capital is the interest rate charged. Physical capital shows high spatial concentration.

The twin processes of social exclusion and environmental degradation often increase poverty (Duraiappah et. al., 2000). Poverty is a direct cause of environmental degradation. The poor neither have the resources nor the means to cause environmental degradation. The relationship between poverty and environmental degradation is very complex and involves a web of interlinked processes, influences and impacts. Duraiappah et. al., (2000) used a Pressure–State–Activity–Impact–Response (PASIR) analytical framework (OECD, 1994) for studying the complex interlinkage in Kenya, but also incorporated a socio-economic activity component. They observed changes and impacts not only in the ecological system but also in the economic or human system. Figure 5.8 illustrates how the various components in the modified PASIR framework operate in a dynamic environment of feed-forward and feedback causality relationship.

In this model, pressure points are the driving forces which exert some notable impact on both ecological and/or socio-economic states through socio-economic activities. If a pressure point is applied, any changes in the ecological state can only come from economic activities. For example, a tax subsidy cannot by itself cause a decrease in forest cover. Rather, it is the economic activities (e.g., excessive forest clearing encouraged by subsidy) that causes degradation. Also, the inclusion of socio-economic activities allows one to differentiate the degree and the type of activities set in motion by different groups of principles in the economy. Ecological states reflect the characteristics of the ecological systems under study. The major challenge is the selection of appropriate indicators to highlight changes in the ecosystem. The number of trees per square unit area may be one such indicator of changes in the forest cover. Ecological impacts are closely linked with the ecological states, and

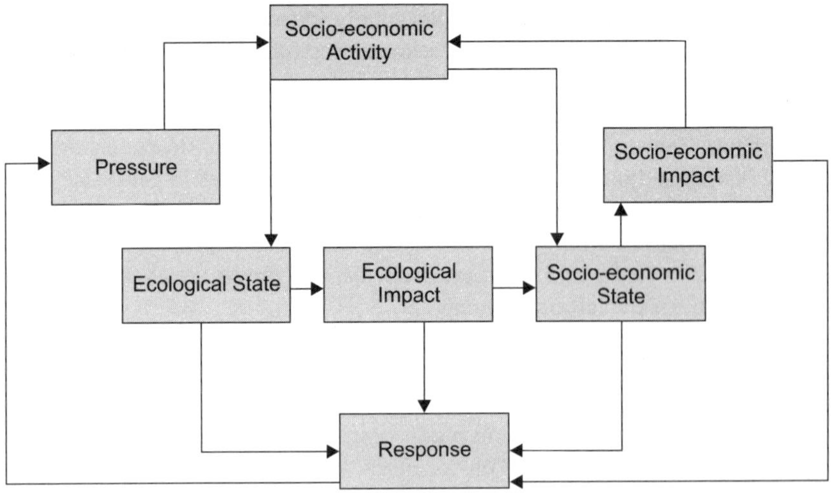

Fig. 5.8 The Pressure-Activity-State-Impact-Response (PASIR) modified framework (After Duraiappah et. al., 2000)

the choice of indicators is crucial. One important ecological impact closely linked to forest cover that has significant impacts on the economic system could be floods or their frequency.

Socio-economic states is a category introduced into the modified PASIR model. It plays a role similar to that of ecological states. Its primary purpose is to monitor level of the economic system. Socio-economic impacts category is a natural extension to the socio-economic states. Changes in socio-economic states by themselves do not mean much, but the actual impacts they have on the socio-economic system demonstrate significance of any changes (Duraiappah et. al., 2000).

Responses are societal reactions to changes and can be formal or informal. Informal responses are captured by the feedback relationship between socio-economic impacts and socio-economic activities. These responses are primarily reactive behaviours on the part of individuals to changes in their environment which can be described in terms of the socio-economic stats and consequently the socio-economic impacts. In contrast, formal responses are classified as official reactions on the part of governmental agencies.

As regards the causality dynamics underlying the PASIR structure, two forces affect socio-economic activity—pressure points and socio-economic impacts. The former captures the responses of the various principles to policy initiatives. For example, an agricultural crop price subsidy may provide the incentive for farmers to grow a particular crop. On the other hand, the socio-economic impacts are more complex as they are caused by changes in the socio-economic states. An example of a change in socio-economic state is a fall in income levels. The corresponding socio-economic impact is poverty if the decline in income causes the acted person to go below the poverty line. The socio-economic impact, in this case poverty, then sets in motion certain socio-economic activities which are expected to help counter the fall in income levels. This cyclical causality link makes up one kind of a feedback loop.

As there are two forces driving the socio-economic activities, so two forces emerge out of the socio-economic activity. One is the causality link between socio-economic activity and ecological states and the other is that between socio-economic activity and socio-economic states.

The last link in the causality chain is the response category. There are four ways in which responses can be triggered:

1. Direct response to change in the ecological state
2. Initiated from impacts as a result of changes in the ecological states
3. Response to changes in the socio-economic state
4. Response to the socio-economic impacts (Figures 5.9 & 5.10)

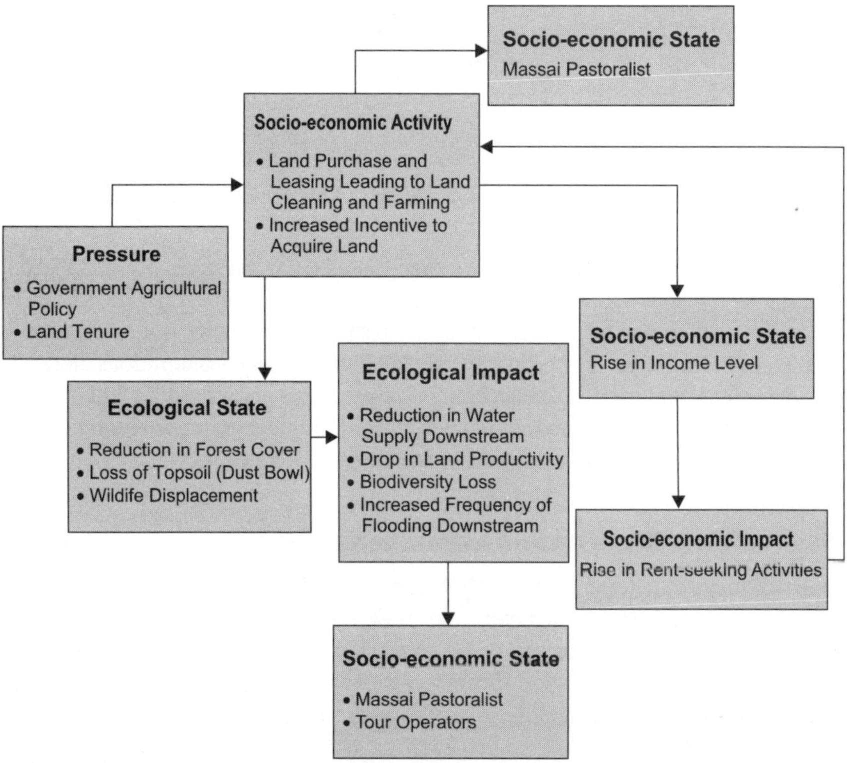

Fig. 5.9 PASIR diagram for commercial farmers (After Duraiappah et. al., 2000)

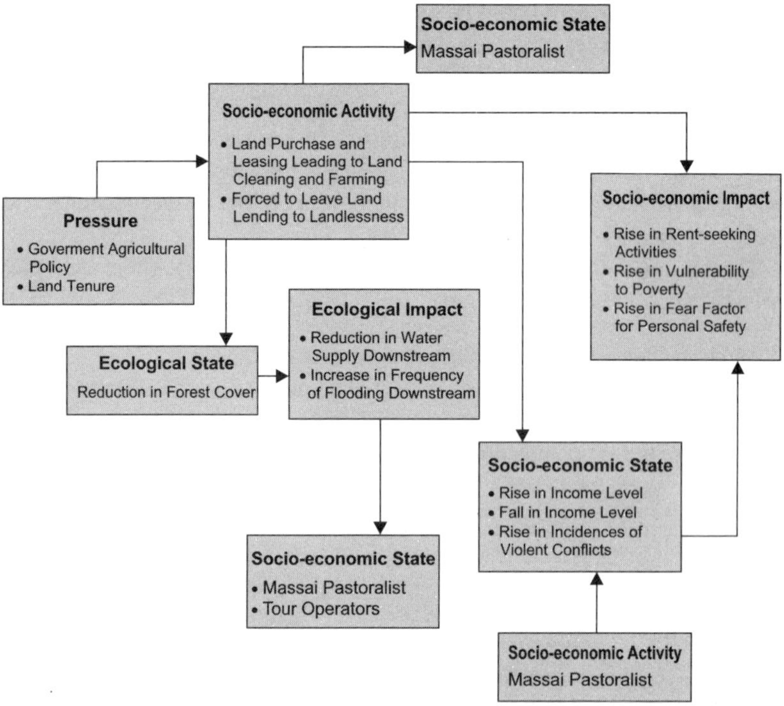

Fig. 5.10 PASIR diagram for mixed farmers (After Duraiappah et. al., 2000)

The ecological impacts caused by changes in ecological states present a strong argument for policy intervention. For example, forest cover reduction can cause a loss in biodiversity or an increase in the frequency of floods. But a response to these ecological impacts is primarily driven by ecological considerations alone. No economic considerations usually come into play at this point (Kumar, 2003).

The modified PASIR model provides a useful framework for analysing the key relationships in the poverty-environmental degradation nexus.

Maximizing Benefits and Minimizing Risks

The two major categories of problems faced by the Third World countries are those related to meeting the basic needs and those related to international trade. Both these categories can at least partly be addressed by biotechnology. Biotechnology offers new opportunities for diversifying economic activity as it deals with persistent environmental problems and improves the living conditions of the Third World population.

Most people in the Third World countries live in villages where agriculture is the main economic activity. The application of biotechnology to small-scale agriculture, for example, can direct the revolutionary potential of the technology towards addressing one of the most persistent problems of the Third World. There is also the potential for dealing with medical problems associated with tropical and other diseases. Thirdly, biotechnology can potentially improve the Third World environment through ecological rehabilitation and pollution abatement.

Biotechnology offers opportunities for developing new agricultural and pharmaceutical products for export. Industrialized countries could eliminate poverty largely through the use of technological innovations coupled with major institutional reforms. The third World countries also cannot avoid pursuing a technological route in their efforts to improve the living conditions of their populations (Clark and Juma, 1990).

However, the challenge is to adopt biotechnology policies that can enable humankind to reap the benefits while reducing the associated risks. In principle, biotechnology is quite consistent with the concept of sustainable development. But its realization for the betterment of humankind can only be achieved through concerted efforts to reshape the direction of technological innovation and the flow of benefits. Science and technology, or innovation broadly defined, is a very important source of economic change. Technology can no longer be viewed as exogenous to economic processes.

Until a few decades ago, environment was viewed as exogenous to economic development. Pollution, for example, used to be considered as external to the process of economic approaches that restore the central role of environmental management in long-term development. Further, environment is not a collection of separate entities but a whole that needs to be considered systemically. Finally, environment is not static but is a dynamic and evolving system. The chief conceptual concerns in technological change are similar to those in environmental management.

The problem, according to Clark and Juma (1990), is that the introduction of technology into the economic system can undermine the environment irreversibly. This seeming contradiction has led to the rise of antitechnology attitudes in certain environmental circles, and attempts are underway to try to reconcile these two seemingly contradictory viewpoints, through the concept of sustainable development (WCED, 1987).

Globalization of markets and privatization of agricultural research, changing patterns of natural resources control and restrictions in access to technologies affect the current global context in which biotechnology has to work. When new technologies are developed, the interests of small-farmer households and resource-poor regions need to be duly protected. According to Altieri (1997), the types of biotechnology most appropriate to the needs and circumstances of the resource-poor farmers need to be identified. Some potential examples are:

1. Development of bioengineered crop varieties that respond to infertile soil or are tolerant to saline or drought conditions and other stresses in marginal lands.
2. Production of improved varieties which are not dependent on agrochemical inputs for increased yields (excluding transgenic crops which may require increased agrochemical input).

3. Development of apomictic crop varieties (that can also develop seeds through sexual reproduction), thus allowing farmers to propagate and maintain superior cultures through seed.
4. Fermentation technologies for large-scale production of microbial insecticides, fungal antagonists and biofertilizers.
5. Tissue and meristem culture techniques for production of resistant varieties or virus-free varieties and clonal propagation for fostering new cultivar development, cautious of the problems arising from genetic uniformity.
6. Development of molecular markers to identify genes of interest in a variety that may be transferred to another for improvement purposes.

Appropriate Biotechnologies

Biotechnology can specially serve small-scale farmers in tropical production systems. Appropriate biotechnologies may be developed on the basis of demand and in consultation with farmers or their representatives. Those modern biotechnologies which require relatively few investments and which can be applied in a country or even in the community have the best chance of being appropriate. In particular, this could apply to plant tissue culture technology to produce healthy, much valued varieties in large enough quantities. The use of monoclonals may enable farmers and extension services to monitor for specific pests and diseases. Artificial insemination could be extended to well-adapted indigenous breeds. Cryopreservation and tissue culture of valuable plant and animal varieties and breeds might also provide the small-scale farming sector a back up for their genetic resources maintained in the field.

However, there are doubts as to whether genetic modification can offer anything to small-scale farmers other than their dependence on the seed industry. For any application in the public domain aimed at benefiting small-scale farmers, co-operation with the private sector will be a must because the private sector owns all the key patents needed to develop GMOs. The case of Golden Rice forms an interesting exception as it is in the public domain and was aimed at alleviating problems of small-scale farmers in developing countries (vitamin A deficiency) through the application of genetic modification.

Appropriate biotechnology is one of the several approaches for agricultural transformation. It is a tool that can complement the landscape of alternative agricultural technologies developed by farmers and NGOs. The peasant farms of traditional agriculture are usually much less vulnerable to catastrophic loss because they grow a wider variety of plants under diversified farming. Many of these plants are heterogeneous landraces grown from seed passed down from generation to generation and selected over the years to produce desired traits. By contrast, a pest or pathogen finds it much less difficult to gain a foothold when it comes in contact with a genetically uniform modern cultivar grown under continuous monoculture over wide areas. Entire crops have sometimes been attacked and seriously damaged or even destroyed by pests and pathogens.

Traditional systems and indigenous knowledge are no panaceas for agricultural problems but they do provide valuable insights into managing soils, water, crops, animals and pests. Research needs to be intensified on the benefits of traditional systems as well as their social and economic characteristics and potential for wider application. Sustainable systems must combine traditional practices and structure with more modern and scientifically derived technologies.

Biotechnology and Biosafety

Modern biotechnology is not just a scientific issue. It is a subject that can generate considerable disagreement and controversy. It has the potential to throw up a variety of moral and ethical concerns on which no consensus can be reached. These concerns mostly emanate from the feeling that biotechnology interferes with the workings of nature, that it involves irresponsible risk-taking for commercial profit or that it exploits and harms economically-vulnerable individuals and communities.

Modern biotechnology can arouse a wide range of intrinsic and extrinsic moral concerns. Biotechnology, in general, and crop biotechnology in particular, for a variety of reasons may be thought to be either intrinsically wrong in itself or extrinsically wrong because of its consequences (Straughan, 1997). The actual and the potential benefits of modern biotechnology, including its potential to increase food supplies and to alleviate hunger, should be weighed against these concerns. The correct balance has to be established in weighing the benefits against the risks of biotechnology. Not all countries have equal opportunity and resources to tap the potential of biotechnology, and the ethical dimension of depriving the poor and destitute of the advantages that biotechnology can bring must be weighed against ethical concerns about tinkering with nature (Straughan, 1997).

6

Sustainable Urban and Rural Development

Sustainable development is a programme for husbanding the earth's sources. Besides the more familiar environmental problems such as ozone depletion, global warming, deforestation, desertification, soil erosion and biodiversity, there is need to take action against poverty, infant mortality, malnutrition, epidemic disease, illiteracy and other afflictions of human population. Countries should join hands to accomplish the task of sustainable development. For the developing nations, the cumulative financial allocations add up to more than three-quarters in the form of labour and resources. For the developed countries, over $100 billion may be supplied principally in the form of essential technologies.

Agenda 21 of the UN Conference on Environment and Development held in Rio de Janeiro in 1992, concerns nothing less than the accommodation of the human species to the resources of the earth. It shows that this goal is both feasible and finite.

In developed countries, industrial revolution has increased people's material well-being and halted their population growth. When they know that their first infants will survive, people decide not to have more children. In countries like India and China, birth rates have been declining as the death rates of children below the age of five have fallen.

In 1992, both the rich and the poor nations agreed for the first time on what it will take to bring the human species to adjust its numbers and needs to the dimensions of a mere planet.

The contribution to sustainable development at a global level can be increased if cooperation to curb climate change is integrated with other efforts to stop environmental degradation and promote social and economic development in the developing countries. Continuous efforts to reduce poverty are essential to tackle the challenges facing mankind. A new and consilient approach is needed to cope with climate change (Kumar, 2006).

Response to climate change must include programmes and investments with a wider range and scope than the first generation of environmental agreements. Even if one cannot today foresee the radical changes in energy systems or production and consumption patterns necessary to meet the challenge of global climate change, a large number of response strategies are available. Many of the strategies could be justified, considering purely economic, development or environmental reasons. In particular, attention should be given to the positive and additional effects on pollution from nitrogen oxides, sulphur oxides, deforestation, erosion and biodiversity that would occur as a result of climate policy measures.

Elements of a comprehensive approach have been suggested and discussed at several international fora. Comprehensiveness relates first of all to flexibility with regard to measures concerning all sources and sinks, and additionally to the political scope of global participation and partnership. The aims and essential elements of a good and comprehensive approach includes:

1. National commitments related to targets
2. Universal participation based on common but differentiated responsibility
3. Additional resources to cover incremental costs of participation for the developing countries
4. Cost-effective implementation on national, regional and global scale

Due to current reassessment of long-term environmental costs of climate change, its limitation and adaptation measures, instant action is warranted on two grounds:

1. Comparatively low cost and multiple benefits of first-phase avertive measures: Cost estimates need to take into account the limitations of economic discounting, which inherently discriminates against future generations. Yet intergenerational equity is usually accepted as an ethical basis of the concept of sustainable development as defined by the World Commission on Environment and Development (WCED).

b. Avoidance of potential threshold effects and uncontrollable or irreversible discontinuities: Some evidence of incipient threshold effects is available (e.g., methane emissions due to tundra warming). But the uncertainty inherent in these risks should not be an excuse to defer precautionary action.

A variety of studies on response strategies that have been done all over the world, suggest that a balance will have to be found between different options on the international, regional and national levels. In the light of the investment cost and other measures which will have to be carried over time, cost efficiency assumes paramount importance.

There is a strong case for 'no-regrets' options. Attention should be focused on feasibility studies of no-regrets and low cost measures in industrial and developing countries alike. In such inventories, there is a need to link climate policy measures to overall economic reform. This would improve economic efficiency and economize the input of natural resources. Reduction of perverse subsidies and market failures would contribute to a wider scope of concrete action.

The no-regrets option accessible through such inventories would include energy conservation through functional energy markets and harmonized carbon taxes connected to appropriate reductions in other tax instruments to avoid inflationary pressures. Subsidies to energy sectors should be directed mainly towards research and development of renewable and other environmentally beneficial energy sources and energy end-use efficiency.

With regard to energy conservation, further clarification of the concept of no-regrets option itself is needed, as well as more empirical research on which options actually qualify as no-regrets.

In industrial countries, the potential for energy conservation is primarily in end-use efficiency. A substantial conservation potential exists in the transformation process from fuel to services. In developing countries, considerable potential exists for energy conservation in the primary production of energy, distribution system and end-use efficiency.

The arguments for economic efficiency of the political and economic instruments of a climate convention may be summarized in the following four aspects:

1. There should be flexibility with regard to different sources and sinks. Climate policies should include all relevant sources and sinks of greenhouse gases. Emission targets should be defined in terms of net emissions of the greenhouse gases that are adequately monitored, measured as carbon dioxide equivalents, taking into account requirements under the Montreal Protocol and the subsequent agreements.
2. Economic instruments should form a basic element in cooperative response strategies from the countries. These instruments will promote cost effectiveness, create incentives for optimal universality in participation and reduce administrative costs of implementation. Since abatement costs differ, uniform standards will be inefficient. Differentiation of behaviour is needed and regulation by incentive is to be preferred to regulation by directives.
3. A system of harmonized national taxes on carbon and other greenhouse gas sources is one alternative to be considered. Alternatively, a system of tradeable permits, on a national, regional or global scale, could gradually be developed. The definitions of tradeable permits should be based either on emission flows over time or definite volumes of emissions.
4. As first step in the direction of more advanced systems, attention should be paid to how countries could widen the field of cooperation by the creation of bilateral or regional alliances in meeting the short-term commitments under the convention. Such alliances will promote mutually beneficial cooperation between industrial and developing countries, between industrial countries and countries presently in economic transition, as well as between industrial countries themselves

Notions of equity or fairness provide important criteria for any policy scheme, including the allocation of quotas or the distribution of reimbursements from an international tax. We are faced with multiple notions of equity that we would consider valid, everything else the same. A starting point may be the notion of equality, parties that are equal in all normatively relevant respects should share the same burdens equally. Today, most of the parties included are not equal in all relevant respects. This calls for criteria for a differentiated approach. Four criterias seem to be particularly frequently invoked are responsibility, contribution, capacity and need. All these criterias are related to cost/benefit and cause/consequence.

Obviously, both the responsibility and the capacity criteria imply that the costs of action to prevent climate change will have to be shared with industrialized countries taking the lead in committing resources. These nations should provide means for technological cooperation and financial transfers as a compensation for incremental costs. Abatement measures should not obstruct economic and social progress in the developing countries.

The Quintessence

The essential meaning of sustainable development, as specified in the Brundtland Report (WCED, 1987), is a type of development which is concerned about responding to the needs of actual population without compromising on the resources required for future generations. The concept of sustainable development arose over a compromise historically negotiated among various social partners on the WCED. According to Vaillancourt (1992), the concept of eco-development was first proposed by Ignacy Sachs and Maurice Strong, among others. This concept combines development with consideration of the basic ecological principles and with an ecological ethic based on the values of autonomy, solidarity and responsibility for the socio-environmental realities. But any clear reference to ecology or environment tends to irritate some politicians and economists. The concept of sustainable development was adopted specifically because of its vagueness about the actual type of development involved, other than that it could be sustained. Thus, "sustainable development" was a shrewd phrase that made it possible to start an intimate dialogue between the worlds of business, politics and environment. It became one of the few keys available for change. Moreover, the strategy proved fruitful, environmental aspects of projects were henceforth recognized as an obligatory concern (constraint) in economic development and so were duly taken into account by decision makers. The concept can be considered as a first step towards the development of a deeper social and environmental ethic. The term "development" brings to mind the trajectory. The expression "sustainable development" neither points to the object nor the direction of this trajectory. It actually means "economic development" and is precisely the conceptual vagueness. So characteristic of this expression gives sustainable development strategy all its strength as it can lead anywhere.

There are several different definitions of sustainable development (Sauvé, 1996). Sachs and Esteva (1996) suggested three ways of looking at sustainable development. The following perspectives are related to a security crisis:

1. **Fortress perspective** The people of the North fear the dangers of the boomerang effect of the misery in the South and view sustainable development as the viability of their own type of development, sheltered from global threats. The North is the saviour and the fortress can resist only, if it propagates its own development model. Several sustainable development training programmes are geared to this instrumental approach (transmission of scientific knowledge, technical expertise and management skills), which proposes a means of achieving a goal that has not been clarified or discussed.

2. **Astronaut's perspective** The entire earth is an object of management with only a new world order can save it and provide the yardsticks which will ensure that development is sustainable. The planetary, global or international perspectives that are proposed for education today often adopt an ethic of the astronaut.

3. **Endogenous perspective** It proposes an alternative form of development. The growth economy threatens subsistence economies and threatens the very basis of human existence and, in the longer term, those of the biosphere. In this context, for many communities, "sustainability" means nothing more than resistance to development. The endogenous perspective involves a search for something beyond development (Esteva, 1996), sheltered from cultural disintegration and the disintegration of small economies (Sauve, 2000).

Although many educationists and champions of education for sustainable development have dissociated themselves from the fortress perspective, it remains the key to explaining many of today's political and economic decisions.

The generally accepted conceptual scheme of sustainable development (Fig. 6.1) represented by three interconnected circles is very problematic because it shows the sphere of the economy as lying outside society and not as an integral component of social choices. It is a supra-entity that governs the relationship between society and the environment, and it is in the economic sphere that development occurs. This, of course, brings out the actual domination of the global economy which is supremely alienating for societies, and which obstructs endogenous development (Sauvé, 2000).

Sustainable development is associated with the sustainability of the development itself as a goal of humanity (UNESCO-UNEP, 1988). Sustainability is

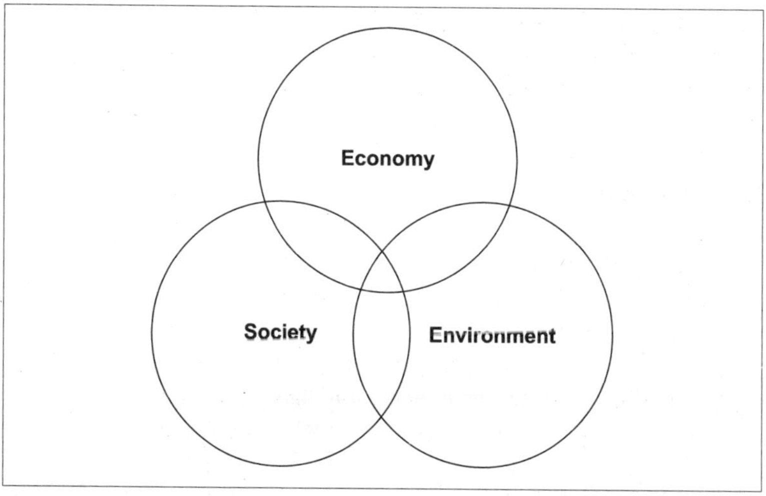

Fig. 6.1 Conceptual structure of sustainable development (After Sauve, 2000)

viewed as a supreme value on which all other values must converge. The relationship with the environment is treated as being subordinate to economic development. The only issue is not to exceed the carrying capacity of the environment while meeting the needs (often not specified) of current and future western-style societies. Besides this kind of ethical problem, the concept is also associated with a cultural issue, "The meaninglessness of such universal statements (found in education for sustainability) and the arrogance of the white, upper middle-class, educated, professional men who develop such statements, shines through. We need to be encouraging people to deconstruct these statements for the value they embody and the perspectives they contain" (Gough, 1998, pp 168)."

Sustainable Future

Because of the conceptual, ethical and cultural problems associated with sustainable development, it has been heavily criticized specifically by some educational professionals. In response to such criticisms, a new expression "Education for a Sustainable Future" has come into being, also referred to as "Education for a Sustainable World or Education for Sustainability" (Sauvé, 2000).

The idea of sustainable future is less loaded with economics than the concept of sustainable development. It refers to the development which provides food and health, so as to sustain human life. It has a more positive halo, including the image of an evolutionary trajectory, particularly appealing for the developing countries. The proponents of education for a sustainable future and education for sustainability have challenged certain narrow conceptions of sustainable development, and emphasize the necessity of a contextually relevant re-definition of sustainability (Tréllez Solis et. al., 1998).

The concept of a sustainable future is based on an essentially anthropocentric and questionable ethic, "It is necessary to imagine a new and sustainable relationship, over time, between humanity and its habitat, a relationship that places humanity at centre stage without forgetting however what is happening in the sides..." (UNESCO, 1997). Faith in technology is crucial to maintain 'the dynamic equilibrium' of sustainable development.

Global Capitalism

Another point of view different from Sauvé (2000) is Huckle (2000), according to whom the globalization of economies is largely responsible for much human misery in several countries. No doubt, structural adjustment programmes, deregulation and opening of markets are sometimes for international capital, but they do increase inequalities, encourage people and countries to overexploit natural resources, and reduce spending on social and environmental welfare.

The global environmental crisis is strongly connected with the global economic crisis and any analysis of the causes and possible solution to environmental problems should start from the fact that the two crises cannot be separated. According to Huckle, the idea of sustainable development has attached prominence in the past two decades when economic liberalism accentuated problems of underdevelopment and environmental degradation.

He feels that only when the economic, political and cultural spheres are fully democratized can people realize their common interest in the kinds of development that are ecologically, economically, socially and culturally sustainable.

Sustainability generates ethical issues when people conserve and enhance ecological capital in ways that either promote or reduce equity. Sustainable development can meet the needs of either the poor or the rich. Huckle advocates a type of citizenship that gives equal attention to rights and responsibilities, embraces the economic, political, cultural and environmental dimensions of citizens' lives at all scales from the local to the global, and prompts action on those forms of governance that can ensure intra and inter-generational and inter-species equity (Lynch, 1992).

Recent decades have brought out certain limits of free market capitalism, state socialism and social democracy, and there is urgent need to address those limits and find alternative ways of regulating economic and social life. A new kind of socialism that includes sustainability and cosmopolitan democracy is badly needed on our political and educational agendas (Tam, 1998; Huckle, 2000).

It is generally agreed that global capitalism (emanating from excessive liberalism) lies at the root of our chief social and environmental contemporary disorders. The socially critical versions of environmental education and education for sustainability converge in several ways and these convergences as well as their differences need to be clarified (Sauvé, 2000a).

The Social Pillar

The World Summit on Sustainable Development (WSSD) advocated proper recognition of the social pillar of sustainable development, including poverty, access and equality, and income-generating employment issues. Trade unions are attempting to integrate these priorities with changes in production and consumption patterns, environmental protection, and water, energy, health, agriculture and biodiversity (WEHAB) areas on a sector-by-sector basis.

For long time, the trade union movement has been much concerned about the social dimension of sustainable development. It has challenged unsustainable forms of development that brought ill health and death, environmental degradation, job dislocation and insecurity to workers. Early efforts in the area of occupational health and safety have developed into accepted models for joint action among trade unions, employers and governments, including retail sector (Gereluk, 2003).

WSSD called for the International Labour Office (ILO) and World Health Organization (WHO) to integrate occupational with public health programmes. It also called upon governments to support workplace-based partnerships that include cooperation between enterprises and communities. International agencies and stakeholders in the retail sector are encouraged to make workplace a foundation for action in areas within their mandate and capacity.

Measuring Poverty

Poverty has been interpreted differently at different times in the past. For many centuries, it was associated with monetary income. The last century saw many methods for its measurement such as the 'population income approach' (daily income per capita), the 'subsistence approach', the 'unsatisfied basic human needs approach', the 'relative deprivation approach', and the 'capabilities and functioning approach' (Mariscal et. al., 2005).

In some very poor countries (e.g., Bolivia), where about 85 per cent of the poor are located in rural areas, the national institutions generally use the population income approach as well as the socio-cultural indicators proposed in the unsatisfied basic needs approach, employment, housing, life expectancy, access to educational and health services, access to drinking water and electricity, and illiteracy (Fig. 6.2). All these conventional indicators are exclusively quantitative.

Four additional indicators related to agriculture that are used to measure rural development are daily income per capita, yield of main crop, production oriented to market, prices of main crop and access to credit (Mariscal et. al., 2005).

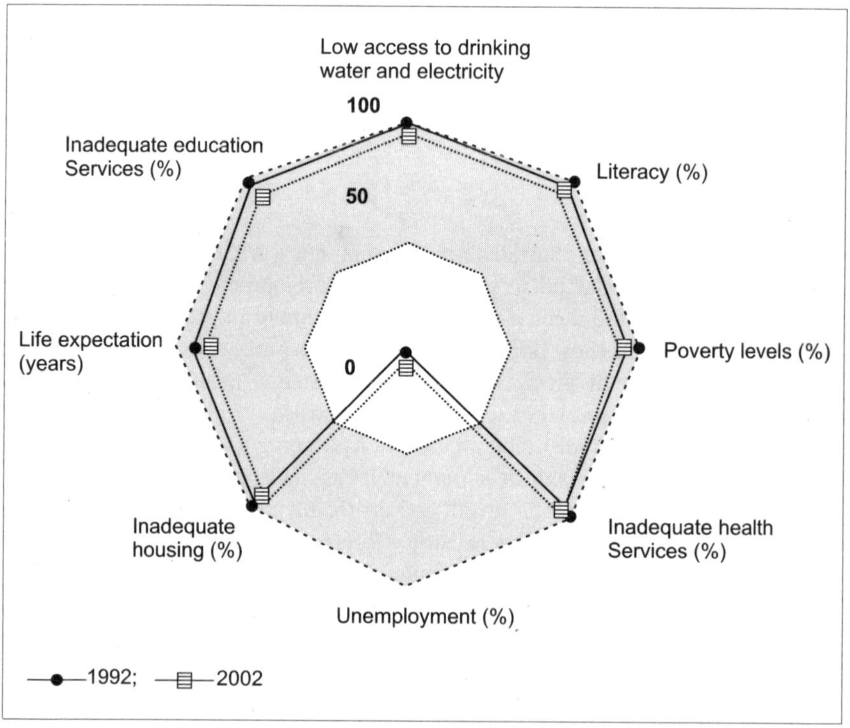

Fig. 6.2 Conventional indicators of unsatisfied basic needs approach (After Mariscal et. al., 2005)

Environmental Indicators

Conventional indicators concerning environmental aspects are lacking. However, the conservation and management of natural resources is crucial in view of the direct dependence of the communities on these resources. This makes 'plant biodiversity', 'animal biodiversity', 'soil conservation and management', 'water conservation and management', and 'land conservation and management' indispensable local (environmental) indicators (Fig. 6.3). Degradation of such natural resources as soil erosion and deforestation is a major contributory cause of poverty.

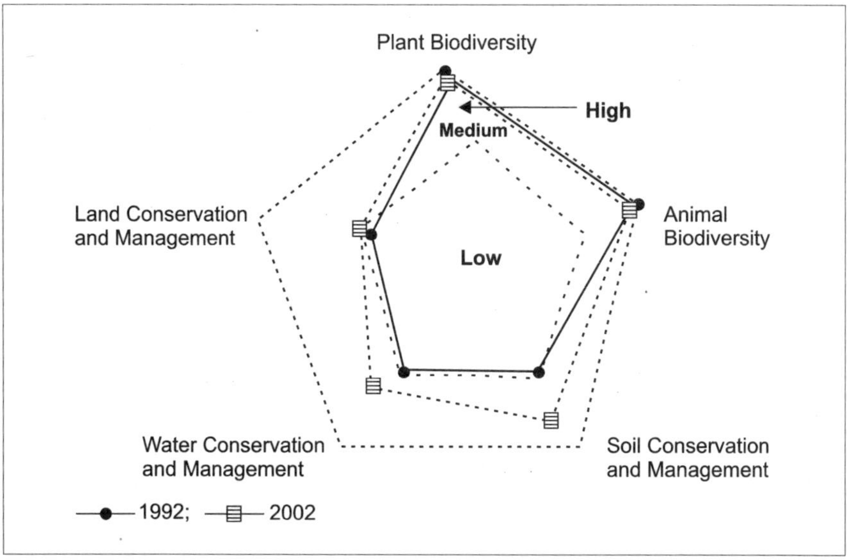

Fig. 6.3 Local indicators of environmental aspects (After Mariscal et. al., 2005)

Development Based on Carrying Capacity

For realizing the goal of alleviating poverty and improving the living standards of the poor, it is extremely important that industrialization and economic development are based on the premise of sustainable development, i.e., in harmony with a nation's carrying capacity (supportive and assimilative).

The idea of sustainable development has given the world's growing population some hope for prosperity in the absence of planetary degradation. Sustainable development demands an effective restructuring of the neoclassical economic structure based on open-ended consumption of material resources. Doctrines of carrying capacity-based development call for ecological economy, wherein the use of renewable resources would only be at the rate no greater than the regeneration of resources, and the use of exhaustible resources would not exceed the rate of their substitution by renewable resources. Ecological economy should help to preserve biodiversity and may produce waste only at a rate at which the waste can be assimilated by the biosphere.

The environment, including both its biotic and abiotic components, provides the basic resources that support production and consumption activities, and assimilates the residues or waste byproducts generated during the course of these activities. The limits to development are therefore defined by the supportive and assimilative capacities of the environment. The crux of the carrying capacity-based sustainable development lies in the quantification of supportive and assimilative capacities of the environment and optimal allocation of resources to stakeholders for various developmental activities (Himesh, 2001).

Sustainable development attempts to identify physical limits to economic growth and extraction of natural resources. It embodies the symbiotic relationship between the consumer human race and the producer natural systems.

Equity and social justice, economic efficiency, ecological harmony and endogenous choices make up some essential ingredients of sustainable development. The underlying correlation between population, poverty and pollution must be analysed against the backdrop of ecosystem capacity to support the development and assimilation needed for the maintenance of an acceptable environmental quality.

Development and Quality of Life

Although a precise meaning of quality of life (QOL) is not explicit, all or most developmental activities are usually justified against the backdrop of this dubious benchmark. The benchmarks are usually borrowed from the Western mindset. It is high time that nations establish an unambiguous and realistic benchmark of QOL, exclusively within the framework of the needs and priorities of the concerned society, consistent with its resource base and the ecosystem's resilience in the concerned region. The economic goal and any kind of developmental activity must be viewed with respect to this benchmark.

The basic elements of a good QOL include safe drinking water, food security, safe shelter and proper sanitation. It is shocking that 20 per cent of the world's population from developed countries should consume some 80 per cent of the total world resources. Mahatma Gandhi once proclaimed that, if the population of the entire world were to go in for this kind of QOL, we would need at least five globes to meet the requirement of resources (Himesh, 2001).

It is appalling that over 50,000 new chemicals are being introduced into the environment every year. Most of these are synthetic organic chemicals. As many of these are neither degradable nor safely disposable, an imbalance arises in natural material cycles. It is this imbalance that ultimately induces instability in the symbiotic relationship existing between the consumer human race and the ecosystem. The issue is whether we really need any of these novel chemicals for sustaining our lives? The scientific and technological abilities in producing such a vast array of chemicals/products should not be simply equated with development without understanding their potential risk to human health and irreversible long-term ecological impacts. Most of these new chemicals are used for making pesticides, herbicides, dyes, paints, cosmetics and drugs. These products did not exist before and have now invaded the consumer sector and are part and parcel of our lives. There is need to re-assess our current priorities so as to conform them in tune with sustainable development. The following are the two important issues that need to be addressed in this context:

1. How many synthetic chemicals and products are really needed by the common man?
2. Whether the products indispensable for life, but not eco-friendly, be substituted with other eco-friendly products by restructuring and reorienting our scientific research and technological efforts?

Infusion of ecological concerns into industrialization is an innovative, effective and efficient strategy for enhancing the competitive edge of the industrial sector in the fast changing global market and economic scenario, with highest concern for the environment. Any industrial or development sector that remains insensitive to environmental concerns is bound to suffer in the newly emerging era of Industrial Green Revolution.

Internalizing ecological concerns into industrialization need not necessarily slowdown the economic growth. Rather, it can trigger a new breed of industries and products expected to be inherently competitive and eco-compatible. Environmental concerns thus pave the way for a sustainable development in which eco-industry, eco-products, eco-market and eco-consumerism are the transformed and essential elements (Himesh, 2001).

There is a clear need to determine the kind of development appropriate for a given country or region which is still striving for basic needs. The developing countries cannot eliminate poverty by adopting the rusted technology left behind by industrialized nations.

Rather, they require home-grown solutions which are in harmony with their opportunities and environments. Irrespective of the mode of approach, the achievement of an ecologically sustainable form of development can be interpreted as a process that seeks to achieve high standard of living for human beings by enhancing their capabilities to live well. But this cannot be achieved at the expense of environmental and ecological integrity. Strategies for achieving an ecologically sustainable mode of development would undoubtedly differ from country to country as each would face somewhat different geo-environmental and socio-economic conditions and even conceptually different development goals (Himesh, 2001).

Current Sustainability Agendas

Some major trends in policy and business aspects in current sustainability agendas created by stakeholders (e.g., political institutions, consumer associations, NGOs and businesses) are:

- Wider application of economic instruments to environmental management
- Encouragement of eco-efficient production patterns and corporate social responsibility
- Adoption of supply and demand side management strategies
- Growth in public participation for business and policy development
- Information dissemination and public awareness programmes, setting product performance targets and policies, and guidelines for reporting

Figure 6.5 compares different kinds of information that stakeholders expect from the aluminium industry (Kuhndt et. al., 2002). Some recent surveys have shown that there is greater consensus on environmental information and less consensus on social and economic information. This may be because environmental information and indicators has long been a subject of public discussion and scientific reviews, but economic and social information/indicators played a less important role in stakeholder discussions until recently.

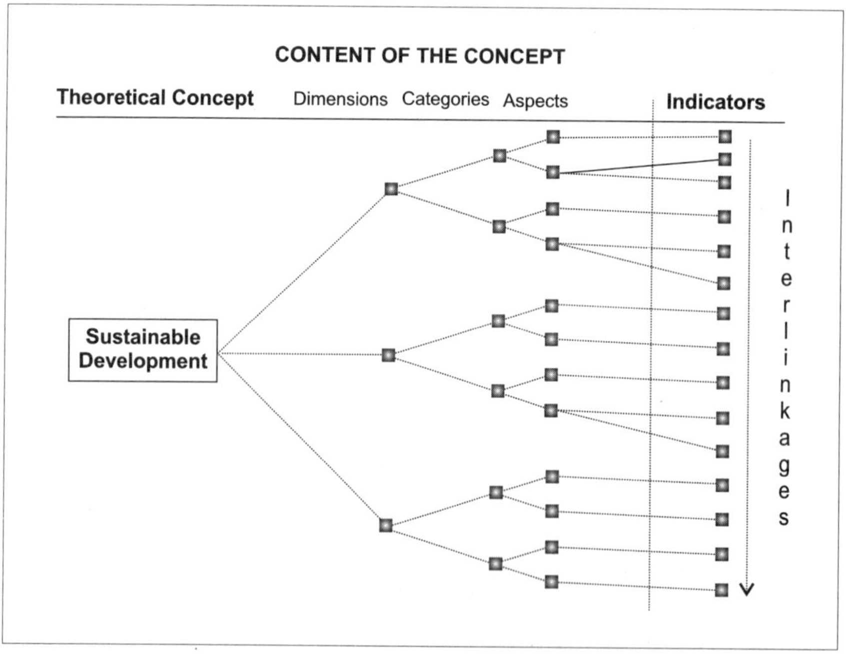

Fig. 6.4 Concept specification: Splitting the sustainable development concept into dimensions, categories and aspects (After Kohler, 1987; Kuhndt et. al., 2002)

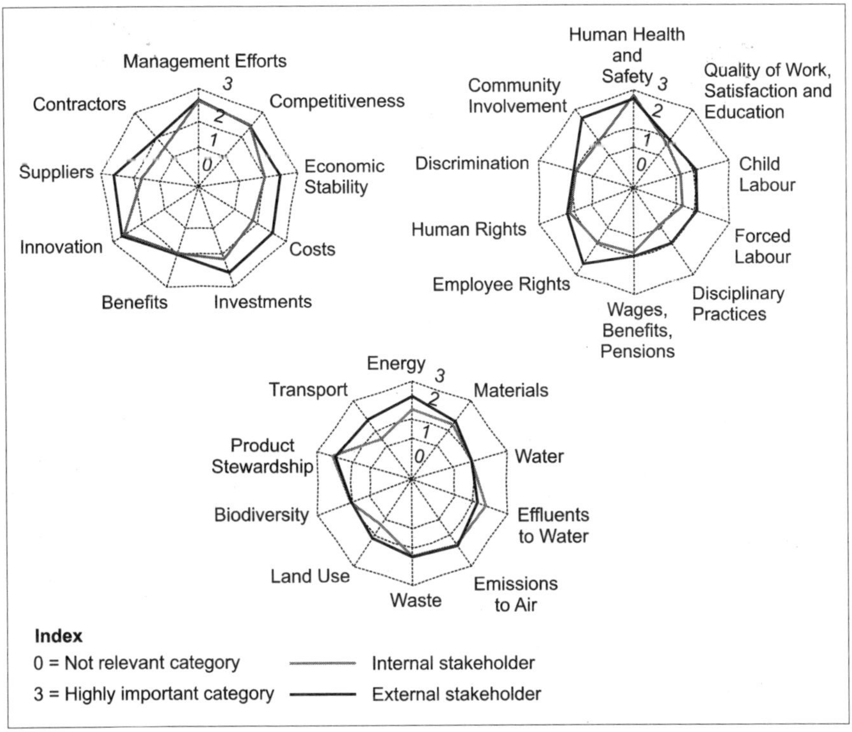

Fig. 6.5 Types of information that internal and external stakeholders expect from the aluminium industry (After Kuhndt et. al., 2002, 2002a)

Sectoral Sustainability Indicators

One of the main challenges in selecting sustainability indicators for business is the diversity of business characteristics. No single "universal" set of indicators can apply to all sectors. Decision makers must distinguish between core and specific sustainability indicators. The former are generally internationally agreed and relate to global sustainability concerns or values and are relevant and meaningful virtually to all businesses. These indicators provide data that can be taken from micro to meso or macro-level. Specific indicators depend on the business's specific nature and provide information at micro or meso level. Aggregation to macro-level is usually not possible. Some questions related to sustainable development of industry are listed below:

- What are the current trends in the international sustainability debate?
- What do they mean for a particular industry in terms of actions?
- Does the industry's strategy reflect these issues?
- What do stakeholders demand of companies and whole business sectors concerning sustainable development?

- Is it possible to transfer general sustainable development objectives to the specific industry under consideration?
- What are the stakeholders' expectations?
- Where do governments, NGOs, research institutes, universities, trade unions, consumer organizations and individual business enterprises and business associations address sustainability targets and indicators relevant to the industry?
- What are priority issues for the particular industry?
- How can environmental, social and economic sustainability be measured?
- What are indicators' potential and limitations?
- Is it possible to give equal consideration to environmental, social and economic aspects while considering a particular industry?

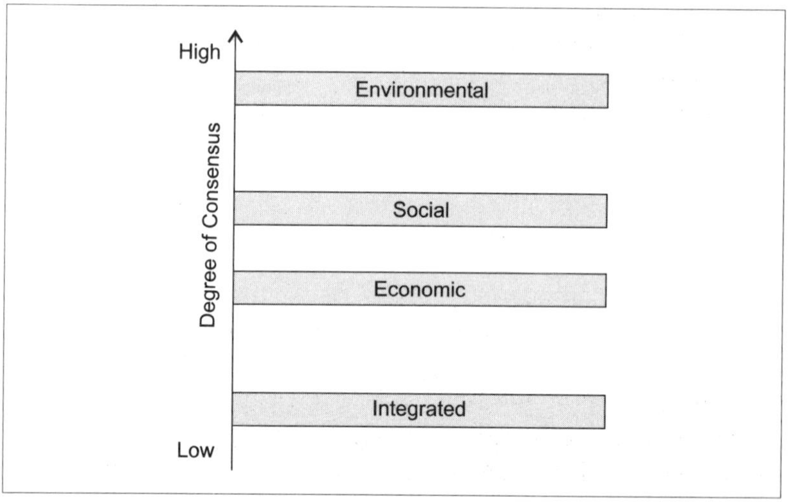

Fig. 6.6 Degrees of international consensus on four types of sustainability indicators

Suitable indicators are available for the categories and aspects listed in Table 6.1. The indicator set designed should be interpreted in its entirety. All categories, aspects and indicators should be examined when using the indicator system. To show the complexity of sustainable development, interlinkages within the indicator system must also be considered.

Further, any indicator set needs to be revised from time to time to adapt it to changing stakeholder demands, significant modifications in the underlying sector e.g., technological innovation and progress made in research on sustainability indicators. Revision on a regular basis is a common management practice aimed at continuous improvement (Kuhndt et. al., 2002).

Table 6.1 List of Sustainability Categories and Related Aspects (After Kuhndt et. al., 2002)

1.	Management efforts	**4.1**	Financial performance	**9.**	Discrimination
1.1	Sustainability policy and strategy	**4.2**	Risk management	**10.**	Human rights
1.2	Corporate economic performance	**5.**	Competitiveness	**11.**	Employee rights
1.3	Corporate social performance	**5.1**	Long-term profit	**12.**	Forced labour
1.4	Corporate environmental performance	**5.2**	International competitiveness	**13.**	Child labour
1.5	Stakeholder dialogue on environmental, economic and social performance	**6.**	Human health and safety (H&S)	**14.**	Community involvement
1.6	Communication	**6.1**	Corporate H&S programmes	**14.1**	Efforts to understand community concerns
2.	Cost	**6.2**	Corporate H&S performance	**14.2**	Corporate role in community/region/ country
2.1	Environmental cost accounting	**7.**	Wages, benefits and pensions	**15.**	Energy
2.2	Social cost accounting	**7.1**	Level of wages	**15.1**	Amount of energy consumed
2.3	External effects	**7.2**	Benefits provided to employees	**15.2**	Energy generation
3.	Investments and innovation	**8.**	Quality of work, satisfaction, education	**16.**	Water
3.1	Investments in research and development (R&D)	**8.1**	Quality of management	**16.1**	Water use
3.2	R&D to improve sustainability performance, best available technology (BAT)	**8.2**	Types of work organization (e.g., teamwork, job rotation)	**16.2**	Effluents to water
3.3	Cooperation with science (external)	**8.3**	Worker participation in decision making	**16.3**	Types of effluents
4.	Economic stability	**8.4**	Education, qualification, training	**17.**	Air emissions

Contd...

Contd...

17.1	Emission types and amounts	**21.**	Raw material availability	**23.3**	After-use phase aspects
18	Waste	**22.**	Suppliers/ Contractors	**23.4**	Life cycle aspects
18.1	Amount of waste generated	**23.**	Product stewardship	**24.**	Transport
19.	Material use	**23.1**	Customers		
20.	Land use	**23.2**	Use phase aspects		

Fig. 6.7 shows some vital components of the concept of sustainable development and resulting demands on its achievement.

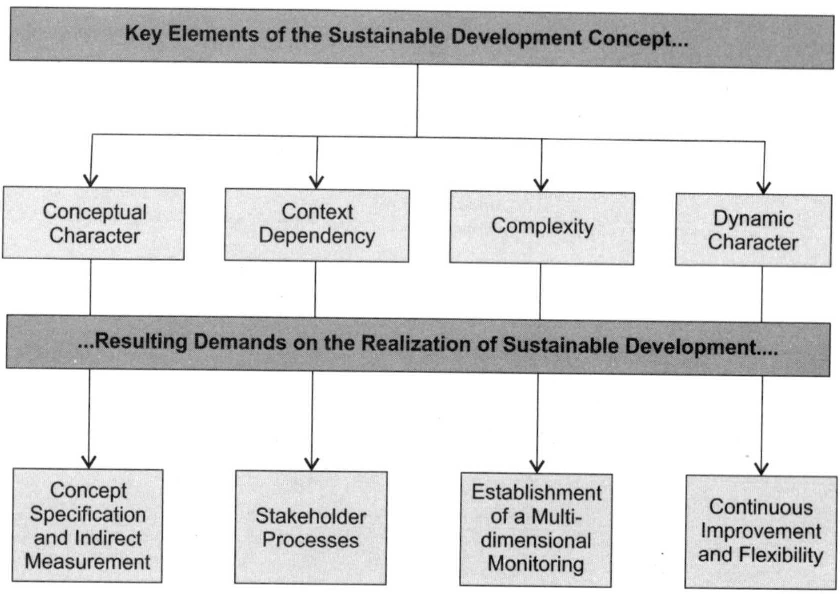

Fig. 6.7 Key elements of the sustainable development concept and resulting demands on its realization (After Kuhndt et. al., 2002, 2002a)

Sustainable Prosperity

Some new hard and soft technologies offer opportunities for achieving sustainable prosperity. Emerging technology areas, including information technology, biotechnology and nanotechnology, can be particularly effective in improving environmental performance, provided that the cleaner production perspective and philosophy is well integrated into the development and implementation of the technologies.

Appropriate technology is a prerequisite for sustainable prosperity. But the social component, in particular, has been largely neglected. Effecting cultural and structural changes is just as important as technological changes.

Transferring obsolete or banned technology from North to South is bad, but is still continuing because companies in developing countries quite often lack capital and hence are willing to buy cheaper, "low-grade" technology. To stop this practice requires effective implementation and enforcement of multilateral environmental agreements. Proposed mechanisms for preventing transfers of sub-standard technology include transparency of transferring processes and extended supplier responsibility. A paradigm shift is necessary, from simple transfer of high-tech hardware (North to South) with no adaptation for local circumstances, towards transfer of knowledge and know-how so that appropriate technology may be developed locally. Capacity building and empowerment of local organizations is also essential.

Human Settlements

The 21st Century is destined to be the century of urban revolution. By the year 2030, more than 60 per cent of the world's population will live in towns and cities and the bulk of the new urban population in the developing countries, where already at least one billion live in life and health threatening conditions.

Some important findings that have emerged in recent years are exemplified by the increasing inter-dependence of countries in the age of globalization and the continuing value of the principle of partnership. There is a continuing commitment to renew and foster political will at all levels to provide security and improve the living conditions for the urban poor, to promote gender equality and inclusiveness in human settlements development, to intensify efforts for ensuring transparent, responsible, accountable, just and effective governance, and a growing recognition of the added significance of international cooperation.

In Africa, the international cooperation focus on poverty eradication has allowed governments to include urban poverty reduction initiatives into their poverty eradication strategies. Enhanced international cooperation and development assistance to improve local capacities and reduce poverty will be required. The Asia–Pacific region is characterized by great differences in socio-economic development. Southeast and East Asia witnessed high economic growth for several decades prior to the economic crisis of 1997, but the economy of China continued to grow well. South Asia's development had been much slower and was less affected by the crisis.

Nonetheless, propelled earlier by economic growth, urbanization continues unabated. While population growth is expected to decrease to 1.11 per cent for the period 2000–2010, the formation of households will continue faster (growth rate of 2.29 over the same period). This will keep housing demand in the developing countries of the region at a very high level. Industrialized countries in the region face different problems such as the changing housing needs of the ageing population and the increase in single person households (Seaforth, 2001).

Among the major trends in the region is the shift of government policy towards an enabling role and more reliance on partnerships with the private sector as well as with NGOs and local community organizations.

Eviction is the greatest threat to most existing slum dwellers in Asia. The rapid growth of motorization in the vast majority of cities has generated much urban air pollution. Industrial pollution of air and water quality also remains an area of major concern requiring legislative action and effective enforcement.

Widespread recognition and understanding of the negative environmental and economic development impact of the overuse of the private automobile is a major concern. Expanding and enhancing access to public transport and light rail transit systems have either already been opened or are being constructed in Kuala Lumpur, New Delhi, Manila, Jakarta, Bangkok and Singapore. However, the widespread use of two-wheelers or motorcycles in the largest cities of Asia is having a negative impact on emissions levels/air quality, traffic congestion and QOL.

In the West Asian region, environmental issues remain paramount, being exacerbated by harsh climatic conditions which make resources like water scarcity. One of the major issues is the lack of potable water for cities in the entire region. Environmental pollution resulting from the prolific use of the private automobile in urban areas and coastal urban centres (ports dealing in the export of crude oil) causes concern in many countries.

OECD and Transition Countries

The main shelter issue in this region is not construction of new units, but urban renewal and conservation of historic sites and cultural heritage. Conservation, renovation and modernization of existing housing stock seems to be the main area of activity in the shelter sector in Western Europe, and even more so in Eastern Europe and the Commonwealth of Independent States (CIS), where the quality of many old dwellings is generally poorer than in many countries in Western Europe (Seaforth, 2001).

In all countries in this region, the population is ageing with its related consequences for the type of dwellings required. With growing numbers of older people, demand for smaller housing units close to services in densely developed inner cities will rise.

Countries with economies in transition where social welfare systems have declined considerably, there is a strong need to address the needs of tenants as housing markets are becoming increasingly commercialized. Western European countries are attempting to improve the situation of homeless people and refugees.

Issues related to urban transport systems are high on the agenda of many European countries. New technologies have led to improving transport systems towards more environmentally sound options.

Many countries are emphasizing on privatization and competition in the delivery of urban services.

Technology-driven Development

The major challenge of the 21st Century will be how to make both urbanization and globalization work for all. Globalization and urbanization have a symbiotic relationship–the characteristics of cities help shape and promote globalization. Global forces are centred in cities which provide the infrastructure and labour on which globalization depends. Many innovative ideas emanate from intense urban activities.

Also, the impact of globalization is most acutely felt in cities. The global economy has changed the structure of employment and altered the demographic makeup of the cities. Globalization has placed cities in a competitive framework of inter-city linkages and networks (Anonymous, 2001).

It appears that technology-driven options for growth and development, which stimulate globalization have led to more lines of stratification among people, places and groups. The costs and benefits of globalization are unevenly distributed within and between cities. Homeless people are living in cardboard boxes alongside towering corporate skyscrapers whose budgets exceed even those of some countries. Enclaves of highly affluent people, firms and institutions, increasingly connected to the world via Internet and mobile phones, exist cheek by jowl with large numbers of poor people who have never even once made a phone call. The social and economic cores and peripheries of the global information age and the global economy are not only continents apart but can now also be found geographically adjacent to each other in some individual cities.

According to Anonymous (2001), cities localize democratic processes in ways in which global and national institutions cannot. Globalization has paradoxically created a condition where civil order is simultaneously becoming more global and more local. For instance, globalization has often nurtured, rather than destroyed, the organizational capacity of the poor. While the urban poor may have little influence over global economic forces, they can plan an active role as agents of their own development.

Of course, in many cases existing approaches do not effectively address urgent issues of access to adequate housing, infrastructure and basic services, and many current developments are not only harmful to the poor but are also detrimental to the long-term sustainability of cities. Therefore, there is a need for new ways of managing and governing cities. The following four new elements of urban governance have emerged in the last decade:

1. Decentralization (devolution of power and resources from central to local governments)
2. Civil society participation in policy making
3. Multi-level governance and partnerships (public, private and civil society institutions joining forces to resolve urban problems)
4. Process driven and territorially based decision making and policies (the development of regional blocs and area-based initiatives)

There is no doubt that social justice and environmental sustainability in cities can only be advanced if cities are viewed not as 'engines of growth', but as 'agents of change'. This requires new political strategies for urban living and new forms of governance. The change would involve reconstituting relationships between the public and private sectors and civil society through the formation of broad-based cooperative partnerships. The challenge is to ensure that the fruits of globalization are shared more equitably.

The role of central governments in ensuring sustainability and equity in cities is also quite important. While national governments must facilitate the functioning of global markets and forces, they must also take responsibility for social cohesion, equity and conflict resolution in cities. In the long run, governments have the ultimate responsibility of managing the benefits and mitigating the risks of globalization.

Current State of the World's Cities

The United Nations Centre for Human Settlements (UNCHS), in its Report in 2001 summarized the state of the world's cities as follows:

Shelter

- Seventy-five per cent of the world's countries have constitutions or national laws that promote the full and progressive realization of the right to adequate housing.
- Sixty-one per cent of countries in the world have constitutions or national laws that protect against forced evictions.
- Households in cities of the developing countries need an average of eight times their annual income to buy a house whereas in Africa, one needs an average of 12.5 times of his annual income. Further, to buy a house in Latin America people only need 5.4 times their annual income. The highest rents are in the Arab states, where a household spends an average of 45 per cent of its monthly income on rent.
- One out of every four countries in the developing world have constitutions or laws that prevent women from owning land and/or taking mortgages in their own names
- Real estate costs are highest in Asia and the Pacific where one square metre of land for a serviced plot costs an average of US $ 3.1. In Africa, the average price is US $ 0.15 per square metre
- Less than 20 per cent of households in Africa are connected to piped water and only 40 per cent have access to water within 200 metres of their house

Society

- In the developing world, 5.8 per cent of children in cities die before they reach the age of five years

- In cities of the developing world, one out of every four households lives in poverty. About 40 per cent of African urban households and 25 per cent of Latin American urban households are living below the locally defined poverty lines

Environment

- City dwellers in Africa use only 50 litres of water per person per day. The highest median price of water is also highest in Africa
- In highly industrialized countries, almost 100 per cent of households are connected to piped water. The average water consumption for these households is 215 litres per person daily
- Less than 35 per cent of cities in the developing world have their wastewater treated
- In countries with economies in transition, 75 per cent of solid wastes are disposed of in open dumps
- Seventy-one per cent of the world's cities have building codes with anti-cyclone and anti-earthquake building standards based on hazard and vulnerability assessment
- Buses and minibuses are the commonest mode of transport in the world's cities, cars the second most common mode, and walking is the third common mode. Travel time in Asian cities is the longest with an average of 42 minutes per trip

Economy

- Thirty-seven per cent of the population in cities of the developing world is employed in the informal sector
- Seventy per cent of the world's cities have developed city-to-city international cooperation
- Sixty-three per cent of the world's cities have established new public private partnerships (PPPs) in the last five years

Governance

- About forty-nine per cent of the world's cities have established urban environmental plans
- Absolute quantity of local government income varies greatly, with total local government revenue per person in cities of highly industrialized countries being nine times that of cities in the developing world
- Sixty per cent of the world's cities involve civil society in a formal participatory process prior to the implementation of major public projects
- Seventy per cent of cities in the world undertake regular independent auditing of municipal accounts, 78 per cent publicly announce contracts and tenders for municipal services, 55 per cent have laws that govern disclosure of potential conflict of interest

Social Development and Eradication of Poverty (Urban Inclusiveness)

Until recently, nobody considered about how to respond and effectively incorporate social diversity in our cities. Most urban development policies were concerned with infrastructure and necessities such as food, housing and education. The larger issues were 'supply driven' rather than 'demand driven' from the viewpoint of agencies and governments.

In 1970s, the typical urban project which responded to this development logic was the large-scale 'sites and services' project. Large-scale projects which needed to deal expeditiously with many thousands or even hundreds of thousands of people in one fell swoop had little ability to look at the very complex reality of how individual people or small groups of people organized themselves in real life (Stren, 2001). This situation gave way in the 1980s to 'urban management', which was essentially a technical approach to improved management of urban services. Issues of social policy did not become prominent until the 1990s.

Decentralization and the Opening of Political Space

From the late 1980s, many countries started adopting plans for the decentralization of important functions and powers from the national to the local level of government. These decentralization plans varied greatly, from new policy emphases at one extreme, to entirely new constitutions or constitutional amendments empowering local authorities, on the other. By around 2000, a large number of developing countries had undergone real decentralization and considerable opening up of political and economic space had taken place at the local level. Smaller local government groups (whose elected members responded to their constituents) took over important policy functions. Many of the new municipal councils with elected mayors and councillors began to take interest in the plight of the poor and other vulnerable groups.

Another factor that strengthened the tendency of municipalities and local governments to pay heed to social differences and inclusivity in their policies is globalization. Cities all over the world (in both North and South), must compete with each other in the international arena, if they wish to prosper.

Diversity and Innovation

In both North and South, cities are more socially and economically diverse than small towns, villages and rural areas with large cities being even more diverse than small cities. Urbanization as a process brings groups of diverse people together, producing 'agglomeration economies', or economies which operate at a higher level of complexity and sophistication because they contain more specialized economic and social functions. This process adds value to national economies, to the extent that the largest cities typically account for a very high proportion of the Gross Domestic Product (GDP) in most of the countries.

Throughout the centuries, cities have been a source of both social stress and innovation. The latter has been the chief strength of the city and the former i.e., social stress being its greatest challenge. Greater social diversity brings inevitable conflict, higher and more aggressive levels of civil society organization, and more political contention. All things being equal, there is more crime and violence in bigger cities. This tension between diversity and productivity, on the one hand, and political conflict, on the other, must be managed well if we wish to get the maximum benefits from these cities.

An effective integration of diverse social groups into the political and policy framework is quite essential, if cities are to be sustainable over time. Not only is the proper treatment of social diversity essential to economic productivity, but it is also essential to environmental sustainability, since the recognition of and sensitivity to diversity form the basis of all efforts to preserve the natural environment (Stren, 2001).

'Socially sustainable cities' need to be managed in such a manner which is compatible with the harmonious evolution of civil society, fostering an environment conducive to the compatible cohabitation of culturally and socially diverse groups while at the same time encouraging social integration.

Many cities in the poorer parts of Asia operate with extremely limited revenues. Their ability to improve public services is limited or virtually non-existent. This leads to a vicious cycle whereby the less governments can do for their citizens, the less their citizens will be prepared to pay taxes and grant them legitimacy. Inclusive governance is most difficult to achieve in large cities, where it may be hamstrung by strong political influences.

However as the world globalizes, diversity is going to be more important and the successful governance of diversity will distinguish the most accomplished and creative cities from the rest (Stren, 2001).

Environmental Management

Cities play crucial role in social and economic development everywhere. Urbanization builds diversified and dynamic economies which raise productivity, create jobs and wealth, provide essential services, absorb population growth, and become engines of economic and social advancement. Productive cities and towns are essential for economic growth and welfare, both at national and local level. Strong urban economies generate the resources needed for public and private investments in infrastructure, education, health and improved living conditions.

Unfortunately, the development potential for cities is increasingly threatened by environmental deterioration. Apart from its known effects on human health and well-being, environmental degradation directly hinders socio-economic development. Water, air and soil pollution impose extra costs on business, industry, households and public services. Inefficient use and depletion of natural resources raises input prices and operating costs throughout the economy, and deters new investment. Enhanced risk from environmental hazards has the same effect. It is usually the poor who directly suffer from environmental degradation, although the lives and health of non-poor urban residents are also affected. Ad hocism or failing to deal with the problem today leads to much greater problems (and costs) in the future. For development achievements to be truly 'sustainable', cities must find better ways of balancing the needs and the pressures of urban growth, and change with the opportunities and constraints of the environment.

Happily, there are some encouraging signs that environmental deterioration may not be a necessary result of urbanization and economic change. Some cities have succeeded in striking the right balance in finding development paths which are more effectively attuned to environmental opportunities and constraints. The basic challenge has to do with urban governance, learning how to plan better and manage more effectively the process of urban development, avoiding or alleviating problems while realizing the positive potentials of city growth and change. New and more positive approaches to urban management can help mobilize and effectively apply local resources.

Successful environmental planning and management require understanding, agreement and coordinated action by the full range of public, private and popular sector groups and organizations (stakeholders) at neighbourhood, community, city and national level.

To identify relevant stakeholders for a specific issue, cities around the world can ask the following questions:

- Whose interests are affected by the environment-development issue at hand or by environmental management strategies and actions that may be decided?
- Who possesses the information and the expertise needed for strategy formulation and implementation?
- Who controls the relevant implementation instruments or has the means to significantly influence environment-developmental interactions?

No city can tackle successfully all its environmental and development issues at once. It has to be selective and needs to set priorities so that attention and action may be focused on a limited array of problems and tasks in a strategic sequence. The criteria for prioritization have, in many cases, been worked out through a participatory process and typically derive from consideration of both the impacts associated with each environmental problem and the local capacities to respond.

Global Networking

The 'democratization' of environmental planning and management has led naturally to a global network joining all those in cities and international programmes who wish to have more accessible and effective facilities for information exchange, mutual learning and collaboration in urban environmental planning and management. This global network, called 'Urban Environment Forum', links cities and their partners in international support programmes in their common commitment to improve social and economic conditions in cities through better urban environmental planning and management. The forum was established in 1996 and is supported by the UNCHS or Habitat and the United Nations Environment Programme (UNEP).

It is hoped that this global network will become a primary means through which our collective knowledge can deepen and through which the successes of cities can be made known and replicated in large number of cities all over the world.

Sustainable Cities

The *Oxford English Dictionary* defines civilization as a civilized condition or state, a developed or advanced state of human society. To civilize may also be defined as to bring out of a state of barbarism, to instruct in the art of life and thus elevate in the scale of humanity, to enlighten, refine and polish. The word 'city' from the same Latin root has come to mean the town or physical space occupied by the community. Civilization, civilized, civil and city have a common root for related concepts that imply a developed, advanced and enlightened community of people living in an environment which supports and nurtures continuing development to a state more and more distant from the state of 'barbarism' (Masterton, 2002). A city expresses human achievements in the built environment, born in terms of the physical building, and human deeds and words.

Civilizations happen to be fragile and can be destroyed. Great civilizations of the past have been destroyed. Some have cited the enemies of civilization as fear and exhaustion. For instance, fear of war, invasion, epidemic diseases and famine. Exhaustion expresses itself as a sense of hopelessness in a society even if it has a high degree of material prosperity.

According to Masterton, civilization requires enough prosperity to provide some leisure, but above all it requires confidence and belief, confidence in the values of society, confidence in humanity's powers and abilities, and belief in laws and philosophy. Vigour, vitality, and zeal and commitment for achievement and excellence matters. Fine art, fine sensibilities and good conversation are not what make civilization. Rather, it is the energy and the confidence of people to develop, question, challenge, create and build. It is the strong expression of the human spirit in its buildings and its cities which catches the real spirit of civilization.

Is civilization worth sustaining? A negative response to this question can greatly undermine our fundamental self belief, which is an essential ingredient for civilization. Sustainability depends on the wish to sustain. Nihilism and anarchy are the enemies of civilization.

Decline of Big Cities

Several big cities are now in a state of decline and are struggling to cope with the massive influx of rural workers. Transport, street cleaning, building, drainage and schools are becoming inadequate to meet the needs of the ever growing population. A good drainage system and clean water supply can dramatically reduce waterborne diseases such as cholera and typhus, and the construction of better houses, underground railways and new highways—often with the beneficial byproduct of the clearance of appalling slums and criminal nests—can make mobility within the city much easier. In the 1850s, London faced immense problems which some believed to be intractable. Today, we can say that London in 1850s was not sustainable. But with the introduction of improvements in the civil engineering infrastructure on a large-scale, London became sustainable and flourished throughout the rest of the 19th and all of the 20th Century (Masterton, 2002).

The problems that London faced in the 1850s are not very different from those facing Accra, Delhi, Mumbai and many other cities in the developing world today. The rate of growth of modern developing cities is faster, but the technology is still more advanced, it is only the gap between wealth creation and population growth which prevents us from achieving sustainable solutions for cities (Masterton, 2002).

The 'Quantum Jump' Model of Civilization

Some changes are 'earth changing' rather than incremental (Fig. 6.8). Schrödinger's model of the quantum jump (Schrödinger, 1944) represents the energy threshold **(3)** between two atomic energy levels **(1)** and **(2)**. When sufficient energy is supplied, there is a quantum jump from state **(1)** to state **(2)**. The energy needed for the transition is not the actual difference in levels between the two steady states, but the step from the initial level to the threshold. When changes with no threshold do occur, they are almost immediately followed by a relapse to the initial state.

According to Masterton (2002) we can use this model of the quantum jump in considering life changing events in QOL or in our life support systems. Take transportation for instance. Without the quantum jump intervention of the motor car, we would still be reliant on horse drawn vehicles for secondary transport links to supplement the rail network. The motor car and the development of an advanced

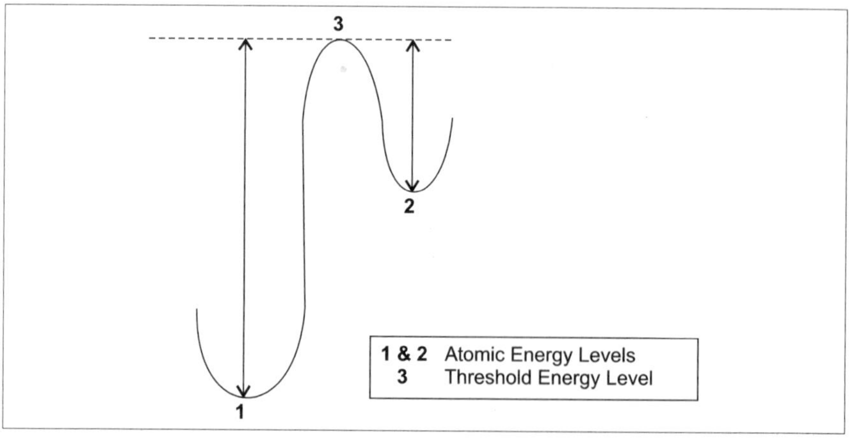

Fig. 6.8 Illustration of the 'quantum jump' (After Schrödinger, 1944)

road network to support it was a quantum jump. When the supply of intellectual energy exceeded the threshold between two levels of life support system, the British people could jump quickly from a transport system based on horses to a transport system based on horsepower.

Quantum Jumps on Civilization

According to Masterton (2002), some good examples of notable quantum jumps in civilization are large-scale wastewater treatment and disposal, large-scale water supply and distribution, rail transportation, motorized vehicles and the motorway and road network, providing rapid inter and intra-city communications, steel and its application to long span bridges, large-scale generation and distribution of power, powered flight, the development of airports to permit large aircraft to operate and electronic computers. Whether that be politicians, lawmakers, doctors, writers, artists, scientists, economists or civil engineers, all have contributed in achieving a civilized society, at least in the industrialized world. The story for many cities in the developing world (most of them in India) is very different. Here the high prevalence of corruption, right from clerk and contractor to chief engineer and minister, means that no high quality roads, buildings, waste treatment systems, water and power supplies, and other infrastructure facilities can be provided to the citizens. The stink of corruption, so common in many walks of life in the developing world precludes any quantum jump in civilization in the developing cities—big or small.

Are Our Cities Sustainable

Meadows et. al., (1972) predicted the collapse of civilized life on the earth around the middle of the 21st Century. This prediction disturbed adherents to uninterrupted economic growth and advised self-restraint on growth to preempt collapse. It aroused great opposition, not least because of its positive feedback loops in which secondary effects tend to reinforce the basic trends. It also presumed no quantum jumps in technology. Despite the opposition, two decades later the authors of the report updated the model, with no less sombre forecasts (Meadows et. al., 1992).

But other future forecasters were more optimistic and believed that when the need arises, new technologies will be developed. These optimists favour the Gaia hypothesis of James Lovelock, with mother earth as a complex integrated feedback system that seeks an optimal physical and chemical environment—essentially a self-regulating process.

Also in 1992, over one hundred heads of states met in Rio de Janeiro for the United Nations Conference on Environment and Development (the Earth Summit), and signed the Framework Convention on Climate Change and the Commission on Biological Diversity. They also adopted the so-called 'Agenda 21' for achieving sustainability in the 21st Century. Sustainability has been placed firmly on the UN agenda. The big question is whether it is on the agendas of individual nation states,, whatever their state of current development is (Masterton, 2002).

The UN established a Sustainable Cities Programme (SCP) in 1990, concentrating on 14 project cities. The priority issues identified for a few of them are shown in Table 6.2.

Table 6.2 Priority Issues Identified by the UN's Sustainable Cities Programme for Three Cities (After Masterton, 2002)

City	Priority Issues
Accra	Sanitation, solid waste management, liquid waste management and drainage
	Pollution of Korle lagoon
	Servicing urban land
	Disarray in institutional arrangements
	Enforcement of regulations and laws
Chennai	Surface water pollution
	Groundwater contamination and scarcity of potable water
	Inadequate solid waste management
	Air and noise pollution
Tunis	Degradation of Sejouri lake
	Loss of agricultural land
	Poor drainage creating flooding and health hazards Uncontrolled urban growth

Ecological Sustainability

The need to develop and transform cities and urban communities in an ecologically sustainable way cannot be over-emphasized. This task involves an extensive process of societal transition that cannot take place overnight as it requires a careful consideration of the whole technical infrastructure for energy, water, wastewater and solid waste management, as well as daily life, habits and values of all the actors involved, including residents. It is this multitude of issues with which we as citizens in a technological world are often confronted with. The problem focus, together with its emphasis on local problems and local solutions, makes it necessary to handle multi-technological and even non-technological problems. The task force engaged in making a city ecologically sustainable has to organize plans that could provide for:

- The creation of new knowledge on locally existing visions, barriers and opportunities to realize vision
- The production of policy proposals—who must do what to accomplish the changes required
- A more qualified debate based on an increased exchange of experience and knowledge. This is very important if changes are to stabilize over time (Anderson and Jaeger, 2001)

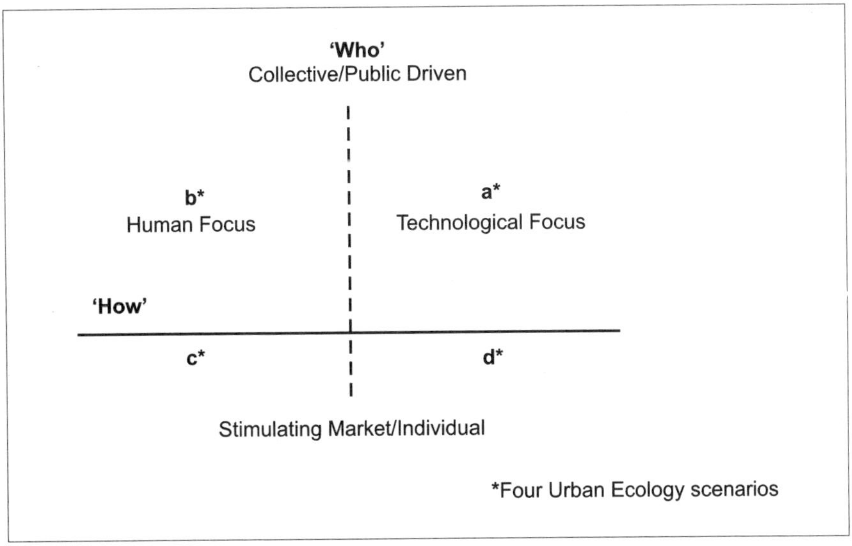

Fig. 6.9 Two-dimensional representation of four urban ecology scenarios (a, b, c, d) (After Andersen and Jaeger, 2001)

To fulfil the above objectives, it is not sufficient to only consult engineers and other technical experts. Local actors need to be consulted to get the knowledge and experience required. It is assumed that the meeting of a variety of social actors from different places and sectors in society can generate new ideas on visions and barriers and produce proposals for sustainable urban development. Figure 6.9 describes some plausible scenarios of a day in the life of a certain family in year 2010, portraying four different kinds of life in future housing areas. It shows alternative ways of solving urban ecology problems in residential areas and individual houses. These scenarios present visions and not predictions, and can be:

1. Block of flats
2. Low-rise high-density housing area
3. People's solar house
4. Intelligent house

Urban Governance

It is the sum of the many ways in which public and private individuals and institutions plan and manage the common affairs of the city. It is a continuing process through which conflicting interests may be accommodated and cooperative action taken. It includes formal institutions as well as informal arrangements and the social capital of citizens.

Urban governance differs from the broader governance agenda (which has tended to concentrate on macro levels), in that it focuses on the meso levels. It also differs from the urban management perspective of operation and maintenance of infrastructure and services. Such governance acknowledges that one should not ignore the complex social and political environments in which these services are being managed. At the city level, good governance is not only concerned with good urban management but also with interactions between all stakeholders in the city. Therefore, political, contextual, constitutional and legal dimensions need to be considered (Van Etten and Van den Dool, 2001).

What is needed is a transparent, responsible, accountable, just, effective and efficient governance of towns, cities and metropolitan areas through enabling local leadership and the promotion of democratic and participatory processes. Public authorities should use public resources in all public institutions to further these objectives. The need for participatory approaches in human settlements development and management should be stressed.

Elements of Good Governance

According to the United Nations Development Programme (UNDP), a good governance process includes the following elements:

1. **Participation** Everybody should have a voice in decision making, either directly or through legitimate intermediate institutions that represent their interest. Local democracy and decentralization are prerequisites for participation.
2. **Strategic vision** Leaders and the public should have a broad and long-term perspective on governance, human development and the development of their cities along with a sense of what is needed for such development.
3. **Rule of law** Legal frameworks should be fair and enforced impartially, particularly the law on human rights.
4. **Transparency** Processes, institutions and information should be directly accessible to all stakeholders, and enough information is provided to understand and monitor governance processes.
5. **Responsiveness** Institutions and processes should try to serve all stakeholders.
6. **Consensus orientation** Different interests should be mediated in order to reach a broad consensus on what is in the best interest of the group and where possible, on policies and procedures.
7. **Equity building** All men and women should have opportunities to improve or maintain their well being.
8. **Effectiveness and efficiency** Processes and institutions should produce results that meet needs while making the best use of resources.

9. **Accountability** Decision makers in government, the private sector and civil society organizations should be accountable to the public, as well as to the institutional stakeholders.

Good urban governance is characterized by the following seven interdependent and mutually reinforcing norms:

- Sustainability in all dimensions of urban development
- Subsidiarity of authority and resources at the closest appropriate level
- Equity of access to decision-making processes and the basic necessities of urban life
- Efficiency in delivery of public services and in promotion local economic development
- Transparency and accountability of decision makers and all stakeholders
- Civic engagement and citizenship
- Security of individuals and their living environment

These norms are supported by a wide range of operational principles that are based on lessons of experience and reflect regional conditions. Their implementation must be grounded in the local reality of urban planning and management.

A future challenge is to translate each component into practical tools and have benchmarks for each component (Van Etten and Van den Dool, 2001).

Traffic Sector

A few years ago, a Swiss Institute called PROGNOS, studied the efficacy of several measures for the reduction of CO_2 emissions in the transport sector. The salient findings of this study are illustrated in Fig. 6.10 (Tauscher and Pollak, 1994).

Sustainable Transportation for India

Most cities and towns in India suffer from high air and noise pollution caused by petrol/diesel-powered two and three-wheelers. An improved and electric cycle rickshaw can provide a non-polluting and noiseless transport system for these areas besides generating good employment opportunities for millions of urban and rural poor. Nimbkar Agricultural Research Institute (NARI) has developed two types of rickshaws—improved pedal cycle rickshaw (IMPRA) and motor-assisted pedal cycle rickshaw or MAPRA (Rajvanshi, 2002). These rickshaws can provide a safe, environment friendly, energy-efficient and cost-effective transport system in cities and towns.

In India, at present there are nearly 18 million petrol-powered two-wheelers and about 1.5 million petrol and diesel-powered three-wheelers and their population is growing at a rate of about 15 per cent per annum (Rajvanshi, 1999/2000). During traffic jams in congested areas, these vehicles produce tremendous air pollution. Even in villages, the spread of diesel/petrol three-wheelers has started affecting air

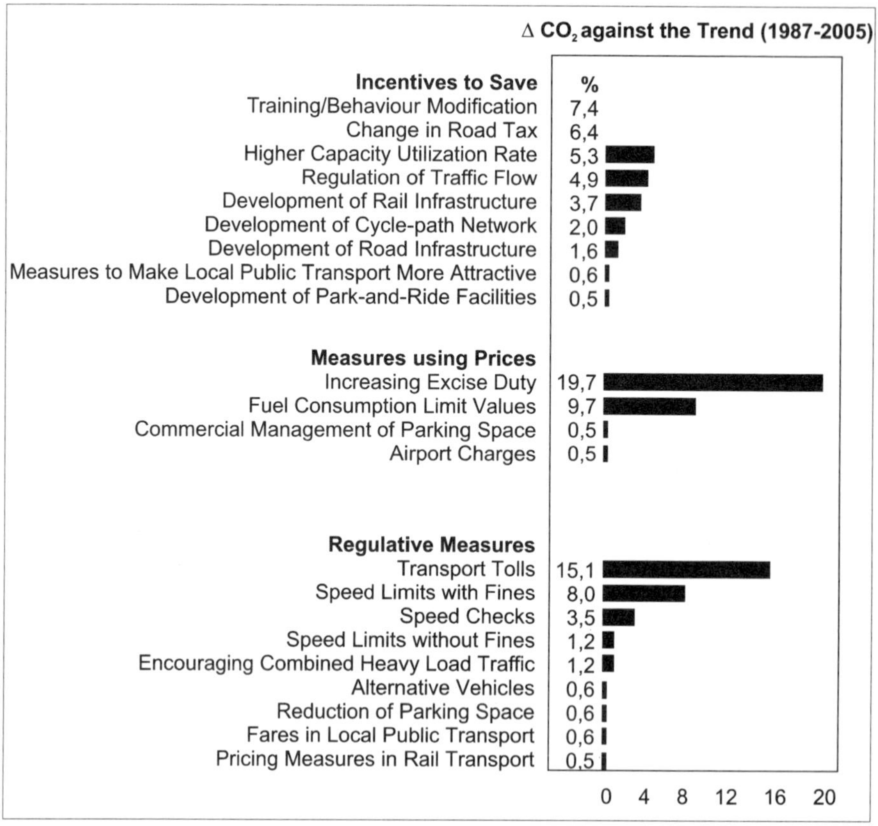

Source: PROGNOS, October 1991

Fig. 6.10 Measures for reduction in traffic sector

quality. Work done at NARI in Phaltan (Maharashtra) has shown that an improved cycle rickshaw powered by an electric motor and batteries is an attractive alternative to petrol and diesel-powered three-wheelers, besides providing extra income to the rickshaw puller.

Nearly two million cycle rickshaws ply on Indian roads, carrying about six to eight billion passenger km per year. In some cities and small towns, they are the major means of transport. They provide employment to over two million rickshaw pullers, are manoeuvrable, and non-polluting. In the narrow lanes of towns and cities, they facilitate point-to-point travel. It is however, unfortunate that in many urban towns of developing countries these rickshaws are being phased out and are being replaced by polluting petrol or diesel-powered three-wheelers (Rajvanshi, 2002). Also, the existing rickshaws are so badly designed that running them on the bad roads so typical of many Indian towns takes a heavy toll on the health of the rickshaw puller. The gearing and the mechanical advantage of the pedal is poor.

Hence, the rickshaw puller has to toil hard. The braking system is also poor, with only front brakes on the rickshaw. The seating arrangement is uncomfortable, and the aerodynamic drag of the system is high. It is humanly degrading to ply the existing inefficient cycle rickshaw. Yet because of poverty, migrant labourers become rickshaw pullers and suffer adverse health consequences. There is a strong need to improve the design of the existing rickshaw to make it user-friendly. The two new types of rickshaws designed by NARI are:

1. Improved pedal cycle rickshaw (IMPRA)
2. Motor-assisted pedal cycle rickshaw (MAPRA)

Improved pedal cycle rickshaw

The existing cycle rickshaw has been re-engineered for the safety and comfort of passengers, and to reduce the work burden on the rickshaw puller. IMPRA has three-speed gears, reduced length of long chain drives, back-wheel shaft braking, better suspension and less aerodynamic drag than the existing rickshaws. It enables a puller to take two passengers on a 6–10 per cent slope quite easily, without getting down from his seat. This rickshaw is made of mild steel angles, is light in weight, sturdy and has ample luggage and leg space. It weighs 85 kg as compared to 90–95 kg of the existing rickshaws. Its life is estimated to be between 7–10 years and costs Rs 7,000 in mass production, this compares well with Rs 4,000–6,000 the cost of existing cycle rickshaws (Rajvanshi, 2002).

Motor-assisted pedal cycle rickshaw

The drudgery can be reduced drastically, if a small motor is attached to the rickshaw, so that it can assist pedaling while going uphill. The extra power may also allow the puller to ply the rickshaw over longer distances and thus increase his earning per day. The MAPRA has the following components:

1. IMPRA chassis with seating arrangement and an extended hood for both passenger and driver.
2. A 375 W, four-pole permanent magnet DC (PMDC) motor attached to a planetary gearbox.
3. Gear drive train so that both pedal and motor power work in tandem.
4. Two 40 Ah, deep discharge lead acid batteries to drive the PMDC motor.
5. A stand-alone battery charger to charge the batteries overnight.
6. High current switches (Rajvanshi, 2002).

The MAPRA weighs 150 kg with batteries. It can carry two passengers at a speed of 10–15 km per hour to 40–45 km in continuous running and 50–60 km in stop/start mode, as experienced in congested city traffic conditions. At present, the cycle rickshaws ply a distance of about 20–25 km per day, since plying longer distances is too strenuous for the rickshaw puller. MAPRA can double the distance that a rickshaw puller can cover in one shift. A simple strategy allows the motor to be switched on by the puller by a high current switch whenever he experiences increased loading conditions. On level roads or while going downhill, he may only pedal the rickshaw.

Twenty MAPRAs have been fabricated at NARI, tested under varying conditions, and have logged over 5,000 km in trial runs. Five of them are running in the Pune University campus and a couple of them are running in Phaltan.

The retail price of a MAPRA has been estimated to be Rs 27,000. Economic analysis of running a MAPRA shows that an owner can make a net profit of Rs 25,000 per year.

According to Rajvanshi, in the case of MAPRA:

- Efficiency of electric power plant, including transmission and distribution losses is 0.255
- Charging/Discharging efficiency of batteries is 0.64
- Takes two passengers to a distance of 40 km per battery charge
- Its puller consumes 8.3 MJ of energy in food per day. Since rickshaw puller will have to pedal continuously, this energy input has also been taken into account
- This contrasts with petrol autorickshaws
- Average mileage is 25 km per litre of petrol
- Calorific value of petrol is 31.5 MJ per litre

Sustainable Rural Development

The term 'local' or 'indigenous knowledge' (IK) is used to distinguish the knowledge developed by a given community from international knowledge systems or scientific knowledge (Warren, 1991). The latter, sometimes referred to as Western knowledge systems (WKS), are generated by universities, government research centres and private industry. The IK can also refer to the 'technical' insight or wisdom gained and developed by people in a particular locality, through years of careful observation and experimentation with the natural phenomena around them.

According to Dewes (1993), the knowledge of local people is an enabling component of development. He compared indigenous knowledge to the feathers of a bird, since a bird can only fly if it has feathers. The terms 'indigenous knowledge' and 'local knowledge' are synonymous. However, what development experts may object to is the use of 'traditional' to qualify the knowledge peculiar to a people, since in some circles 'traditional' evokes 19th Century conceptions of simple, savage and static societies (Kolawole, 2001).

The WKS and the IKS can be distinguished on contextual, substantive and methodological grounds. First, Western knowledge systems are universal due to the fact that Western education is entrenched in many world cultures. And second, they have long been noted for their rigorous observation, experimentation and validation procedures, all very carefully documented. The same cannot be said of IKS, at least in respect of documentation.

Indigenous knowledge is related to the entire culture of people, including its identity and spiritual and religious beliefs. While some scientists and development planners may see traditional knowledge (TK) as a means of resolving certain development problems, indigenous people see it as part of their overall culture, vital to their survival as people (Dewes, 1993). The Western world must respect the cultural values of this knowledge, and the right of indigenous people to maintain those values should be acknowledged and protected within the development process.

Regardless of whether or not these knowledge systems are recognized or not, at the grass root level what has been tested and proved under local socio-economic, political and ecological conditions tends to be preferred to a foreign idea. The insistence on the use of indigenous technological knowledge (ITK) is rooted in the concept of a 'culture lag' that changes in non-material culture (ideas and social arrangements) always lag behind material culture (technology and inventions). Regardless of the degree to which they have embraced modernity, local people continue to prefer concrete knowledge, which belongs to them in time and space, and which they deem suitable for particular purposes. For people who live by tradition and folklore, change involves risk and they trust what has been tried and tested by long-established custom.

Culture is a way of life that is transmitted from one generation to the other. To meet various needs, rural communities make use of certain curiosity, problem-solving and adaptation experiments (Rhoades and Bebbington, 1995). Once validated, the results are added to the body of ancient wisdom. Through socialization and oral tradition, this wisdom is handed down from the old to the young. Insights gained in this way are not easily compromised.

Farmers in the developing countries have a good knowledge of agriculture and natural resources. This knowledge is based on many generations of insights gained through their close interaction with the natural and physical micro-environment. Variations in environmental conditions from year to year make the farming systems dynamic, if only to ensure sustainability. Cultivator experimentation is a normal part of agrarian change. The knowledge systems upon which farming decisions are based must be both reactive and proactive, relying on indigenous experimentation and innovation, as well as technologies made available through external channels, to cope with and adapt to changes (Warren, 1996).

The stages of local knowledge development have been identified as observation (of the environment leading to insight), experimentation and validation (through results). The utilization of local knowledge passes through five stages:

1. Awareness (of a particular phenomenon)
2. Perception (of the phenomenon as a problem)
3. Motivation (to seek a solution)
4. Evidence (arising from a specific approach employed to find solution)
5. Utilization (of the tried and tested approach)

Rural development aims at improving the QOL of low income group is multi-faceted and is best achieved by taking into account disciplines like agriculture, medicine, technology, politics, economics, sociology and education. At the grass root level, it focuses on the enhancement of agricultural production, improvement in literacy level, technological growth, improvement in healthcare services and reinforcement of leadership structures within the community (Kolawole, 2001). The starting point must be people themselves, because they possess the intrinsic knowledge of the conditions and phenomena which affect them. The socio-economic, cultural, ecological and political background must be considered by development agencies when seeking to improve their living standards.

In the past, development programmes were usually approached by governments through a top-down strategy. The building of infrastructure and the provision of social amenities alone were thought to be capable of providing solutions to rural problems. Policy makers were soon proved wrong as development is all about people. If infrastructures are put in place without getting the beneficiaries involved in the process of development, all efforts to bring about improvement in people's daily lives will be futile. People must be encouraged to participate actively as stakeholders and power wielders.

Development may be said to be sustainable when it has become self-perpetuating, self-regulating and beneficial to future generations (Alao, 1996). Some factors which are crucial to this process include good resource management, an effective flow of information and good leadership. Participatory approaches are the most appropriate measures to achieve that aim, particularly in rural areas, where over 70 per cent of the people in the developing world live.

The introduction of the farmer-first (FF) approach in the late 1980s represented a reversal for agricultural research and extension bodies. The starting point of development then became an active and equitable partnership among rural people, researchers and extension workers.

The FF approach concentrated on the technical side of local knowledge, and the followup movement Beyond Farmer-First (BFF), launched in the early 1990s, has expanded this perspective. Indigenous knowledge is seen as the cultural knowledge of rural people, promoting understanding and identity among the members of a farming community, where local technical knowledge and skills are inextricably linked to non-technical issues. The BFF programme incorporates a socio-politically differentiated view of development where factors such as gender, ethnicity, class, age and religion are highlighted. This has had major implications for research and extension practice (Röth, 2001).

According to the principles of BFF, new participatory approaches have been developed for agricultural research. These involve a soft-systems approach that centres on networks, relations of power and dynamic performance. Participatory action research (PAR) and increasingly, farmer participatory research (FPR), participatory technology development (PTD), participatory rural appraisal (PRA) and farmer field school (FFS) all share elements of this new style. These programmes encourage farmers to generate and evaluate indigenous technologies on the basis of their own knowledge and value system (Röth, 2001).

Today in India, villagers struggle to make ends meet in the rapidly developing country. Their ecological resource base is threatened and national and international legislation tend to ignore their major concerns. The Green Foundation is an NGO, situated in the dryland region of South India. It works to enhance biodiversity as a means of sustaining the livelihood of the rural people. Innovative methodologies have been developed to recover traditional crop varieties, medicinal plants and sustainable ways of producing food, within the cultural context of the people (Ramprasad et. al., 2003). The introduction of monocultures and high yielding varieties, along with frequent application of external inputs, have not only increased the economic dependence of farmers but also eroded the rich and diverse bio-genetic base.

Bio-cultural Seed Villages

The concept of the 'bio-cultural seed village' refers to a single market area that acts as a centre for endogenous development. It has been developed over the years. Some villages were identified in the midst of indigenous communities and tribal groups. Initiatives undertaken include community organization, seed conservation, strengthening health traditions, promoting kitchen gardens, reviving the cultural heritage, children's activities and marketing. On-farm conservation and multiplication of traditional crops such as paddy, foxtail millet, areca, chilles, and red gram are promoted (Ramprasad et. al., 2003). Even children groups are encouraged to grow traditional crop varieties of paddy, finger millet and vegetables on community lands. Composting by means of earthworms has been adopted by several farmers.

Marketing of Organic Products

Farmers, who grow food crops like ragi, rice and minor millets organically, retain what they need for their own consumption. The rest is collected and sold to consumers of organic food in nearby Bangalore. Women are encouraged to add value by making organic food products that are also marketed. For example, ragi and rice *pappads*, ragi flour mixed with edible spices and jaggery, ragi and pulses are fried and flavoured with edible spices. Products like honey, chilli powder, tamarind and pickles are also included. Though the demand for organic products is rather low, the sale of organic food has generated an income for farmers and improved the economic and social status of women (Ramprasad et. al., 2003).

Soil Erosion and Agricultural Sustainability

The detrimental influence of accelerated soil erosion on agricultural societies has been recognized since times immemorial (Lowdermilk, 1953). Several studies have suggested that erosion rates from conventionally plowed agricultural fields are much greater than rates of soil production, erosion under native vegetation and long-term geological erosion. However, pronounced historical episodes of soil erosion have been generally attributed to the effects of deforestation (Williams, 2003) and the role of agriculture in maintaining accelerated erosion in upland environments has been neglected.

The complex process of soil erosion depends strongly on soil properties, ground slope, vegetation, and amount and intensity of rainfall. Changes in land use can greatly accelerate soil erosion, and erosion in excess of soil production eventually results in decreased agricultural potential (Shaler, 1905). Although soil fertility usually declines with accelerated erosion, soil fertility itself is a function of agricultural methods and site conditions such as type, nutrient and organic matter content. This points to the importance of the issue of soil erosion, as the long-term maintenance of soil fertility still requires maintenance of the soil itself.

Until recently, very few quantitative data were available on natural rates of soil production or long-term geological erosion rates against which erosion rates from agricultural fields might be compared.

Instead, estimates of anthropogenic increases in soil erosion typically depend on the universal soil loss equation, developed as a planning tool to provide a common empirical framework within which to evaluate local controls on soil erosion rates (Wischmeier and Smith, 1978). However, it is important to bear in mind that erosion rates determined from small plot studies cannot always be extrapolated across large spatial scale (Trimble and Crosson, 2000).

Considered globally, hillslope soil production and erosion evolve to balance geologic and climate forcing, whereas conventional plow-base agriculture increases erosion rates enough to become unsustainable (Dale and Carter, 1955; Perlin, 1989). In contrast to how net soil erosion rates in conventionally plowed fields (≈1 mm/year) can erode through a typical hillslope soil profile over time scales comparable to the longevity of major civilizations, no-till agriculture produces erosion rates much closer to soil production rates and therefore could provide a foundation for sustainable agriculture (Montgomery, 2007).

According to Montgomery (2007), a direct implication of the imbalance between agricultural soil loss and erosion is that, over a time period, continued soil loss will become a critical problem for global agricultural production under conventional upland farming practices.

In view of the acute shortage of new land that could be brought under sustained cultivation and a projected increase in global population to more than 10 billion later this century, the issue of long-term agricultural sustainability will become increasingly pressing. Although, maintaining soil health and agricultural productivity additionally requires preventing nutrient depletion. Yet, if agricultural erosion rates continue to be higher than those of soil production, global society will eventually need to either adopt agricultural methods that sustain the soil or face increasing competition over a shrinking agricultural land base (Derspeh, 2001; Montgomery, 2007, 2007a).

Indigenous Knowledge

Indigenous knowledge is a kind of local know-how about cultural practices. It is a tool that communities use to manage their natural resources, including genetic resources, and building blocks of biodiversity and agriculture. A growing number of global institutions are now defending, promoting and using IK more widely. Recognition of IK of biodiversity has now moved into several hitherto neglected areas. Recently, the World Intellectual Property Organization (WIPO) has recognized the applications of traditional knowledge and the need to acknowledge local systems of innovation and intellectual property. WIPO's Intergovernmental Committee on Intellectual Property and Genetic Resources, Traditional Knowledge and Folklore (IGC) and the World Bank's growing investment in the application and dissemination of IK through fora like the Development Gateway constitute strong evidence of how far IK has moved onto global development and biodiversity agendas.

Participation is a vital element in successfully implementing rural development projects and programmes. Over the past decade, the practice of participation has grown to include local people's involvement in virtually every aspect of development, from conceptualizing, planning and implementation to monitoring and evaluation.

There is a strong role of IK, including the understanding of pre-existing, traditional systems of social organization. Participation brings IK to the forefront of development.

To gain a true understanding and wisdom in development it seems more important to know what questions to ask (and whom to ask) than to have a kit bag full of ready answers. Some important issues that need to be raised include those concerning accountability, power relationships, conflict, institutional learning, change and flexibility in applying participatory monitoring and evaluation (PME), 'ownership' of process and results, trust and trustworthiness, issues of political and social context, enabling policies, capacity needs, leadership and champions and linkages (learning from others) (Marisol, 2000).

Nuclear Technology for Sustainable Development

Nuclear techniques are being widely used, especially in the area of health care and sterilization of medical products. In agriculture, nuclear techniques are used for insect pest control, irrigation management, enhancing genetic diversity through induced mutations, and also as tracers in studies on soil, water, plant and environment. These techniques have contributed much towards increasing crop productivity, improving human and animal health, and promoting sustainable growth.

Some questions concerning food security have cropped up, related to the new realities of globalization, integrating the world's poor into the global economy, and producing food needed for 800 million people in a sustainable way.

For instance, tsetse fly is the carrier of parasitic microorganisms (trypanosomes) which cause sleeping sickness in humans and equally devastating nagana disease in domestic animals. An area of over 10 million square kilometres in 37 countries of sub-Saharan Africa is infested with the tsetse fly. It is because of these flies that horses and animal-drawn farm implements are not seen in most of Africa. All productive breeds of cattle are susceptible to nagana and can therefore be raised only in those highlands which are free from tsetse. Sterile insect technique (SIT) has been used in Zanzibar (Africa), and tsetse could be eliminated from the island. In the post-tsetse era, milch cattle are thriving in Zanzibar and livestock population is increasing the income of poor farmers. Successful eradication of tsetse in Zanzibar has led to the implementation of similar programmes in many African countries. Joint efforts have been initiated for a phased systematic elimination of tsetse from the African continent.

Seventy-five species of plants with economic value which include tropical and temperate fruits and vegetables are infected by fruit flies in 77 countries (Bhatia, 2001). SIT has been used for the control of fruit flies for the past five decades. Currently, it is used in 13 countries which have more than 40 'fly factories' with capacities to raise up to 500 million flies per week. The cost-effectiveness of SIT for the control of fruit fly in citrus plantations has been demonstrated in Israel and Argentina.

More than 2,250 new cultivars in different crops and ornamental plants have been developed globally using induced mutants. A hundred and fifty malting barley cultivars used for the production of beer in all five continents carry the denso semi-dwarfing gene. Durum wheat cultivars in Italy contribute to an additional annual income of US $ 180 million, mutant rice cultivars in Japan US $ 937 million and in California US $ 20 million. The black gram (*Phaseolus mungo*) cultivar TAU-1 developed at the Bhabha Atomic Research Centre (BARC), Trombay has contributed to additional production of 1.3 million metric tonnes in Maharashtra, amounting to nearly Rs 260 billion, while the total investment on mutation research for black gram at BARC would not exceed Rs 10 million. In a model project on the utilization of saline water and land in nine countries of North Africa, West and South Asia, it has been demonstrated that saline water can be fruitfully utilized in the wastelands to grow several salt-tolerant grasses, shrubs and trees. The sustainability of the system depends upon the use of groundwater and irrigation management in such a way that salts do not accumulate in the top soil. This is a low-cost technology.

Use of isotopes in hydrology studies has increased our understanding of the groundwater resources, flow and quality in arid regions of Ethiopia. Nuclear techniques are helping in identification of arsenic-free sources of water in Bangladesh.

Nuclear techniques find good applications in human health. Radiation therapy for treatment of cancer and nuclear medicine are well known, but the role of nuclear techniques using stable isotopes in human nutrition is less known.

Malnutrition (hidden or silent hunger) is receiving much attention since the 1990s. Nuclear and isotopic techniques have emerged as a valuable tool to address the problems of malnutrition such as micronutrient deficiencies, estimation of energy expenditure, determination of lean body mass, nutrient absorption and utilization, analysis of food and detection of stomach infections. These techniques use stable isotopes of iron, zinc, carbon, oxygen and deuterium. When rice labelled with C-13 is cooked and eaten, the degree of malabsorption can be estimated by the proportion of tracer carbon to the total carbon in the stool.

The market forces do not drive the nuclear technologies in most developing countries. At the same time, the private sector provides the best mechanism for the delivery of the products and services, both in the developed and developing countries. The question, therefore, is how to motivate the private sector to provide these technologies in the developing countries. It is conceivable that success may come from adopting the principle 'globalize opportunities and nationalize problems' as the national problems will have to be solved by the local efforts.

Sustainable Development in Asia

One major challenge facing sustainable development in Asia is reaching small and medium-sized enterprises (SMEs), many of which are family-run and have 10–100 employees. SMEs supply goods and services to local markets and larger corporations and play vital economic and social roles in the local community. However, recognition of SMEs is limited on the international scale. This unfortunate "facelessness" internationally makes it difficult to implement cleaner production directly in Asian SMEs. Understanding of cleaner production operations is low and penalties for violations are difficult to enforce. While cleaner production and the quest for decent work conditions are laudable, most SMEs tend to be reluctant to incorporate such agendas because they assume that this would increase the expense of running their business. Disenfranchisement of SMEs occurs regularly. Grievances are not often addressed or even recognized. Furthermore, SMEs are usually operated by women.

By contrast, large multinational companies competing in the global market have thousands of employees and well-trained management. They can be better partners for initiating and implementing widespread change. Large companies frequently have self-sufficient facilities providing an extensive range of on-site services. They are ISO certified and their work ethics, systems and procedures comply with "best practice" standards. A disproportionate majority of businesses in Asia are SMEs facing competition from other markets which readily provide cheaper goods. Thus, SMEs are primarily concerned with immediate fiscal responsibilities and initiatives such as cleaner production are relegated to a lower rank. Bigger businesses find it easier to implement such initiatives.

Ms Isabelita Sy-Palanca, Chairperson, National Steering Committee on the Global Compact, Philippines points to the Global Compact and its activities in stressing the need for private business to become involved in sustainable development and to comply with the aims and objectives of the Global Compact, which relate to human rights, labour rights and the environment. She described how Global Compact is reaching out to involve SMEs through such initiatives as:

- Speaking the language of business through presenting the Global Compact as a call to share the benefits of the New Global Economy. The outreach messages cite cases in which suppliers have been banned or ostracized because of their non-adherence to protection of human rights, labour rights or the environment

- Synergizing limited resources by using Global Compact as theme of employer federation's national annual convention and fostering adherence to Global Compact via preparatory regional consultations leading to national convention
- Establishing business-initiated, multi-sectoral committees designed to foster consensus-building among employers, employees, NGOs, the media, academia, churches and local government units. The committees have been organized through partnerships with large corporations, as well as organizations with Chapters throughout the Philippines and with many SME members—chambers of commerce, industry associations and the Women's Business Council of the Philippines. This strategy is based on using the synergy of partners
- Planning for a media campaign and endorsement by popular personalities. Strategic plans include monitoring schemes, documentation processes and systems and incentives for compliance.

Mrs Palanca has linked Global Compact and cleaner production to goals of organizations she works with to help women and SMEs enter global business and once there and transform the human face of globalization into a happy one.

In the industrialized world most people are now convinced that something must be done to save the environment. In Europe, North America and several other developed countries, global warming has become a general subject of discussion.

However, what exactly should be done to tackle the problem, and how best to do so, is not very clear. Technology enthusiasts believe that the world can be saved by grand technical solutions. CO_2 emissions from coal-fired power plants can be checked through carbon capture and storage. Cars and trucks can be powered by electricity from such renewable sources of energy as solar, wind and biofuels.

While effective improvements in technology are essential, the recent reports by the Intergovernmental Panel on Climate Change (IPCC) make it very clear that the trend of increasing emissions will need to be quickly reversed before 2015—we do not have enough time to wait for novel technologies to mature slowly before they can be fully implemented. There is no doubt that more energy from renewable sources is a necessity, but we also need to become much more efficient by minimizing the wastage and squandering away of energy and other resources. We must learn and avoid wasteful habits and behaviour. Historically, the current concerns were preceded over two decades ago by those of acid rain and Stratospheric ozone depletion.

Air pollution has moved from local to global scale in half a century. Understanding the intriguing connections between the aforesaid concerns can be highly rewarding and useful for addressing the matters of cleaner production and sustainable trading in the century of the environment. None of the cries of outrage that cleaning up would be impossibly expensive and damaging to national economies, voiced during the past pollution crises, turned out to be correct. This generates considerable optimism. Action has very often turned out to be painless. Indeed, it was quite profitable for the companies involved. Those who want to avoid taking action on air pollution come up with the same pathetic excuses every time. Analogous comments may well be equally relevant to cleaner production processes.

7
Industrial Ecology

Industrial ecology is a new approach to industrial design of products and processes and implementation of sustainable manufacturing strategies. In fact, an industrial system cannot be viewed in isolation from its surrounding systems, but in concert with them. Industrial ecology seeks to optimize the total cycle from virgin material to finished material, to component, to product, to waste product, and to ultimate disposal (Jelinski et. al., 1992).

In other words, industrial ecology is to highlight the totality or the pattern of relationship between various industrial activities, their products and the environment. Traditional ecological activities focuses on two aspects of interactions between industrial activities and environment–the past and the present. Industrial ecology, a systematic view of the environment, pertains to the future (Patel, 1992).

The concerns about the past are characterized by remediation of problems created by yesterday's industries such as the cleaning up of dumping sites. The issues of the present are typified by a series of activities that address the current problems. The goals of industrial ecology include:

- Maximimum use of resources and at the same time minimum disruption to the environment
- Integration of an entire industrial process, determination of maximal beneficial use of a resource, optimum utilization of resource, minimum waste generation during the procurement and processing of the resource, minimum waste during manufacture, maximum reuse of waste resulting from manufacture, maximum ultimate recycling or disposal of the product, and minimum consumption of energy throughout the process.

Frosch (1992) defined industrial ecology as the network of all industrial processes as they interact with each other and and live off each other, not only in the economic sense, but also by direct usage of each other's material and energy wastes. In this context, Ausubel (1992) posed the following questions:

1. Do socio-technical systems have long-range environmental goals?
2. Is there a systematic way to choose among alternatives for improving the ecology of technology?
3. How to measure performance with respect to industrial ecology?
4. What are the sources and rates of innovation in environmental technology?
5. How is market economy performing with respect to industrial ecology?

6. What will be the effect of the ecological modernization of the developed nations on the developing countries?

Industrial activities include treatment, storage and disposal of diverse wastes. This adds net cost to industrial production since they address the problems after the act. Industrial ecology focusses on future by addressing those issues that will impact future production, utilization and disposal technologies. One expects to devote significantly less resources to potential remediation in future. Since, the first two represent net cost increase and the third aims to obviate the necessity of the first two in the future, industrial ecology would add net value and reduce the cost. The following facts describe the current situation of manufacturing industries:

1. During production of manufactured goods, industry generates huge amount of non-hazardous and hazardous wastes which need to be treated, stored or disposed.
2. Manufacturing industry spends huge amount annually on pollution control to meet existing regulations.
3. The disposal of wastes is an expensive proposition and these costs are rising. This raises the spectre of disposal costs becoming the dominant cost of production, if nothing is done.
4. No magic bullet is available.

In 1970s, the chief objective of many industrial concerns was to manufacture products using minimum possible energy. Environmental issues and use of natural resources were secondary concerns. Using less energy (and creating less waste) attracted higher priority.

For sustainability, it is necessary to manage our affairs, including industry, so as to minimize direct destruction of resources (for instance, the destruction of forests, agricultural lands and soils) by poisoning the world with pollutants or by using up materials. Energy sources and systems are very important, but the management of materials in both industrial and consumer activities is crucial to the avoidance of unsustainable practices. Therefore, attempts have been made to develop concepts and operating systems to achieve more sustainable practices for the handling and use of materials. These cover, life cycle analysis, "green" (environmentally sensitive) design, knowledge about the use of materials in product designs and manufacturing processes, industrial metabolism (analysis of the flow of materials through the industrial system and into the environment), the reuse and recycling of subsystems, parts and materials, and the control and elimination of waste materials and pollution (Frosch, 1998).

Industrial ecology brings these developments in a systematic view of industry, seen by analogy with natural ecosystems as a collection of industrial organisms organized into a network through which flow energy, used and reused materials, and products and services come from. It is like studying material civilization as an ecological network involving industry, consumers and the natural environment. This large-scale system view raises new possibilities for connections in material and energy web, and novel ways to minimize or eliminate environmentally destructive effects of human activities.

Today, consumers are more environmentally conscious and are demanding products with reduced impact on the environment. Life cycle assessment (LCA), diagnoses the effects a product or process may have on the environment from the time raw materials are removed from the ground, through the manufacturing process, until the product's ultimate disposal. That way, a manufacturer can make changes to a product to reduce its environmental impact. For instance, LCA has shown that most of the energy used over a laundry detergent's life cycle is by the consumer heating washing machine water. Thus, researchers explore different ways to address the energy impact of the detergent beyond just manufacturing it, by creating detergents that work in cold water.

The LCA consists of an inventory analysis, which looks at what goes into the product, an impact assessment, which determines what the product does to the environment, and an improvement assessment, which examines how to reduce the product's burden on the environment. The first part is well-established. The other two are still developing.

The inventory analysis involves measuring product inputs and outputs. An emerging key sector of economic development in several developing countries is the manufacture of chemicals and pharmaceuticals. In these countries, these industries have begun to generate income and contribute to improve their balance of trade. Unfortunately, sustained development depends on good infrastructure and capabilities to treat hazardous wastes generated by these industries, and neither the adequate infrastructure nor the capabilities have grown commensurately.

Biotechnology makes possible complete biodegradation of these wastes to CO_2 and H_2O. It has moved into its third and the most important domain, after its bio-pharmaceutical and agri-food applications, the protection and restoration of the environment has become the priority goal of biotechnology efforts. Although biotechnology is not the only technology to help keep the environment clean, it is an essential one, and its importance, in conjunction with other tools, is expanding.

Environmental biotechnologies have vast long-term market potentials. The current preferences for environmental biotechnologies for prevention, treatment and remediation of environmental damage stem from the relative cost-effectiveness of biological clean-up methods as compared to traditional chemical and physical methods. Several useful technologies have developed in the industrialized nations and these could be fairly easily adapted in the developing countries where prevailing atmospheric temperatures are more conducive to faster biological reaction rates. This is best illustrated by chlorophenols and other phenols which are common pollutants in effluent streams from the chemical industries. These compounds harm aquatic and human life as well as the general environment. Quite often, these hazardous wastes are collected in barrels prior to disposal in liquid dump sites. Development of novel bioprocesses for complete degrading these hazardous compounds would spell economic growth in developing nations and minimize the detrimental effects associated with Persistent Organic Pollutants (POPs).

For some materials, databases are being developed that list standard values for certain materials. The American Plastic Council has created a database covering some top plastic resins. This base allow users to access datas such as how much energy is used and what wastes are released into the air and water per pound of a given plastic. The outcome of an inventory analysis is large volume of numbers—representing amount of raw materials needed, energy used to gather and manufacture those materials and more—for one product. An impact assessment translates the inventory data into human health, ecological, resource and social ramifications. For example, an impact assessment of cloth diapers has shown that a large volume of waste water is generated from repeated washings over the course of their lifetime. In contrast, for disposable diapers the chief impact is solid waste.

Some companies have LCA for their internal use only, for designing products and processes. The consumer only sees the end result and does not notice any difference between a product that has been assessed and one that has not been. Other business houses have gone public with assessments to show how their version of a product compares with others and to clarify the actual impacts.

In the case of detergents, for example, most consumers do not realize that their use of detergent exerts greater environmental impact than the manufacturing process. Heating the water to use laundry detergent has more environmental impact than making the detergent.

In the long run, a company may develop products that have the least impact on the environment at the lowest possible price by using an LCA.

Environmental Goals of Socio-technical Systems

Some major goals of many societies are reduction of poverty, universal education and health care, population stabilization, and enhancement of environmental quality. Highways and water supply systems are periodically built. But what are the general long-range goals of such systems as agriculture, transport, energy and production? There was never a goal to become reliant on fossil fuels, this reliance was reached through dynamic optimization of the energy system with respect to transport and storage of energy and other factors (Ausubel, 1992). Society has directions in which it is driven but is it driven by intent? It is not clear to what extent socio-technical systems are directed towards an end or shaped by purpose. Societal development appears to be fundamentally evolutionary and thus to a larger degree without purpose.

The teleological question raises some issues for industrial ecology. One is the capacity for coordination and creative design in the economy. On the one hand, there is the recognition of a need for some kind of larger-scale optimization of industry which takes better account of environment. On the other hand, there is some myopia in economic systems. Moreover, how far into the future can social radar look? How far into the future can societies sensibly plan? What products and services do people need according to various criteria? Most organizations want to sell more of any particular product they make and to have more products. The issue of long-term public good is rarely asked in fundamental ways of technological or environmental impact assessments.

The issue may be interpreted as the traditional one in living systems of difference between growth and development. Growth implies an increase in size i.e., a quantitative phenomenon, while development implies additionally a realization and enhancement of potential. It is a qualitative phenomenon. According to Speth (1992), the *ad libitum* feeding of the industrial economies involves great environmental cost. The rise of industrial ecology may indicate the maturity of industrial society to ask questions seriously not only about growt but also development and its consequences.

Industrial ecology also implies concern with equity, not only over time but also as the current network of production and consumption distributes goods and bads. It suggests not only some broad goals for socio-technical systems such as waste reduction and dematerialization but also revised rules of selection for the technologies, products and enterprises that should survive. The goal for technologists should be to make possible greater efficiency and productivity in serving human needs with reduced environmental impact, reduced consumption of raw materials, and substitution of more for less-abundant raw materials, as well as inclusion of wastes and products at the end of their lives in the industrial food web as both material and energy.

Ecology considers how organisms are embedded in their environment and how they interact with it (Kumar, 1995). Ecosystems are defined from the inner surface of their environment or their ecological niche. The key is that the parts are conceived with respect to the whole and not other way around. Ecology recognizes connectedness as the condition of existence. At the same time, existence itself is constantly evolving.

Ecology is not the only discipline to make claims for a sound model of flows of energy, resources and information. Its nemesis and economics also does so. Chemical engineering also stresses dynamical systems. The value of industrial ecology will depend on the extent to which it can provide grounds for synthesis and interrelation of the variables normally incorporated or ignored in each of these and other relevant fields. It is about deepening appreciation of technology and extending what is valued in economics, broadening the domain of what must be considered in engineering design and practice, and ending the isolation of ecology from the man-made world (Ausubel, 1992).

This multiplication of needs means that we need science and industry for a small planet. Industrial ecology can contribute both understanding and solutions. If the current ratio of emissions, pollution and waste creation to production and consumption is maintained, the environmental problems are to be worse. It is possible to increase efficiency in many systems. The question is whether the introduction and diffusion of technologies, including social technologies, will proceed in directions and at rates such that there is net improvement. Industrial ecology may be vividly illustrated by the sequence that started with textiles. The arrival of the spinning wheel in Europe in the 13th Century speeded up yarn production, lowered the price of cloth and increased its consumption. By the 14th Century there was great increase in linen shirts, bedding and towels. Increased use meant not only more but also cheaper rags, which formed the best material for making paper. The burgeoning paper industry expanded and prices fell. Earlier, it used to take the skins of about 220 sheep or calves to provide sufficient vellum to produce a copy of holy Bible. With cheaper rags, books could be produced more cheaply. Thus, it was the wastes created by the spinning wheel that created the conditions for success in writing. We live inevitably in such a web of connections. We live off each other and sometimes off one another's wastes.

Some environmental technologies remedy, some conserve and some prevent pollution. While others define environmentally sound technologies by their quality or performance relative to present practices. For example, as diverse as compact, efficient lighting devices (Hoffman, 1992) and completely biodegradable plastic materials produced by bacteria from agricultural raw materials rather than petro-chemicals (Luzier, 1992). There are environment-friendly technologies that relate to manufacturing and operations such as just-in-time (JIT) inventory and on-demand generation of toxic chemicals to obviate mass storage and transport.

Choice of Alternatives for Improving Ecology of Technologies

According to Patel (1992), the crucial elements in industrial ecology are selection of materials with desired properties at the outset, use of JIT materials philosophy, substitution of processes to eliminate toxic feedstocks, modification of processes to contain, remove and treat toxics in waste streams, engineering of robust and reliable processes, and consideration of end-of-life recyclability.

Measurement of Performance in Industrial Ecology

There are many indicators of environmental quality and of economic performance. There are also some specific, promising reports of change. However, few indicators represent effectively the network of industrial processes and how they are changing (Duchin, 1992).

Industrial ecology may promote a transition from materialization to dematerialization. Dematerialization could translate into less waste from both production and consumption. The shift from increasing reliance on carbon fuels to "decarbonization" of the energy system might be another key transition (Fig. 7.1). Carbon is the main element used in spinning the industrial web and is also associated with greenhouse warming, smog and deforestation. Coal, an environmentally damaging fossil fuel, contains more carbon and would weigh the same as natural gas, which is mostly hydrogen. During 1973–1986, several advanced countries, in absolute terms large polluters, nonetheless moved on toward high energy efficiency and low carbon intensity. Meanwhile, Mexico and India moved in the reverse direction (Fig. 7.1A). An alternative formulation of decarbonization includes biomass (fuelwood and hay) in addition to fossil fuels. By this measure all nations have proceeded at different rates and by different routes (Fig. 7.1C) (Ausubel, 1992).

(A)

(B)

(C)

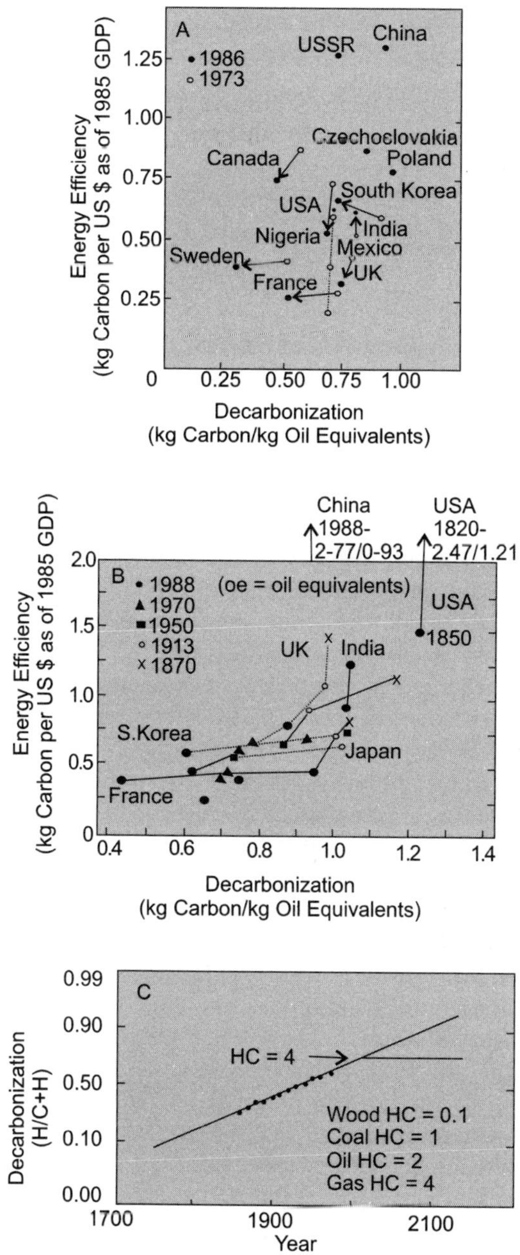

Fig. 7.1 Three views of decarbonization. (A) Decarbonization refers only to fossil fuel carbon used in energy supply, in units of kg carbon per kg of oil equivalent, (B) Decarbonization indicates total amount of carbon, including carbon in noncommercial wood and hay used in energy supply, (C) Decarbonization refers to evolution of the atomic ratio of hydrogen to carbon in the world fuel mix, where gas (methane) for example, is CH_4 (After Ausubel, 1992)

Performance of Market Economy with respect to Industrial Ecology

The higher-level environmental effects that the invisible hands of the market have produced from the multitude of decentralized decisions include both success and tragedy. The economic system needs complete internalization of social costs. Modern societies have become accustomed to the idea of social overhead. Disability insurance and pensions have been internalized in the course of the 20th Century, whereas, comparable adjustment on the environmental front has started only recently.

Effect of Ecological Modernization of the Developed Nations on the Developing Countries

In general, industrial plants in the developing countries use abnormally high levels of energy per unit of output because most of these plants have obsolete equipment designed with outdated, material-intensive technology. One such example is the mini-cement technology used in China and India. This technology is relatively small-scale, low-tech, labour-intensive and energy-intensive. It may be appropriate in those locations which have limited market potential and have low accessibility (high transport costs). Under such conditions, the mini-cement technology can be most energy-efficient on a delivered product basis.

The cost of energy inputs may be the single most important factor limiting an effective energy drive. This applies particularly to cement and other energy-intensive industries. In developing countries, domestic energy prices are often highly subsidized. This undermines the desire or efforts to bring down high levels of energy consumption. To redress this situation, there is need to implement sound and stable macro-economic policies and a sound and predictable regulatory environment so as to promote individual energy efficiency.

South is mostly an exporter of energy and nature, in the sense of wood, minerals and other primary products. In fact, carbon (as fossil fuels) is by far the largest export of the South to the North. If energy demand is substantially reduced in Europe and America, if the demand diminishes for resource inputs, if the North need not buy oil from Nigeria, Mexico or Venezuela, if the market is reduced for tropical woods, at least the near-term outcome could be impoverishment of the South. Although it is desirable for the entire planet to move in the direction of accelerated efficiency, the short-term effects of a move by the North could widen its economic gap with the South (Ausubel, 1992).

Industrial ecology encompasses the cradle-to-grave production philosophy, except that in an ideal circumstance there is no grave. Such a philosophy includes industrial processes that are environmentally benign during the manufacturing phase, products that are environmentally benign and safe during their use, and products that at the end of their useful lives can be economically recycled without adverse impacts on the environment and without adding net cost to the society (Patel, 1992).

Industrial ecology is a system that integrates all aspects of an industrial process so that optimization of the total occurs rather than minimization or maximization of individual components. This requires a broadening, in general, of environmental consideration beyond the approaches required by government and taken by industry over the last several decades. There is a need for the intertwining of previously separate environmental and technological problem. This is because an industrial process is thought of and solved as a continuum. Industrial ecology will require an understanding of the environmental impacts and interrelationships related to mining, transport, process, manufacturing and disposal. A system approach to an industrial process must form the foundation of industrial ecology (Troxell, 1992).

Many of the industrial processes that have benefitted society have also created problems. "Business as usual" is not an option that industry maintains for long. Nonetheless, the complexities involved in new approaches to industrial design and operation are many and very few individuals are adequately equipped to make decisions with the full spectrum of those complexities in mind.

It is now widely recognized that new approaches are required for the industrial design of products and processes and the implementation of sustainable manufacturing strategies.

Traditional biological ecology is defined as the scientific study of the interactions that determine the distribution and abundance of organisms. The relationship between this concept and that of industrial activities has been discussed by Frosch and Gallopoulos (Frosch, R A. Gallopoulos, N, paper presented to the Royal Society, London, February 21, 1990).

"In a biological ecosystem, some of the organisms use sunlight, water and minerals to grow, while others consume the first, alive or dead, alongwith minerals and produce wastes of their own. These wastes are in turn food for other organisms, some of which may convert the wastes into the minerals used by the primary producers, and some of which consume each other in a complex network of processes in which everything produced is used by some organism for its own metabolism. Similarly, in the industrial ecosystem, each process and network of processes must be viewed as a dependent and interrelated part of a larger whole. The analogy between the industrial ecosystem concept and the biological ecosystem is not perfect, but much could be gained, if the industrial system were to mimic the best features of the biological analogue".

The material cycles involved with the earliest earth's life forms were simple, and the usable resources were so large and the amount of life so small that the existence of life forms had essentially no shortage of available resources. The flow of materials from one stage to the next was independent of all other flows. A contrasting picture is an ecosystem in which resources are limited and the resulting life forms become strongly inter-linked, forming the complex networks called 'biological communities'. In this system, the flows of material within the proximal domain may be quite large but the flows into and out of that domain (i.e., from resources and to waste) are quite small. This type of system is shown in Fig. 7.2. Even this system is not sustainable for long-term because all the flows are in one direction. To be ultimately sustainable, biological ecosystems have evolved to be almost completely cyclical in nature, with "resources" and "waste" being undefined, since waste to one component of the system represents resources to another. The exception to the cyclicity of the overall system is that energy in the form of solar radiation is available as an external resource. This type of system is illustrated in Fig. 7.3. The cycles within the system function on widely differing temporal and spatial scales.

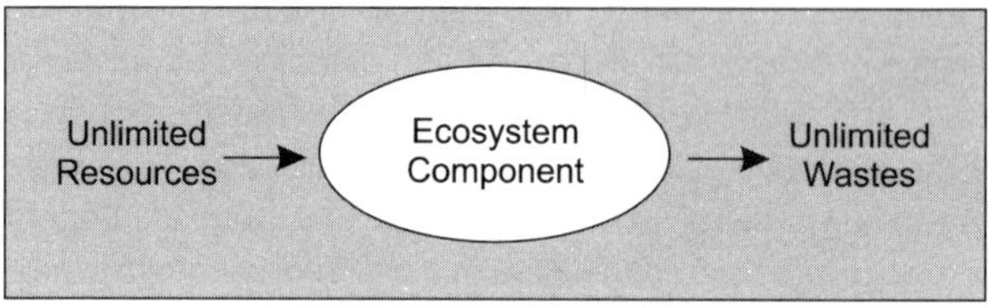

Fig. 7.2 Linear material flows in Type I ecology

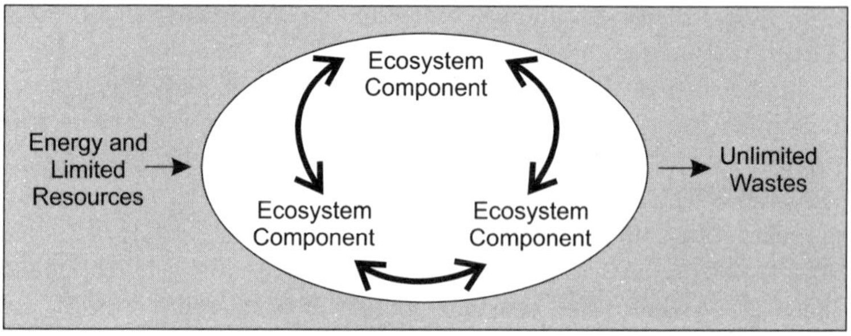

Fig. 7.3 Quasi-cyclic materials flow in Type II ecology

The ideal anthropogenic use of materials and resources available for industrial processes (including agriculture and the urban infrastructure) would be one that is similar to a good biological model. Many materials are degraded, dispersed and lost in the course of a single normal use. This trend can be associated with the maturation of the Industrial Revolution of the 18th Century which, together with exponential increases in human population and agricultural production, took place essentially in the context of global plenty in which copious quantities of energy and raw materials were available. Many present day industrial processes and products still remain largely disruptive. For example, lubricants, paints, pesticides and automobile tires (Jelinski et. al., 1992).

Specific materials are sufficiently precious, some show ecological type II behaviour, at least in part. For example, precious metals recovery. The flows in many industrial ecosystems are so large that resource limitations are setting in: the rapid changes in atmospheric gases and the filling of available waste disposal sites are examples. Accordingly, industrial systems will increasingly be under pressure to evolve from linear to type II modes.

The central domain of industrial ecology is conveniently pictured with four central nodes: the materials extractor or grower, the materials processor or manufacturer, the consumer, and the waste processor (Figures. 7.4 and 7.5). They evolve into cyclic models of operation that are more efficient, have less disruptive impact on external support systems, and are more like type III ecological behaviour. Examples range from the recycling of iron scrap by the heavy metals industry to the popularity of garbage sales for the reuse of products within the consumer domain (Fig. 7.5). The flows within the nodes and within the industrial ecological systems as a whole are much larger than the external resource and waste flows.

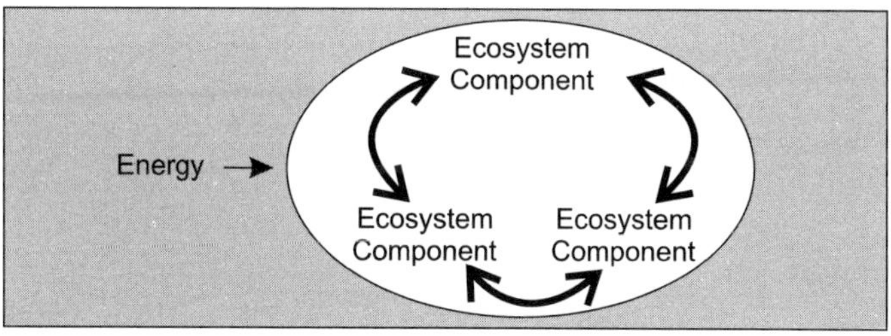

Fig. 7.4 Cyclic materials flows in Type III ecology

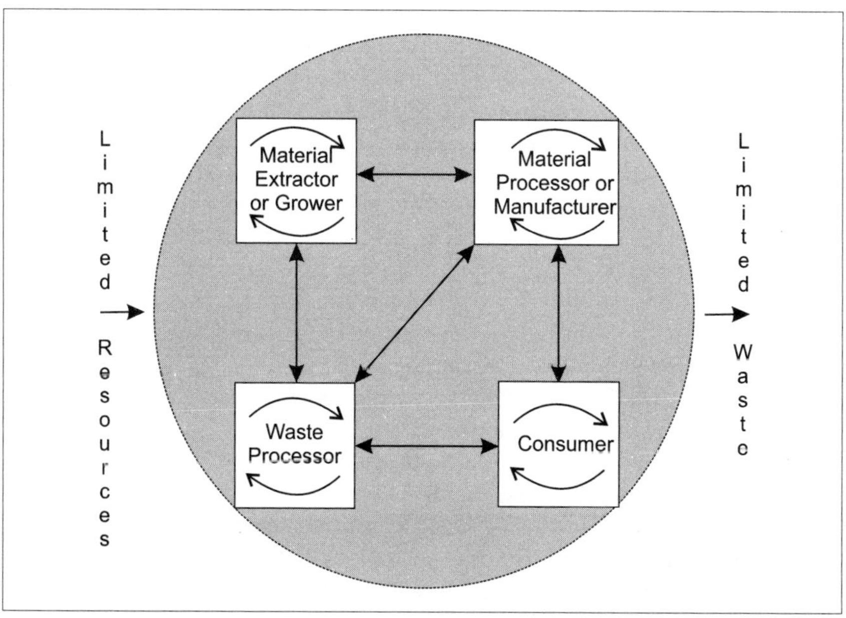

Fig. 7.5 Type III model of the industrial ecosystem

According to Frosch (1992), natural ecosystems, evolving over millions of years have produced every entity needed for a type III ecosystem. The industrial ecosystem, in contrast, is a system moving from type I to type II ecology. If we wish it to approach a type III system, we will have to artificially create some of the missing entities. Frosch regards a healthy recycling and remanufacturing entity as an example of a missing entity, and may need creation, if industrial ecology is to progress rapidly.

Industry is considered as a strong analogous to the behaviour of the natural world with regard to the use of materials and energy. The idea of an industrial ecology is based upon straightforward analogy with natural ecological systems. In nature, an ecological system operates through a web of connections in which organisms live and consume each other and each other's waste. The system has evolved so that the characteristic of communities of living organisms seems to be that nothing which contains available energy or useful material will be lost. There will evolve some organism that will manage to make its living by dealing with any waste product that provides available energy or usable material. Ecologists talk of a food web i.e., an interconnection of uses of both organisms and their wastes. In the industrial context, we may think of this as being use of products and waste products. The system structure of a natural ecology and the structure of an industrial system, or an economic system, are very similar (Frosch, 1992).

The ecological analogy is somewhat beyond the metabolic analogy in carrying the analogy to another level. Frosch (1992) thinks of the organism as being the industrial process or the set of industrial processes that leads to a particular product or product family and of the ecology as being the network of all industrial processes. Because they may interact with one another and live off one another, not just in the economic sense but also in the direct use of one another's material and energy wastes and products. We have not generally been able to integrate the waste fully into the web of industrial relationships. We must include wastes and products at the end of their lives in the industrial food web both as material and as energy.

Wastes may be thought of not only as outputs to be prevented by proper choice, but also as part of the industrial process product stream that is to be designed. They are not just things to be got rid of but are part of some potential product stream. Rarely, some companies look for particular waste streams, and the wastes are routinely bordered, brought and sold, or handled by waste exchanges. For example, the wastes from the acid "pickling" of steel are used as materials for water treatment, and are sold in the chemicals market. These wastes are the cheapest available source of ferrous sulphate and ferrous chloride.

Processes can be and at times already are designed so that they will accept wastes that are known to be coming from other processes, and new processes can be designed so that their wastes are designed to be useful to other processes.

One possibility for products at the end of their lives is that they may cascade down a kind of industrial food chain through a series of more degraded uses.

Plastics are extremely difficult to recycle into direct uses largely because they turn up in products mixed together and are not identified as to chemical type. The various chemical types require different kinds of treatment for reuse, so they can be very difficult to recycle when mixed, although new methods are continuously being found. In a plant, it is frequently possible to reuse the plant waste if it is a reusable material because we know what it is (Frosch, 1992). Plastics are not easily reusable for anything that is involved with food because they generally do not survive good sterilization temperatures without severe degradation. Of course, the tale of some of the industrial uses of iron is the same as in plastics. All iron and steel waste can be used directly by the industry which produces it.

How do we encourage the growth of the web of interaction of waste product and waste use, as well as waste prevention and some inevitable disposal to grow into a better integrated and a more elaborated system? There is need for more waste being prevented and more of it being cycled through the industrial web and thus less of it appearing at the end of the industrial system to become a disposal and an environmental problem. In several ecological systems, if a certain system component or an organism disappears, the entire nature of the system changes and other organisms may also vanish. This appears to be the case with predatory fish in lakes and ponds, the absence of a predator can make the whole pond "sick". Sometimes, one can correct the problem in such a system by specifically introducing a species that will fill the particular link in the system web. We might consider the problem of "stocking" the industrial pond to make other parts of the web material cycling operate correctly.

The problem of cost has been much studied in its system aspects by both ecologists and economists, but the problem of internalizing the costs of handling external wastes, and particularly the internalizing of societally diffused costs into the internal cost management systems of industrial enterprises, has not been solved (Frosch, 1992).

Certain incentive systems are better than direct regulation. For example, we can induce a differential cost between virgin materials and waste or recycled materials. The business community must think about internalizing the waste problem by shifting from disposal to prevention. We now have to think about the problem of using each other's wastes, of designing wastes to be useful as part of designing product, and of designing product so that when it becomes waste it is easier for the industrial system to use and accept it. Business should provide appropriate information during the design and manufacturing cycle.

Life Cycle Inventory

Life cycle inventory (LCI) which quantifies the energy needs and emissions relating to specific packages and/or products, constitutes one of three parts of a full LCA. A fundamental tenet of LCA is that every material product must eventually become a waste. To choose the 'greener' of two products or policies it is necessary to take into account its environmental impacts from 'cradle to grave'. This includes not only indirect inputs to the production process, and associated wastes and emissions, but also the future (downstream) fate of a product (Ayres, 1995). The first stage in the analysis is quantitative comparisons of materials flows and transformations. LCA has focussed on the second stage of analysis, namely the selection and evaluation of different, non-comparable environmental impacts. The only approach that can succeed is one that utilizes monetization to the limits of its applicability, rather than one that seeks to by-pass (or 're-invent') economics (Ayres, 1995). Nevertheless, the evaluation problem is second in priority, for the simple reason that LCA has utility even if the evaluation technique is imperfect. On the other hand, LCA has no (or even negative) utility if the underlying physical data are either wrong or unreliable with respect to critical pollutants (Ayres, 1995). Most life cycle studies consists of two components i.e., an inventory of all the energy and resources used and environmental releases to the air, water and land for a given product, process or package, and subsequent improvement analysis (Fig. 7.6). There is no scientific consensus on how to perform impact assessment which conceptually is an assessment of the effects of environmental releases and resources usage identified in the inventory (Kuta et. al., 1995).

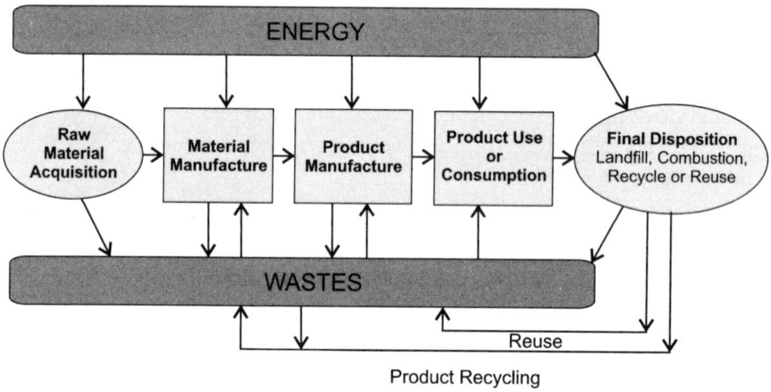

Fig. 7.6 General materials flow for 'cradle-to-grave' analysis of a product system (After Kuta et. al., 1995)

Hunt et. al., (1992) described an LCA methodology that first identifies the materials and products in the system to be analysed. A materials flow diagram is then drawn to describe the key elements of a typical product system. This generalized system is specified in detail for every package and/or product option to be studied. The result of this approach is a complete and systematic accounting of the material requirements, energy consumption and emissions for each step of the sequence from cradle to grave (Kuta et. al., 1995).

Furuholt (1995) made an LCA to compare production and use of three different fuel products, viz., regular gasoline, gasoline with methyl tertiary butyl ether (MTBE), and diesel. Figure 7.7 gives an outline of the system studied by him. Figure 7.8 illustrates how a refinery may be partitioned into several sub-processes. He quantified energy consumption and potential through the production chain and assessed the potential impacts to the environment. His work indicates that production of gasoline with MTBE exerts potentially greater environmental impacts than production of regular gasoline. The results also indicate that production of diesel leads to significantly lower potential impacts than the gasoline (Furuholt, 1995).

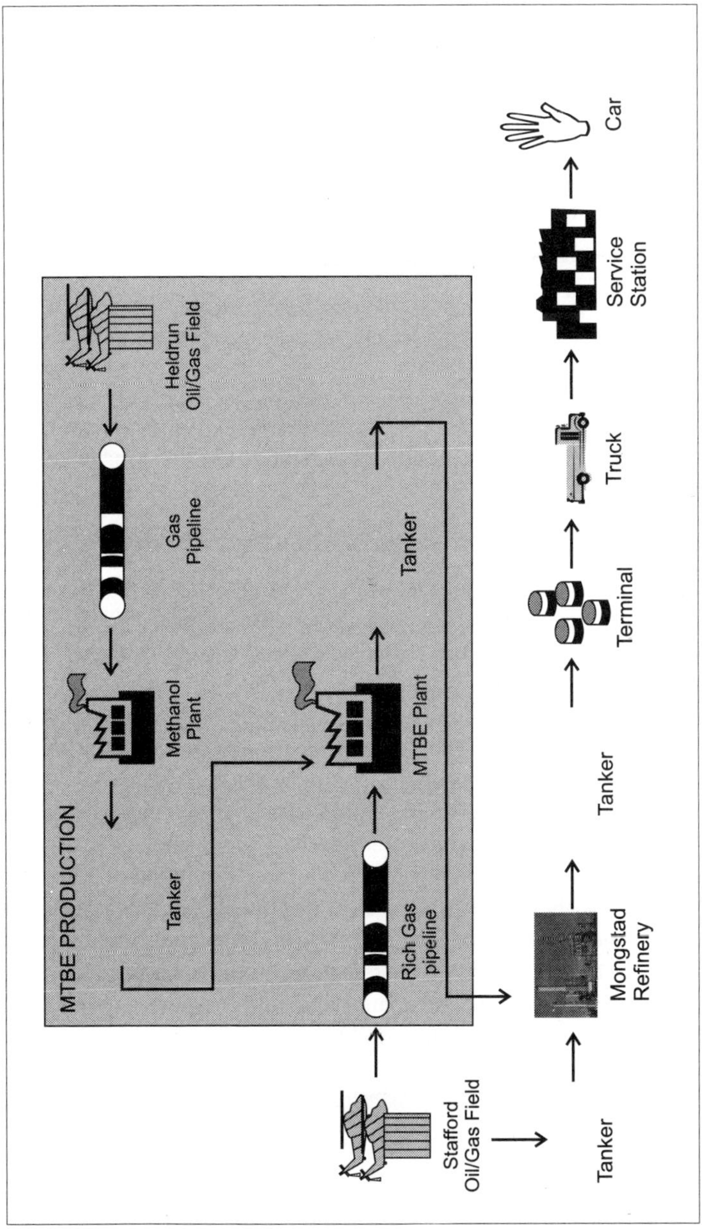

Fig. 7.7 System description and boundaries (Studied by Furuholt in1995)

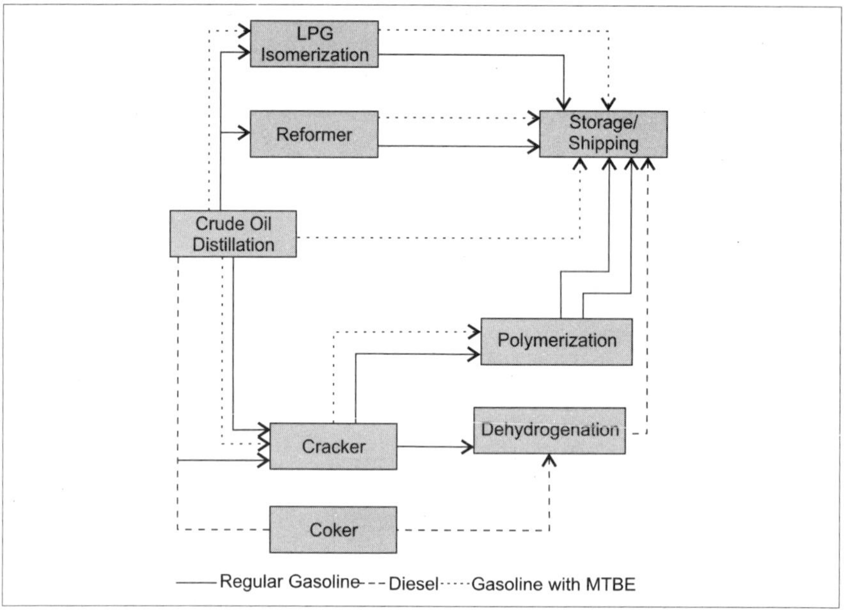

Fig. 7.8 Partitioning the refinery into eight sub-processes (After Furuholt, 1995)

The Adoption of Life Cycle Approaches by Industry

Sustainable industrial development is a process in which resource flow through and emissions from developed economies are modified. This includes a reduction of materials and energy intensity, increasing cyclicity of material flux and a reduction of dissipative uses of toxic materials. Life cycle assessment activities in large European firms in six industrial sectors were reviewed (Tables 7.1–7.3) by Berkhout and Howes (1997). They found that market and regulatory pressures on firms to adopt life cycle approaches differ greatly between industrial sectors and across national markets. Producers of final products can make improvements in the life cycle environmental performance of products while making gains in dynamic competitiveness simultaneously. Upstream producers of commodity products have used life cycle approaches defensively against negative environmental claims and in seeking to influence the policy process. Despite widespread adoption of life cycle approaches, changes in product system ecoprofiles may occur slowly in view of technological trajectories, infrastructural and resource endowments, and the fragmentation of environmental responsibility across the product chain (Berkhout and Howes, 1997).

Table 7.1 Some Approaches to LCA Adoption by European Firms (After Berkhout and Howes, 1997)

A

Characteristics of LCA Adoption	Chemicals		Aluminium	Building Materials
	Plastics	Surfactants		
Position in product chain	Upstream	Upstream	Upstream	Intermediate
Level of LCA activity	High	Intermediate	High	Variable
Key Driver				
Regulatory or market?	Regulation	Market competition	Market competition	Market competition
Appropriability of result	High	Intermediate	High to intermediate	Variable
Data availability	Good	Good	Good	Variable
Cost	Intermediate (shared)	Intermediate (shared)	Low (shared)	Variable

B

Characteristics of LCA Adoption	Automobiles	Electronic Goods	Personal Products	
			Hairspray	Diapers
Position in product chain	Central	Central	Central	Central
Level of LCA activity	Intermediate to high	Low to intermediate	Low	Low
Key Driver				
Regulatory or Market	Regulation	Regulation	Eco-labelling	Market competition
Internal/External Oriented	Internal	Internal	Both	Both
Appropriability	Low	Low	Intermediate	Low
Data availability	Good to poor	Poor	Good	Good
Costs	High	High	Intermediate	Intermediate

Table 7.2 Pattern of LCA Activities in European Industrial Firms (After Berkhout and Howes, 1997)

Activities	Commodity Product	Intermediate and Simple Product	Complex Product
Orientation of life cycle activities	External	External and internal	Internal
Study structure	Collaborative	Collaborative and independent	Independent
Study practitioner	In-house and third party	Scoping total product cycle LCI	In-house total product cycle LCI/LCA
Study type	In-house and third party	In-house	Cradle-to-grave LCI
Data origin	Cradle-to-gate LCI, internally generated	Internally and externally generated (upstream)	Externally generated (upstream and downstream)
Evaluation	None	Limited	Some
Collaboration	On data	On data	On methodology

Table 7.3 Life Cycle Environmental Impacts across Five Generic Product Groups (After Berkhout and Howes, 1997)

Product	Major Environmental Impacts	Key Players
Commodity	Raw materials extraction and production	Mining extraction firms, commodity producers
Intermediate	Production and use	Commodity producers, final consumers
Simple (short-use life)	Production and end-of-life	Commodity producers, waste handlers
Simple (long life)	Use	Final consumers
Complex	Use	Final consumers

Life cycle approaches make up the core of developing more integrated, product-oriented environmental policies, the aim being to reduce the resource and pollution intensity of the delivery of 'functions' provided through goods and services to the consumer. These include both upstream and downstream resource and pollution aspects. Today, the rate of improvement in the 'eco-efficiency' of goods and services can outpace the rate of growth of demand for them, thereby yielding environmental gains.

Patterns of applications of life cycle approaches in industry are determined chiefly by the nature of competition in an industrial sector. Application of life cycle approaches is therefore highly differentiated between sectors.

A full-scale LCA study should include a description of the product system and its mass and energy balances (inventory stage), an accounting of the environmental and resource impacts of the system (classification and characterization) and, finally, some valuation of the different impacts (normalization and valuation). In actual practice, however, most life cycles deal will only a limited set of life cycle components. More limited 'cradle-to-grave' LCI studies typically provide mass and energy balances and environmental emissions inventories for the production of intermediate products, such as commodity thermoplastics. Downstream assembly, use and waste management steps are not considered, and there is no attempt at valuing impacts.

Life cycle studies can help us to understand three kinds of problem:

1. Assessments of single products to learn about their eco-profiles.
2. Comparisons of process routes in the production of substitutable products or processes.
3. Comparisons of alternative ways for delivering a given service or function (mobility, warmth).

Some LCA activity is now going on in most sectors of industry: agriculture, mining and oil and gas extraction, construction/the building materials sector, manufacturing industry (except tobacco products) and retailing.

Berkhout and Howes (1997) simplified the analysis of LCA approaches to bring out dominant characteristics, by clubbing together industrial sectors in three broad life cycle categories i.e., commodity producer, intermediate goods producers and final goods producer [Table 7.1(A & B) and Table 7.2].

Social Impact of Life Cycle Assessment

Life cycle assessment has registered considerable progress in providing data, management tools, software and methodologies for more precise measurement but some issues have yet to be addressed such as worldwide dissemination of LCA methods and how to adapt them for developing countries through building databases and customizing management tools to suit local demands (Pommez, 2002).

Addressing such issues requires investments that must be shared among industry, government and international agencies. Sustainability may be considered as the ultimate aim of product development. LCA initiatives focus on measuring the economic and environmental impacts of a product over its entire lifetime, whereas, sustainability implies a human factor that is quite difficult to assess. This gap represents a drawback in the current methodology for evaluating the impact of the product's life cycle.

No effective methodology yet exists for accurately assessing the social impact of a sustainable development project. However, some have examined the development of such a methodology. For instance, Robert Chambers and Gordon Conway defined a sustainable livelihood as one that integrates justice, capability and sustainability.

According to Ian Scoones of the University of Sussex, sustainable livelihood can be quantified by assessing five types of capital i.e., natural, financial, human, social and physical. Using this method, in cooperation with a community, the degree to which a given project has affected the community's access to any of these types of capital may be assessed. In fact, these capitals may serve as a basis for developing social life cycle indicators. These indicator capitals may be described as:

1. **Natural** Levels of deforestation and maintenance of stocks of animals and fish.
2. **Financial** Access to credit.
3. **Human** Literacy.
4. **Social** Participation in decision-making processes.
5. **Physical** Roads, hospitals and other infrastructure.

However to holistically consider the chain of relationships throughout the life cycle, LCA must integrate the social aspects of development, preservation of the culture in question and traditional knowledge (Pommez, 2002).

Life cycle thinking is the key to changing production and consumption patterns, and life cycle approaches provide people and groups from all walks of life with the means to do so. Life cycle approach allows tackling environmental issues and opportunities holistically, and to design product service systems with the aim of reducing potential environmental impacts over an entire life cycle. The impacts of all life cycle stages should be considered to take informed decision concerning product development, policies and management strategies aimed at changing consumption patterns.

Life cycle thinking can involve several life cycle approaches such as LCA, design for environment, life cycle management, product service systems and integrated product policy. All of these, except LCA, are triple bottom line tools incorporating social, economic and environmental issues.

Life cycle assessment is an objective process to evaluate the environmental burdens associated with a product, process or activity by identifying energy and materials used and wastes released to the environment. It also evaluates and implements opportunities to affect environmental improvements.

Design for the environment (DFE) means the systematic integration of environmental and social considerations into product and process design.

Life cycle management is an integrated framework of concepts, techniques and procedures to tackle environmental, economic, technological and social aspects of products and organizations to achieve continuous environmental improvement from a life cycle perspective.

Product service system (PSS) is defined as a marketable mix of products and services that can jointly fulfill a client's need with minimal environmental impact.

Integrated product policy (IPP) has been developed by the European Commission. It aims to stimulate each part of each individual phase of a product or service's life cycle—from extraction of natural resources through design, manufacture, assembly, marketing, distribution, sale and use to eventual disposal as waste—so as to improve environmental performance.

Production systems have been experiencing structural changes worldwide. As a consequence of globalization, consumer tastes and habits are changing and converging. Production has become more efficient, but consumption of goods and services has also increased. Life cycle tools provide a crucial support for making these trends visible to consumers and producers.

Some developed countries are fairly advanced with respect to cleaner production, but in the last decade have suffered "rebound effects", in which improvements in efficiency are offset by increased consumption (efficiency improvements may even stimulate consumption). The effect of these improvements on both society and the environment is minimal (Matthews et. al., 2000). Rebound effects can be dealt with by changing consumption patterns.

Consumer organizations are evincing interest in knowing more than just the environmental burden of a product. Consumers often ask about social considerations. They wish to know how and where a product has been produced, for example, preferably label. These organizations are increasingly incorporating environmental issues among their criteria for product comparison.

Eco-labelling and environmental product declarations, used in combination with other tools, constitute one strategy for providing information about the product to consumers. Consistent product criteria and information should be conveyed through eco-labels and product declarations. However, eco-labelling and product declaration should not hinder trade or severely skew the market. Rather, eco-labelling should be supported, developed and applied to provide new business opportunities. Consumers ought to be provided with a consistent set of signals in a common language.

The major challenge for business and industry is to secure and increase market share, to protect and propagate business values and to achieve a competitive edge that goes beyond legal compliance and short-term cost savings. Incorporating life cycle and sustainability management not only improves image and brand value for world market players, but also for smaller suppliers and producers. By integrating the life cycle perspective into overall management and orienting product and process development in a more sustainable direction, business can contribute benefits to environmental, occupational health and safety, risk and quality management, as well as developing and applying cleaner process and product options.

There is a pressing need to make life cycle tools more easily accessible in developing countries, where small and medium-sized enterprises (SMEs) could especially benefit. Also to assure a global change towards sustainability, developing countries need to "leapfrog" with more sustainable technologies. Yet, most developing countries lack these.

In summary, life cycle approaches can be advantageous by:

- Providing reliable information in an accessible format, improving communication and contributing to awareness raising and more informed decisions by consumers, governments and industry
- Preparing industry for increasingly aware consumers by facilitating more efficient communication strategies and stakeholder involvement to be implemented by both the public and the private sector

- Supporting good business practices and thereby contributing to "leapfrogging" both within and among regions (North and South), countries and industries
- Contributing to continuous improvement i.e., adaptation of existing methods to the triple bottom line creates a truly holistic way of thinking and thus generates efficient structures for improvement
- Ensuring global applicability and dissemination i.e., efficient implementation of the life cycle approach to optimize usability and prevent duplication of work

Steel for Industries

Steel is used more extensively than any other metal or alloy as a structural material. New steel technologies frequently enable new or improved products in a broad range of industries. For example, the development of novel sheet steels is driven primarily by the demands of car manufacturers. Development of advanced high-strength steels with low carbon content (less than 0.2 per cent by weight) will permit significant vehicle weight savings, thereby reducing fuel consumption (Anderson et. al., 2002; Militzer, 2002). Some novel steels are multiphase steels such as dual-phase (DP) and transformation-induced plasticity (TRIP) steels. These steels combine high strength with excellent formability. As tensile strength increases, conventional steels show a decrease in elongation to failure—a measure of formability, i.e., the higher its strength, the less formable is the steel. The DP and TRIP steels deviate from this general rule by combining high strength with significantly higher elongation values than those of conventional steels of the same strength level (Militzer, 2002). The DP steels are likely to become a key component (74% by weight of the proposed vehicle body structure) in new automobile designs.

All low-carbon steels undergo processing steps like hot rolling at temperatures where the face-centered cubic crystal phase (known as austenite) is stable. During subsequent cooling the high temperature-phase austenite decomposes into a body-centered cubic phase (ferrite). The properties of steel depend mostly on the microstructure resulting from austenite decomposition. By tightly controlling this phase transformation, superior steels with multiphase microstructures can be produced. A detailed knowledge of the austenite decomposition kinetics in iron and steel is of crucial importance to the development of new steel grades and the design or optimization of industrial processing routes to consistently produce high-quality steels.

Nanoscale Zerovalent Iron

Nanoscale Zerovalent Iron (ZVI) is attracting attention for degradation of agrochemicals for the purpose of developing a cost-effective treatment technology. Joo and Cheng (2006) identified byproducts produced from the ZVI-mediated degradation process of particular contaminants and clarified the reaction mechanism by which ZVI degrades a chosen contaminant. They also described how the ZVI-based technology may be applied in complex, natural systems, limitations to implementation and possible avenues for further research which might improve the viability of the process.

Pulp and Paper Industry

According to Kerski (1995), dispossession, deforestation and pollution caused by the pulp and paper industry is tied to a dynamic and ever-increasing scale, concentration and capital intensiveness. The paper industry and its allies attempt to refashion the infrastructure through which they work, capturing subsidies, managing demand, centralizing power, and evading, digesting and regulating resistance. Expansions of the pulp and paper industry have aroused increasing opposition throughout the world. Campaigns are gaining momentum to reduce dioxins and other toxic compounds produced by the use of chlorine in the paper-making process. The Indonesian people are alarmed at the pulping of thousands of square kilometres of native hardwood stands in Sumatra. The expansion of monoculture pulpwood plantations is being opposed in Chile, Brazil, India and Australia. The pulp and paper industry's argument is that through seeking profits it is merely increasing society's efficiency in meeting the pre-existing needs of its members. The industry's drive towards larger scale and global expansion cannot be explained solely by economics. Social structures that are sensitive to the needs of pulp and paper elites are promoted through the political efforts of many agents working together against an ever-varying background of resistance. Due attention to this dynamic is crucial to the success of environmentalist's efforts to reduce the damage done by the industry (Kerski, 1995).

Commercial techniques for pulping of wood were developed over a century ago. As wood is a material which could be harvested at any time and easily stored and shipped in great volume, the switch to wood as a raw material has reinforced paper makers' reliance on large, highly-mechanized mills.

Today, most paper pulp is made of wood, either by grinding it or chipping and boiling it in strong chemicals. Large quantities of fresh water and energy are needed and the process annually uses the rough equivalent of the timber that would cover 20,000 square kilometres of woodland. Paper manufacture is estimated about 10 per cent of total wood use and represents one per cent of the world's total economic output. Most of the pulped wood used for manufacturing newsprint, packaging board and writing paper comes from a small number of sprawling plants, using very costly computerized machinery.

Pulp mills do not share landscapes with local communities pursuing a variety of agricultural, fishing and subsistence-gathering activities. For example, large mills work better with simplified, compact population of factory-friendly trees than with native woodlands reserved for a variety of uses. They promote the growth of mill towns where virtually everyone works for the industry rather than communities with diverse livelihood.

Ever since wood-based pulps ushered in an age of cheap, large-scale paper production. In the mid-1800s, new commodities ranging from building materials, bags, toilet papers, drinks cartons, nappies, fax and computer paper and export packaging, have been embedding paper use ever more thoroughly into business and home activities. In 1991, 40 per cent of world paper production was used for packaging and wrapping, while only 30 per cent went for printing and writing and 13 per cent for newsprint, with increasing volumes of all the three categories going for advertising (Wright, 1993).

As native forests become depleted and local resistance increases, pulp and paper industries turn to industrial tree plantations to furnish large amount of fresh, uniform raw material on a smaller land base, avoiding conflict with other land uses. Although industrial plantations supply less than a quarter of world demand for pulpwood, this proportion is bound to rise in the face of deforestation, the limitations of recycling (fibres can only be reused a few times before disintegrating into dust), and the resistance of much of the industry to non-wood materials (Kerski, 1995).

Soda Ash Industry

Soda ash industry generates a large quantity of solid, liquid and gaseous effluents which are non-toxic. These effluents do not contain any organic matter. Gaseous emissions mainly consist of carbon dioxide emitted from the top of kilns. Table 7.4 shows the norms stipulated by Central Pollution Control Board (CPCB) as the minimal national standards. Some dust is emitted from the solid-handling section of the Solvay process, but no separate standard has been laid down. The tolerance limit for particulate matter in atmospheric emissions is 250 mg/Nm^3.

Table 7.4 Mineral National Standards for Soda Ash Effluents

Parameter	Quantitative Limit
Total suspended solids	Not to exceed 600 mg/L
pH	Up to 9.5
Nitrogen as ammonia	15 mg/L
Temperature	45°C

Caustic Soda Industry

Emissions from the diaphragm and mercury cell plants include chlorine and hydrogen. Gaseous chlorine occurs in the blow gas from liquefaction, vents in tank cars and tank containers during loading and unloading and in storage tanks and process transfer tanks. Other emissions include mercury vapour from mercury cathode cells and chlorine from various seals, and the air-blowing of depleted brine in mercury cell plant.

In India, the specific consumption of asbestos per tonne of caustic soda in the diaphragm cell process is about 48 kg, which is extremely high as compared to the world standard of about 15 kg. The CPCB has suggested the permissible emission of asbestos to be around 0.3 kg/t of caustic soda in the diaphragm cell using metallic anodes and modified diaphragm (Table 7.4).

The emission of mercury into the environment constitutes the chief problem with the mercury cell process. Most Indian mercury cell process plants have adopted pollution control measures and many have already reduced mercury consumption from 350 gm/t of caustic soda to about 90 gm/t. Lower consumption of mercury amounts to lesser mercury losses from the process. Units having the lowest specific consumption of mercury per tonne of caustic soda usually recirculate the largest amount of mercury-bearing waste brine. In developed nations, the level of specific consumption of mercury has been brought down to less than 20 gm/t of caustic soda. In contrast, the average mercury discharge by Indian caustic soda units is more than 100 gm/t of caustic soda produced.

Petrochemical Industry

The petrochemical industry covers a broad spectrum of synthetic chemicals. Many processes including polymerization, hydrogenation, halogenation, epoxidation, alkylation, nitration, hydrocarboxylation, sulphonation, distillation, isomerization and crystallization are operated by this industry. Hence, there exists much potential for the production and release of pollutants. Many of the products and intermediates are toxic. The types and nature of various pollutants are given in Table 7.5.

Table 7.5 Pollutants from Petrochemical Industry

Product	Process	Pollutants
Ethyl benzene	Alkylation	Tar, HCl, caustic oil, HCN, unreacted soluble hydrocarbons
Butadiene	From n-butane and butylenes	Residue gas, tars, oils, soluble hydrocarbons
Styrene	From ethyl benzene	Spent catalyst, aromatic hydrocarbons
2-Ethyl hexanol	Hydrocarboxylation (oxoprocess)	Soluble hydrocarbons, aldehydes
Acrylonitrile	Hydrocyanation	Cyanides, organic and inorganic compounds
Benzenexylene	Isomerization	Aliphatic and aromatic hydrocarbons, derivative tars
Ethylene oxide ethylene glycol	Oxidation	$CaCl_2$, spent lime, hydrocarbon ethylene polymers, ethylene oxide, glycols
Aldehydes, alcohols, acids	From hydrocarbons	Acetone, formaldehyde, acetal alcohols, methanol, higher alcohols and organic acids
Acids and anhydrides	Aromatic oxidation	Acids, aromatics

Nonferrous Metals Industry

Traditionally, single-medium approaches have been used to protect the environment, i.e., air, water and land environments were created as if they are isolated compartments. This approach has given way to environmental policies based upon comprehensive analysis of air, water and land pollution as an inevitable logical supplement to single-medium approaches. Pollutant releases to each environmental medium (air, water and land) affect each other, so environmental strategies must identify and address these inter-relationships by designing policies for the "whole" facility. One way is to design environmental policies for similar industrial facilities (EPA, 1995). By doing so, environmental concerns that are common to the manufacturing of similar products can be addressed in a comprehensive manner. The designing of comprehensive and sensible environmental protection measures for specific industries depend on knowledge of several inter-related topics. Some key elements include general industry information (economic and geographic), a description of industrial processes, pollution outputs, pollution prevention opportunities, and statutory and regulatory framework.

Several establishments are engaged in the primary and secondary smelting and refining of ferrous and non-ferrous metals from ore or scrap i.e., rolling, drawing, and alloying as well as the manufacturing and casting of basic metallic products such as nails, spikes, wires and cables. Primary smelting and refining produces metal directly from ores, while secondary refining and smelting produces metals from scrap and process waste. Scrap means small pieces of metal parts, bars, turnings, sheets and wires that may be damaged or worn-out but can be recycled.

Two metal recovery technologies are generally used to produce refined metals. Pyrometallurgical technologies use heat to separate desired metals from undesirable materials. These processes exploit the differences between constituent oxidation potential, melting point, vapour pressure, density, and/or miscibility when melted for example, drying, calcining, roasting, sintering, retorting and smelting. Hydrometallurgical technologies differ from pyrometallurgical in that the desired metals are separated from undesirables using techniques that differentiate between constituent solubilities and/or electrochemical properties while in aqueous solutions. Leaching, chemical precipitation, electrolytic recovery, membrane separation, ion exchange and solvent extraction are a few examples.

During pyrometallic processing, after being concentrated by benefication (crushing, washing and drying), an ore is sintered or mixed by heat, with such other materials as baghouse dust. The concentrate is then smelted in a blast furnace so as to fuse the desired metals into an impure molten bullion which is then subjected to a third pyrometallic process to refine the metal to the desired level of purity. Each time the ore or bullion is heated, waste materials are created. Air emissions like dust may be captured in a baghouse and are either disposed of or returned to the process depending upon the residual metal content. Sulphur is also captured, and when concentrations exceed four per cent, it can be converted into sulphuric acid. From certain ores, various metals including gold and silver are sometime produced as byproducts. Some hazardous wastes are produced during primary refining operations which require the heating of ores to remove impurities. Large amounts of sulphur are released during copper, lead and zinc smelting operations.

Aluminium Industry and Aluminium Processing

Environmental hazards due to the aluminium industry in India basically emanate from the mining of bauxite, the chief raw material produced through open-pit mining which produces much dust. This ore is subjected to grinding and granulometric sorting which also generates dust. Being chemically very active, fresh bauxite is readily attacked by oxygen, moisture and microorganisms. During the rainy season, the water draining over the ore becomes acidic and seeps into the underground water table. Water runoff from the mines pollutes both groundwater and surface water.

At the alumina refining stage, the environmental problems are created by disposal of red mud–a waste product of the process of refining alumina from bauxite and pollutants such as coal dust from steam generators, alumina dust from calcining and stack emissions of SO_2 from the refinery and other miscellaneous wastes. Red mud is composed of oxides of aluminium, iron, titanium and silicon as major constituents and oxides of vanadium, gallium, calcium and magnesium as minor constituents. The ratio between these and the end product tends to be 1:1. The residue from aluminium-rich liquor is dumped into tanks which generate

Table 7.6 Types of Pollution and Pollutants in a Typical Aluminium Plant (After Ganapathy and Padmanabhan, 1992)

Types of Pollution	Materials Produced
Gaseous emissions	Carbon monoxide, carbon dioxide, hydrogen fluoride, sulphur dioxide, carbon disulphide, silicon tetrafluoride, carbon tetrafluoride, hexafluroethane, water vapour
Solid emissions	Alumina, cryolite, aluminium fluoride, calcium fluoride, carbon, iron oxide
Liquid effluent	Fluorine compounds, hydrocarbons entrained water
Smelter wastes	Spent potlinings anode butts from prebaked pots, dust from gas cleaning, sludge from cleaning and scrubbing water, material from pot skimming, spills
Paste preparation emissions and wastes	Coke and coal dusts, hydrocarbon fumes
Anode baking emissions and wastes	Hydrocarbons, fluorides, sulphur
Cast house emissions and waste	Fluxing fumes (primarily aluminium and chloride) trace fluorine, sulphur dioxide
Ancillary operations	Dust from bulk material handling, demolition of old pots and cleaning of prebaked anode butts to recover carbon

dust and pollute groundwater through seepage. When the ponds get filled up, new disposal sites are selected and this land cannot be used for growing crops.

The major pollutants released during smelting are gaseous and particulate fluoride emissions. About 780 cubic metre of gases are produced per tonne of alumina from cryolite, aluminium fluoride, calcium fluoride and sodium fluoride used in the electrolytic process. A list of the type of pollution and pollutants in the aluminium industry is given in Table 7.6.

The primary and secondary aluminium industry produces highly pure (99%) ingots of aluminium that act as feedstock for other materials and processes. The leading end-users of aluminium come from three industries, containers and packaging, transportation, and building and construction. Some materials containing aluminium are sheet metal, aluminium plate and foil, rod, bar and wire, beverage cans, automobiles, aircraft components and window/door frames (EPA, 1990, 1995).

Primary Processing

Primary aluminium producers usually use a three-step process to produce aluminium alloy ingots. First, alumina is extracted from bauxite ore using the Bayer process (Fig. 7.9). Finely crushed bauxite is mixed with an aqueous sodium hydroxide solution to make a slurry which is reacted at a high temperature under steam pressure in a digester vessel. This produces a mixture of dissolved aluminium oxides and bauxite residues. Most of the impurities such as silicon, iron, titanium and calcium oxides settle at the bottom of the digester during the reaction and form a sludge. The remaining sodium aluminate slurry is then flash-cooled by evaporation and sent for clarification. During clarification starch is added due to which fine impurities that remain in the slurry like sand drop out, further purifying the sodium aluminate solution. The solution is then fed into a precipitation tank and crystallized. In the precipitator, the solution is allowed to cool by adding a small amount of aluminium hydroxide "seed" which stimulates the precipitation of solid crystals of aluminium hydroxide and sodium hydroxide. The aluminium hydroxide crystals settle to the bottom of the tank and can be removed. They are washed to remove any caustic soda residues, vacuum dewatered and sent for calcination. In the calciner (a type of rotating kiln), the aluminium hydroxide is roasted to further dewater it.

In the second step, aluminium oxide (alumina) produced during the Bayer process is reduced to make pure molten aluminium. Alumina has a strong chemical bond between aluminium and oxygen which makes separating them difficult—pyrometallurgical separation requires a temperature of 3600°F. However, alumina can be dissolved when placed in molten metal cryolite at only 1745°F. Once dissolved, the aluminium oxide is readily separated into aluminium and oxygen electrically by means of the Hall-Heroult process which begins with the placement of the alumina into electrolytic cells or "pots" that are filled with molten cryolite. The process requires at least six kilowatts of electricity per pound of aluminium produced but only a low voltage. This permits the pots to be laid out in a series along one long electrical circuit to form what is known as a "potline". Within

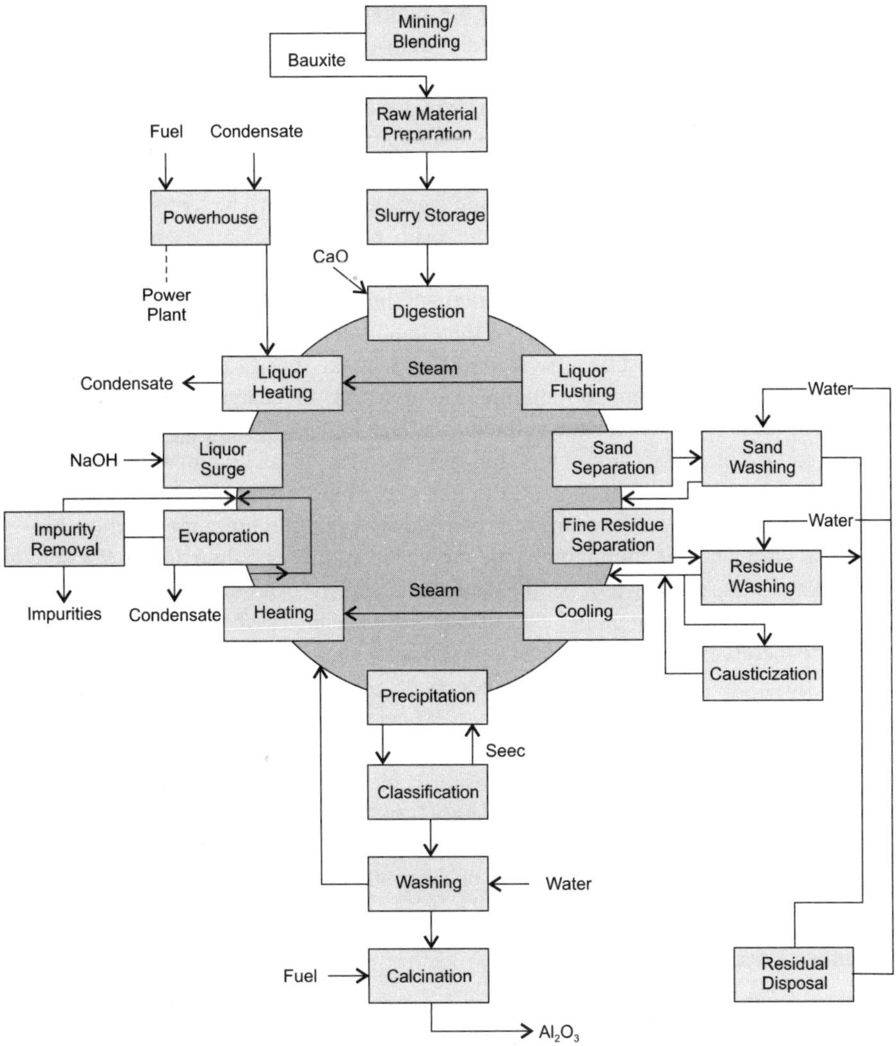

Source: Buonicore and Davis, 1992

Fig. 7.9 Bayer process for alumina refining

each pot a positive electric current is passed through the cryolite by means of a carbon anode submerged in the liquid cryolite. The oxygen atoms, separated from aluminium oxide, carry a negative electrical charge and are attracted to the carbon anodes. The carbon and the oxygen combine immediately to form carbon dioxide and carbon monoxide which bubble out of the melt. Pure aluminium collects at the bottom of the pot is siphoned off, placed into crucibles and then transferred to melting holding furnaces.

Step three involves either mixing the molten aluminium with other metals to form alloys or casting it into ingots for transport to fabricating shops. Casting involves pouring of molten aluminium into molds and cooling it with water.

Some fluorides are produced as waste material during the primary production of aluminium, chiefly during the reduction process. In secondary production, aluminium scrap is melted in large gas or oil-fired reverberatory furnaces which have one or two charging wells separated from the main bath by a refractory wall that admits only molten metal into the main bath. Magnesium is removed by treating the molten bath with chlorine or with various fluxes of aluminium chloride, aluminium fluoride or mixtures of sodium and potassium chlorides and fluorides. For convenient handling, some part of the old aluminium scrap is melted to form sweated matter that must be processed further to make specification-grade ingot.

Another method employs aluminium drosses as the charge instead of scrap. The term dross has been usually defined as a thick liquid or solid phase that forms at the surface of molten aluminium and is a byproduct of melting operations. It is formed with or without fluxing and the free aluminium content of this byproduct varies. Dross is usually taken to mean as being lower in aluminium content, while the material with a higher aluminium content is called "skim" or "white dross". If a salt flux is used in the melting process, the byproduct is called "black dross" or "salt cake". Drosses containing about 30 per cent metallics are usually crushed and screened to raise the metal content to over 60 per cent. They are then melted in a rotary furnace, where the molten aluminium metal collects on the bottom of the furnace and is tapped off. Salt slags containing less than 30 per cent metallics are leached with water to separate the metallics. In addition to this classic dross-recycling process, a new dross treatment process using a water-cooled plasma gas arc heater (plasma torch) installed in a specially-designed rotary furnace has been patented in the USA. The new process eliminates the use of salt flux in the conventional dross treatment process and claims recovery efficiencies of about 90 per cent.

Primary Processing

Primary aluminium processing results in air emissions, process wastes and other solid-phase wastes. Particulates are released during the calcining of hydrated aluminium oxide, but extensive controls are applied to reduce emissions to relatively small quantities. Some particulates are emitted from the bauxite grinding and materials handling processes. Emissions from aluminium reduction processes are primarily gaseous hydrogen fluoride, particulates fluorides, alumina, carbon monoxide, volatile organics, sulphur dioxide and vaporized organics. Wet scrubbers can be used to abate emissions.

Wastewaters generated from primary aluminium processing are produced during clarification and precipitation, but much of this water is reused. Solid-phase wastes are generated at two stages in the primary aluminium process, red mud produced during bauxite refining and spent potliners from the reduction process. Red mud contains iron, aluminium, silicon, calcium and sodium.

Secondary Processing

Secondary aluminium processing also results in air emissions, wastewaters and solid wastes. Atmospheric emissions from reverberatory (chlorine) smelting/refining make a significant fraction of the total particulate and gaseous effluents generated in the secondary aluminium industry. Furnace effluent gases contain combustion products, chlorine, hydrogen chloride and metal chlorides of zinc, magnesium and aluminium, aluminium oxide and various metals and metal compounds. Emissions from reverberatory (fluorine) smelting/refining are similar to those from reverberatory (chlorine) smelting/refining. Fluorides are emitted as gaseous fluorides or as dusts. Baghouse scrubbers are used to control fluoride emission (EPA, 1990, 1995).

Solid-phase waste or the slag generated during smelting contains chlorides resulting from the use of fluxes and magnesium. Wastewaters are also generated when water is added to the smelting slags to facilitate the separation of metallics.

Raw Material Inputs and Pollution Outputs

Table 7.7 shows the material inputs and pollution outputs resulting from primary and secondary aluminium processing.

Table 7.7 Aluminium Process Materials Inputs/Pollution Outputs

Process (For Alumina)	Material Input	Air Emissions	Process Wastes	Other Wastes
Bauxite refining	Bauxite, sodium hydroxide	Particulates		Residues of silicon, iron, titanium, calcium oxide and caustic soda
Clarification and precipitation	Alumina slurry, scratch, water		Wastewater containing starch, sand and caustic	
Primary electrolytic smelting	Alumina, carbon anodes, electrolytic cells, cryolite	Fluorides, CO_2, SO_2, CO_2, C_2F_6, CF_4, and perfluorinated carbons (PFC)		Spent potliners
Secondary scrap smelting	Aluminium scrap, oil or gas, chlorine or other fluxes	Particulates and HCl/Cl_2		Slag containing Mg and chlorides
Secondary recycling	Aluminium dross, water	Particulates	Wastewater, salts	

Copper Processing

Copper has high electrical conductivity. The leading consumers of refined copper are wire mills and brass mills producing copper and copper alloy. The dominant end-users of copper and copper alloy are the construction and electronic product industries and transportation equipment like radiators. Copper and copper alloy powders are used for brake linings and bands, bushings, instruments and filters in the automotive and aerospace industries, for electrical and electronic applications for anti-fouling paints and coatings, and for diverse chemical and medical uses. Copper sulphate and cupric and cuprous oxides are widely used as algicides, fungicides, wood preservatives, copper plating, pigments, electronic applications and many special applications.

Primary Processing

Depending upon the ore grade and the nature of the ore deposit, copper is mined in both open pits and underground mines. Copper ore contains less than one per cent copper as sulphide minerals. The ore is brought to the ground, crushed and ground to a powdery fineness, then concentrated. During concentration, ground ore is slurried with water. Chemical reagents are added and the slurry is aerated. The air bubbles attach themselves to the copper minerals and are then skimmed off the top of the flotation cells. This concentrate contains 20–30 per cent copper. The "tailings" from the ore drop to the bottom and are removed, dewatered by "thickness", and transported as a slurry to a tailings pond for disposal. All water used in this operation from dewatering thickeners and the tailings pond is recovered and recycled back into the process.

Depending on the ore type used as a charge, copper can be produced either pyrometallurgically or hydrometallurgically. The ore concentrates containing copper sulphide and iron sulphide are subjected by pyrometallurgy to yield high purity copper products. Oxide ores (copper oxide and other oxidized waste materials) are subjected to hydrometallurgy to yield high purity copper products (Fig. 7.10).

Copper conversion is done by a pyrometallurgical process known as 'smelting' during which the concentrates are dried and fed into one of several different types of furnaces. There the sulphide minerals are partially oxidized and melted to yield a layer of 'matte', a mixed copper iron sulphide, and 'slag', an upper layer of waste.

The matte is further processed by 'converting'. The slag is tapped from the furnace and stored or discarded in slag piles on site. Some slag may be sold for railway ballast and for sand blasting grit. Smelting process also produces SO_2 which is collected, purified and converted into H_2SO_4.

The copper matte is fed into a converter by pouring into a horizontal cylindrical vessel fitted with a row of pipes known as 'tuyeres', which project into the cylinder and are used to introduce air into the converter. Lime and silica are added to the copper matte to react with the iron oxide produced in the process to form slag. Scrap copper can also be added to the converter. The furnace is rotated so that the tuyeres are submerged. Air is blown into the molten matte. This makes the remaining iron sulphide combine with oxygen to form iron oxide and sulphur dioxide. Following the "blow", the converter is rotated to pour off the iron silicate slag.

After removing all the iron the converter is rotated back and given a second blow during which the leftover sulphur gets oxidized and is removed from the copper sulphide. The converter is rotated to pour off the molten copper (called 'blister copper'). Sulphur dioxide is converted into sulphuric acid. Due to its residual copper content, slag is recycled back to the smelting furnace.

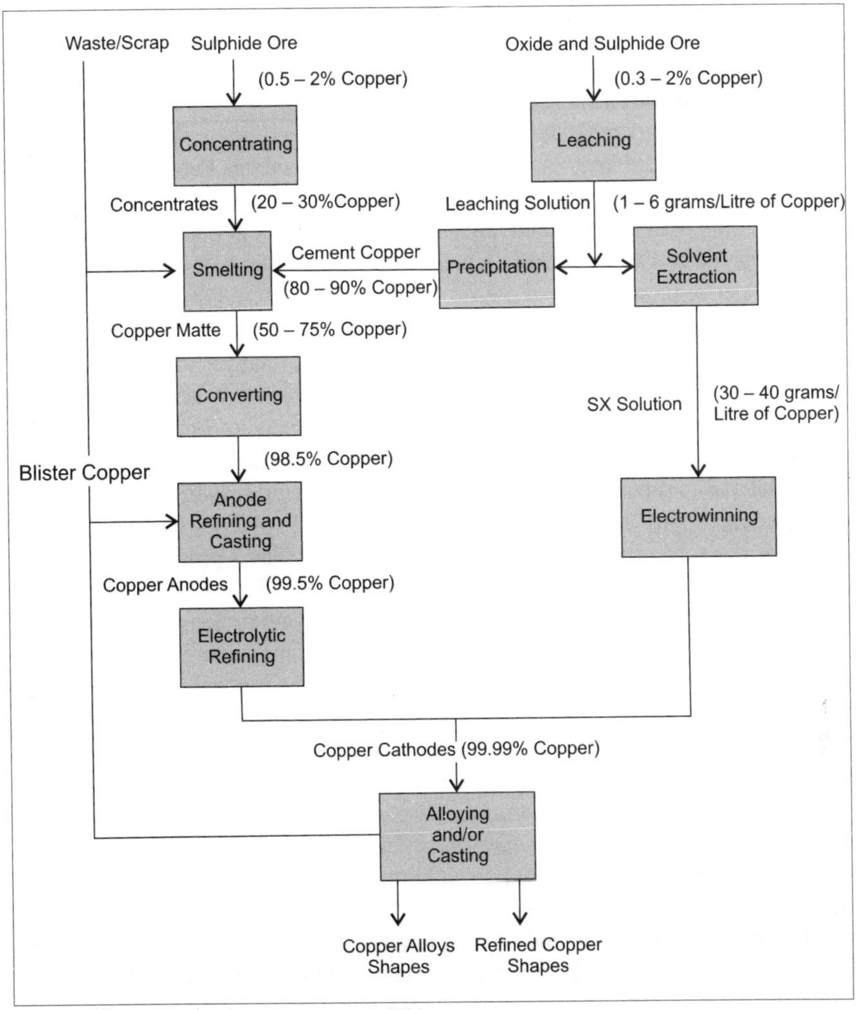

Source: Office of Technology Assessment, USA

Fig. 7.10 Copper production by pyrometallurgy and hydrometallurgy

Blister copper contains at least 98 per cent copper. It is further refined to high purity copper in two steps:

1. **Fire refining** Here, the molten blister copper is poured into a cylindrical furnace, where at first air and then natural gas or propane are blown through the melt to remove the last of the sulphur and any residual oxygen from the copper. The molten copper is then poured into a casting wheel to form anodes pure enough for electrorefining.
2. **Electrorefining** Here, the copper anodes are loaded into electrolytic cells and interspaced with copper 'starting sheets' or cathodes in a bath of copper sulphate solution. Passing direct current (DC) through the cell dissolves the copper from the anode. It is transported through the electrolyte and re-deposited on the cathode starting sheets. The cathodes become thicker, and are removed and replaced by fresh starting sheets. Solid impurities in the anodes fall to the bottom of the cell as a sludge where they are ultimately collected and processed for the recovery of precious metals such as gold and silver. This material is called 'anode slime'. The cathodes removed from the electrolytic cell are the primary product of the copper producer and contain 99.99 per cent copper.

In the hydrometallurgical process, the oxidized ores and waste materials are leached with sulphuric acid. Leaching is either done in situ or in special piles by distributing acid across the top and allowing it to percolate down through the material. The ground under the leach pads is lined with an acid-proof impermeable plastic material to prevent leach liquor from contaminating ground water. Once the copper-rich solutions are collected they can be processed by either the 'cementation' process or the solvent extraction and electrowinning (SXEW) process. The former process is rarely used today and hence is not described. In the SXEW process, the pregnant leach solution (PLS) is concentrated by solvent extraction during which an organic chemical that extracts copper, but not impurity metals (iron, etc.) is mixed with the PLS. The copper laden organic solution is separated from the leachate in a settling bank. Addition of sulphuric acid to the pregnant organic mixture strips the copper into an electrolytic solution. The copper-rich solution is passed into an electrolytic electrowinning cell which differs from an electrorefining cell in using a permanent and insoluble anode. The copper in solution is then plated onto a starting sheet cathode in the same way as on the cathode in an electrorefining cell. High purity copper is produced. Copper smelting and converting generate over half a tonne of SO_2 per tonne of copper concentrate. SO_2 releases need to be controlled, by elaborating gas collection and filtration systems after which the SO_2 contained in the off-gases is converted to H_2SO_4. Generally, if the SO_2 concentration exceeds four per cent, it should be converted into H_2SO_4, which is an ingredient in fertilizer. Fugitive gases containing less than four per cent SO_2 are either released to the atmosphere or scrubbed to remove the sulphur dioxide (EPA, 1994).

Secondary Processing

The basic processes in secondary copper recovery are scrap metal pretreatment and smelting. Pretreatment means cleaning and concentration to prepare the material for the smelting furnace. Pretreatment of the feed material is achieved by using several different procedures. Feed scrap is concentrated manually and by mechanically sorting, stripping, shredding and magnetic separation. It is often briquetted in a hydraulic press. Pyrometallurgical pretreatment includes sweating, burning of insulation from scrap wire and drying (burning off oil and volatiles) in rotary kilns. Hydrometallurgical methods include flotation and leaching with chemical recovery.

After pretreatment the scrap can be smelted. The general fire-refining process is essentially the same as for the primary copper smelting industry.

Raw Material Inputs and Pollution Outputs

The material inputs and pollution outputs resulting from primary and secondary copper processing are shown in Table 7.8.

Table 7.8 Copper Process Materials Input/Pollution Output

Process (Copper)	Material Input	Air Emission	Process Wastes	Other Wastes
Concentration	Copper ore, H_2O, chemical reagents, thickeners		Flotation wastewaters	Tailings containing waste minerals e.g., limestone and quartz
Leaching	Copper concentrate, H_2SO_4		Uncontrolled leachate	Heap leach waste
Smelting	Copper concentrate, siliceous flux	SO_2, particulates containing arsenic, antimony, cadmium, lead, mercury, zinc		Acid plant blowdown slurry/sludge slag containing iron sulphides, silica
Conversion	Copper matte and scrap, siliceous flux	SO_2,particulates (as above)		Acid plant blowdown slurry/ sludge slag containing iron sulphides, silica
Electrolytic refining	Blister copper		Process wastewater	Slimes containing impurities e.g., gold, silver and various other impurities
Secondary processing		Particulates	Slag granulation waste	Slag

Lead Processing

The power storage battery industry is probably the largest end user of lead. Industrial demand for lead acid batteries has increased greatly due to the growth in demand for stationary batteries used in telecommunications as well as back up power systems for computers, lighting and security systems. The demand is more also due to an increased need for mobile batteries used in forklifts and other battery-powered vehicles. Some other end uses are ammunition. Lead oxides are used in television glass and computers, construction (including radiation shielding) and protective coatings. Miscellaneous uses include ballasts, ceramics and crystal glass.

Primary Processing

The primary lead production process consists of four steps: sintering, smelting, drossing and pyrometallurgical refining (Fig. 7.11). A feedstock of lead concentrate is fed into a sintering machine. Other raw materials may be added including iron, silica, limestone flux, coke, soda, ash, pyrite, zinc, caustic and particulates gathered from pollution control devices. In the sintering machine, the lead feedstock is exposed to blasts of hot air which burns off the sulphur producing SO_2. The sinter is then fed along with coke, various recycled and cleanup materials, limestone, and other fluxing agents into a blast furnace for reduction. Here, the carbon acts as a fuel and smelts or melts the lead.

The molten lead flows to the bottom of the furnace where four layers form: (i) 'speiss' (the lightest material, basically arsenic and antimony), (ii) 'matte' (copper sulphide and other metal sulphides), (iii) blast furnace slag (primarily silicates) and (iv) lead bullion (98 per cent lead by weight). All layers are then drained off. The speiss and matte are bought by copper smelters for recovery of copper and precious metals. The blast furnace slag containing zinc, iron, silica and lime is stored in piles and partially recycled. Rough lead bullion from the blast furnace needs some treatment in kettles before undergoing refining operations.

The lead bullion is refined using pyrometallurgical methods to remove any remaining non-lead saleable materials (e.g., gold, silver, bismuth, zinc and metal oxides like those of antimony, arsenic, tin and copper). The lead is refined in a cast iron kettle during five stages. Antimony, tin and arsenic are removed first. Then gold and silver are removed by adding zinc. Next, the lead is refined by vacuum removal of zinc. Refining is continued by adding calcium and magnesium. These two materials combine with bismuth to form an insoluble compound that is skimmed from the kettle. Lastly, caustic soda and/or nitrates are added to the lead to remove any remaining traces of metal impurities. The lead refined in this way has a purity of up to 99 per cent, and may be mixed with other metals to form alloys or it may be directly cast into desired shapes.

The above processes create waste streams of considerable concern. Some hazardous wastes include smelting plant wastes that are sent to surface

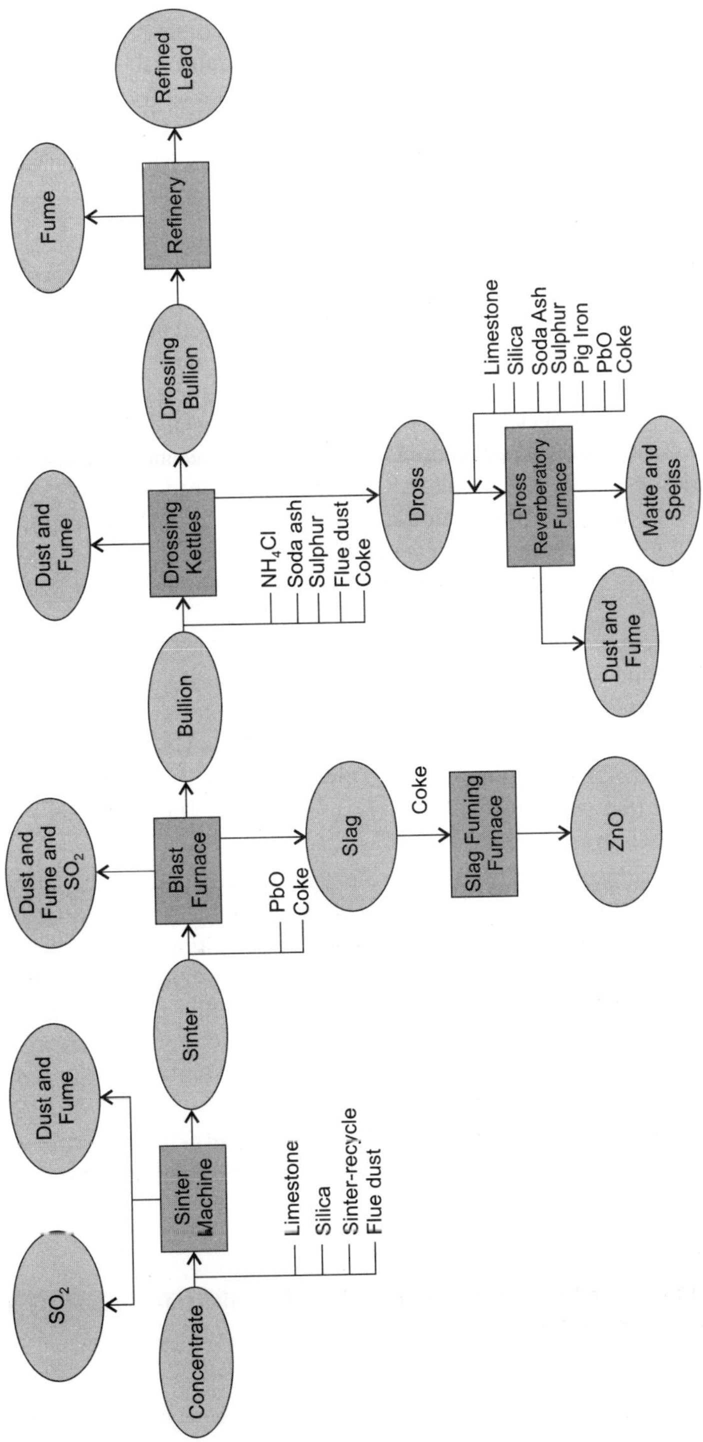

Source: Buonicore and Davis, 1992

Fig. 7.11 Primary lead production process

impoundments to settle. Acid plant blowdown is formed during the production of lead in the same way as produced at a copper plant, i.e., during the recovery of SO_2 emissions. Slag granulation water is produced when hot slag from the process is sprayed with water to be cooled and granulated before being transported to a slag pile. Plant washing is a housekeeping process and the washdown normally contains a substantial amount of lead and other process materials.

Secondary Processing

The secondary production of lead begins with the recovery of old scrap from worn out, damaged or obsolete products and new scrap that is made of product wastes and smelter-refinery drosses, residues and slags. While some secondary lead is recovered directly for special products such as Babbitt metal, solder, remelt and copper-based alloys, over 95 per cent of it is recovered at secondary lead smelters and refineries as either soft (unalloyed) or antimonial lead, most of which is recycled directly back into the manufacture of new batteries. Unlike copper and zinc, where scrap processing varies greatly depending on scrap type and ultimate use, the dominance of lead battery scrap makes possible a more standard secondary recovery process.

Blast furnaces produce hard lead from charges containing siliceous slag, scrap iron, limestone and coke. Most of the charge comprises oxides, pot furnace refining drosses and reverberatory slag. Some of the coke in the furnace combust to melt the charge, while the remainder reduces lead oxides to elemental lead.

As the lead charge melts, limestone and iron float to the top of the molten bath and form a flux that retards oxidation of the product lead. The molten lead flows from the furnace into a holding pot.

Refining/Casting involves the use of kettle type furnaces for remelting, alloying, refining and oxidizing processes. Materials charged for remelting are usually lead alloy ingots that require no further processing before casting. Alloying furnaces simply melt and mix ingots of lead and alloy materials. The most common alloying materials are antimony, tin, arsenic, copper and nickel. Refining furnaces are used either to remove copper and tin, arsenic, copper and nickel. Refining furnaces are used either to remove copper and antimony to produce soft lead, or to remove arsenic, copper and nickel for making hard lead.

Improved and modern secondary recovery plants use lead paste desulphurization to reduce sulphur dioxide emissions and waste sludge generation during smelting.

Raw Material Inputs/Pollution Outputs

The material inputs and pollution outputs relating to primary and secondary lead processing are shown in Table 7.9.

Table 7.9 Lead Process Materials Input/Wastes Output

Process (Lead)	Material Input	Air Emissions	Process Wastes	Other Wastes
Sintering	Lead ore, iron, limestone, flux, coke, soda, ash, pyrite, zinc, caustic, bag-house dust	Sulphur dioxide, particulates (cadmium, lead)		
Smelting	Lead sinter, coke	Sulphur dioxide, particulates (cadmium, lead)	Plant washdown wastewater, slag granulation water	Slag with impurities e.g., zinc, iron, silica, and lime, surface impoundment solids
Drossing	Lead bullion, soda, ash, sulphur, baghouse dust, coke			Slag with impurities e.g., copper, surface impoundment solids
Refining	Lead drossing bullion			
Lead acid battery breaking	Lead acid batteries			Polypropylene case fragments, dilute sulphuric acid
Secondary smelting	Battery scrap, drosses, oxides, iron, limestone coke	Sulphur dioxide particulates, cadmium, lead)		Slag, emission control dust

Primary Processing

Primary lead processing operations produce air emissions (SO_2, particulates), process wastes and other solid-phase wastes. About 85 per cent of the sulphur found in the lead ore concentrate gets removed during sintering. Particulate emissions from sinter machines may range between 5–20 per cent of the concentrated ore feed. Some of the sulphur in the ore concentrate fed to the sinter machine is eliminated in the blast furnace. Particulate emissions from blast furnaces contain many different kinds of material, including a range of lead oxides, quartz, limestone, iron pyrites, iron-limestone-silicate slag, arsenic and other metallic compounds associated with lead ores. These emissions can be controlled by means of fabric filters and electrostatic precipitators.

Smelting of primary lead produces wastewaters and slurries. Slag granulation water arises when slag is disposed. Plant washdown water is generated from plant housekeeping and contains lead and other process materials. Acid plant blowdown comes from the conversion of SO_2 to H_2SO_4.

Secondary Processing

Secondary lead processing generates air emissions and solid-phase wastes. Reverberatory and blast furnaces used in smelting account for most of the lead emissions. Other emissions include oxides of sulphur and nitrogen, antimony, arsenic, copper and tin. Smelting emissions can be controlled with a settling and cooling chamber followed by a baghouse. Other air emissions (chiefly H_2SO_4, dirt and lead compounds) are generated during battery breaking. Crushing emits mainly dusts.

The solid-phase wastes produced during secondary processing include dust and slag. The latter is generated from smelting.

Zinc Processing

Zinc is the fourth most widely used metal after iron, aluminium and copper (lead is fifth). Most zinc is used in metal form and some is used in compound form. Zinc metal is used for galvinizing (i.e., protection against corrosion) steel and for alloys, and is used in the automotive, construction, electrical and machinery sectors. Zinc compounds are used in the agricultural, chemical, paint, pharmaceutical and rubber sectors.

Primary Processing

The first step involves the reduction of zinc concentrates to metal either pyrometallurgically by distillation or hydrometallurgically by electrowinning. Hydrometallurgical refining is more common and popular than pyrometallurgical. Hydrometallurgic refining uses four processing stages, calcining, leaching, purification and electrowinning. Calcining (roasting) removes sulphur, forming leachable zinc oxide. Roasting at high temperature converts zinc sulphide concentrate to impure zinc oxide called 'calcine'. Calcining begins with the mixing of zinc-containing materials with coal. This mixture is then heated (roasted) to vapourise the zinc oxide which is then moved out of the reaction chamber with the resulting gas stream. The gas stream is directed to the baghouse (filter) area where the zinc oxide is captured in baghouse dust. Multiple hearth, suspension and fluidized bed roasters are used for calcining (roasting).

Electrolytic processing of desulphurized calcine involves leaching, purification, and electrolysis. Leaching means the dissolution of the captured calcine in a solution of H_2SO_4 to form a zinc sulphate solution. The latter is purified in large agitation tanks by adding zinc dust. The solution is purified as the dust forces deleterious elements to precipitate so that they can be filtered out. The elements recovered during purification include copper as a cake and cadmium as a metal. Electrowinning in an electrolytic cell involves running an electric current from a lead-silver alloy anode through the aqueous zinc solution. This charges the suspended zinc, forcing it to deposit onto an aluminium cathode immersed in the solution. The zinc-coated cathodes are removed and rinsed, and the zinc is mechanically stripped from the aluminium plates. The zinc concentrate is then melted and cast into ingots which can be even 99 per cent pure.

Much SO_2 is generated during the primary zinc refining process. Its concentrations in the off-gas vary with the type of roaster operation. Typical concentrations for multiple hearth, suspension and fluidized bed roasters are 4.5–6.5 per cent, 10–13 per cent and 7–12 per cent respectively. This SO_2 can be converted into H_2SO_4.

Primary zinc processing operations create air emissions, process wastes and other solid-phase wastes. Air emissions come from roasting, which accounts for over 90 per cent of the potential SO_2 emissions. Up to 97 per cent of the sulphur in the feed is emitted as sulphur oxides. SO_2 emissions from the roasting process are recovered at on-site H_2SO_4 plants. Much of the particulate emitted from primary zinc facilities also comes from roasters.

Wastewaters are generated during the leaching, purification and electrowinning stages when electrolyte and acid solutions become too contaminated to be reused again. This waste water has to be treated before discharge. Solid wastes, some hazardous, appear at various stages in primary zinc processing.

Secondary Processing

The secondary processes use scrap metals for recovering zinc as zinc slabs, zinc oxide or zinc dust. Zinc recovery involves pretreatment, melting and refining. Secondary recovery begins with the separation of zinc-containing metals from other materials, usually by magnetics, sink-float or hand sorting.

Mostly, the zinc materials recovered from secondary materials such as slab zinc, alloys, dusts and compounds are qualitatively similar to primary products.

Secondary processing creates air emissions and solid-phase wastes. Air emissions include particulates, zinc fumes, other volatile metals, flux fumes, and smoke generated by the incomplete combustion of grease, rubber and plastics in scrap. Substantial emissions come from incomplete combustion of carbonaceous material in the zinc scrap and are controlled by afterburners. Particulate emissions are usually recovered by fabric filters.

Slags containing hazardous metals such as copper, aluminium, iron and lead are also generated.

Constraints and Incentives

Industrial ecology cannot be studied and optimized in isolation from human institutions of various kinds that promote or constrain some materials or energy flows.

Legal constraints to industrial ecology were discussed by Henrichs (1992). Regulations based on incentives rather than on sanctions have proven to be the most effective. Also, such legal approaches are far easier to change as knowledge changes than are those that dictate every detail of the industrial process they seek to regulate.

According to Speth (1992), solution to today's environmental problems lie mostly outside the established 'environmental sector'. Industrial ecology requires not only fresh approaches to technology, but also institutional innovations in management.

General Characteristics of Industrial Ecology

1. It is proactive, not reactive. It is initiated and promoted by industrial concerns because it is in their own interest, not because it is imposed by external factors.
2. It is designed-in, not added-on. Many aspects of material flows are defined by decisions taken early in the design process and optimization of industrial ecology requires every product and process designer and every manufacturing engineer to view industrial ecology with the same intensity that is brought to bear on product quality or manufacturability.
3. It is flexible, not rigid.
4. It is encompassing, not insular. It calls for approaches that not only cross industrial sectors, but national and cultural boundaries as well.

Taxonomy of Advanced Materials

Advanced metal alloys are generated by manipulating defects in the crystalline structure so as to produce desirable properties in terms of ductility, low brittleness, and performance at high temperature vibration and corrosive environments like in aircraft engine applications.

Most research and development of advanced metals has been guided by the increasingly stringent requirements for high temperature performance as producers are striving for higher energy efficiency in aerospace. New alloy developments and new advanced processing techniques for cost-competitive metal production have also responded to demands for higher performance materials coming from other industries such as oil companies drilling in deeper and hostile environments and the chemical processing industry's search for improved process efficiency and corrosion resistance.

A search is on for new cost-effective high temperature stainless steel alloys. Duplex stainless steels have been improved and are used increasingly in severe corrosion environments and in chemical processing.

High-strength Low Alloy Steels

High-strength Low Alloy (HSLA) steels are sophisticated mass produced materials used in the construction of ships, oil platforms and cranes by adding miniscule amounts of at least two metallic (such as niobium, aluminium, titanium, vanadium) and two non-metallic (such as carbon and nitrogen) components to the iron elements during hot rolling. A very fine grain structure is produced, conducive to high and good wearability. The extremely fine and stable distribution of tiny particles 'nanoparticles' (about 50 atoms in diameter) prevent grain coarsening during heat treatment as in welding. This fine grain structure is effectively pinned down by carbide or nitrite particles of high strength and fracture toughness (Easterling, 1988).

HSLA steels provide various opportunities for developing countries with existing or planned steel capacity such as more effective utilization of existing equipment capacity, production without licensing agreements, added value for production, upgrading of local engineering standards, import substitution of costly heat-treated alloy steels and improved competitiveness in world export markets.

Superalloys

Advanced metals have generally been aimed at high-temperature and extreme condition applications. Superalloys are nickel-based materials developed for just such uses. Nickel is melted down and mixed with aluminium and small amounts of chromium to impart anti-corrosive properties, and other metals such as titanium and tungsten for hardening. The superalloy is then cooled to form a gamma-phase nickel-aluminium, and then further cooled in its solid state (Kaounides, 1989).

Superalloys have made much of modern high temperature engineering possible. They form essential components of the gas turbines that power jet aeroplanes. It is these engines that have provided the technological pull for the development of superalloys. Besides use in gas turbines, they serve in rocket engines and spacecraft, nuclear reactors, submarines, steam power plants, petrochemical equipment and corrosion-resistant applications.

Advanced Ceramics

Advanced ceramics show distinct advantages over metals or some plastics in a number of demanding applications because of their density, resistance to stress, corrosive properties and high-temperature operational ability. They comprise a large number of materials derived from the oxides, nitrides and carbides of silicon, aluminium, titanium and zirconium, which are processed or consolidated at high temperatures. These inorganic and non-metallic advanced materials have been developed in response to needs arising from specific industrial and high-technology applications as summarized below:

1. **Electronics** Advanced ceramics are used in integrated circuit (IC) packages, capacitors and resistors, and have enormous potential in the high growth market of electronic components. Another application is in integrated optics which will play a revolutionary role in fibre-optics communications systems, the major telecommunication technology. They will be increasingly used in sensors in robotics, cars, automation, medical implants (bioceramics) and other industrial and consumer applications.

2. **Engines** An important structural application in the form of silicon nitrite, silicon carbide and zirconia is in gas turbines, diesel and gasoline engines.
3. **Cutting tools and machine parts** Tools made from advanced ceramics show distinct advantages over metallic counterparts, facilitating higher speed, cost reduction and enhanced productivity gains.
4. **Industrial products** Their resistance to corrosion and erosion has won new applications in the metals industries, chemical processing, oil and gas industries and precision jigs in the manufacture of electronic components.
5. **Consumer products** In Japan, advanced ceramics are used in sporting equipment, scissors, knives and other consumer products.
6. **Energy** Applications of advanced ceramics in this sector include batteries, fuel cells and solar collectors.
7. **Space, aerospace and defence** Heatshields and tiles for space missions and re-entry vehicles, infrared windows, armour and military engines, etc.

Advanced ceramics possess properties that make them superior for many high-temperature, high stress or corrosive applications which subject materials to intense wear and heat. They can be lighter than metals, thus offering energy saving potential. Their use may offer cost advantages to the user industry via process and product redesign. Overall systems costs taking into account integrated design, fabrication, installation and life cycle costs would render advanced ceramics competitive with conventional materials and metals in many applications (Table 7.10).

The use of advanced ceramics in industrial processes could result in dramatic gains in fuel efficiency, permitting the raising of their maximum operating temperatures. Tremendous gain can accrue in terms of engineering efficiency, higher productivity and lower costs in a multitude of industrial applications.

Table 7.10 Some Properties of Advanced Ceramics (After Kaounides, 1989)

Advantages		
High melting point	Wear and corrosion resistance	Ion-conductor properties
High stiffness	Low density (light weight)	Magnetic properties
High hot strength	Good dielectric properties	Biocompatibility
High compressive strength	Thermal/Electrical insulators	
High hardness	Semiconductor properties	
Disadvantages		
Susceptibility to thermal and mechanical shock (brittle)	Poor reproducibility	High cost
Difficulty in fabrication		

Commercialization Barriers

The major problems preventing widespread use and diffusion of advanced ceramics are the poor manufacturing techniques and their brittleness. Ceramic materials are very susceptible to small flaws such as cracks, voids and inclusions. Flaws can occur at any stage of the multistage fabrication process from power production, power conditioning, shaping and designing, and cannot be corrected at later stages. In fact flaws will always exist in ceramic parts, whose design therefore becomes a statistical process as compared to metals in which it is a deterministic process. It is important to identify those conditions in the early processing stages that create defective products and to detect critical flaws in the fine powder itself. Another method to reduce the probability of failure is to design the microstructure of the materials so as to increase resistance to fracture (increasing toughness), through a refinement of the polycrystalline grain size and shape, transformation toughening and composite reinforcement.

Another major problem is the difficulties encountered in their additive manufacturing processes. A central need in designing such materials is to consolidate as many components as possible into a single structure. This is because finishing and fabricating are extremely difficult in view of the hardness of the material. Hence, the aim of design and fabrication is always near-net-shape processing so as to produce a final product that requires very little machining.

Engineering Plastics

Polymers (Baer, 1986), commonly called 'plastics', are organically-derived and synthesized materials that can be moulded at high temperatures and will then retain their shape when cooled. 'Commodity' plastics such as polyethylene, polystyrene and polyvinyl chloride (PVC) have formed the backbone of a large and growing plastics industry for the last few decades. Commodity plastics are high volume, low cost materials in contrast to the modern engineering polymers or plastics which have low-volume output and high-unit value.

Engineering or high-performance plastics possess exceptional strength and/or heat resistance in comparison with commodity plastics, and are increasingly used in automobiles, aircraft and many other applications. They include polyphenylene oxide, polyethylene terephthalate, polyacetal and alloys and blends of these polymers. Performance polymers with decomposition temperature as high as 350°C include fluoropolymers, polyarylate, polyetherketone and others. Such materials can be reinforced with a variety of fibres to form polymer matrix composites with applications in both exterior and interior component of aircraft, automobiles and other structural applications with high expected growth rates.

Thermoplastics can be repeatedly resoftened and rehardened. Resins are organic liquids or solids that are plastic materials which can be used to build more complex plastic compounds.

The major plastics producers are large oil companies since the principal raw materials for plastics are petrochemicals derived from petroleum.

Polymer science can now tailor-make polymer molecules. The latter are made from smaller units called 'monomers'. The way monomers are chosen and assembled determines the properties of the bulk material which comprises them. The polymers so structured or engineered can then be tailored via processing on a larger scale, like a metal or a composite and given a desired microstructure.

The shape of the polymer molecule and its chemical make-up affect the properties of the bulk material. And by varying the characteristics of polymer chains one can create a desired microstructure. Polymer matrix composites imitate the structures of biological tissues or cells. Biology has pointed the way to design polymers as systems for particular use, where polymers in the 21st Century will not be used as monolithic materials, but as materials systems in complex and delicately structured combinations of materials.

Composite Materials

Advanced composite materials may be used in situations where extreme performance requirements cannot be met individually by monolithic materials. As they can be tailored to meet specific need, they are likely to become the main structural materials of the future, displacing monolithic materials from many applications (Fig. 7.12).

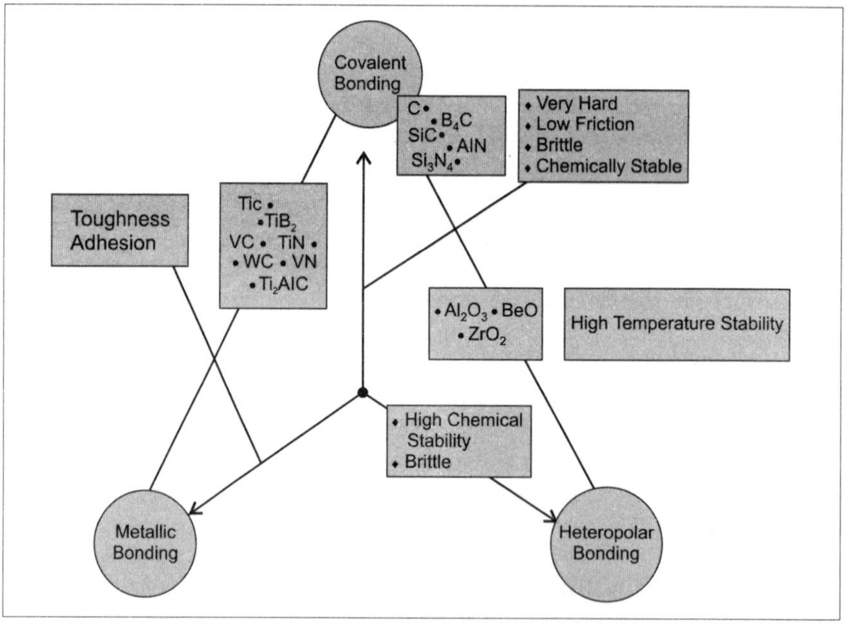

Fig. 7.12 Some advanced composite materials and their properties

Composites make it possible to synergistically combine materials so as to take advantage of the enhancement properties of fibres. For this, the fibres are embedded in a matrix of another material, so that the latter binds and protects the former. The reinforcing material contributes the main characteristics in terms of strength and stiffness but the matrix also affects the properties such as heat and electrical conductivity. The determinant of matrix material choice is the temperature to which the material will be exposed in use.

Engineering design is being transformed because of the degree of control over properties that can be achieved in composite design. The design of a component and of the material are now a unified simultaneous process. Material scientists can tailor the microstructure of a composite according to the distribution of stresses it will be subjected to. Moreover, it is the ability to tailor that distinguishes composites from other materials and can therefore lead them to dominate the materials market.

Polymer Recycling

The disposal of trash is a serious problem as the available landfills are becoming exhausted. While polymers compose only about 80 per cent by weight (20% by volume) of landfills, there is much focus on polymer accumulation because of their high visibility. This has stimulated the formulation of considerable restrictive legislation regulating polymer use. A response has been the consideration of alternatives for polymer disposal. The principal means are source reduction, incineration, bio or photodegradation, composting and recycling (Stein, 1992).

Source Reduction

Elimination of unnecessary packaging and the packaging of products as concentrates is one approach. Another is the replacement of polymers by alternative materials. The replacement is not always ecologically desirable and is sometimes functionally inadequate. The abandonment of plastic in packaging can result in a great increase in the weight of waste, energy consumption in making the alternatives, and in cost (Association of the Plastic Products Industry, 1987). Alternative materials are sometimes heavier, more permeable, more water absorbent and weaker than their polymer counterparts, and so may not function as well. For example, the replacement of synthetic fibres such as nylon and Dacron with "natural degradable" fibres like cotton and wool. A proper analysis of the ecological effect would require consideration of the agricultural implications of growing the required amount of cotton and raising the sheep, the fertilizer needed the fuel for the tractors, differences in energy requirements for processing, and differences in the care required for maintenance and laundering. The choice is indeed not simple (Stein, 1992).

Incineration

Incineration is widely used in Asia. It releases toxic fumes and ash. These problems may be avoided through use of current technology in incinerator design and by employing some degree of separation of feedstock.

A polymer of concern for incineration is PVC where hydrochloric acid can be produced with improper incineration. A main product of incineration is CO_2, which contributes to global warming. However, since a relatively small fraction of the petroleum supply is used to produce polymers and only a fraction of that would be incinerated, this source should not be a major factor in comparison with CO_2 production arising from the burning of fossil fuels.

Bio and Photodegradation

There is skepticism as to whether the employment of degradable polymers can reduce the buildup of landfills. Usually, degradation rates in landfills are low. Modification of polymers so as to increase degradation rates often leads to the problem of their degrading under normal conditions of use. Furthermore, degradation is in opposition to possibilities for future recycling of the polymers. A usual product of degradation is CO_2, so it parallels incineration in this respect (without the advantage of possible energy recovery).

There is a definite role for degradable polymers. One should distinguish between intrinsically degradable polymers and those to which a degradable material is added. An example of the latter type is polyethylene to which starch has been added. The polymers do not disappear on degradation of the additive, but just fall apart into small bits. This may have cosmetic value or may serve to release the contents of a plastic bag to exposure for composting, but it is not a means for disposal of polymers.

Intrinsically degradable polymers include polylactic acid and bacterially synthesized polyalkonates. These convert completely to nonpolymeric products on degradation. The principal drawback is cost. Unless this can be significantly lowered, the use of the class of materials will be limited to specialized applications.

A promising development is the formation of intrinsically biodegradable polymers by the reforming of starch (Starch Research Group, 1991). The starting material is sufficiently cheap that there is hope of producing an economically competitive material. The amount of degradable synthetic polymer in use today is negligible.

Composting

Yard and agricultural waste constitutes a much larger part of the solid waste burden than polymers, and composting seems to be the right approach for these. It is feasible to add biodegradable polymers to the composting mixture. Also cellulosic wastes could be included. Wastes of these types have to be separated from nondegradable material.

Recycling

Recycling implies reuse of the polymer as polymer. Two types of recycling are recycling of industrial scrap (sometime called 'prompt scrap') and post-consumer recycling.

The former involves recovering and reusing waste polymer resulting from processing operations. Recycling of industrial scrap is simpler than the post-consumer recycling as the polymers are usually of particular kind and are collected in a central location. The practice is motivated by economics.

Post-consumer recycling of co-mingled plastics is more difficult. Here, plastics of a variety of types are in the hands of consumers after being used for a variety of purposes. The consumer may be motivated to recycle these articles by monetary rewards or legislation. Citizens can usually separate polymers from nonpolymeric components. If this is not done, some separation may be accomplished after rubbish collection. Polymers normally have lower densities than other components and are usually nonmagnetic and nonconducting. Such separation usually results in co-mingled plastic as opposed to separated. Co-mingled plastics can be fabricated to make articles such as 'plastic lumber', fence posts and traffic barriers.

Milk and water jugs have proved a good source of recyclable high density polyethylene (HDPE). There has been public reluctance toward imposing deposits on these, so their return rate is not as high as for soda bottles. Recycled HDPE cannot be used for food containers.

For other polyethylene sources like shopping bags, the economics of recycling is less favourable. Since the amount of polymer per article is small, the cost of collection represents a greater fraction of the value of the recycled polymer. Where possible, the reuse of such articles should be encouraged. Multiple use of a shopping bag is probably a more effective use of the polymer than would be possible by collection and recycling (Stein, 1992).

Photodegradation is also a viable disposal approach for polyethylene mulch. A similar situation may exist for other recycled polymers. Polypropylene is extensively used industrially and as strapping or binding in agriculture.

For polystyrene also recycling has been successful. Styrofoam is commonly used for coffee cups, hamburger shells, insulation and cafeteria trays. Its recycling is feasible, if sources of ready collection can be identified.

The processing behaviour and product properties of polymers produced from a variable feedstock are often inconsistent and difficult to control. There is need to monitor properties and to modify these by adding virgin polymer to the recycle feedstock (Stein, 1992).

The separation of polymers into constituents often proves difficult. The need for sophisticated separation techniques can be minimized, if recycling is considered in product design. The contribution of polymeric parts of junked automobiles to the solid waste stream is an increasing burden. In cases where there is a combination of polymers that contain nonpolymeric additives, fillers, and reinforcing fibres, the separation is not possible or economically feasible. This source will grow with the increasing use of polymer-based composites in automobiles and housing.

Polymers can be degraded to low molecular weight species by pyrolysis, hydrolysis or methanolysis. This could be done for mixed polymers leading to mixture of low molecular weight materials. These may be of sufficiently low viscosity so that they may be separated from insoluble nonpolymeric additives by filtration. The low molecular weight mixture could be regarded as an organic feedstock which could be separated into components by fractional distillation.

Polymer dissociation is an endothermic process and converts a low-entropy polymer molecule into higher entropy dissociation products. Since energy conservation should deal with conservation of free energy that implies minimizing entropy production, this aspect is ecologically undesirable. However, it is a price to pay for enabling separation (Stein, 1992).

Input-Output Analysis

Industrial metabolism may be conceived as a systems approach to modifying the production, use and disposal of goods to greatly reduce the generation of wastes (Ausubel and Sladovitch, 1989; Frosch and Gallopoulos, 1990). Industrial ecology is intimately related to human ecology because significant reductions in waste will require changes in people's private and social habits, not only in industrial life cycle planning and production (Duchin, 1992).

Reducing waste can simultaneously conserve energy and other materials of mineral and biological origin, save money and reduce pollution. The biosystem analogy also exemplifies a complex system that operates in such a way that wastes are reduced and recycled as the system proceeds to a higher degree of organization. According to Duchin (1992), "Natural systems evolve over long stretches of time, and false starts are weeded out by trial and error. Actual outcomes may be optimal responses to particular narrowly defined problems: but it is not clear what the "optimal" evolution of an entire ecosystem might mean, and there is no mechanism assuring its occurrence. In human affairs social institutions are dominant agents of selection. They also proceed by trial and error and are able to respond optimally to certain problems, especially problems that are narrowly defined and have short-time horizons".

The marketplace is an efficient mechanism for selecting profitable alternatives, but it certainly is not the only relevant institution, the governments can direct the ecologically sound evolution of an economy. Nonetheless, an outcome that goes against the logic of the marketplace is not likely to be sustainable.

Then the challenge to industrial ecology is two-fold:

1. It needs to generate workable concepts and actual methods for reducing wastes and recycling those that are generated.
2. It also needs to include a coherent operational framework for examining potential long-term advantages and disadvantages of alternative webs of industrial changes and identifying the short-term bottlenecks that may emerge.

Industrial ecology can benefit from the long experience with the analysis of industrial interdependence, e.g., operational system-wide frameworks for analysing the interrelationships among production processes and the associated flows of materials.

Structural Economics

Like industrial ecology, structural economics combines old and new ideas to help us understand and tackle current issues including environmental pollution. The differences between structural economics and 'mainstream' economics are mainly differences of emphasis. Structural economics is concerned with a detailed, disaggregated description of an entire economy in terms of its concrete and observable constituent parts and their interrelationships. Prominent among these constituents is the material infrastructure of a society. This includes not only natural objects like soil and those made of bricks and mortar, but also specific technologies and social institutions. Because some of these components are not fundamentally economic objects (unlike prices or interest rates those are the work of the structural economist typically crosses disciplinary borders) (Duchin and Lange, 1991). Structural economists study the material world and are concerned with information and data. These are described and measured in physical units as well as in money values when the latter have meaning.

Structural economics is concerned with structural change and, therefore, with dynamics rather than only, or mainly, with static analysis or with 'equilibrium' states. Interest is typically in the longer term more than the short-term, and the focus on technological and institutional structures provides a firm 'handle' for projecting parameters several decades into the future according to alternative assumptions about structural changes (Duchin, 1992).

Many of the economic mechanisms are the same as in mainstream (or neoclassical) economics, but with one fundamental difference. In neoclassical economic models, a variety of optimization problem are solved simultaneously under a system of constraints that is expected to yield a unique solution. The formal structural economic models, on the other hand, are used so as to yield a set of possible solutions rather than a single optimal one. Within the set, trade-offs are believed to operate that are not reducible to monetary bottom line. In addition, economic feedback mechanisms are generally believed by structural economists to be more complex than the work of neoclassical economists would suggest. A critically important example is the substitution of less expensive for more expensive inputs both in personal consumption and in production. The incorporation of technological information into an input-output database has been developed especially in Japan where the collaboration of engineers with economists is encouraged.

Implications for Industrial Ecology

Raw materials are processed into finished products whose life cycle can end in different ways. The use of the constituent materials can be reduced at the source and materials used can be recovered for reuse in less demanding applications. The following questions need to be posed to economists.

1. How much will it cost to reduce wastes of particular materials?
2. Will the value of the benefits be greater than the cost?

3. Who would end up paying?
4. What financial incentives could be offered that the "optimal" amount of recycling does occur?
5. How would source reduction and recycling be achieved?

This question of "how" has been largely ignored by economists. An economic analysis is generally based on the conviction that individual decision makers have the right to decide for themselves the "how" question, what techniques they will use for production and consumption? The decision makers' ingenuity to seek out the best approach consistent with cost minimization is said to be unleashed if decision makers are provided with incentives, but not constrained by prescriptions. Therefore, the analysis usually focusses on incentives and not on techniques. In this view, the "right" incentives can make it possible to achieve virtually any social objectives. If the prices are right, new techniques will be forthcoming (Leontief and Duchin, 1986; Duchin, 1992).

This reasoning proved fruitful in many contexts, especially those involving adjustments in the economic environment within a relatively unconstrained physical environment. But these mechanisms are not sufficient for tackling unusual problems or practices. The analysis of alternative techniques in their interaction within the economic system can provide valuable input to industrial ecology and can also serve as the basis for the subsequent development of incentive schemes. Once this work has been done, the market mechanisms will do their job. Input-output economics, an important formal model within structural economics, can trace the stocks and flows of energy and other materials from extraction through production and consumption to recycling or disposal. The concept of input-output economics has been extended to address increasingly complex questions, notably the fully dynamic physical/price/income model and the engineering/input-output database. Economists need to be able to assess the costs of cleaning up and to develop incentive schemes to increase the likelihood that this will happen. To do this, they need to address the difficult "how" questions that concern industrial ecologists since the cost and indeed the wider implications of cleaning up depend upon how it is done. Structural economics, modern input-output models and databases, in particular, can help meet this challenge.

The importance of a physical basis for economic analysis becomes clear when one is concerned with alternative arrangements for the handling of materials and their effects on the environment. However, the advantages of asking the "how" outcomes should allow a more realistic assessment of production alternatives more generally.

8
Energy Use and Industrial Ecology

Industrial ecology is concerned with the relationship among economic activities, society and nature, through the application of ecological principles to contemporary society while treating society as an ecosystem having a defined boundary, inputs, outputs, components, regulators, internal flows, transformations and feedbacks of energy and materials. This new multidisciplinary area has recently aroused much interest in view of its utility in addressing the problem of how to restore the balance between society and nature (Penny, 2003).

Over the millennia human beings have developed the capacity to control energy and matter to create modified ecosystems such as cities and farms so as to support their cultural and metabolic needs and desires. With increasing population and growing civilization, societies have increasingly diverted energy and materials away from their natural organization. Also the ecological services of natural ecosystems have been diverted toward technical activities that stabilize society. This has benefitted the society, but has given rise to environmental problems that are increasingly manifesting themselves as economic and social costs and have been exerting a cumulative impact on global environmental change. The pertinent principle is that we do not consume energy, but rather transform high-grade energy into waste heat i.e., dissipated into the environment (Penny, 2003). We do not consume resources but alter the organization of matter, relocating and rearranging it and discarding some parts of it into the environment—parts which may not be of immediate use to us. According to the first law of thermodynamics (the law on conservation of energy), we consume states of order, not matter. This law postulates that energy can be transformed from one form into another, but it can neither be created nor destroyed. For instance, the chemical energy in petrol is converted into kinetic energy of motion, heat energy, sound energy and potential energy in a motor vehicle. However, the potential for each subsequent form of energy to do work is not the same as at the start of the process. This is enunciated in the second law of thermodynamics (the entropy law) according to which all processes proceed in such a way that the availability of energy decreases or entropy (disorder or chaos) increases. Humans prevent society from falling into chaos and disorder by applying more and more energy to maintaining the structures which allow desired functions to occur (Penny, 2003).

The relationship between society and environment is sometimes described as existing in a state of (thermo) dynamic equilibrium (Fig. 8.1). Increasingly, however,

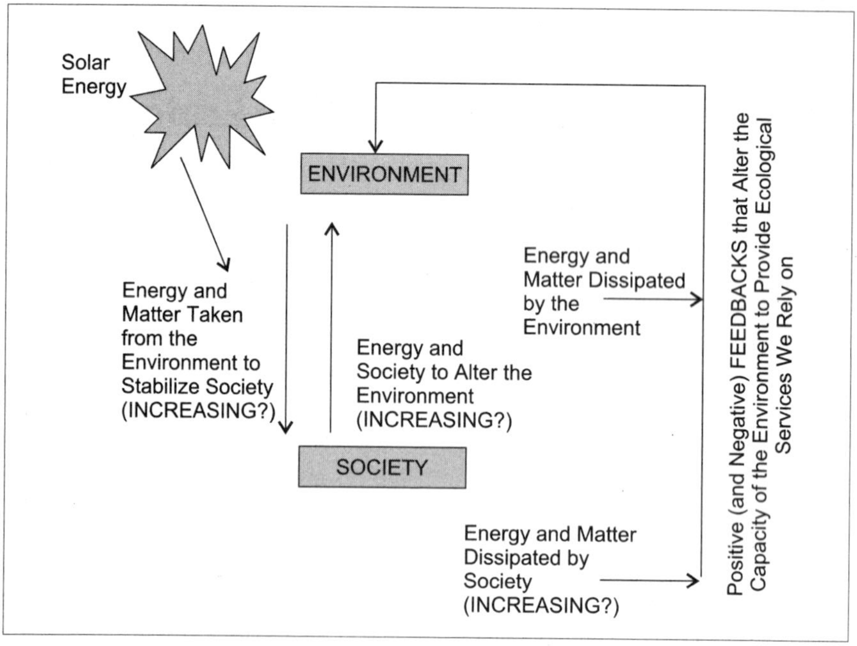

Fig. 8.1 Society and environment in a state of (thermo) dynamic equilibrium (After Penny, 2003)

energy and matter imbalances between society and nature have been causing marked environmental changes. As our natural capital consisting of renewable and non-renewable resources and ecological services is transferred to social capital (e.g., knowledge, skills, organizational and adaptive capacity) and economic capital (like wealth generated through economic activity), the environment becomes more and more unstable by losing its capacity to fight entropy (chaos) as per the second law of thermodynamics. Humans now dissipate so much energy and disorganized matter into the environment that they undermine the capacity of the global environment to maintain the state of order needed to produce the ecological services upon which we depend for our basic needs. A positive-feedback energy and materials cycle between society and nature has emerged, which is strongly unsustainable in view of the fact that the two systems are evolving at different speeds, creating a grave problem for the society.

We will have to address this positive feedback cycle, if we wish to prevent a new equilibrium with reduced social, economic and natural capital. This is possible only by making sacrifices and by effecting changes both to our current energy generation and use, and in associated changes to industrial processes and resources consumption patterns. Such changes account for the effects and byproducts of all processes and how they provide feedback to modify states of order in the environment and society. Industrial ecology may prove helpful in this endeavour—ecological sustainability of living systems (including societies and agricultural ecosystems) is related not only to their compatibility with surrounding environment but also to their ability to maintain their organized pattern in the face of changing environmental conditions. One example of estimating the ecological sustainability of changing agricultural land-use systems is shown in Fig. 8.2.

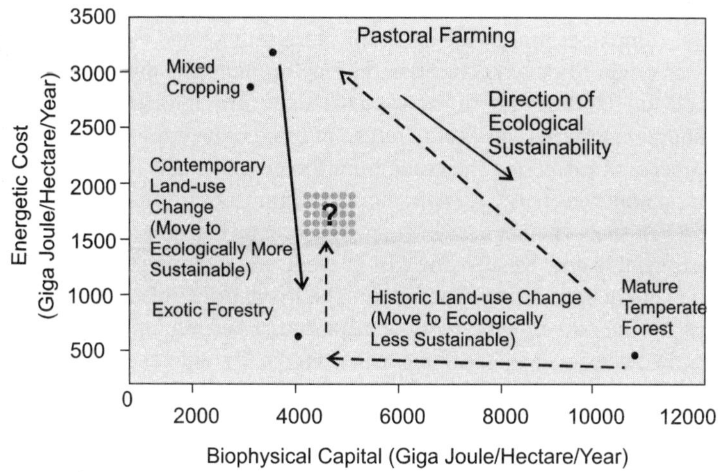

Fig. 8.2 Measuring the ecological sustainability of land-use change in the Gisborne Region (After Penny, 2003).

Global demand for energy is growing and is expected to be 50 per cent higher by 2030 than it is today, it is likely to be met largely by fossil fuels for some years. This spells rising greenhouse emissions and increasing competition for energy resources, which has ominous implications for both climate change as well as security of supply.

According to S D Freeman, one-time advisor to American Presidents Johnson, Nixon and Jimmy Carter, continued heavy use of fossil fuels and nuclear power is almost sure to cause havoc and destruction of the high-energy civilization we cherish. The worrying problem about fossil fuels is that in the very near future there could be no security of supply, in view of their impending scarcity.

Without doubt, oil has already peaked. Less and less crude is being found, and known deposits have been exaggerated. Price is hovering around US $100 a barrel. It is really peak oil that is behind the car wheel. Peak oil pushes the rise in price. Demand does not matter. We are in the very beginning of entering a new era. Some experts warn that the export capacity of OPEC, Russia and Mexico will drop by 2.5 million barrels per day by the end of this decade. According to J Rubin, domestic demand growth of as much as five per cent per year in key oil-producing countries is already beginning to cannibalize exports and will increasingly do so in the future as:

production plateaus or declines in many of these counties. "OPEC members, together with independent producers such as Russia and Mexico, consume over 12 million barrels per day, surpassing western Europe to become the second largest oil market in the world."

If current rates of domestic consumption continue, the future export capacity of OPEC, Russia and Mexico will certainly become questionable. These chilling trends could even sharply escalate world oil prices in the next few years.

As oil companies search the earth for more remote and ever more expensive reserves of crude, they also consider the environmentally devastating option of making oil for fuel from tar sands and coal shale. The industry's own optimistic figures show that there is an energy return of three units out for every one unit in, for the process of extracting the crude from the tar and shale alone. And if we also take into account the energy used in mining and transportation, the true return will at best be half that—the net gain in energy is perhaps just half a unit. This alchemy could prove viable only because the cost of crude will continue to rise.

Oil is chiefly used for transportation. The likely price-hike will hit the pumps and push up the cost of everything transported, wherever transported. If supply suddenly becomes scarce, rationing will have to be enforced. An International Energy Agency (IEA) Conference on "Cutting Oil Use in a Hurry" concluded in 2005. "The future is emergency rationing, tele-working and car-pooling. Besides these, the oil crisis will also push up the cost of food production. Oil has been food since the 'Green Revolution'—oil, in the form of petro-chemical fertilizer, increased crop yields. Today we depend on these oil-based yields, but they may vanish in the years to come" (Hughes and Anslow, 2007).

Natural gas also has peaked like oil. We are using more than we are generating. As per the most optimistic forecasts, we may rely on supplies for about 130 years on current rates of global usage. However, being the cleanest of all fossil fuels, the US has seen its domestic supplies peak, global demand has skyrocketed, and its long-term availability may well be only half that. The IEA recently warned that 'there are prospects of even tighter natural gas markets at the turn of the decade'.

Then, coal may be the last fossil-fuel source. 'Clean coal' is a nice phrase, but in reality, coal is not clean. Rather, the CO_2 from burning coal is removed from the exhaust gases in the process of carbon capture and storage or Zero Emissions Technology (ZET). Once the emissions are captured, the carbon is either piped or transported by tanker to some pump station where it is driven under pressure to some exhausted oil well. The east coast of USA has several such wells. However, the 132 coal plants currently planned for America are in the mid-west and none has this technology installed yet. Furthermore, there is a fundamental issue about the viability of CCS: How to police it? How to calculate emissions where production is not constant? How best to ensure that it is tankered and delivered, especially in times of energy shortages? (Hughes and Anslow 2007).

Coal deposits only look attractive when compared to the dwindling supplies of oil and gas. From what little is known about mechanism of producing clean coal, the process reduces its efficiency as a powder generator, further reducing its prospective long-term viability. Considered on its own, coal can only be a crutch to maintain our current way of life for only a few more years.

Energy Wastage and Energy Poverty

The two outstanding energy challenges of today are energy waste and energy poverty. Prevailing waste patterns of over one and a half century of industrialization have resulted in unhealthy air, water and soil, climate-changing greenhouse gas (GHG) emissions, and losses from inefficient fuel conversion, transmission, distribution and end-use (LaRocco, 2003). The task of providing sufficient energy to people who live in energy poverty has become daunting and difficult. As about 1.6 billion people in the world today do not have access to electricity and 2.4 billion depend on traditional fuels for cooking (IEA, 2002). One effective way to tackle this challenging task of eradicating energy poverty and ending energy waste is to tap the potential of Small and Medium-sized Enterprises (SMEs). SME initiatives offer a very effective means to tackle energy waste and energy poverty but it is unfortunate that this has been widely ignored. Modern civilization is an energy guzzler. It uses energy to reduce threats to health and environment, and energy is an essential ingredient of quality of life (QOL) improvements for the poorest people. Energy poverty interconnects the issues of environment, development and QOL (LaRocco, 2003).

Clini and Moody-Stuart (2001) made an energy assessment to suggest a strategy for eliminating both energy waste and energy scarcity. They suggested a target of providing clean energy to 800 million people over 10 years (non-electricity improvements for 200 million people, off-grid electricity for 300 million, and on-grid clean energy for another 300 million).

SMEs are the untapped resource that needs to be brought to centrestage, if the energy provision target is to be met. They can make this target practical, through people and institutions combining resources and experience (LaRocco, 2003).

LaRocco (2003) proposed an enterprise-centred model of modern energy production and use those which are market-driven and technology-neutral. The key characteristics of the enterprise-centered model are:

- Technologically neutral (within the broad category of clean energy, technology choices are driven by local market conditions)
- Specialized intermediary organizations provide services and capital to entrepreneurs before and after investments are made
- Implementation partnerships tackle policy, sustainability and expansion issues
- Local presence assures hands-on implementation
- Tools and training cost-effectively identify entrepreneurs, enabling them to frame a business plan or investment proposal at their own pace

Consumer finance is critical to eliminating energy poverty. Many households could afford modern energy today, if they are able to finance it over periods ranging from a few months to a few years. It is a dangerous myth to assume that poor cannot afford modern energy. They already paid heavily in time, health and cash for dirty, dangerous and inefficient energy sources (e.g., generators which emit toxic fumes).

Undoubtedly, SMEs represent a largely ignored but potentially potent instrument to tackle the twin problems of energy waste and energy poverty. Working with specialized intermediaries, they constitute the linchpin that connects the objectives of funders, policy makers and large corporations with the hundreds of millions of citizen customers who can benefit from the elimination of energy waste and energy poverty (LaRocco, 2003).

Alternative Energy Technologies and Materials

Modern lifestyles based on high mobility, prosperity and comfort demand a steady and assured supply of energy. But this energy security cannot be taken for granted. Energy sources are usually divided into three main categories. The first is chemical or photophysical energy that relies on oxidizing some reduced substance, usually a hydrocarbon, or absorbing sunlight to generate either heat or electricity (Dresselhaus and Thomas, 2001). The energy involved here is that of a chemical bond or fraction of an electron volt (eV). The second comes from nuclear reactions that release energy

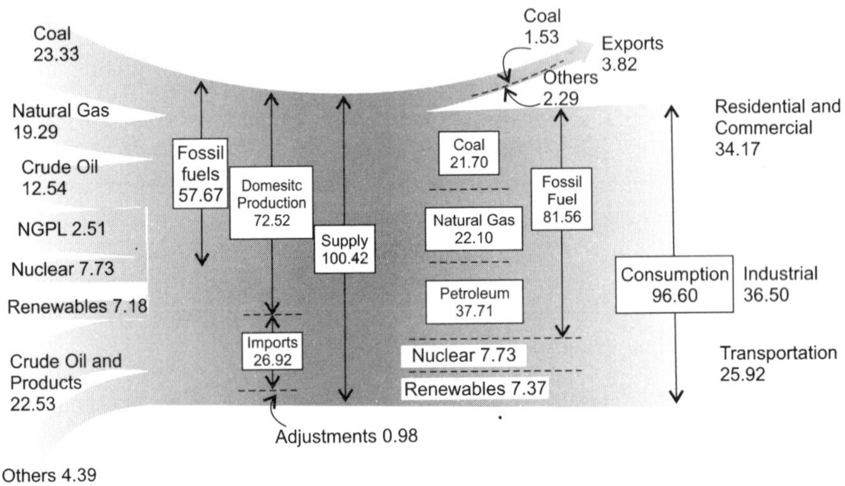

Source: Nature 414: 332, 2001

Fig. 8.3 Energy flow diagram of the United States for 1999, in quads (1 quad = 10^{15} British thermal units = 2.9 x 10^{11} kWh). The average energy consumption in the United States is 0.4 x 10^{-6} quads/person/year, and the US population is about 5% of that on the planet Earth. The energy consumption is large as compared to the food consumption (1.2 x 10^4 kJ/day/person, which translates to only 0.4 x 10^{-8} quads/person/year). Some corresponding numbers for world energy consumption for 1999, in quads, are: Petroleum 149.7; Natural gas 87.3; Coal 84.9; Nuclear 25.2; Hydro, Geothermal, Solar, Wind and other renewables 29.9; Total world energy production is 377.1 quads (After EIA, 2000 and 2001)

either by splitting heavy nuclei or by fusing light nuclei. This energy is in the region of 10^6 eV (i.e., 1 mega electron volt, MeV) per nuclear reaction. The third type is thermomechanical as wind, water or geological sources of steam or hot water. This type of energy is in the milli electron volt (meV) region e.g., water falling from many metres. The current usage of the various energy sources is illustrated in Fig. 8.3.

Each energy source has some undesirable characteristics. Any process using fossil fuels produces CO_2 and possibly also some other contaminants e.g., NOx, SOx and ash. Nuclear plants make radioactive fission products. Hydroelectric plants require dams or large lakes. Solar energy and wind energy require large areas and suffer from geographical limitations. Geothermal sources occur at only a few locations.

Currently, most of the world's energy supply comes from fossil and nuclear sources. As these sources will continue to be important in providing energy worldwide at least for the coming few generations, it is crucial to tackle the issue of CO_2 sequestration now, while also keeping the nuclear energy option open. But to meet increasing global demands for energy, it is also important to develop alternative clean energy sources, which do not depend on fossil fuels and have a fairly significant environmental impact. Grätzel (2001), Steele and Heinzel (2001), Tarascon and Armand (2001), Schlapbach and Züttel (2001), and Larbalestier (2001) have reviewed the current status of several such sources. Renewable means of producing and storing electricity are likely to acquire greater importance in the coming years, and in view of the recent progress in condensed-matter physics and materials technology could well compete with existing technologies. For technologies using renewable energy sources, notable advances are taking place in the fields of fuel cells and solar cells. To use renewable sources effectively, dependable ways of storing energy (e.g., hydrogen storage) are required.

Fossil Energy

Supplies of fossil fuels are finite, at present there is no shortage of fossil fuels. While world reserves of oil are about 1.6×10^{14} litres (1×10^{12} barrels), world consumption is about 1.2×10^{10} litres/day. World reserves of natural gas are about 1.4×10^{14} m^3, gross production of gas is about 2.4×10^{12} m^3 per year. World coal reserves are about 9.1×10^{11} tonnes, and annual consumption is about 4.5×10^9 tonnes per year (Dresselhaus and Thomas, 2001). The chief problems with fossil fuels for the near term are distribution and recovery.

All fossil fuels produce CO_2—natural gas the least, coal the most. For example, the CO_2 can be sequestered by storing it as a gas or in solution underground or in the deep ocean, but high costs are involved in the energy expended in pumping the CO_2 from where it is produced to where it is going to be stored.

Electric cars represent one approach to reducing undesirable emissions from conventional internal combustion engines in densely populated places. Since about two-thirds of the world's total electric power is generated from fossil fuels, electric cars ultimately consume mostly fossil fuels. But it is possible to produce electricity in areas of low population density. It can be generated from sources such as hydroelectric and nuclear energy that do not produce GHGs (Dresselhaus and Thomas, 2001). The major problem with electric cars relates to the storage of electric power. There is no battery that has the energy density of petrol, and battery recharging is much slower than filling a petrol tank. The lifetime of batteries need to be increased and much lighter and non-toxic battery materials should be found to replace lead. A novel concept now being tested is a hybrid vehicle with a small and highly efficient petrol engine to recharge its batteries and to drive the vehicle after the electric motor has accelerated it. Work is underway to develop better catalytic converters for removing toxic chemicals from automobile exhausts while optimizing fuel efficiency. Even highly efficient engines produce oxides of nitrogen and carbon monoxide and require the use of catalytic converters.

Nuclear Energy

In the United States, nuclear energy has traditionally been produced by fission which does not emit any CO_2, and from the standpoint of global warming, nuclear energy provides an ideal source. But the public has genuine fears of nuclear energy. Reactors must be made safe and the nuclear waste must be disposed of safely.

Fusion is another nuclear process that could potentially generate much power. It is basically a physics problem but the engineering challenges are substantial. Fusion reactors using magnetic confinement technology as currently contemplated may use a mixture of deuterium and tritium as fuel. Tritium is formed by bombarding lithium (either ^{6}Li or ^{7}Li) with a neutron to yield tritium (T) and a-particle (^{4}He), it would need to be recovered and injected into the plasma (Dresselhaus and Thomas, 2001). Some difficult materials problems relating to radiation damage on exposure of the materials to the energetic plasma will have to be addressed before fusion energy is harnessed.

Solar Energy

Our world (especially the tropical countries) is blessed with abundance of sunlight. Capturing just some of this solar energy could make a significant contribution to fulfilling the energy requirements of many countries.

Solar thermal technology that produces hot water is highly efficient even in northern climates. Modern versions using evacuated glass tubes can supply a substantial amount of domestic hot-water needs.

Solar photovoltaic panels generate electricity but are quite costly both financially and in respect of the heat energy used to melt the silicon in the cells. But this may change with the commercialization of 'thin-film' photovoltaics that use conducting chemicals which can be 'sprayed or 'printed' onto glass or plastic backings, thereby avoiding the high-energy processes associated with conventional manufacturing. Unfortunately, these new thin-film technologies depend either on heavy metals like cadmium, or on nanoscale particles such as titanium dioxide molecules or carbon nanotubes. To ensure the efficiency benefits of these technologies, manufacturers need to enforce stringent 'end-of-life' procedures for safely recycling these dangerous compounds.

Concentrating solar power (CSP) is another area where the sun's energy can be very rewarding. It involves focusing solar radiation by means of curved or parabolic reflectors onto specially designed surfaces containing molten salts. These salts are then used for boiling water, driving steam turbines and producing electricity (Hughes and Anslow, 2007). Covering an area of 254 × 254 (km) of Sahara desert with CSP plants could possibly generate power equivalent to the entire world demand for electricity. Using high-voltage DC power transmission would then allow electricity to be transmitted from North Africa to London with no more than about 10 per cent energy loss.

Alternative Energy Sources

With the dwindling supplies of fossil fuel and increasing environmental concern in the coming decades, there is bound to be increasing dependence on energy conservation and alternative energy sources. The most obvious alternative energy source is the sun. When the sun is directly overhead and the sky is clear, radiation on a horizontal surface is about 1,000 Wm^{-2}. Some of this can be captured in the form of solar thermal energy and solar photovoltaics that convert sunlight to electrical energy. Sunlight may be used for heating, lighting and electricity generation, when concentrated, it provides steam to run turbines. The disadvantages of solar energy are the conversion efficiency of sunlight to electric power is low and sunlight varies with time of day, weather conditions and season.

Photovoltaics and photoelectrochemical cells have not so far proved very useful as energy supply because of their low conversion efficiencies and relatively high cost. Research is being done on developing improved materials (Grätzel, 2001). According to Grätzel, it is advisable to use existing roofs as solar collectors because solar roofs tied to a grid may reduce peak daily electricity demand significantly. Also certain multi-junction photoelectric devices have been designed that use III-V compound semiconductors (Wei and Zunger, 1990) to achieve conversion efficiencies of about 30 per cent. Also advances are being made by using novel classes of materials such as films containing nanocrystalline structures, quantum dots and nanostructured conducting polymers. These films typically contain nanoparticles with a size distribution showing a wide range of electronic band gaps and that allow much of the solar spectrum to be captured by the solar cell. Attempts are being made to make such films cheaply.

Fuel cells convert fuel or chemical energy directly to electric energy. The main chemical reactions involve the oxidation of CO_2 and H_2 (Steele and Heinzel, 2001). Fuel cells consist of an anode, cathode and electrolyte. Being expensive, fuel cells have not yet been widely used. To make this technology commercially competitive, better anode, cathode and electrolyte materials and processes are needed. Work is being done on polymeric electrolyte membranes and phosphoric acid fuel cells, both operating under ambient conditions, and the solid oxide and molten carbonate fuel cells, operating at higher temperature. Phosphoric acid fuel cells are commercially available and generate electricity at about 40 per cent efficiency. Polymer or proton-exchange-membrane fuel cells operating at about 90°C are quite suitable for automotive use (Steele and Heinzel, 2001).

If hydrogen could be stored well, then hydrogen-based fuel cells would be much more promising. Hydrogen is currently made by steam reforming of hydrocarbons. It can also be made by heating coal to about 1000°C in the absence of oxygen, by partial burning of coal in the presence of steam or by electrolysis (Dresselhaus and Thomas, 2001). The reactions with coal yield H_2, CO, CO_2 and other gases, which need to be separated from hydrogen. Production of CO_2 can be avoided only if the electricity is generated from nuclear, hydroelectric, wind, solar or geothermal energy. There is some potential for photochemical production of hydrogen, using sunlight to dissociate water (Grätzel, 2001). Also microbial pathways for the production of hydrogen are being considered.

Hydrogen is attractive as a fuel, but its storage is problematic (Schlapbach and Züttel, 2001). Use of carbon nanotubes as a storage medium, making use of their high surface area and light weight may be an option but reversible hydrogen storage may be achieved in carbon nanotubes under reasonable operating conditions. According to them, light weight metal alloy hydrides are the most promising materials for hydrogen storage.

One commercially successful recent alternative energy storage technology is the rechargeable lithium-ion battery, being used widely in portable computer and telecommunication devices. Demand and competition is driving the search for higher storage capacity, longer operating times and faster recharging times. According to Tarascon and Armand (2001) three areas of opportunity (also common to most of the other alternative energy technologies) are: advances in nanostructured materials providing a chance to improve both anode and cathode performance, new *in situ* characterization techniques helping in identifying materials problems in a format that permits rapid assessment of possible solutions and advanced computer simulation modelling promising rapid progress in surveying new combinations of materials and geometries (Tarascon and Armand, 2001; Dresselhaus and Thomas, 2001).

To optimize any alternate energy technology, improvements need to be made in energy storage and energy transmission. Superconductors may possibly perform both these roles. For superconducting magnetic energy storage (SMEs), electric energy is stored by circulating a current in a superconducting coil. As there are no resistive losses, the current persists indefinitely. The efficiency of charging and discharging is very high because no energy conversion is involved. For the same reason SMEs responds rapidly, the only limitation being the time required for conversion between DC and AC power. SMEs can also be used for load levelling and for frequency and voltage control, which are expected to be the first applications of this technology.

Substantial improvements need to be made in materials that are needed to increase efficiency in the generation, conversion, transmission and use of energy. The most effective way to increase fuel economy in automobiles is to lower their weight, so more and more vehicle components are being made of light weight, tough and strong composite materials. Happily, physics, chemistry, biology and engineering research are now meeting at nanoscale. Many of the subcellular components that nature uses to make fuels and composite materials e.g., wood, bone and shell) exist at the nanoscale, including vital enzymes, molecular motors and cell membranes. These living models should inspire assessment of alternative energy sources that are scientifically conceivable, environmentally acceptable and technologically promising (Dresselhaus and Thomas, 2001).

Energy Efficiency

The ways in which energy is captured, stored, allocated and transformed indicate a system's health and sustainability. As an ecosystem develops its energy use per unit biomass is continuously reduced. This energetic cost (Joules/kg/year) is the energy required to sustain the organization of 1 kg of biomass for a year, and is a measure of the ecosystem's internal energy allocation and so its complexity. Ecosystems also tend to maximize their total energy storage (kg/m^2). This is called 'biophysical capital' and is an indicator of the ecosystem's stability—its compatibility with processes sustaining environmental equilibria.

Systems that lack these two development characteristics tend not to survive. On their own, these two measures point to an ecosystem's energetic characteristics. However, when measured over time or when comparisons are made between e.g., different land-uses—these provide valuable insights into an ecosystem's ecological sustainability (Penny, 2003).

Industrial companies use up about 33 per cent of world energy. To assure tomorrow's industrial growth, production patterns need to be changed. Energy efficiency should form a vital part of an overall "cleaner production approach" aimed at preventing pollution at source and reducing the use of raw materials, both in production processes and in products. Such an approach makes good environmental sense as well as good business sense.

Japan succeeded in reducing its industrial energy consumption from 61 per cent of national energy consumption in 1970 to 47 per cent in 1987. Industry in the United States and the European Community accounts for about 33 per cent of the national total. Elsewhere, industry's share often reaches 50 per cent or more. This is the case in some industrialized countries as well as in countries that are industrializing (e.g., Mexico, India and China) or in transition (e.g., Russia and Hungary). Industrial energy efficiency in developing countries is also vital to reduce global GHG emissions (Kumar, 2006). In many developing countries, the use of old and ill-maintained equipment often causes industry to consume two to five times as much fuel as necessary for a given industrial process. Luckily, many opportunities are available for more efficient energy use in all industrial sectors. Good housekeeping alone can improve corporate energy efficiency by at least 10 per cent and process improvement can do so by a further 15 per cent. Similar measures could reduce industrial energy consumption by some 15–25 per cent.

There are strong pressures for increased commercial energy consumption as countries industrialize. The rate of growth of both economy and energy overall slows down as economies mature. It is not known whether energy use in post-industrial societies is likely to continue with slow growth, plateau, or may even decline. Also nothing is known about how the fuel mix may evolve. Some projections of high baseline emissions growth for industrialized countries seem improbable because they emanate from unrealistic perceptions and models. If a baseline trend of emissions is assumed to be near the 1990 levels for industrialized countries, then implementing progressive reductions may be more manageable (and less costly) than projections of exponential increase.

With increasing attention being focused on emissions of CO_2, more precise national accounting will become necessary. National estimate of CO_2 emissions can be based on energy statistics for consumption of coal, oil and natural gas. However, not all of this consumption consists of combustion that leads to CO_2 emissions. Some part of oil remains as asphalt or is used to manufacture plastics, fertilizers and other chemical products that can be made from natural gas.

Most of the carbonaceous matter in fossil fuel becomes CO_2 through combustion. This flow includes leakage and the products of incomplete combustion which are oxidized into CO_2.

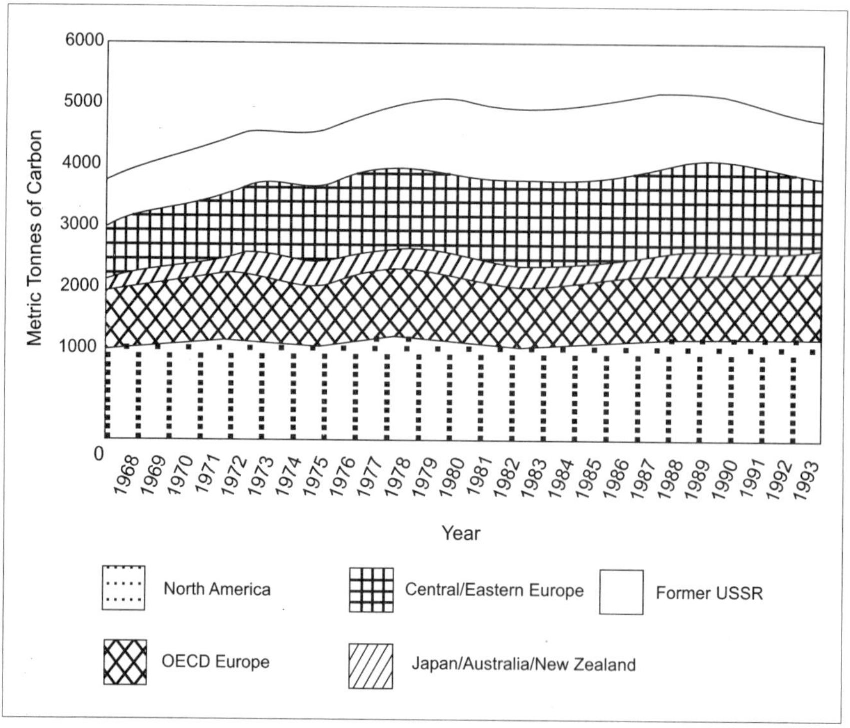

Fig. 8.4 Carbon emissions (1968-93) for industrialized countries

Of the non-energy portion, a certain fraction becomes oxidized to join the carbon dioxide stream which includes fertilizers, lubricants, solvents and detergents. The other fraction contains highly viscous solid materials e.g., plastics, monomers, synthetic rubber, asphalt, bitumen, formaldehyde and silicon carbide that are not readily oxidized. These products fall into two classes—disposable or durable. Most of the disposable products and some of the durable ones are incinerated to add to the CO_2 stream. The remainder is sequestered in landfills or building materials, where the carbon molecules will not break down for centuries. For national accounting, this stream also includes carbon contained in exports of products and wastes. At various points, the carbonaceous material may be recycled, delaying its eventual fate and reducing the consumption of fossil fuel.

The Energy Audit

Besides using energy efficient technologies, companies can improve their energy management systems through an energy audit and an efficiency plan. Audit centres around four key questions:

1. Do we have to do things the way we do them now?
2. What do we measure and how do we do it? How energy is used (or wasted) must be analysed in detail?
3. How should we design our energy plan?
4. How can we put the plan into action?

A close monitoring and review system should ensure that progress is maintained. The plan must be seen as an ongoing process and should be regularly updated.

Cleaner Production

The cleaner production approaches involve redesigning products and processes to reduce the use of raw materials and energy per unit of output. The benefits include reduced costs, improved productivity, less waste and pollution and lower GHG emissions.

Potential for Increasing Efficiency

According to IEA (2007), industrial energy efficiency can be potentially increased by up to 26 per cent, even without introducing new technologies. Areas where further improvements can be achieved immediately are conventional factory systems such as motor and steam systems, combined heat and power generation, and materials efficiency and resource use.

Manufacturing industries use nearly a one-third of world energy production while releasing 36 per cent of the global emissions of the GHG carbon dioxide. Chemicals, petrochemicals, iron and steel, cement, paper and pulp, and certain other minerals and metals, account for more than two-thirds of this amount.

Fossil Fuel Efficiency

Any projects that increase the combustion efficiency of fossil fuels qualify for registration under the Clean Development Mechanism (CDM).

A methodology for monitoring emissions from fossil fuel efficiency projects and for setting the emissions baseline against which their emission reductions can be measured has been approved. Such projects can prevent from inadvertently prolonging the use of fossil fuel or competing against renewable sources of energy. This can be done by building in a phase-out feature that limits the number of certified emission reduction credits (CERs) that can be earned. Another way involves limiting the number of projects eligible in a given country, based on a percentage of the fossil fuel (covered by the project) used in the country.

The methodology approved by the executive board of the CDM can be applied under the following conditions:

- Project activity is the construction and operation of a new fossil fuel fired grid-connected electricity generation plant that uses a more efficient power generation technology than that which would otherwise be used with the given fossil fuel.
- Project is not a co-generation plant
- Data on fuel consumption and electricity generation of recently constructed power plants is available
- Identified baseline fuel is used in more than 50 per cent of total generation by utilities in the geographical area *(Greenhouse Issues 88, pp 17, Dec. 2007).*

Under the CDM, projects in developing countries can earn saleable CERs by reducing GHG emissions. Industrialized countries can use these CERs to meet a part of their commitments under the Kyoto Protocol. The potential to earn CERs is expected to help reduce the high cost barrier to developing and then deploying clean-burn technologies.

As of September 2007, there were more than 780 CDM projects registered in 48 countries. These projects, and roughly 1,320 others in the registration pipeline, are expected to generate 2.2 billion CERs, each equivalent to 1 tCO_2, by the end of the first commitment period of the Kyoto Protocol in 2012 *(Greenhouse Issues, Dec. 2007).*

Power Plants as Global Warming Factories

Power plants burning coal, oil and gas account for a substantial part of the emission of CO_2. Because they waste far more of the fuel's energy than they transform into electricity, an average power plant emits millions of tonnes of CO_2 annually while converting less than 40 per cent of the fuel's energy into electricity. Indeed, power plants may be considered as virtual global warming factories. Electricity is only a byproduct from such a global warming factory.

An evaluation of American experience that was commissioned by Greenpeace has showed that investment in the more efficient use of electricity did more to encourage economic growth and generated more employment than the expenditure on new power stations did. Each dollar spent on saving electricity made it possible to avoid spending $ 1.75 on electricity supply. In Europe also, there is much potential for energy saving and there may be a marked fall in the demand for electricity even with continued economic growth. By around 2010 AD, electricity consumption in Europe could lessen by 45 per cent. From the point of view of CO_2 emissions, if maximum use of the available measures for promoting demand side energy efficiency, renewables and gas co-generation takes place, by the year 2020 the power sector could be emitting 85 per cent less CO_2 than it did in 1985. If only half of the potential for more efficient use of energy were to be exploited, the emissions could still be reduced by 55 per cent, in the same period (Agren, 1994).

It appears that Europe could reduce power needs by between one-third-and -a-half without compromising growth. A ban on power-plant construction would prevent significant amount of pollution from a relatively small number of sources. Energy saving programmes also generate more employment while creating a more efficient modern infrastructure.

Industry as a Metabolic Activity

The concept of "industrial economic metabolism" acts as a bridge between environmentalists and industry. In nature each individual or species reacts to natural stimuli, competing with others for resources, extending its domain until it loses comparative advantage and comes to equilibrium with an adjacent competition. Those species that succeed over time flourish and those that do not suffer or disappear.

Corporate metabolisms are remarkably similar to those of nature. They too react to stimuli, collect and use resources and grow or perish based on how effectively they compete. Corporate management recognizes and responds naturally and efficiently to cost and price signals. Through them it selects resources and converts them into useful products. The efficiency with which this is done is measured by profit. Profit thus provides a discipline on its absence, weeding out others. Unfettered by influences other than economic, the path of corporate success is unlikely to be a compassionate one. The environment and the economy are not separate systems but intertwined to form a complex natural and social setting. The human designed economic system depends on natural resource inputs and, in turn, its metabolic waste can overload the ecological system, threatening the long-term survivability of both (Smart, 1992).

Increasing concern for the environment gives the farsighted manager new latitude. There are competitive benefits in some pollution prevention. But these are not sufficiently strong forces to correct all current ills. In addition, we must harness the metabolism of the industrial world to the realities of the natural one by recognizing the immense value of depletable natural resources and ecosystems (Kumar, 2008). Considering these resources as "cheap" or "free" encourages their overuse. What is needed are adjustments that price these resources at their true long-term value. Corporations will respond naturally, quickly and efficiently to such signals. If we can send our metabolic industry the economic signals it can understand, we can retrofit our human economic system to live in harmony with the natural ecosystem of which we are a part. If we do not, nature will not accommodate our failure by changing its ways (Smart, 1992).

Most of the developed world's environmental problems are caused by economically successful technologies that carry with them unintended harmful ecological side effects whose roots lie in excessive use of resources or restorative systems that are treated as cheap or free, as now measured, but are precious in a long-term environmental sense.

Many socially responsible managers recognize this but their hands are tied by the need to remain economically competitive and by the need to respond to the economic metabolism of the industrial world. Increasing public knowledge and respect for the environment gives the farsighted manager some new latitude. There is a competitive benefit in some pollution prevention measures a cost saving in reduced resource inputs, a more attractive work environment, increased investor support for the company, increased consumer appeal of "greener" products, or lessened exposure to future liabilities (Smart, 1992).

Responding to these shifts in public attitude and to the economic opportunities they provide is a welcome chance for the responsible manager to move a company's environmental policies beyond compliance with existing regulations. We must recognize the value of depletable natural resources and ecosystems and how essential they are to human survival. Economic adjustments can price these resources at their true long-term value, prices high enough to lower the demands to sustainable levels. The economic metabolism of corporations will respond naturally, quickly and efficiently to such signals. Better technologies now on the shelf will be deployed and new ones developed in a vigorous cooperative effort will remain economically competitive. Companies and industries that react best to these changed conditions will thrive. Those that do not will fail.

Examples of Industrial Ecology in Manufacturing

Industrial ecology may be approached in either of the two ways, material-specific or product-specific. An example of a material-specific analysis is that given by Boyhan (1992) concerning the way in which AT & T revised its approach to cleaning electronic circuits while eliminating the use of chlorofluorocarbons (CFCs). McFarland (1992) exemplified a product-specific analysis by mentioning DuPont's analyses of possible replacements for CFCs by more environmentally benign substances.

Mitchell (1992) described a technique for eliminating the hazards in the transportation and storage of harmful chemicals by synthesizing them as a part of the industrial process.

According to Ross (1992), much of the energy used in industry is concentrated in very few sectors, e.g., aluminium smelting and cement production. Major reductions in energy will follow from the declining quantities of materials use as modern technologies are less energy intensive than the processes they replace.

Fuel Cells

Fuel cells are electrochemical devices that extract hydrogen gas from fuel, join it with oxygen from the air and generate electricity and heat, with water as the only byproduct. They work in the same manner as conventional batteries, but have the major merit of not running down over time. They go on producing electricity as long as their fuel supply does not exhaust. Using reformer technology, fuel cells can use hydrogen from any hydrocarbon fuel such as natural gas, gasoline or even methanol (Francis, 2002).

A fuel cell consists of two electrodes, usually platinum coated, separated by a Polymer Electrolyte Membrane (PEM). Hydrogen gas from the fuel source is fed over the anode and oxygen from the air is likewise fed over the cathode. At the anode, the platinum splits the hydrogen gas into protons and electrons, which go to the cathode by two different paths. The protons pass through the electrolyte to the cathode, whereas the electrons cannot take this route through the electrolyte and so move to the cathode via an external circuit. It is this current that is used to power a variety of electrical devices. At the cathode, the protons, electrons and oxygen are catalysed by the platinum coating to form water. Fuel cells can then be combined together in a stack to give the required voltage (Francis, 2002).

Fuel cells possess three chief advantages over traditional power sources:

- They lack moving parts and so are quiet and reliable
- They do not produce any harmful pollutants, relying on electrochemistry
- Since fuel is converted directly to electricity, the efficiency of fuel cells is much greater than that of internal combustion engines

With heat recovery, fuel cells can convert over 75 per cent of the available fuel to electricity, compared with only about 20 per cent conversion achieved by conventional combustion-based power generators (Francis, 2002).

One important factor driving fuel cell development, particularly in the automobile industry, is the more stringent environmental controls on exhaust emissions and the desire to reduce noise pollution. Indeed, it is now emerging that fuel cell vehicles may at last end the century-old reign of the internal combustion engine as the dominant source of power for personal transportation—consumers can look forward to getting an efficient power source, and communities can get zero emissions.

The major factor that holds back the development of fuel cells is cost. Hydrogen is more expensive than coal and oil. Scientists are seeking cheaper feedstocks, including reformers, enzymes, solar and wind-powered hydrogen generation. Further development of fuel cells will require the integration of such disparate disciplines as materials science, surface science, catalysis, processing, thermal engineering, reformer engineering, electrochemistry, control engineering and sensors (Francis, 2002). Computational chemistry techniques, in particular molecular modelling and simulation, will aid in this diverse field by helping scientists in understanding processes better, and experiment with new approaches (Francis, 2002).

Many of modern fuel cells have either solid oxide or polymer electrolytes. The performance of the electrolyte, both in restricting the flow of electrons and hydrogen, and facilitating the flow of protons, strongly influence the performance of the fuel cell.

So far, fuel cells have found only limited use as the primary or back-up power source in hospitals and homes, cellular phones and landfill/wastewater treatment plants (consuming the methane produced). Their full potential in these and many other applications is yet to be realized and our dream of the quiet and pollution free surroundings may not be too far around the corner (Francis, 2002).

Microfuel Cells

These are a new class of miniaturized power supply for portable electronic devices being brought to market in the near future. A traditional electrochemical battery generates electricity from an internal chemical reaction whereas a fuel cell produces it by decomposing a fuel like methanol. Once the fuel is exhausted, it is replenished by either replacing a cartridge or by refilling a reservoir—an operation that only takes seconds rather than hours needed to recharge a battery. It appears that users of mobile electronics will no longer depend on batteries. The microfuel cell may provide electricity for a hand-held radio frequency identification (RFID) tag reader for use in stores and warehouses. Toshiba is planning to introduce a laptop computer powered by a microfuel cell that will operate for about 10 hours before requiring refuelling *(Sci. Amer. pp 56, Dec. 2004).*

Electric Vehicles for a Decarbonized Economy

Competitive electric vehicle technology is now looming large on the horizon and within a few years we may see widespread uptake of electric vehicles. Before that, one question that needs to be answered is: What electricity system would be required to support the increasing numbers of electric vehicles? Social issues such as what types of cars will people be prepared to drive in the future and what distances will people want to travel by car, also will require consideration.

Substantial advances in electric vehicle technology have occurred in recent years. Many of the drivetrain systems (the components from the electric motor to the driving wheels, including the control systems) have been tested in the mainstream hybrid vehicles being marketed by Toyota and Honda. Future advances in battery technology, fuel cells and general vehicle technology will further improve these. Problems concerning the weight of batteries and limited range of electric vehicles will be solved.

Rapid recharging to minimize loss of current refuelling convenience has several technical implications, as also the batteries of electric vehicles becoming an integral component of a country's electricity system. The average energy economy of electric vehicles, and therefore the load on the network, will vary significantly from country to country depending on people's choices.

The problems posed by batteries may be dispensed with using on-board fuel cells to power electric vehicles. Fuel cells can run on hydrogen or liquid fuels. They can be refuelled eliminating the need for batteries and their recharging. Several automobile companies are engaged in producing fuel cell electric vehicles and the refuelling infrastructure.

Clean (Hydrogen) Energy

Hydrogen is an attractive option in search of clean, secure energy, especially for transport. Imagine running a car which emits only water vapour—no lung irritants, no carcinogens and no toxic gases. Hydrogen can be produced from all the energy sources a country possesses, reducing the expense and insecurity that comes from dependence on imported fossil fuels. However, there are many technical challenges with hydrogen, and most technologies for delivery, storage and use of hydrogen will probably be developed through international research efforts. When the challenges have been tackled, hydrogen cars will kick off the production line. Until then, it would be wise for any country to have already done the planning and built the expertise to ensure a smooth transition to a hydrogen economy.

Considerable progress has been made in some countries (e.g., New Zealand) in producing pure hydrogen by converting lignite into 'syngas' from which pure hydrogen can be extracted. In this effort, the essential 'partner' technology is carbon capture and storage. There are currently three large-scale sites around the world (Canada, the North Sea and Algeria) where CO_2 is removed from gas streams and stored geologically. Carbon dioxide emissions may be significantly reduced by use of carbon capture and storage, provided that suitable geological sites have been identified and tested.

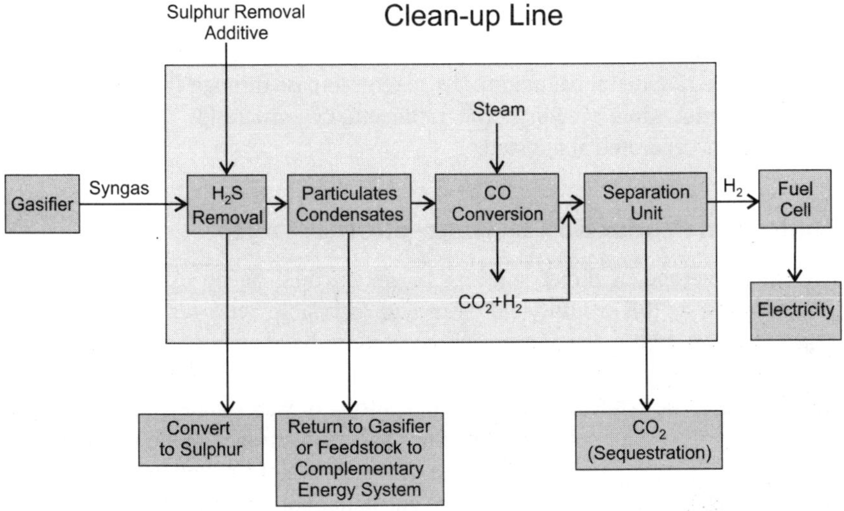

Fig. 8.5 Protocol for feeding coal into a gasifier for the production of hydrogen stream

Lignite yields high purity hydrogen suitable for fuel cells to generate electricity—for distributed and large-scale applications, and for running vehicles. Basically, the process involves feeding coal into a gasifier to produce syngas which is primarily hydrogen, carbon dioxide and carbon monoxide (Fig. 8.5). The syngas is then cleaned to produce a pure hydrogen stream.

In New Zealand, CRL Energy Ltd has already built and commissioned a 'fluidized bed' gasifier and associated computer control system. The pilot plant is large enough to power about 20 houses. A reliable and consistent stream of syngas of known quality can be generated from New Zealand lignite.

Compared to other advanced gasification technologies, fluidized bed gasification is relatively simple in design and construction and suitable for distributed generation and industrial scale facilities. Several lignites are well-suited to this technology.

Breakthroughs in Clean-up

An alkaline fuel cell package which requires extremely high purity hydrogen is being developed in New Zealand. Substantial progress has been made in removing impurities and maximizing the amount of hydrogen produced.

1. **Particulate and condensables** A combination of a high efficiency cyclone and a Venturi scrubber (both well-established technologies) works well.
2. **Sulphur** A new desulphurizing system has been designed, built and tested. Sulphur gas can now be fully removed from the syngas.
3. **Water gas shift reaction** Syngas contains carbon monoxide which can be converted into more hydrogen and CO_2 by running the syngas and steam over a catalyst bed (known as 'water gas shift reaction').
4. **Producing pure hydrogen stream** To separate the hydrogen from CO_2, work is underway in the Netherlands (ECN), using new ceramic 'membranes' coated with the rare metal palladium. Hydrogen can pass through the membrane but CO_2 cannot. More proven, but less efficient, CO_2 separation technology is also being incorporated and tested.

Hydrogen Production by Nano-photocatalyst

One good method of direct splitting of water could be by using a particulate photocatalyst as this would yield clean and recyclable hydrogen on a large-scale (Bard and Fox, 1995). A variety of photocatalysts have been found, that function under visible light (Kato and Kudo, 2002). Now Maeda et. al., (2006) have described an advance in the catalysis of the overall splitting of water under visible light. The new catalyst is a solid solution of gallium and zinc nitrogen oxide (Maeda et. al., 2005), $(Ga_{1-x}Zn_x)(N_{1-x}O_x)$, modified with nanoparticles of a mixed oxide of rhodium and chromium. This mixture is an efficient nanophotocatalyst that promotes the evolution of hydrogen gas.

$(Ga_{1-x}Zn_x)(N_{1-x}O_x)$ is a yellow powder with an absorption edge at about 510 nm. By itself, it has virtually no photocatalytic power. But Maeda et. al., impregnated it with nanoparticles of rhodium-chromium mixed oxide. Scanning transmission electron microscopy revealed that fine (10–20 nm) particles were distributed uniformly on the $(Ga_{1-x}Zn_x)(N_{1-x}O_x)$ surface and that the loaded nanoparticles were crystalline. These nanoparticles contained both rhodium and chromium. It is this photocatalyst modification that enhances the overall splitting of water driven by visible light.

The quantum efficiency of overall water splitting by the photocatalyst is a function of the wavelength of the incident light. It decreases with increasing wavelength and the longest wavelength suitable for overall water splitting coincides with the absorption edge of the $(Ga_{1-x}Zn_x)(N_{1-x}O_x)$ solid solution. This suggests that the reaction proceeds through light absorption by the solid solution. The quantum efficiency of overall water splitting on this catalyst is about 2.5 per cent at 420–440 nm, which is about an order of magnitude higher than the previously reported activity of photocatalysts used in overall water splitting under visible light (Maeda et. al., 2005a).

The photocatalyst remains stable during overall water splitting that is driven by visible light (Maeda et. al., 2006). Using silver nitrate as a sacrificial electron acceptor raises the quantum efficiency for oxygen evolution to 50 per cent at 420–440 nm, i.e., about 20 times higher than that for overall water splitting. Therefore conceivably, the photocatalytic activity of the modified $(Ga_{1-x}Zn_x)(N_{1-x}O_x)$ solid solution might be increased further by improving the hydrogen evolution site. Its composition could also be modified to extend the absorption edge to longer wavelengths. These results point to the feasibility of using photocatalysts and solar energy to produce hydrogen from water.

Hydrogen Storage Materials

Hydrogen atom has its electron (for charge neutrality) accompanied by only one proton. It has the best ratio of valence electrons to protons (and neutrons) of all the elements and so the energy gain per electron is very high. Although hydrogen is the most abundant element on earth, less than 1 per cent of it occurs as molecular hydrogen gas H_2, the rest being either chemically bound as H_2O in water or bound to hydrocarbons. A clean method to produce hydrogen from water is to use sunlight in combination with photovoltaic cells and water electrolysis.

There are two principal methods to run a road vehicle on hydrogen. In the first method, hydrogen in an internal combustion engine is burnt quickly with oxygen from air. The efficiency of the transformation from chemical to mechanical through thermal energy is slightly better for hydrogen-air mixtures (around 25%) than for petrol-air mixtures. When a lean mixture is used, the exhaust gas contains only water vapour, richer mixtures also produce NO_x. In the second method, hydrogen is 'burnt' electrochemically with oxygen from air in a fuel cell that generates electricity (and heat) and drives an electric engine. Here, the efficiency of the direct process of electron transfer from oxygen to hydrogen can reach 50–60 per cent, twice as much as the thermal process (Schlapbach and Züttel, 2001).

For on-board energy storage, vehicles need compact, light, safe and affordable containment. A modern, commercially available car optimized for mobility with a range of 400 km burns about 24 kg of petrol in a combustion engine. To cover the same range, 8 kg of hydrogen are needed for the combustion engine version or 4 kg of hydrogen for an electric car with a fuel cell (Schlapbach and Züttel, 2001). At room temperature and atmospheric pressure, 4 kg of hydrogen gas occupies a volume of 45 m^3, corresponding to a balloon of 5 m diameter. This rules it out as a practical solution for a vehicle. Compacting H_2 as liquid or as metal hydrides reduces its volume considerably. Liquid hydrogen has been used as a fuel in aircraft and space shuttles. Some car companies have built an automated liquid-hydrogen filling station and developed cars that can run with hydrogen.

Many metals and alloys can reversibly absorb large volumes of hydrogen. Charging may be done either by using hydrogen gas or hydrogen atoms from an electrolyte. Molecular hydrogen becomes dissociated at the surface before absorption—two H atoms recombine to form H_2. In metal hydride formation from gaseous hydrogen, metal initially dissolves some hydrogen as a solid solution (a-phase). As the hydrogen pressure along with the concentration of H in the metal increases, interactions between hydrogen atoms become locally important and there is nucleation and growth of the hydride (b-phase). The two phases coexist. In the pure b-phase, the H_2 pressure rises sharply with the concentration. At higher H_2 pressure, more hydride phases may be formed. The two-phase region ends at a critical point above which the transition from a-phase to b-phase occurs continuously (Schlapbach, 1988, 1992). Hydrogen is deposited in the form of atoms (not molecules) on interstitial sites of the host metal lattice.

Metal-hydrogen bonds have very high hydrogen density at moderate pressure. Many elemental metals form hydrides e.g., $PdH_{0.6}$, rare earth REH_2, REH_3 or MgH_2, none exist in the pressure and temperature range attractive for mobile storage.

Alloys derived from $LaNi_5$ show some very promising properties, including fast and reversible sorption with small hysteresis, and have good cycling life. The volumetric hydrogen density (crystallographically) of $LaNi_5H_{6.5}$ at 2 bar equals that of gaseous molecular hydrogen at 1,800 bar. Happily, all hydrogen desorbs at a pressure of 2 bar. The density for practical purposes is reduced by the packing fraction of $LaNi_5$ powder, but still remains above that of liquid hydrogen. Storage in these intermetallics allows very safe hydrogen handling. But this is not suitable for gaseous hydrogen fuel tanks to be used in vehicles. The low mass density is a common weakness of all known metal hydrides working near room temperature. Some intermetallic compounds and alloys do form hydrides with high mass per cent hydrogen (like $Li_3Be_2H_7$) and 4.5 H atoms per metal atom ($BaReH_9$), but they are not reversible within the required range of temperature and pressure (Schlapbach and Züttel, 2001).

Attempts are underway to finds ways to enhance the mass density—new families of alloys based on vanadium, zirconium and titanium are being tested in several Japanese laboratories (Akiba and Iba, 1998; Tsukahara et. al., 2000).

Hydrogen Energy Technology

Systems for producing pure hydrogen for fuel cells from methanol can face problems with energy efficiency and short lifetime unless the right catalyst is combined with the right purification membrane.

The power demands of portable electronic gadgets such as laptops, mobile telephones, iPods, etc., have skyrocketed in the recent past, but the storage capacity of the batteries which power them has not kept pace. This has directed increasing attention to systems based on fuel-cell technologies, which have much higher energy-storage densities (Masel, 2006).

Wilhite et. al., (2006) have developed a catalytic system that allows production of pure hydrogen, the basic power source of proton-exchange membrane fuel cells, from methanol at a much higher rate per unit volume than could be achieved in the past. In their mode of working, fuel cells are quite like batteries—they use electrochemical reactions to produce electricity. A reaction on an anode coated with a catalyst like platinum produces electrons which pass through a circuit and deliver power to a device. They then return to the fuel cell, where they are gathered by a second reaction on a catalytic cathode that generally produces water as a waste product. In proton-exchange membrane fuel cells, the reactions are:

(At anode) $2H_2 \rightarrow 4H^+ + 4e^-$

(At cathode) $4H^+ + 4e^- + O_2 \rightarrow 2H_2O$

Hydrogen is quite light (not dense). The large amounts of heat energy which it releases on combustion supply much more energy per unit weight than the lithium batteries traditionally used in laptops and similar electronic devices. In fact, hydrogen fuel cells can be very suitable for supplementing or even replacing lithium batteries. Their only drawback is that it is difficult to find a way to store or produce enough pure hydrogen in the laptop. One possibility may be placing a tank of very pure hydrogen in the laptop and refilling it at filling stations, like those for cars. But this is ruled out by the explosive nature of hydrogen. Hydrogen cylinders, metal hydrides and borohydrides are banned on aeroplanes. Therefore, a hydrogen-powered laptop would have to generate its hydrogen internally from methanol or formic acid.

Some suggestions on how to generate hydrogen from methanol (CH_3OH) have been reviewed by Masel et. al., (2005). One option is to perform 'steam reforming' via the reaction:

$$CH_3OH + H_2O \rightarrow CO_2 + 3H_2$$

The problem here is that carbon monoxide is yielded by a side reaction:

$$CH_3OH \rightarrow CO + 2H_2CO$$

Carbon monoxide is highly poisonous for the catalysts used in fuel cells. Even trace amounts of CO_2 can be fatal, as this generates carbon monoxide through the reverse water-gas shift reaction:

$$CO_2 + H_2 \rightarrow CO + H_2O \qquad \text{(Masel, 2006)}$$

Differentially permeable membranes have previously been used to purify hydrogen of such trace gases with some limited success. Palladium and palladium-silver membranes do produce pure hydrogen, but they degrade quickly in the presence of carbon monoxide and methanol. Also, it takes much energy to push hydrogen through a membrane that is of the thickness required for mechanical stability. Thus, it has not so far been possible to produce hydrogen of sufficient purity at a high enough rate to power a laptop for an extended period.

Wilhite et. al., (2006) addressed this issue by building a composite structure combining a hydrogen-permeable palladium-silver membrane with a catalyst for the hydrogen-producing methanol-oxidation reaction:

$$2CH_3OH + O_2 \rightarrow 2CO_2 + 4H_2$$

This prevented the membrane from degrading. As described by Khaladkar et. al., (2000), protective layers can be used in commercial applications to protect sensitive materials from corrosive gases as they form an impenetrable barrier in front of them. But such an impermeable system has no use in a fuel-cell system where hydrogen must pass through both the protective layer and the membrane to reach anode of the fuel cell.

Therefore, Wilhite et. al., used a permeable catalytic layer that aids the oxidation of most carbon monoxide and methanol, thereby making them harmless before they reach the membrane while letting hydrogen past. Any traces of corrosive gases that reach the membrane are small enough to be oxidized there before doing any damage, leaving the hydrogen to filter through. Thus, hydrogen can be both produced and purified in one stage. Hence, this is not only important for portable devices but is also useful in many other chemically reacting systems.

Wilhite et. al., demonstrated that their membrane is stable for some days, as opposed to a few hours with an unprotected membrane. But a laptop's power supply needs to be stable for years and better thermal management is also needed. The temperature in the system employed by Wilhite et al. is about 400°C, too high for comfort in one's lap or pocket. Nevertheless, this step does represent considerable advance towards practical portable fuel-cell power systems.

Strategies for Demand-side Management

Demand-side management (DSM) programmes are aimed at managing the timing or amount of electricity demanded by customers. They are developed and implemented within a certain geographical area, usually by the utility that serves the area. In some countries, government agencies also participate in DSM.

DSM strategies involve certain initiatives that change the shape of the load curve or the total area under the load curve (the integral of the load curve gives the total energy consumed) or a combination of both goals. The classical DSM strategies are illustrated in Fig. 8.6. For instance, the peak of the load curve is reduced by raising tariffs during peak hours. Reducing the peak does not necessarily decrease overall energy consumption. Certain amount of energy consumed during peak hours can be

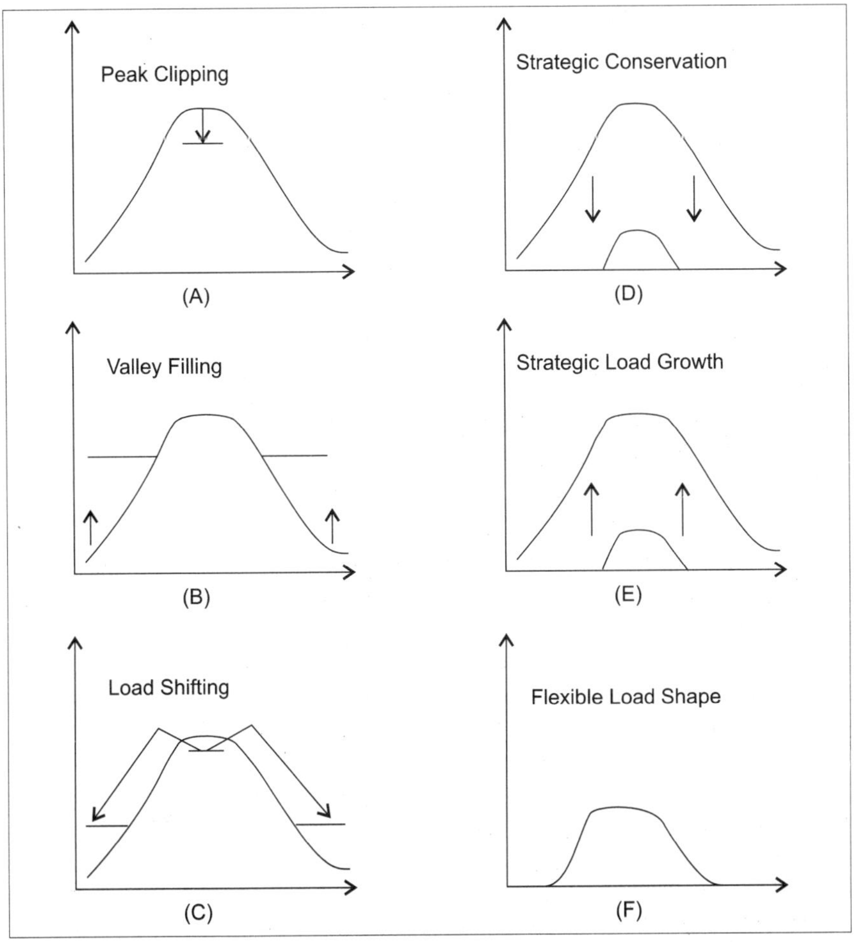

Fig. 8.6 DSM load shape objectives (After EPRI, 1990)

shifted to other periods, for example, using thermal energy storage. Some strategies (Fig. 8.6B&E) involve increasing electricity sales. In first case, load growth is directed toward specific periods and in the second case, general load growth is promoted. In some cases, increased electricity use can result from fuel switching that reduces direct fuel use so that electric load growth does not always increase total primary energy consumption (Swisher et. al., 1997). Fig. 8.6D illustrates the situation where energy conservation, through improved end-use efficiency, is the primary objective of the DSM effort (EPRI, 1990).

Impact Evaluation of DSM Programmes

Impact can be evaluated by examining the programme results in terms of energy saved and load reductions. Costs and benefits, participation rates and customer acceptance are also evaluated. The impact evaluation approach, being quantitative, uses advanced statistical analyses (Hirst and Reed, 1992). The results obtained can prove useful for new programme design and for making load and energy projections. The cost-benefit ratio of DSM programmes depend on the achievable market penetration over time and the administrative costs and uncertainties associated with implementation.

The amount of potential achievable savings is estimated (pre-evaluation), and after the DSM programme has been launched the actual savings achieved through it (post-evaluation) are determined. Evaluation methods include:

Measurement pre and post-programme(whole building metering, end-use metering is:

- Analysis of customer billing data
- Engineering analysis that uses physical models based on weather data, customer surveys, facility and equipment inventories and operating patterns
- Statistical modelling that employs statistical techniques to evaluate changes through billing data, demographic characteristics and economic variables (Swisher et. al., 1997)

Engineering analysis, the simplest and least expensive approach to impact analysis, is done on information about the technical characteristics of end-use equipment and data on customer participation in the programme. Its limitation is that it fails to catch changes in customer behaviour e.g., to increase comfort in an efficiently air conditioned building.

Direct measurements can show the evolution of the load profile and involve instrumentation and collection of data by individual end-use or by a whole building. Energy use should be quantified before and after the implementation of the conservation measure. In this case, data are obtained through sampling involving programme participants and non-participants.

DSM programmes contain both direct and indirect cost components. Direct costs include those directly associated with efficiency measure. A good illustration is that in a rebate programme it will include the amount of capital spent by the utility to subsidize the purchase of new equipment. Here the cost component includes the financial incentive paid by the utility for the materials and installations needed to acquire the conservation resource. Indirect costs include both fixed and variable costs for managing the programme. In our example of a rebate programme, indirect costs will include costs of an information campaign, utility staff salaries and costs of evaluating or monitoring the programme results. Some of these costs are fixed but others vary depending on the duration of the programme, for instance, staff salaries, (Swisher et. al., 1997).

Integrating Options on Supply and Demand Sides

An integrated resource planning (IRP) process can bring together, for comparison, various programmes for energy efficiency and load management with options for electricity supply. The basis of comparison should contain a societal perspective and also include environmental and social costs. IRP should be used to bring new elements such as energy efficiency programmes and environmental constraints into electricity supply planning.

The traditional electric planning model includes projections of demand growth, expansion planning to determine available resources and when they are needed, production cost analysis to rank supply options by cost and calculation of required revenues and rates.

The chief objective of traditional power planning is to meet the projected demand for electricity at the least cost. This goal needs to be modified in the IRP context to meet the demand for energy services, facilitating the inclusion of DSM and energy efficiency programmes. Under IRP, it should be cheaper to meet the demand for energy services by improving energy efficiency rather than by building additional supply capacity, then the energy efficiency resource would be selected (Swisher et al., 1997).

In the IRP process, besides the conventional thermal and hydroelectric power supply options, it is quite possible to include such options as DSM, supply-side loss reductions, cogeneration of heat and power, and intermittent renewable resources (solar, wind, etc.). All these different options can be compared on the basis of the (long-run) marginal cost of energy. The long-run marginal cost governs the planning of new resources but the choice of which existing resources should operate or be dispatched, at a given time is determined by short-run marginal costs (variable costs for fuel, operations and maintenance). A traditional economic dispatch strategy ranks supply resources by variable costs to determine the dispatch order. The most expensive source operating at a given time is the marginal resource which varies with the system load. On the other hand, an environmental dispatch approach considers the emissions from available sources and ranks them according to a combination of cost and emission rates, depending on how the pollution is valued. IRP allows the use of environmental impacts for ranking new supply resources according to the cost of avoided emissions, or by adding emission charges or externality values to the economic cost values (Swisher et. al., 1997).

Marginal Energy and Capacity Cost

The least cost combination of different resources is one where the marginal cost of each resource is equal (assuming diminishing returns to scale). With the increasing total supply, this marginal cost threshold increases, indicating how much of each resource needs to be included in the least cost mix and it can be determined by ranking the available resources in order of marginal cost and selecting those with the lowest marginal cost. Resources of increasing marginal cost are added until the total supply satisfies the total projected demand. If in the process of expanding total supply to meet the projected demand, the projected tariff changes enough that projected demand also changes, then the projected total supply would also need to change.

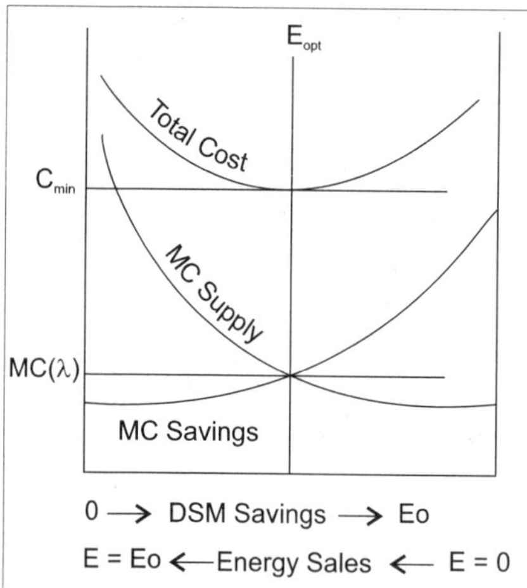

E = Energy Consumption

E_{opt} = Optimum Energy Consumption

E_o = Total Energy Demand

C_{min} = Minimum Total Cost

MC = Marginal Cost

As DSM savings increase toward a maximum of E_o, the marginal cost of savings (MC savings) increases. Simiarly, as the DSM savings decrease toward zero and the energy sales increase toward a maximum of E_o, the marginal cost of supply increases. The optimum mix of energy sales and DSM saving occurs at E_{opt} and results in the minimum total cost.

Fig. 8.7 The least-cost combination of energy supply and DSM savings is at the level where the marginal cost of increasing either resource is equal. In an actual IRP analysis, multiple options of both types would be considered and evaluated in this framework (After Swisher et al., 1997)

Figure 8.7 shows how the optimum mix of energy supply and energy savings (e.g., DSM) occurs at the point where the marginal cost of adding an extra unit of energy supply equals the marginal cost of adding an extra unit of energy savings.

Environmental and Social Cost Analysis

One very important aspect of IRP is to account for environmental impacts and to weigh these impacts against the costs of relatively clean options such as DSM and renewable sources.

Impacts of Electricity Production

The electric power sector creates many different kinds of environmental impacts, particularly in the process of generating electricity. The impact may be classified as:

Land use

The large amount of land devoted to electric generation and transmission increasingly make these facilities difficult or controversial to site. Some facilities discourage residential or commercial use in the surrounding area. People are often concerned about the magnetic fields created by high-voltage transmission lines or about the possibility of accidents at nuclear generation plants.

Coal mining that provides the majority of fuel for the electric utility industry in many countries, also has severe impacts on land use, especially in areas where surface mining is predominant. There has been increasing concern about the need to reclaim land that has been mined.

Land areas, e.g., Pristine river valleys, of high scenic and recreational value, can be flooded to provide hydroelectric storage reservoirs. The areas inundated depend on the flow, the design storage capacity and the steepness of the watershed.

Waste disposal

Generation of electricity produces several different types of wastes which must be handled safely. The large volumes of ash created by coal combustion and the sludge waste from air pollution control equipment create the problem of disposing of solid and liquid wastes, including radioactive and highly toxic wastes. The long-term disposal of radioactive wastes from nuclear power plants is still unresolved.

Cooling

All coal and nuclear power plants, and some gas and oil-fired plants, use Rankine cycle steam turbines to convert thermal energy into electric power. These cycles require extensive cooling to maintain efficient operating conditions, usually about 2 MW (thermal) for each 1 MW (electrical) in nuclear plants, and somewhat less in fossil plants. Large volumes of cooling water have to be provided. In fact in the US, electricity generation is the second largest use of water after agriculture.

Air emissions

The most serious impact of electric generation, in countries where it is predominantly fossil fuel-based, is the emission of various trace gases into the atmosphere as byproducts of combustion. Some emissions result from impurities in the fuel such as particulates and sulphur dioxide (SO_2) from coal. The other impurities come from the air used in the combustion process like oxides of nitrogen (NOx) or the inherent end-product of hydrocarbon combustion like carbon dioxide.

Until this time, utility regulations and expenditures have focused on reducing the rates of emission of particulates, SO_2 and NOx. Particulates include both visible and microscopic dust particles emitted from the combustion process, especially when the fuel is coal or diesel oil. The smaller microscopic particulates pose a strong health hazard because they readily enter human lungs. The most common method for removing small particulates is the electrostatic precipitator.

Sulphur dioxide is a corrosive and hazardous gas at high concentration, especially in the presence of high particulate concentrations. Also, it undergoes reactions in the atmosphere that produce sulphuric acid, which is deposited over large distances downwind from the original source. SO_2 is removed from coal-fired plant emissions through various processes. In the conventional wet scrubber technology, a pulverized limestone slurry is mixed with the flue gases to absorb most of the SO_2. However, they are expensive, consume about five per cent of the plant's electric output and produce large quantities of waste sludge.

Some other technologies include regenerative scrubbers that recover the sulphur for other commercial uses. Contrary to wet scrubbles, dry scrubbers use lime as a sorbent to remove 40–60 per cent of the SO_2 at a lower cost. In fluidized bed combustion, pulverized coal or biomass plant emissions are mixed with limestone and fluidized by up-flowing combustion air so that the limestone reacts with SO_2 during combustion to form a dry byproduct, reducing emissions by 90 per cent.

Nitrogen oxides emitted from power plants include mostly nitric oxide (NO) and some amount of nitrogen dioxide (NO_2). Additional NO_2 is formed in the atmosphere, which along with other secondary byproducts such as N_2O, nitric acid (HNO_3) and peroxyacetyl nitrate (PAN) reduces visibility. PAN is an eye irritant. NOx react with hydrocarbons in the presence of sunlight to form ozone that can damage plants and materials.

Like sulphuric acid, nitric acid can be deposited as acid precipitation far from the original pollution source. This precipitation threatens freshwater life and affects forest health both directly and through increased leaching of hazardous minerals like aluminium.

Emissions from NOx may be controlled by modifying the combustion process or by post-combustion control. Accurate control of combustion air to minimize excess air reduces NOx emissions by 15–50 per cent. New low NOx burners using multi-stage combustion provide 40–60 per cent reductions. Post-combustion technologies include urea injection to reduce 35–75 per cent of flue gas NOx to nitrogen and water, and selective catalytic reduction, which can accomplish 80–90 per cent NOx removal by mixing the flue gas with ammonia in the presence of a vanadium catalyst (Swisher et. al., 1997).

Greenhouse gases

The increasing atmospheric emission of CO_2 have aroused concerns about the potential threat of global climate change. The chief source of CO_2 is fossil fuel combustion and electric utilities that contribute to one-third of global CO_2 emissions. Coal burning utilities produce the most emissions because coal produces roughly 24 kg of carbon per GJ energy, compared to approximately 20 kg/GJ for oil and 14 kg/GJ for natural gas.

Industrialized countries have made voluntary commitments to stabilize or reduce future carbon emissions. To stabilize the CO_2 concentration in the atmosphere, emissions from the developing countries will also have to be minimized. Several national and multilateral efforts are underway to identify emission reduction options and develop national strategies in the developing countries. Energy efficiency and non-fossil generation technologies are core components of such a strategy.

Carbon Capture and Storage & Clean Coal Technology

Humanity's extravagant use of fossil fuels is squarely to blame as the cause of climate change. Unless urgent measures are taken to reverse this trend, a climate catastrophe seems imminent. The trouble is that energy also happens to be the lifeline of modern society. Without it we do not have heat, light, cars and computers. If we consider currently known and proven reserves as well as predicted usage of the world's remaining reserves of fossil fuels and uranium, we may somehow keep these functions going in as little as only three decades. So, we only have this short span of time in which we need to tackle the converging crises of energy security and climate change by protecting the climate and ending the energy crisis. If we could stop using oil, gas and coal, we might just be able to stabilize carbon emissions at a level to keep global climate temperature from rising significantly above a genocidal 2°C by 2050.

Carbon Capture and Storage (CCS) technology is used for stripping CO_2 from the exhaust gases of fossil fuels. The CO_2 is then buried underground in liquid form.

Coal constitutes the most abundant fossil energy source on earth and its reserves are reasonably well distributed throughout the world. Carbon has previously been successfully buried at three locations worldwide. The best known is the Sleipner gas rig in the North Sea, operated by oil giant Statoil. The natural gas, which the rig was built to extract, was found to have a CO_2 level too high to pump into people's homes. Statoil stripped out this excess CO_2 and pumped it straight into the atmosphere. It then learnt that the company could benefit by saving thousands of euros in carbon taxes, if it captured CO_2 and pumped it into a saltwater aquifer deep under the North Sea.

Another project is located in US (North Dakota). It takes the CO_2 produced by a coal gasification plant built to produce synthetic natural gas from coal. The CO_2 is piped up to Weyburn in Canada, where it is used to force extra oil out of an ailing well. The third site is Salah in Algeria. It adopts the same strategy as the Sleipner project for natural gas refining.

All the three projects share one thing in common, none of them generates electricity. The technology needed to either strip CO_2 from the toxic, complex fumes of a coal power plant or to extract the CO_2 before burning the coal has not so far been tested on a commercial scale. Another problem is the difficulty experienced in locating geologically suitable strata in the liquefied and highly pressurized CO_2 has to be injected. The UK does own some spent oil and gas fields in the North Sea which might be suitable, but feasibility and viability of CCS for these fields is somewhat uncertain. A lack of suitable sites means that longer pipelines have to be used to transport the carbon to wherever it can be buried (and hence more energy), or where liquefied CO_2 can be transported by ship to a suitable repository.

Some experts on CCS have estimated that a 'clean coal' plant may require around 25–30 per cent more fuel than a conventional one to capture and store 90 per cent of its CO_2 (Hughes and Anslow, 2007).

Both these are vital to future prosperity. If not earnestly tackled, climate change poses catastrophic human consequences and economic cost. Several countries have launched serious efforts to improve energy efficiency with a view to reduce GHG emissions from industry through the application of CCS in the power sector and by increasing research and development for iron and steel plants as well as an aggressive policy on the introduction of renewable energy technology and hybrid fuel cell technology in the transport sector. In Korea, where the power sector is the major emitter of CO_2, CCS is deployed to effect marked cuts in these emissions. Unfortunately, the current cost are high and attempts are afoot to bring them down to \$ 25–30/t CO_2 with wet scrubbing. Dry sorbent technology and chemical looping combustion may even enable reducing the costs to less than \$ 20/t CO_2.

Small-scale CO_2 Capture and Collection

Considerable interest is being evinced in the technology and cost of capturing and collecting CO_2 from smaller emission sources. Most studies of CO_2 capture processes have previously focused on capture from large power plants or other large-scale industrial processes. It has usually been assumed that capture and collection from smaller sources would be significantly more expensive and hence not worth further investigation. To eliminate or reduce their emissions, small-scale facilities are thus left with the options of converting to carbon free carriers such as electricity and hydrogen. There is need to better understand the relative cost and difficulty of implementing small-scale capture by examining the type and size of small-scale industrial CO_2 emission sources and the technology options which might become available in the future for capturing this CO_2. Another approach may be to examine the design, construction and cost of CO_2 collection networks to collect CO_2 from distributed sources in a typical industrial area.

Technologies for Small-scale Capture

Some work has been done on 'medium-scale' combustion installations in the industrial and commercial sectors. The commercial sector includes offices, retail and wholesale premises, hotels, hospitals and educational institutions as well as supply of energy to the residential sector through district heating schemes. Installations with a fuel input between 1 and 100 MW(Th) have been considered. These cover CO_2 emissions in the range 1500 to 250,000 tonnes per annum (TPA). Publicly available information on the capacities of medium-scale sources of CO_2, particularly from the US, the Netherlands and China, have been appraised *(Greenhouse Issues, 88, Dec. 2007)*.

The main applications of medium-scale CO_2 capture for GHG abatement, if any, are likely to materialize after the year 2020. Some novel capture technologies now being developed may become commercially available by that time. The following promising technologies suited to small-scale capture in this market have been identified:

- Natural gas and diesel oil fired reciprocating engines [1.5 MWe] with post-combustion membrane assisted liquid absorption for CO_2 capture
- Natural gas fired gas turbine [5 MWe] with pre-combustion PSA capture of carbon dioxide
- Oxy-combustion coal boiler [50 MW(Th)] with membrane oxygen production

- Oxy-combustion natural gas boiler [5 MW(Th)] with membrane oxygen production
- Solid oxide fuel cell [0.5 MWe] with oxygen conducting membrane after burner

Costs of Small Scale CO_2 Capture

A critical analysis has been made of a 50 MW(Th) oxy-combustion coal boiler using an integrated dense membrane oxygen separation (Fig 8.8). Two designs, one burning only coal and the other using supplementary natural gas, to assist in heating air to the separation membrane, were considered. The economic analysis estimated capture cost of the order of only around \$ 22 per tonne compares with estimated \$ 70 per tonne for the equivalent system using current MEA scrubbing technology. This compares with capture cost estimated to be around \$ 35 per tonne for a large-scale power plant with MEA scrubbing, suggesting that small-scale capture may prove quite economical.

It appears that the cost of capturing and collecting CO_2 from medium sized distributed industrial sources using future technology may well be affordable. Once a backbone CCS system consisting of a few major sources connected to nearby geological storage is in place, the marginal cost of CO_2 capture and collection from nearby smaller sources could be quite economical. These smaller industrial and commercial emitters will be faced with ever reducing emission caps. The sensible option for them will be to buy emission certificates. Another option for the industries would be to purchase supplies of hydrogen produced in centralized capture plants or capture CO_2 emitted from the fuel they use and pipe it into the capture network.

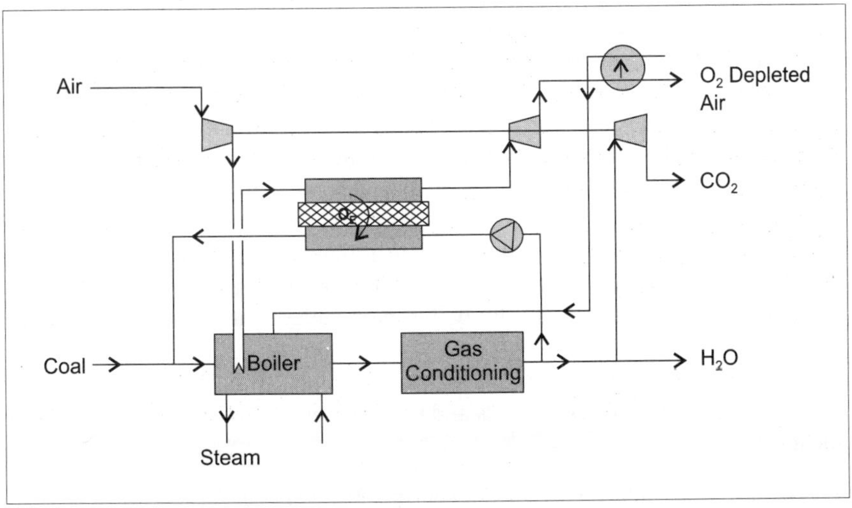

Source: Greenhouse Issues No. 88, p. 5, Dec. 2007

Fig. 8.8 An oxy-combustion coal boiler with membrane oxygen production

Yet another alternative could be to switch to electric power which again places the burden of emission control on the supplier. And, of course, other option could be cutting consumption of fossil fuel energy through efficiency improvements, relocating or even to close down!

Companies thinking of building CCS plants and marketing of "emission mitigation products" can gain much from knowing what the future local demand for electricity, hydrogen and CO_2 storage will be. This would offer a realistic choice of type of installation and capacity and the option value of future markets to be factored into investment decisions. At the same time, those on the demand side of the equation will profit from knowing the relative price and availability of the various options, including the timing. They should also critically evaluate which of the options will be more technically feasible for their operations. It needs to be kept in view that not every process can be successfully converted to electric power or hydrogen, and that capture of CO_2 from some processes could be particularly difficult.

Reducing CO_2 Emissions

Reducing CO_2 emissions can benefit the world in several ways. In the European Union (EU) alone, CO_2 emissions can be reduced by at least 30 per cent by the year 2020 (as compared to 1990). Some additional benefits of the low-carbon option will be lowered emissions of common air pollutants as well as a reduction in the import of fuels into the EU. The security of energy supplies will also improve (Barrett, 2007). It is well known that energy use is the chief cause of emissions of the main GHG like CO_2 and a range of health damaging air pollutants.

Alternative energy strategies that include behavioural change, demand management, energy efficiency and low-carbon fuels can go a long way in achieving a low-carbon economy. Besides abating GHG emissions, these strategies make possible cheaper and stronger abatement of other atmospheric pollutants as compared to higher carbon scenarios. This interaction between strategies to limit global warming and strategies for achieving other environmental objectives such as reduced acidification and improved air quality is highly attractive.

In recent years, the marginal cost of applying end-of-pipe (EOP) emission control technologies have increased as also the concern about global warming. Consequently, a greater emphasis is placed on developing integrated policies which can tackle the multiple environment problems of global warming and air pollution. This is important because controlling GHGs also brings down the level of air pollution. Stringent targets for both can be achieved at a lower total cost than when addressed separately.

All non-end-of-pipe (NEOP) solutions, except switching between fossil fuels, decrease dependence on fossil fuels and improve security of supply. NEOP options include:

- Behavioural change (e.g., smaller cars and lower speeds)
- Demand management (e.g., building insulation and low energy appliances)
- Fuel switching from coal and oil to gas and renewables

Emissions Accounting and Environmental Impacts

A chain of analytic techniques and models can relate environmental impacts on ecosystems and/or human health to emissions from the operation of electric power stations:

- Emissions are related to concentration and deposition by transport processes
- Concentration and deposition are related to dosage by exposure relationships
- Damage is related to dosage according to dose/response relationships

Swisher et. al., illustrated the above as, "Emissions from a source of SO_2 must be analysed to determine how the pollutants and byproducts formed by atmospheric reactions are transported, resulting in a pattern of local airborne concentration or deposition on land. A given concentration causes human exposure depending on the relationship between where it occurs, and where and how people spend their time, while deposition causes exposure to plant and animal species depending on where they are located and come in contact with the pollutant. Exposures lead to health damage or ecological impacts according to the sensitivity of the individuals exposed (age, diet and other parameters) or of the ecosystem (nutrition, chemical buffering, etc.)".

Methods and models exist to translate emissions into impacts and (at least in theory) to environmental and social cost values. In the context of IRP, potential energy supply or demand-side options can be compared on the basis of environmental as well as economic cost. Even if the environmental cost cannot be monetized reliably, they can be assumed to be proportional to emissions, allowing one to rank different measures according to their emission values. The analysis of environmental costs, whether monetized or not, requires a consistent accounting of emission rates.

Reducing Carbon Footprint in the Fuel Chain

Reducing CO_2 emission during the fuel life cycle is much more important than increasing the use of biofuels. In keeping with this view, a fuel quality directive presented by the EU Commission in January 2007 recommended giving fuel suppliers the responsibility for reducing the carbon footprint of their road fuels by 10 per cent by the year 2020. Specifically, they must cut the life cycle GHG emissions of their fuels by one per cent every year from 2011 onwards. The market could then decide for itself whether the fossil fuel chain or biofuels are more cost effective in reduction of emissions.

The proposal received support from the environmental movement, which has always criticized biofuel initiatives that do not consider the benefit they deliver. The sustainable biofuels can be part of the solution, but unsustainable biofuels are even worse for the environment than not producing them. The use of "well-to-wheel" calculations and sustainability criteria ensure that the most appropriate fuels receive priority (Corbey, 2007).

The EU has set country-specific targets for the proportion of biofuels used by the transport sector. In March, leaders of EU agreed to a legally binding

10 per cent biofuel target by the year 2020. The binding nature of the target is subject to sustainable, second-generation biofuels being actually available. However, the goal of decarbonization is to be achieved solely through an increased share of biofuels. It will certainly require a higher proportion than 10 per cent by the year 2020.

Integrating Energy Demand and Supply

A production cost analysis of the performance of existing and new electric supply alternatives facilitates the ranking of various alternatives according to marginal cost, including environmental and social costs. These results are then compared to the marginal cost of the demand-side options. The two sets of options are combined to make the "integrated" least cost electricity plan—"integrated" in the sense that unlike traditional least cost planning, it includes demand-side options, non-utility supply options, as also the environmental cost and other societal impact of all the options considered.

Northwest Power Planning Council (NWPPC) (1991) summarized the process of developing an integrated least cost energy plan in the following steps:

Step 1 Develop scenarios of energy service (not kWh) growth over time, and sensitivity analysis

Step 2 Assess the size, timing, cost and risk of energy supply and energy efficiency options

Step 3 Rank the options by marginal costs to develop integrated energy service "supply curves"

Step 4 Evaluate environmental and economic risk and reorder options to include policy issues

Step 5 Develop plans to implement energy savings and integrate with supply resources

An important basic assumption of IRP is that the benefit of electricity service should be measured in terms of the energy services provided, not simply the amount of energy sold. Therefore, the scenarios are based on projections of the growth in energy services (**Step 1**), and the need to maintain the required level of energy services irrespective of which particular combination of DSM and supply resources is used to meet the demand for energy services. As in the case of energy efficiency and DSM scenarios, the integrated energy scenario begin with baseline projections of energy service demand growth (Swisher et. al., 1997). Now, the assessment of an "integrated" set of options, including utility and non-utility energy supply sources as well as energy efficiency and load management options is done (**Step 2**). The ranking of both supply and demand-side options according to their marginal cost (**Step 3**) makes it possible to develop an integrated marginal cost function, or "supply curve", for providing electric services in future. The resources available and their relative ranking not only depend on the existing resources but also the new options considered, the time frame, the economic and energy-service growth rate and other economic parameters and the use of environmental or other external cost values. The integrated electricity plan is subjected to further policy studies, financial evaluation, sensitivity analysis and implementation planning before a final plan can be completed **(Steps 4 & 5)**. The incorporation of these issues can sometimes change the ranking order of the integrated plan somewhat or may even exclude certain resources from the plan.

Scenario analysis allows comparison of alternative combinations of technological options to provide the same level of energy services. The scenarios can be defined and differentiated under the following:

1. The level of projected energy service growth (e.g., high, medium, low).
2. The degree of implementation of energy-efficiency improvements (e.g., efficiency standards scenario, DSM scenario, etc.).
3. The energy supply strategy applied (e.g., least cost, least emissions, high renewables, etc.).

Baseline scenarios serve as the starting point in the analysis of energy-efficiency improvements. Other scenarios describe various levels of improved energy efficiency, meeting the same level of energy-service demand. A starting point might be a scenario

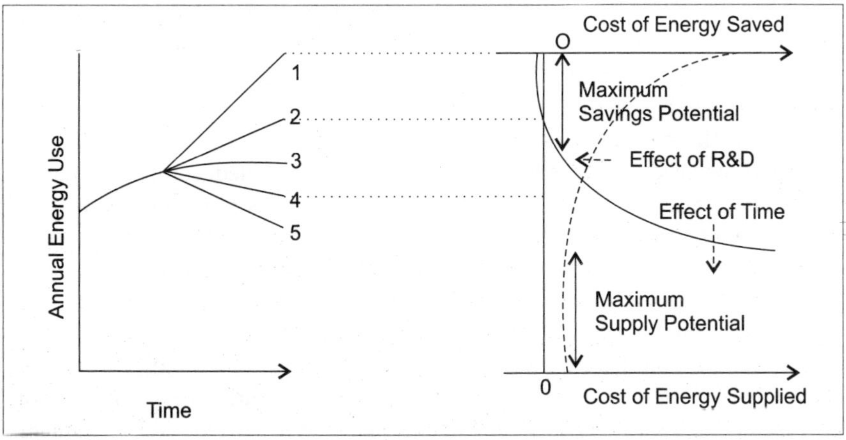

Fig. 8.9 The relationship between energy demand scenarios and marginal costs. The left graph illustrates the development of energy use up to the base year of the study, and shows five scenarios with different levels of energy demand for the end year of the study. All values apply to a given year. The upper half of the right figure shows the energy efficiency supply curve. This is drawn from the level of base-year frozen efficiencies, starts with negative cost measures (i.e., measures that will reduce the costs of obtaining the energy services). Energy service demand that is not met by end-use energy efficiency measures has to be met by supply options whose costs are shown by the energy supply curve in the bottom half of the right figure (After Swisher et al., 1997)

that reflects a marginal cost threshold of zero for energy-efficiency measures. This threshold might represent existing trends in energy-efficiency improvement, which would be expected with no policy change or new utility programmes (Fig. 8.9, Scenario 2). These criterias are often described as a reference scenario. Other scenarios might include greater efficiency improvement at higher cost (Swisher et. al., 1997).

Multiple scenarios allow identification of a least-cost scenario which combines the most cost-effective supply and demand options, where increasing the electric supply would cost more than increasing savings through energy efficiency and vice versa (Fig. 8.9). Linear optimization models are used to help identify the least-cost energy system.

Ecological Engineering

Mankind is now at the crossroads, searching for answers to the current pressing ecological problems. On one side are "deep ecologists" who patiently await the reactions of global Gaia. On the other side are 'biotechnologists' who would design and build new organisms and new ecosystems. The first approach is defeatist as it awaits the decimation of the human population. The other is activist but will it work? Berryman et. al., (1992) considered the idea of ecological engineering, which offers some promising solutions to our problems if it can integrate the practical sides of ecosystem, landscape, community and population ecology with relevant formal concepts from the engineering sciences.

Odum (1971) introduced the concept of ecological engineering. Engineers are frequently draw upon nature in the design and construction of their structures and machines. Odum's vision of mutually beneficial partnership between humans and nature is—blending of the gentle organizational capacity of nature with human technology. This may be feasible.

The three basic views of ecological engineering may be called ecothermodynamics, ecodynamics and ecodesign. Ecological thermodynamics is concerned with the flow of energy and materials through ecosystems and is commonly applied to the problems of waste disposal, environmental reclamation and the recovery or development of degraded or unproductive ecosystems. The thermodynamic approach has evolved from the concepts and methods of ecosystems ecology and borrowed many of its conventions from electrical engineering (Mitsch and Jorgensen, 1989; Berger, 1990). It attempts to optimize production, recycling and successional processes by controlling inputs such as pollutants, fuel and fertilizers. Thermodynamic ecology concentrates attention on the force functions of the ecosystem (rather than its endogenous feedback structures) and on the photosynthetic engine that drives it (Berryman et al., 1992).

Ecological dynamics has been widely applied to the management of resource and pest population, but the concept has been ignored in the ecological engineering texts. The ecodynamic approach focuses on the interactions between specific components of the ecosystem and its goal is to achieve optimal steady-state harvest or pest control. It derives its conventions from mechanical engineering and adopts the concepts and methods of population and community ecology. Its emphasis is on the interactions and feedback of the ecosystem (i.e., structure) rather than its forcing function. This approach is commonly encountered in textbooks aimed at resource and pest managers (Berryman, 1981; Deangelis et al., 1986).

Finally, design or architectural view of ecology emphasizes spatial structure and pattern of the ecosystem. This permeative has become popular as landscape ecology. Architectural design is an essential part of any engineering problem.

Engineers design and build machines to perform useful functions. Like ecologists, some engineers concentrate on thermodynamics, others are concerned with dynamics, and yet others deal with design. All three groups are necessary for solving complex engineering problems and all usually work cooperatively. In contrast, ecologists with different viewpoints seem more interested in popularizing their particular perspective, sometimes by inventing new jargon rather than new ideas (Berryman et. al., 1992). In fact, all three kinds of ecologists should cooperate to design and construct stable self-sustaining ecosystems.

One of the most challenging engineering problems is the control of the space-time dynamics of the machine. This is a 'dynamics' job and the discipline that helps solve this problem is called 'control theory'. Ecodynamics is made more difficult by the fact that ecosystems involve nonlinear interactions which can have very complex dynamical behaviour (Logan and Hail, 1991).

Stability is one of the most important problems faced by the engineer. Stability under disturbance is also a major problem for the ecodynamicist. Unfortunately, the concept of stability has been misunderstood. However, some ecologists even deny the existence of stability and equilibrium in ecosystems and there is no mention of the term stability in the textbook on ecological engineering by Mitsch and Jorgensen (1989).

Control engineers deal with the problem of stability by building negative feedback regulators into their machines such as autopilots, gyroscopes and thermostats. They build negative feedback regulators and 'feedforward' predictors to stabilize their machines or attenuate their behaviour and positive feedback devices to destabilize them or to amplify their behaviour (Berryman et al., 1992).

Natural ecosystems contain many feedbacks between their biotic components, e.g., negative feedbacks between predators and prey and positive feedbacks between competing species. The ecological engineer can likewise manipulate these feedbacks to regulate the system at desired steady states or to amplify certain components.

Thus, predaceous or parasitic insects can be added to an ecosystem with a view to regulate pests or weeds at non-damaging levels (Van den Bosch et. al., 1982). This biological control utilizes the negative feedback between prey and predator populations to regulate the variables at desirable steady states i.e., low densities of the pest or weed. Two of the many ways to achieve these ends include the introduction of new species from exotic lands or augmenting populations of native species by rearing them or by providing them with refugees (Hawksworth, 1991).

Landscape design is an integral part of the control and stability problem. The layout of habitat reserves, the distances between reserves and the corridors linking reserves are important components of a biological control project or species conservation (Berryman et al., 1992).

Even genetic engineering may have a role in the development of stable, self-sustaining ecosystems. There is a need not only to continue breeding pest-resistant plants, but also to engineer more effective predators, parasites and pathogens. It is likely that someday ecological engineers may be able to order 'designer' plants or natural enemies from bioengineering firms. However, the decision of when and where to release such organisms should be made by the ecodynamicist.

Green Design

A concept of green design is being advocated in several countries to produce products that are high in quality, have little environmental impact and cost less to produce. Green design means incorporating environmental objectives while maintaining product performance, useful life and functionality.

Green design considers not only the end product and its disposability, but also the byproducts and waste generated by producing and using the item. Getting and processing materials during manufacture of products is when serious environmental effects usually occur. Also, some products release materials during use that are harmful to the environment.

Ultimately, green design means waste prevention. This may be done by substituting less hazardous materials for more hazardous ones, by designing materials and products that use materials more effectively or by designing products that can be recycled or remanufactured more easily.

The major opportunities for design changes come in the cycle where one begins to design a new product. In several cases, proper product design can reduce manufacturing costs through consolidation of parts and modular assembly, increase serviceability while the product is in use, and recapture the value of the material through recycling and reuse it.

From the chemical industry to the automotive industry, implementing green design poses many challenges and requires companies to re-examine their processes. However, designing product that are "green" from production to disposal can be virtually impossible because trade-offs exist not only between traditional design objectives, but also sometime between environmental objectives themselves.

In some cases, toxic or hazardous chemicals are used to make benign end products. For example, ethylene oxide is used in the production of crayons. In other cases, materials used in the process may have negative environmental effects while the products they make are environment friendly. For instance, heavy metals (like mercury) are used to make energy-efficient lighting. However, while green design is certainly a step in the right direction for creating less waste and less hazardous waste, it alone cannot solve the world's environmental problems. It is only a necessary part of a larger and holistic environmental policy.

Shoes with soles made out of recycled tyres are already being sold in Europe. People have been trying for years to come up with a way to reuse tyres. There are literally over a billion used tyres in the world. Not only are the soles made of recycled tyres, the shoe is held together with non-toxic glue and the leather is treated with a vegetable tanning process. Even the packaging is in the recycling spirit, where the shoe boxes and papers are made from recycled papers and cardboards and the boxes are printed with water-base colours. Before the tyres become shoe soles, they are inspected, cut, washed with water and then dried. The scraps are reformulated into rubber to be injected in the heel of the shoe.

Not only shoes but belts, knapsacks and briefcases are being made from recycled tyres, as well as leather and suede byproducts of shoe making.

Rural Energy Transitions for Clean Energy Systems

Fuelwood, agricultural residues, dung cakes and other biomass are the chief sources of fuel and contributors of the total cooking energy in Indian villages (Census of India, 2001). Mostly women and girls produce, collect and use these fuels. But incomplete burning of these fuels in traditional cookstoves not only causes economic losses but also creates indoor air pollution and consequent health hazards. Indiscriminate use of fuelwood causes deforestation and desertification. In this context, technological solutions, institutional arrangements, awareness raising and training schemes for promoting affordable clean energy systems and services have great significance in the rural energy sector.

Some attempts have been made in India with a view to increase energy supply to rural households in a sustainable manner by introducing renewable energy technologies with a focus on improving energy use efficiency of cooking, pumping and lighting devices. For this purpose, improved *chulhas* (stove), biogas, kerosene lanterns or lamps, and solar lanterns were introduced and popularized in many villages (Prasad, 2005). Some financial subsidies are given to bring down their prices so that poor people can afford them. Additionally, greening of villages through plantations has been promoted to ensure availability of sufficient sources of biomass.

Decentralized participatory methods have been adopted for planning, implementation and project monitoring. The emphasis on participatory approach seems justified on the following grounds:

1. Energy intervention cannot be considered in isolation from the wider development priorities of the people.
2. Rural energy issues/patterns of consumption are localized and so the strategies to tackle these issues should be planned at that level. Indigenous knowledge of the people is valuable in understanding rural energy systems and identifying workable solutions (Prasad, 2005).

Benefits

Successful implementation of such projects has yielded good dividends in many villages with substantial fuelwood saving that helps to grow and raise the productivity of trees. Maintenance of tree growth reduces soil erosion, increases water infiltration, improves soil nutrient cycle and mitigates global climate problems (Prasad, 2005).

Potable drinking water has become available in the village through the installation of solar pumps. Likewise, installation of biogas plants provides high quality manure and enough cooking gas for daily cooking. The improved, fuel-efficient approaches such as biogas, improved *chulhas*, solar lanterns and improved kerosene lanterns reduce indoor pollution levels considerably.

Clean Energy for Chilling Milk

In Peru, many small farmers work in milk chilling business. Hundreds of dairy farmers from nearby villages bring their milk to a nodal farm where it is stored in milk chilling tank until it can be collected by some milk enterprises which collect and process the milk. Use of diesel engines to power the milk chilling is expensive. Besides the high cost of the diesel, transporting the diesel fuel to a farm is also expensive. The process is labour consuming and difficult, especially during the rainy season when road conditions become worse. A diesel engine also requires frequent maintenance and repairs.

These problems can be addressed by tapping a local energy source (Herrera and Ramirez, 2005). A project of the intermediate technology development group (ITDG) in Peru has promoted small hydroelectric power plants as an energy alternative for isolated areas. It has offered technical and financial assistance for the installation of small-scale hydropower turbines. Some farmers have installed a small hydro turbine on their property. The power generated by this turbine not only chills the milk but also provides electricity for other uses.

By mid-2003, a 30 KW hydropower plant had been constructed, a small electricity grid installed and the farmers are trained in the operation, maintenance and management of the plant. This small hydropower plant provides all the electricity for the milk chilling unit, and there is still some surplus power available for other activities. Also, the plant supplies electricity to several neighbouring families and even a school. It also powers a battery charging unit that is now used by 60 families living in the neighbouring village of Quinuamayo. In fact, thanks to the electricity generated by the hydro plant, the neighbouring families also could buy televisions and radios, which educate the farmers who learn new information about issues that affect their lives e.g., concerning education and health (Herrera and Ramirez, 2005).

Economic Efficiency and Energy Security in India

India is adopting various kinds of fuel options and forms of energy, including emerging technologies to meet economic efficiency, environment protection and energy security (3-E) goals. The country should seek clean coal technologies to tap its vast coal reserves by using conventional technologies (IEE, 2001). Not only medium to long-term challenges of ensuring competitive energy supplies from other nations need to be met (Table 8.1), but the immediate and pressing problem of power and coal shortages also requires policy actions (Venkaiah et. al., 2007).

India is facing a formidable challenge in meeting its energy requirement over the coming 25 years to support its anticipated eight per cent growth rate (Parikh et. al., 1994, 1996). This challenge may possibly be met by accelerating power sector reforms, cutting power cost, rationalization of fuel prices that promote efficient fuel choice and substitution, promoting energy efficiency and conservation, augmenting energy resources and supply, encouraging renewables, enhancing energy security, and creating an enabling and conducive environment and regulatory oversight for competitive efficiency (Venkaiah et. al., 2007).

Clean Energy Technology

There is considerable scope for effective international collaboration in areas such as clean and efficient coal combustion, coal conversion, CO_2 capture and storage, renewable energies such as wind, solar, geothermal and bioenergy, heat pumps, hydrogen and scenario analysis.

Serious efforts need to be made for improving energy security and services while reducing cost and vulnerability. In this context, Patterson (2007) points out that we are making an unnecessary mess of electricity supply largely due to the legacy of the old large power stations and transmission network. Patterson stresses that electricity needs a new story. In the traditional version, electricity is a fuel like any other. Someone makes electricity in power stations and delivers it to users over networks of cables. A better power station is usually a bigger one, farther away. Producers and users sell and buy electricity as a commodity, by the unit. Building power stations and networks requires heavy funds. Electricity users buy their own electrical equipment and attach it to the system as loads. As they switch loads on and off, the rest of the system must respond accordingly. Someone has to keep the system stable and ensure that the system has enough generation and network capacity to meet the maximum possible load that users can connect. Someone else has to keep your lights on.

In reality, one-third of the world population has no electricity and the rest have trouble keeping the lights on. The main technologies of traditional electricity—large dams, coal-fired and nuclear power stations, and overhead transmission lines—face strong financial and environmental troubles *(Greenhouse Issues 88, pp 16–17, Dec. 2007).*

According to Patterson, electricity is neither a fuel nor a commodity. It is a process that occurs simultaneously and instantaneously throughout an entire and interconnected circuit. A process cannot be stored. A fuel like coal comes out of the ground and is taken somewhere to be used. But we can start the electricity process anywhere, in various ways. Electricity exists only in the infrastructure of assets that generate it, deliver and use it, and through which it flows. Electricity is a function of infrastructure. While electricity can be produced and used without

Table 8.1 Demand Projection of Coal in India by various Industries in million tonnes (After Venkaiah et. al., 2007)

Source	Sectors/ Period	Base Year	2006–07	2010	2011–12	2015	2016–17	2020–21	2021–22	2024–25	2025
Tenth Plan Working Group	Power		322		469		617				
	Captive Power		28		32		37				
	Steel		43		40		40				
	Cement		25		24		25				
	Fertilizer		4		5		5				
	Others		51		50		56				
	Total	**2001–02**	**473**		**620**		**780**		**981**	**1126**	
Coal Vision 2025* 8% GDP	Power		322		427		553		699	804	
	Captive Power		28		44		63		90	112	
	Fertilizer		4								
	Steel		43		54		69		90	105	
	Cement		25		39		61		95	123	
	Others		51		65		82		106	123	
	Total	**2006–07**	**473**		**630**		**828**		**1079**	**1267**	
		1998–99						**1118**		**1402**	**1483**

Contd...

Contd...

Source	Sectors/ Period	Base Year	2006–07	2010	2011–12	2015	2016–17	2020–21	2021–22	2024–25	2025
Hydrocarbon Vision 2025, India Vision 2020	Best Case Scenario	1997–98						538		659	
	Business as usual	(311)						688		971	
EIA	High	2000		408		473		548		611	629
	Low			374		411		447		481	490
	Reference			390		439		493			
IEA		2000		484				623		713	
P&E Division, Planning Commission		2001	481		612		764	920	957		

* Projection made by TERI for Coal Vision 2025

fuel, it cannot be produced without infrastructure. The flow of electricity through the infrastructure is easy to measure. But the price of a unit of electricity is ultimately arbitrary and depends on the price of any fuel, and on asset accounting, taxation, regulation, risk, subsidies, network and system effects, and some other factors that are usually not stated.

The crucial issue here is the infrastructure of the electricity system—who owns it, who has access to it, who uses it and on what basis. To deliver electricity services more reliably and sustainably, not only the electric infrastructure, especially the end-use technologies needs to be upgraded, but it also needs to be transformed. The old centralized system of large remote power stations and a network including long high-voltage transmission lines used to make sense some decades ago but it no longer does so today. Most central station generators operate either intermittently or at only partial load most of the times misusing costly assets. Fuel-based central generators waste two-thirds of the fuel energy before it even leaves the power plant. On many systems, line losses are quite significant. The configuration is strongly vulnerable to disruption. Traditional electricity assumes that every load being essentially equivalent requires the same high quality of electricity. In fact, much is used for undemanding services such as heating and cooling.

Patterson suggests a better way. Wind turbines, microhydro, biomass generators, photovoltaics, gas engines, microturbines, fuel cells, stirling engines and microcogeneration all show economies not of unit scale but of series manufacture. Small-scale generators can usually be located close to loads, even on site, dramatically altering network requirements and operation. Instead of a radial one-way network, a decentralized system would have a two-way meshed network, with loads and generators of broadly comparable sizes more or less uniformly distributed across the system. Monitoring and control technologies allow for creating fully self-stabilizing systems in which loads and generators interact continuously and react accordingly.

Clean Energy & Geothermal Power

Although geothermal power holds enormous potential in the burgeoning clean-energy market, it has not attracted much interest for many uses. Iceland is quite rich in geothermal energy as the country is located on a geological hot spot which provides enough power not only to generate one-quarter of its electricity but also heat most of its homes. In fact, geothermal energy may play a more important role in world energy production. For a utility, the first choice of renewable energy is geothermal. Many energy analysts believe that geothermal companies have a substantial long-term potential.

Nevertheless, with less than 10 gigaWatts of installed capacity, geothermal energy accounts for only about 0.2 per cent of all electricity produced around the world. In theory, geothermal heat can be found anywhere in the world if we dig deep. But in reality, it has only been worth harnessing in those regions where water is found in combination with hot, porous rock close to the surface (Kleiner, 2007).

For example, just to the north of San Francisco, the geothermal field named 'The Geysers' generates 760 megaWatts of electric power. The plants there exploit an extensive naturally occurring underground steam reservoir which can be tapped by drilling fairly shallow wells.

The Geysers exemplify 'dry-steam' power plants. The steam from the reservoir contains little or no liquid water, and so can be routed directly to a turbine to generate electricity. But most plants are of the 'flash-steam' type. They use water that has been heated to about 180°C, but still is liquid because it is highly pressurized underground. This water is then pumped to the surface. Since the pressure there is lower, most of the water 'flashes' into steam, which is then used to operate a turbine.

When the water is around 100–180°C, 'binary' plants are used—they use hot water to heat a working fluid like isobutene, whose boiling point is lower than that of water. This vapourized working fluid can be used to drive the turbine.

Geothermal power requires high capital cost—the cost of digging deep wells are high. The lower fuel costs, however, balance the high cost of digging a well. An Australian firm called 'Geodynamics' is developing a new technique that exploits geothermal energy in the absence of a ready-formed reservoir of water. This company intends to use the Cooper Basin, a geological feature of the Australian interior, in which rocks with a temperature of about 270°C are found very near the surface.

Geodynamics aims to drill two wells to a depth of 4.3 km. The hot granite in the rocks is being fractured by pumping down cold water. When the rock becomes permeable, the system will serve as a heat exchanger, i.e., water will be pumped down one well, migrate through the rock to the other well, from where it may be extracted and used to generate electricity (Kleiner, 2007). The company estimates the potential capacity of the Cooper Basin at 10,000 megaWatts of power, which could be realized by drilling hundreds of wells. The Geodynamics project exemplifies a technology called 'hot-dry-rock' or 'hot-fractured-rock' geothermal. This type of 'enhanced' geothermal power generation is expected to greatly enhance our ability to tap geothermal energy.

In the United States, enhanced geothermal electrical capacity could reach 100 gigaWatts in the next five decades and will meet about 10 per cent of the country's electricity needs.

The flexibility of such systems could prove to be economical from a very large scale, all the way down to a relatively small, 1-megaWatt plant that also provides direct heating to buildings. Indeed, this combined heat-and-power approach substantially increases the economics of geothermal power.

Appendix
Conversion Factors

Heating Value (Lower Heating Value or Net Calorific Value) of some Fuels

Fuel	GJ/Metric Tonne	MJ/m^3
LPG	49.35	
Kerosene	46.05	
Diesel oil	45.46	
Fuel oil	43.24	
Natural gas		41.23
Gasoline	38.87	
Ethanol	29.68	
Charcoal	29.46	
Coal	28.46	
Piped gas (town or city gas)		17.50
Wood fuel	10.56	

Source: Brasil, Ministerio de Minas e Energia, 1995

Important Conversion Factors

Parameter	Joule	Kilo Watt Hour	Kilo Calorie
1 J	1	2.778×10^{-7}	2.388×10^{4}
1 kWh	3.6×10^{6}	1	860
1 kcal	4186.8	1.163×10^{-3}	1
1 TOE (IEA)*	4.1868×10^{10}	11630	10^{7}
1 TOE (Brazil)*	4.5×10^{10}	12510	1.0835×10^{7}

Source: International Energy Agency (IEA), 1995, except Brazil TOE conversions. from Brasil, Ministerio de Minas e Energia, 1995

* Note, every country's oil products have different calorific values, resulting in different conversion factors for each country between TOE and other units of measurement like Joules, kiloWatt hours, and kilo calories. We present two separate TOE conversions here to illustrate this point. The IEA value is an international average while the Brazil value applies specifically to just one country. In carrying out analyses for specific countries, country-specific TOE values should be used to the greatest extent possible.

Decimal Multipliers

Multiplier	Abbreviation	Meaning
Kilo	k	10^3
Mega	M	10^6
Giga	G	10^9
Tera	T	10^{12}
Peta	P	10^{15}
Exa	E	10^{18}

Terminology for Energy and Electricity

Energy (E) is the ability of a system to do work or to produce heat, measured in J (Joules) or Wh (Watt hours), 1 Wh = 3,600 J. Various forms of energy can be converted into one another.

Efficiency refers to the quality of the conversion process during which some part of the input energy (e.g., radiation) is not transformed into the output energy (e.g., electricity) but is lost into another form (e.g., heat).

Power defines the rate at which energy is supplied, measured in W (Watts). A 60 W light bulb burning for 1 hour consumes 60 Wh, the same energy as a 30 W fan running for 2 hours or 3,600 W motor in 1 minute. Electric power follows the relation P = U * I. Light intensity or irradiance is a form of power. Sunlight delivers up to 1 kW = 1,000 W per square metre. The symbol I refers to current, which corresponds to the flow of electrons through an electric conductor. It is measured in A (amperes). If the electron flow continuously changes direction, it is called AC (alternating current), otherwise, it is DC (direct current).

Voltage is best understood by comparing the current with the flow of water in a channel. The voltage U is then the gradient of the channel which causes the water to flow. It is measured in V (Volts). Appliances are indicated by their power consumption. The current drawn by them depends on the voltage. A 60 W AC lightbulb requires 0.25 A (240 V) while the current for a 60 W DC device is 5 A (12 V).

Resistance determines how many amperes flow at a given voltage. Resistance (R) is measured in Ω (Ohm). According to Ohm's law, R = U/I or I = U/R.

Glossary

Achievable Potential It is an estimate of energy savings based on the assumption that all energy-efficient options will be adopted to the extent that they are cost effective and possible through appropriate utility programmes.

Adaptive Management The process of implementing policy decisions as scientifically driven management experiments that test predictions and assumptions in management plans, and using the resulting information to improve the plans.

Adiabatic Process A thermodynamic process in which no heat is extracted or added to the system.

Administrative Costs In the context of Demand Side Management (DSM), these costs are incurred by a utility for programme planning, design, marketing, implementation and evaluation. They include labour-related costs, office supplies and expenses, data processing and such other costs but exclude costs of marketing materials and advertising, purchases of equipment for specific programmes, and rebates or other incentives.

Agroecosystem An ecological system modified by people to produce food, fibre, fuel and other products desired for human use.

Agropastoralism Land-use system in which arable cropping and the keeping of grazing livestocks are combined.

Air Change A measure of the rate at which the air in a building is replaced by outside air from infiltration and ventilation. It is usually described as air changes per hour.

Alternative Rate Programmes Special rate structure or discount on the customer's electric bill, generally in return for participation in programmes aimed at cutting peak demands.

Annual Energy Effects The estimated change in energy used on an average annual basis associated with participation in a programme or installation of an efficiency measure.

Arid Region A region which is very dry and has little vegetation. Aridity depends on temperature, rainfall and evaporation. An arid area is usually defined as one that receives less than 250 mm (10 inches) of rainfall every year.

Audit Analysis of a home, building or industrial process by an energy engineer to determine ways the customer can improve their energy efficiency.

Availability The ratio of the maximum output of a supply resource to its rated capacity. It is a measure of reliability.

Avoided Cost The incremental cost that a utility would incur to produce or purchase an amount of power equivalent to that saved by a DSM measure.

Balance of Nature The idea that there is an inherent equilibrium in most ecosystems, with plants and animals interacting so as to produce a stable, continuing system of life on earth.

Base Load Generation Those generating facilities within a utility system which are operated to the greatest extent possible to maximize system mechanical and thermal efficiency and minimize system operating costs.

Bench Marking A process for achieving superior performance through rigorous measurement and comparison of operating practices and philosophies in companies organized as "best-in-class", to identify and incorporate the best practices and to surpass the best-in-class performers.

Benefit–Cost Ratio The ratio of the value of a DSM measure's energy savings to its installed cost. The energy savings value is based on the utility's avoided cost.

Best Available Technology (BAT) Definition used in US Public Law 92–500 (Amendments to the Federal Water Pollution Control Act of 1972) as applied to wastewater treatment processes for obtaining effluent limits effective July 1, 1983.

Bidding Programme The utility's issuance of a Request for Proposal (RFP) to acquire demand-side resources. Potential bidders may include energy service companies, installation contractors, material suppliers, customers and other utilities.

Biocentrism A perception of the world that values the existence and diversity of all biological species, as opposed to a human-centred perspective (anthropocentrism).

Biosphere The narrow zone that supports life on our planet. It is limited to the waters of the earth, a fraction of its crust and the lower regions of the atmosphere.

Biotechnology Any technique that use living organisms (or parts of organisms) to make or modify products, to improve plants or animals, or to develop micro-organisms for specific uses.

Capacity Value The contribution of a supply resource to the maximum capacity of the system. It is a measure of reliability and predictability of a resource.

Capacity-limited Resource A supply resource (e.g., thermal) of which the energy output is limited by the rated capacity, regardless of how much energy is available.

Capitalized Equipment or other costs that are considered capital investments to be used over a multi-year period and therefore eligible for inclusion in rate base.

Carbon Cycle Sequence by which carbon circulates and is recycled through the natural world.

Carbon dioxide Fertilization Enhancement of plant growth or of the net primary production by CO_2 enrichment that could occur in natural or agricultural systems as a result of an increase in the atmospheric concentration of CO_2.

Carbon Flux The rate of exchange of carbon between pools (reservoirs).

Carbon Pool The reservoir containing carbon as a principal element in the geochemical cycle.

Carrying Capacity The maximum number of animals of a given species that a particular area can support. When the carrying capacity is exceeded, there is insufficient food (or other resources) for the population. The population may then be reduced by emigration, reproductive failure or death through starvation.

Cash Incentive An incentive in the form of a rebate or cash payment.

Catalytic Converter Device fitted to the exhaust system of a motor vehicle so as to reduce toxic emissions from the engine. It converts harmful exhaust products to relatively harmless ones by passing the exhaust gases over a mixture of catalysts coated on a metal or ceramic honeycomb which increases the surface area and hence, the amount of active catalyst with which the exhaust gases come into contact.

Climate System It includes the five physical components (atmosphere, hydrosphere, cryosphere, lithosphere and biosphere) that are responsible for the climate and its variations.

Coke Clean, light fuel produced by the carbonization of certain types of coal. When this coal is strongly heated in airtight ovens (to release all volatile constituents), the brittle and silver-gray remains are coke. Coke comprises 90 per cent carbon together with very small quantities of water, hydrogen and oxygen and makes a useful industrial and domestic fuel.

Combined Heat and Power (CHP) Generation Simultaneous production of electricity and useful heat in a power station. The heat is often in the form of hot water or steam, which can be used for local district heating or in industry. The electricity output from a CHP plant is lower than from a conventional station, but the overall efficiency of energy conversion is higher.

Commercial Sector A group of non-residential customers that provide services, including retail, wholesale, finance, insurance and public administration.

Competitive Bidding A competitive procurement process for selecting, for instance, some portion of future electric generating capacity that may include the publication of a RFP by an electric utility for the purchase of electric generating capacity, electric energy, and/or DSM products and services, the submission of bids offering to provide such products and services by multiple would be suppliers, and the selection by the electric utility of one or more winning bids subject to appropriate oversight by a state regulatory body.

Compost Decomposition of organic material by bacteria under controlled conditions to make a nutrient-rich natural fertilizer for use in gardening or farming. A well-made compost heap reaches a high temperature during the composting process, killing most weed seeds that might be present.

Connection Charge An amount to be paid by a customer in a lump sum, or in installations for connecting the customer's facilities to the supplier's facilities.

Conservation The protection, improvement and use of natural resources according to principles that will assure their highest economic or social benefits.

Conservation Cost Adjustment (CCA) A means of billing customers to accrue funds to pay for the costs of load management programmes. Utilities defer the cost of building expenses generating capacity by encouraging customers to use energy more efficiently. Customers are encouraged to purchase energy-efficient appliances and machinery to replace less efficient devices. A common example is when a utility advertises that it will pay customers to convert from electric resistance heat to heat pumps. The greater efficiency of the heat pumps reduces peak demand. Applied over large numbers of customers, the lowered demand allows the utility to avoid expensive construction of energy supply units, which more than pays for the cost of the advertising and the rebates.

Conservation Programme It is a DSM programme that attempts to reduce a customer's energy (kWh) consumption over most or all hours of the day.

Contingency Security Criteria Reliability criteria based on a given number of component failures being compensated by other facilities without losing the ability to meet forecasted loads.

Cost of Avoided Emissions The ratio of incremental costs of emission-reducing measures to the incremental quantity of emissions reduced.

Cream Skimming Installing only the lowest cost or easy-to-install DSM measures while ignoring other cost-effective opportunities.

Customer Class A group of customers with similar characteristics such as economic activity or level of electricity use.

Demand The aggregate desire for economic goods and services. The quantity of a good or service that consumers are willing to purchase at various prices. Demand involves the relationship between quantity and price.

Demand Side Management The planning, implementation and monitoring of utility activities designed to influence customer's use of electricity in ways that will produce desired changes in a utility's load shape (i.e., changes in the time pattern and magnitude of a utility's load). Utility programmes falling under the umbrella of DSM include load management, new uses of electricity, energy conservation, electrification, customer generation adjustments in market share and innovative rates. DSM includes only those activities that involve a deliberate intervention by the utility to alter the load shape. These changes must produce benefits to both the utility and its customers.

Demography Study of the size, structure, dispersal and development of human populations to establish reliable statistics on such factors as birth and death rates, marriages and divorces, life expectancy and migration.

Developed World or First World or the North The countries that have a money economy, a highly developed industrial sector, a high degree of urbanization, a complex communications network, high gross domestic product per person, low birth and death rates, high energy consumption and a large proportion of the workforce employed in manufacturing or service industries. The developed world includes the USA, Canada, Europe, Japan, Australia and New Zealand.

Developing World or Third World or the South Countries with a largely subsistence economy where the output per person and the average income are low. Typically have low life expectancy, high birth and death rates, poor communications and health facilities, low literacy levels, high national debt and low energy consumption per person. The developing world includes much of Africa and parts of Asia and South America.

Development The acquisition of industrial techniques and technology by a society. Hence, the common classification of the 'developed' nations of the First and Second Worlds and the poor, 'developing' or 'under-developed' nations of the Third World. The concept has been enlarged recently to include improvements in 'quality of life' e.g., in health care, life expectancy, education and housing. The assumption that development in the sense of industrialization is inherently good has been increasingly questioned since the 1960s, especially as the environmental consequences of industrial growth have gained a higher public profile.

Economic Commission for Europe (ECE) Its headquarters is in Geneva. (Not to be confused with the EEC (European Economic Community) with its own Commission in Brussels).

Ecological Efficiency Percentage of energy in the biomass produced by one trophic level that is incorporated into biomass produced by the next highest trophic level.

Ecology The branch of science dealing with the interactions among all living organisms and their environment.

Economic Potential An estimate of energy savings based on the assumption that all energy efficient options will be adopted and all existing equipment will be replaced with the most efficient, whenever it is cost-effective to do so, without regard to market acceptance.

Ecosystem The complex of an ecological community, together with the non-living components of the environment, which function together as a stable system and in which exchange of materials follow a circular path.

Ecosystem Management An approach to maintain or restore the composition, structure and function of natural and modified ecosystems for the goal of long-term sustainability. It is based on a collaboratively developed vision of desired future conditions that integrates ecological, socio-economic and institutional perspectives, applied within a geographic framework defined primarily by natural ecological boundaries.

Efficiency, First Law The amount of energy service delivered by a machine per unit of energy input. For example, if a 400-Watt electric motor delivers only 280 Watts of mechanical drive power, it has an efficiency of 280/400 = 70%. Under the First Law of Thermodynamics, this efficiency cannot exceed 100 per cent.

Efficiency, Second Law An alternative concept of energy efficiency, based on the Second Law of Thermodynamics. This efficiency is defined as the ratio of the theoretical minimum energy that is required to accomplish a given task to the energy actually consumed. In using the second law efficiency concept, energy consumption has to be measured in units which reflect the quality of the energy involved. For example, a water heater with a first law efficiency of 75 per cent would be compared to an ideal heat pump, operating between the same temperatures as the water heater with a coefficient of performance of 7.5 (750% efficiency). This comparison would give a second law efficiency of 0.7/7.5 = 10%. While the first law efficiency gives the impression that only modest improvement is possible, the second law efficiency indicates a 10-fold potential gain.

Efficient Technologies State-of-art commercially available appliances, equipment, building-shell measures or industrial processes that improve the end-use efficiency of electricity relative to the existing stock of appliances, equipment, measures and processes.

Electrification New electric technologies such as electric vehicles, industrial process heating and automation with the potential for increasing productivity, contributing to strategic load growth or facilitating strategic conservation, peak clipping or load shifting. For example, robotics and industry automation, microwave heating and drain, and freeze concentration of solutions.

Electrostatic Precipitator Device for removing dust or other particles from air and other gases. An electric discharge is passed through the gas, giving the impurities a negative electric charge. Positively charged plates are then used to attract the charged particles and remove them from the gas flow. These devices are attached to the chimneys of coal-burning power stations to remove ash particles.

Emission A discharge of a liquid or gaseous material.

Emission Factor The ratio of emissions to energy produced or fuel consumed, denominated in units of tonnes of emissions per unit of energy.

Energy The ability or capacity to do work. Energy can be categorized in either stored or transient forms. Stored forms of energy include thermal, potential, kinetic, chemical and nuclear. Transient forms include heat and work, mechanical or flow.

Energy Conservation Methods of reducing energy use through insulation, increasing energy efficiency and changes in patterns of use. Profligate energy use by industrialized countries contributes greatly to air pollution and the greenhouse effect when it draws on non-renewable energy sources. Increased energy conservation can significantly cut both air pollution and industrial costs.

Energy Costs Costs like fuel that are related to and vary with energy production or consumption is termed energy costs.

Energy Efficiency Programme DSM programme aimed at reducing overall electricity consumption (kWh), often without regard for the daily timing of the programme induced savings. Generally, such savings are achieved by substituting technically more efficient equipment to produce the same level of end-use services with less electricity.

Energy Efficiency Ratio (EER) A figure of merit of air conditioning or refrigeration performance. The relative efficiency of an appliance in converting primary energy (e.g., electricity) to useful work (like for cooling in the case of air conditioners) at the rated condition. EER (Btu/kWh) is the Btu per hour output provided by the unit, divided by the Watts of electrical power input. The larger the EER, the more efficient is the unit.

Energy Productivity It refers to the productivity of energy as a factor of production and includes the level of economic value produced per unit of energy input. Energy productivity improvements occur when existing energy services (e.g., lighting, heating, cooling, motor drive) are made more efficient and when new energy-using technologies boost economic efficiency (e.g., telecommunications, automation/robotics, information processing).

Energy Services The physical amenity provided by energy-using equipment e.g., cooking, illumination, thermal comfort, food refrigeration, transportation or product manufacturing.

Energy, Alternative Energy from sources that are renewable and ecologically safe, as opposed to sources that are nonrenewable with toxic byproducts such as coal, oil or gas (fossil fuels), and uranium (for nuclear power). At present, the most commercially important and exploited alternative energy source is flowing water, harnessed as hydroelectric power. Other sources include the oceans' tides and waves, wind, the Sun and the heat trapped in the earth's crust (geothermal energy).

Engine A device that transforms energy, especially heat energy, into mechanical work. Among the prime movers, those in which the power originates in a piston and cylinder are classified as engines, while those with purely rotative motion are known as 'turbines'.

Environment A general description of the surroundings of an organism encompassing air, water and land, which support its life and receive its waste products.

Environmental Health The state of being of an individual as influenced by changes in his environment such as a biohazard, hazardous material, pollution, working and living conditions.

Environmental Impact Any action of specific materials or gross pollution upon the environment.

Environmental Quality Characteristics of the environment indicative of its desirability for human activity in general.

Environmentalism Theory emphasizing the primary influence of the environment on the development of groups or individuals. It stress the importance of physical, biological, psychological or cultural environment as a factor influencing the structure or behaviour of animals, including humans. In politics, this has given rise to green parties in many countries, which aim to 'preserve the planet and its people'.

Erosion The natural removal of the surface of land by the action of wind or water.

Eutrophication Natural process of nutrient enrichment of a lake or other contained water body which can be accelerated by uncontrolled wastewater discharges. Typically characterized by increased growth of algae, bacteria, plants, etc.

Evaluation Systematic measurement of the performance of DSM programme.

Expensed Costs Costs that are treated as current expenses rather than as capital costs. Here, the utility cannot earn a return on expensed costs.

Externality A social cost not captured in conventional market transactions.

Feedback A system whose output modifies input to the system. Prices play this role in market systems.

Fine-grained It refers to qualities of the environment that occur in small patches with respect to the activity patterns of an organism and among which the organism cannot usefully distinguish.

Food Technology The commercial processing of foodstuffs to render them more palatable or digestible, or to preserve them from spoilage.

Food Web An abstract representation of the various paths of energy flow through population in the community.

Fossil Fuel These are fuel such as coal, oil and natural gas formed from the fossilized remains of plants that lived millions of years ago. Fossil fuels are a non-renewable resource and will eventually run out. Extraction of coal and oil causes considerable environmental pollution and burning coal contributes to problems of acid rain by releasing sulphur dioxide. All fossil fuels release carbon dioxide when burnt, regardless of whatever anti-pollution measures are in place. Increased levels of carbon dioxide are liable to cause global warming by artificially enhancing of the greenhouse effect.

Friends of the Earth (FOE) Environmental pressure groups that aim to protect the environment and to promote rational and sustainable use of the earth's resources. They campaign on issues such as acid rain, air, sea, river and land pollution, recycling, disposal of toxic wastes, nuclear power and renewable energy, the destruction of rainforests, pesticides and agriculture.

Fuel Any source of heat or energy, embracing the entire range of materials that burn (combustibles). A nuclear fuel is any material that produces energy by nuclear fission in a nuclear reactor.

Gaseous Waste (Gaseous Emission) Discharge of volatile or non-condensable compounds into the atmosphere.

Genetic Resources Genetic material of plants, animals and other organisms, which value as a resource for present and future generations.

Geographic Variation Change in a species' trait over distance or among different distinct population. Measurable character divergence among geographically distinct population that are often, though not necessarily, the result of local selection.

GigaWatt Hour (GWh) One gigaWatt hour is 1,000 megaWatt hours.

Global Warming Projected imminent climate change attributed to the greenhouse effect. By 2030, the average global temperature would have risen by between 0.7– 2.0°C.

Green Manure Green plant biomass used as fertilizer.

Green Party Political party aiming to preserve the planet and its people, based on the premise that incessant economic growth is unsustainable.

Green Revolution The use of a package of inputs, including modern varieties, pesticides, fertilizers and frequently also irrigation, in an attempt to increase farm yields in developing countries.

Green Tax Taxes levied against companies and individuals causing pollution.

Greenhouse Effect Phenomenon of the earth's atmosphere by which the energy of solar radiation, absorbed by the ground and remitted as infrared energy, is prevented from escaping by various gases in the air. This results in a rise in the earth's temperature.

Greenpeace International environmental pressure group with a policy of non-violent direct action backed by scientific research.

Habitat A specific place occupied by an organism or community, where interactions with other organisms and the environment occur.

Hydroelectric Power (HEP) Electricity generated by moving water.

Hydrology Study of location and movement of inland water, both frozen and liquid, above and below ground.

Impact Evaluation Examines the effects of a DSM programme, including quantitative documentation of costs and benefits, programme participation and measure adoption, performance of DSM technologies, and energy and load impacts.

Incentive Programme Awards (either cash or non-cash) to customers, trade allies, or employees to encourage participation in a DSM programme and adoption of recommended measures.

Incremental Cost The difference in costs, particularly between that of an efficient technology or measure and the alternative standard technology. In some early retirements and retrofits, the full cost of the efficient technology is considered to be the incremental cost.

Indigenous/Local Knowledge Knowledge that develops in a particular area and accumulates over time through being handed down from generation to generation.

Industrial Sector The group of non-residential customers that provide products, including construction, mining and manufacturing.

Innovative Rate A rate schedule with rate above or below the associated costs of providing service to the customer. A promotional rate establishes a pricing level which permits sales to be made which otherwise would not occur.

Integrated Resource Planning The combined development of electricity supplies and DSM options to provide energy services at minimum cost, including environmental and social costs.

KiloWatt Hour (kWh) A kiloWatt hour is the standard 'unit' of power that appears on your bill. For example, in the UK, an average household uses 3,300 kWh of electricity and 20,500 kWh of gas every year.

Landfill The disposal of solid wastes or sludges by dumping onto land and preferably covering with a thin layer of soil (sanitary landfill).

Landfill Site Low-lying area used for dumping household and commercial waste. The sites can release toxins and other leachates into the soil. Decomposing organic matter releases methane, which can be explosive, but the gas can be collected and burnt for energy.

Leaching Process by which substances are washed out of the soil. Fertilizers leached out of the soil drain into rivers, lakes and ponds and cause water pollution. The risk of nitrates and pesticides leaching into aquifers is greatest in sandy or shallow soils. In tropical areas, leaching of the soil after the destruction of forests removes scarce nutrients and can lead to a dramatic loss of soil fertility. The leaching of soluble minerals in soils can lead to the formation of distinct soil horizons as different minerals are deposited at successively lower levels.

Leaded Petrol Petrol that contains antiknock, a mixture of the chemicals tetraethyl lead and dibromoethane. The lead from the exhaust fumes enters the atmosphere, mostly as simple lead compounds, and is poisonous to children's developing neural systems.

Least Cost Planning A utility planning method whereby alternative resource mixes, including demand-side options such as conservation and load management, are evaluated along with traditional supply-side options to determine which of them minimizes the overall cost of service. Cost management is the criterion for selecting the resource plan for the utility company.

Livelihood System A combination of people, resources and environment in which the stocks and flows of food and cash are used to meet the basic needs of the people. The livelihood system of a rural household may include cropping, tree-growing, animal-keeping, fishing, hunting, gathering, processing, trading, paid employment and a wide variety of other non-farm activities.

Malthus Theory Projection of population growth made by Thomas Malthus in 1793, based on his theory of the population explosion. He argued that the number of people would increase faster than the food supply. Population would eventually reach a resource limit (overpopulation). Any further increase would result in a population crash, caused by famine, disease or war.

Management Refers to managers' role which consists of the psychometric quantitative analyses of interdependent relationships of indigenous components as deflected by the theoretical analogy of perturbation and adumbration of sagacity.

Marginal Resource The most expensive resource, in terms of short-run marginal (fuel and operating) cost, needed at a given time.

Market Potential An estimate of energy savings that adjusts the economic potential for the likely acceptance by customers of various energy-saving actions.

Market Research The systematic gathering, recording and analysis of data about problems relating to the marketing of goods and services. Refers to the process of developing information and analyses about customers. Includes various subsidiary types of research such as market analysis (a study of the size, location, nature and characteristics of a specified market), consumer research (a study of consumer attitudes, behaviour, reactions and preferences for goods or services), sales analysis (a study of sales data) and advertising research (a study of the effectiveness of the advertising of goods and services).

Marketing Costs It is the costs that are directly associated with the preparation and implementation of the strategies designed to encourage participation in a programme.

Maximum Sustained Yield (MSY) The largest harvestable level of a renewable resource that can be sustained over several generations. Harvest of a natural population at the population size representing the maximum rate of recruitment into population, based on a logistic growth curve.

MegaWatt Hour (MWh) One megaWatt hour is equal to 100 kiloWatt hours.

Monetizing Attaching monetary value on typically non-monetary goods and processes such as biological material or ecological processes. The process of converting values to economic units.

Monitoring and Evaluation Costs The expenditures associated with the collection and analysis of data used to assess programme operation and effects.

Monoculture The growing of a single plant species in one area, usually the same type of crop grown year after year.

Montreal Protocol International agreement signed in 1987 to stop the production of ozone depleting chemicals by the year 2000.

Mulch Protective covering of the soil surface by various substances such as green or dry organic matter, sand or stone applied to prevent evaporation of moisture, regulate temperature and control weeds.

Nature Reserve area set aside to protect a habitat and the wildlife that lives within it, with only restricted admission for the public. A nature reserve often provides a sanctuary for rare species.

Networking Establishing and strengthening links between individuals, groups and organizations with similar interests and objectives.

Non-cash Incentives Incentives in a form other than rebate or cash payment, may include low-interest loans, reduced equipment costs, bill credits or discounts, merchandise or free services.

Non-coincident Demand Maximum demand of a customer or customer class, regardless of when it occurs. Generally, the non-coincident demand is used as the basis for calculating the demand charge.

Non-renewable Resource Natural resource like coal or oil that take millions of years to form naturally and can therefore not be replaced once consumed. The main energy sources used by humans are nonrenewable; renewable resources, such as solar, tidal and geothermal power, have so far been less exploited.

Nuclear Energy or Atomic Energy Energy released from the nucleus of the atom. Energy produced by nuclear fission (the splitting of uranium or plutonium nuclei) has been harnessed to generate electricity.

Oil Natural mineral oil, a thick greenish-brown flammable liquid found underground in permeable rocks. Crude oil is known as 'petroleum'.

Operations and Maintenance Costs Non-capital, equipment-related costs that continue over the life of the equipment; include fuel costs as well as costs for maintaining and servicing equipment.

Overpopulation Too many people for the resources available in an area (such as food, land and water). Although there is often a link between overpopulation and population density, high densities do not always result in overpopulation. In many countries, where resources are plentiful and the infrastructure and technology are well-developed, a large number of people can be supported by a small area of land. In some developing countries, insufficient food, minerals, and energy, and inequitable income distribution results in poverty. Here, even low population densities may amount to overpopulation. Overpopulation may also result from a decrease in resources or an increase in population or a combination of both.

Performance Factor It is the ratio of the useful output capacity of a system to the input required to obtain it. Units of capacity and input need not be consistent.

Petrochemical Chemical derived from the processing of petroleum (crude oil).

Petroleum or Crude Oil Natural mineral oil, a thick greenish-brown flammable liquid found underground in permeable rocks. It consists of hydrocarbons mixed with oxygen, sulphur, nitrogen and other elements in varying proportions.

Photovoltaics Solid state silicon devices which convert sunlight directly into energy. They are popularly known as 'solar cells' and are encountered most frequently in sun-powered pocket calculators.

Pollution Contamination or introduction of undesirable substances or energies into the environment that lower the quality of the environment.

Polychlorinated Biphenyl (PCB) Any of a group of chlorinated isomers of biphenyl $(C_6H_5)_2$, valuable for their fire-resisting qualities. They constitute an environmental hazard because of their persistent toxicity.

Population The number of people living in a country, region, area or town.

Population Control Measures taken by government to limit the growth of their population by reducing birth rates.

Population Density The number of people living in a given area, usually expressed as people per square kilometre. It is calculated by dividing the population of a region by its area.

Population Explosion The rapid and dramatic rise in world population that occurred over the last few centuries.

Precipitation The conversion of dissolved solids into suspended solids which may be concentrated subsequently by flocculation and sedimentation.

Present Worth The equivalent value today of discounted future cash flows.

Primary Productivity Rate of assimilation (gross primary productivity) or accumulation (net primary productivity) of energy and nutrients by green plants and other autotrophs.

Prior Informed Consent Informal policy whereby companies which sell pesticides to developing countries agree to suspend exporting the product, if there is an objection from the government of the receiving country and inform the government of the nature of the pesticides.

Process One or a collective series of defined steps or operations to accomplish a set purpose.

Process Evaluation An independent review of a programme's design, delivery and implementation.

Process water Water within a process that comes in contact with end-products or with material incorporated into end-products.

Production-cost Model An analytic tool that simulates utility loads and the operation and economic dispatch of generating sources to help determine system capacity requirements.

Productivity The relationship between the quantity of goods or services produced and the factors used to produce it. Farm productivity can be expressed as output per unit of land, capital, labour time, energy, water, nutrients etc.

Proximate Factors Aspects of the environment that organisms use as cues for behaviour like daylength (proximate factors are often not directly important to the organism's well-being).

Refuse Generally, all solid waste collected periodically for disposal.

Renewable Energy Power from any source that replenishes itself.

Renewable Resource Natural resource that is replaced by natural processes in a reasonable amount of time.

Resource A substance or object required by an organism for normal maintenance, growth and reproduction. If the resource is scarce relative to demand, it is referred to as 'limiting resource'. Non-renewable resources (like space occur in fixed amounts and can be fully utilized; renewable resources (like food) are produced at a rate that may be partly determined by their utilization.

Resource Recovery Recycling of solid wastes generally at a central processing plant after collection.

Restoration Ecology Use of ecological principles and experience to return a degraded ecological system to its former or original state.

Retrofit Modifications made to update existing equipment or structures.

Rural Depopulation Loss of people from remote country areas to cities, it is an effect of migration. In poor countries, large-scale migration to urban core regions may deplete the countryside of resources and workers.

Standard Industrial Classification (SIC) A system of classification for industry types, for instance that used in the USA.

Smog Natural fog containing impurities (unburned carbon and sulphur dioxide) from domestic fires, industrial furnaces, certain power stations and internal-combustion engines (petrol or diesel). Can cause illness and loss of life, particularly among chronic bronchitics, and damage to wildlife.

Snapback Effect The argument that by undertaking conservation actions, customers perceive a lower (relative) price for energy and therefore, purchase more of the commodity in terms of comfort or appliance use.

Solar Energy Energy derived from the Sun's radiation.

Source and Sink Dynamics Spatial linkage of population dynamics such that high-quality habitat (sources) provide excess individuals that maintain population density through migration in low-quality habitats (sinks).

Statistical Analysis Statistical analysis of whole customers' energy or load data to infer changes in consumption associated with adoption of efficient technologies. Methods range from simple before/after comparisons between programme and control groups, to applications of parametric statistical models (e.g., regression models).

Stochastic Random, any random process, such as mortality due to weather extremes.

Supply The aggregate amount of goods or services available to satisfy economic needs or wants. The quantity of a good or service which producers are willing to sell at different prices. Supply involves the relationship between quantity and price.

Sustainable Development Attempts to meet economic objectives in ways that do not degrade the underlying environmental support system. Also defined as human activities that respect the intrinsic value of the natural world, the role of the natural world in human well-being and the need for humans to live on the income from nature's capital rather than the capital itself.

Sustainable Capable of being continued indefinitely. For example, the sustainable yield of a forest is equivalent to the amount that grows back.

Synergy The action of two or more substances, organs or organisms to achieve an effect which each individual cannot produce.

Technology The combination of knowledge, inputs and management practices that are deployed together with productive resources to produce a desired output.

TeraWatt Hour (TWh) One terawatt hour is 1000 gigaWatt hours.

Third World Term originally applied collectively to those countries of Africa, Asia and Latin America that were not aligned with either the Western block (First World) or Communist bloc (Second World). The term later took on economic connotations and was applied to the countries of the developing world.

Tragedy of the Commons The idea that unregulated use of a common, public resource for private, personal gain will result in overexploitation and destruction of the resource.

Trophic Level Position in the food chain determined by the number of energy-transfer steps to that level.

Turbine Engine in which steam, water, gas, air or nuclear energy is made to spin a rotating shaft by pushing on angled blades like a fan. Turbines are among the most powerful machines.

UNCED (the Earth Summit) United Nations Conference on Environment and Development, which took place in Rio de Janeiro, Brazil in June 1992.

Urban Sprawl Outward spread of built-up areas caused by their expansion as a result of urbanization. Unchecked urban sprawl may join cities into conurbations, the green-belt policies are designed to prevent this.

Utilitarian View A philosophical term applied to any activity that produces a product useful to humans, typically in some economic sense. Also used to describe a system of values which is measured by its contribution to human well-being, usually in terms of health and economic standard of living.

Utility The 'want-satisfying' power of goods; personal satisfaction received through an economic gain.

Zoning A reserve design that controls human activities within and near conservation reserves so that the reserve function may be protected while some human activities, including those supplying some economic benefit may take place.

References

Abram, D; *The Spell of the Sensuous*; Pantheon, New York (1996).

Abramovitz, J N; Putting a Value on Nature's "Free" Services; *World Watch* 10–19 (1998).

Adams, R M C; Dealing with Disaster; *Science* 296: 1404–1405 (2002).

Agren, C; Global Warming Factories; *Acid News*; 2: 1–4 (April 1994).

Ågren, C; Multiple Benefits of Low-CO_2 Policies; *Acid News* 3: 1, 4–5 (Sept 2007).

Akiba, E; Iba H; Hydrogen Absorption by Laves Phase Related BCC Solid Solution; *Intermetallics* 6: 461–470 (1998).

Alao, J A; Sustainable Rural Development for Rural Transformation—Plea for Relevance; pp 3–11 in Adedoyin, S F Aihonsu, JOY (Eds); Proc. *Eighth Annual Conference of Nigerian Rural Sociological Association*; Ibadan (1996).

Allen, D Preventive Environmental Protection: From Waste Reduction to Toxics Use Reduction; National Toxics Campaign; *Third Annual Woods Hole Waste Reduction Conference* (June 1987).

Allen, T F H; Hoekstra, T W; *Toward a Unified Ecology*; Columbia University Press, New York (1993).

Altieri, M A; The CGIAR and Biotechnology: Can the Renewal keep the Promise of a Research Agenda for the Rural Poor? pp 91–95; In: *Ethics and Equity*. Proc. Workshop CGIAR; 21–25 April 1997; Foz do Iguacu; Brazil (1997).

Anastas, P T; Warner, J C; *Green Chemistry: Theory and Practice*; Oxford University Press, New York (1998).

Andersen, I E Jaeger, B; Scenario Workshops and Urban Planning in Denmark; PLA Notes (IIED, London) 40: 53–56 (2001).

Anderson, D; Energy-efficiency and the Economics of Pollution Abatement; *Annual Review of Energy Environment*; 18: 291–318 (1993).

Anderson, D W et. al., (Eds); *New Steel Sheet and Steel Bar Products and Processing*; SAE-SP 1685; Society of Automotive Engineers (SAE); Warrendale; PA; 63–71 (2002).

Anon; Report on the World Food Summit in Rome; *Global Pesticide Campaigner* 12(2): 18–19 (Dec, 2002).

Anonymous; Cities in a Globalization World; *Report on Human Settlements* 2001; Earthscan; London (2001).

Anonymous; Materials for Sustainability; *Nature* 419: 543 (2002).

Anonymous; Small and Medium-sized Enterprises and Sustainability: Facts and Figures; *UNEP Industry and Environment* 26(4): 4–6 (Oct–Dec 2003).

Ashford, N, Zwetsloot; GIJM; Encouraging Inherently Safer Production in European Firms: A Report from the Field; *Journal Hazard Materials* (Amendola, A, Wilkinson, D (Eds); 78/1-3, pp 123–144 (2000).

Association of the Plastic-producing Industry; *Consequences of Abandoning Plastics in the Packaging Sector*; APPI; Frankfurt (1987).

Attaway, D, Zaborsky, O, (Eds); *Advances in Marine Biotechnology*, Vol I: *Pharmaceutical and Bioactive Natural Products*; Plenum Press, New York (1993).

Ausubel, J H; Industrial Ecology: Reflections on a Colloquium; *PNAS* (USA) 89: 879–884 (1992).

Ausubel, J H, Sladovitch, H E (Eds); *Technology and Environment*; pp 23–29; National Academy Press; Washington (1989).

Ayres, R U; Life Cycle Analysis: A Critique; *Resources, Conservation and Recycling* 14: 199–223 (1995).

Aysscough, N J et. al., *Review of Human Pharmaceuticals in the Environment* (P390); Environment Agency of England and Wales; Bristol (2000).

Baas, L, Hofman, H, Huisingh, D, Huisingh, J, Koppert, P, Neumann, F; *Protection of the North Sea: Time for Clean Production*; Erasmus Centre for Environmental Studies; Erasmus University; Rotterdam (1990).

Baer, E; Advanced Polymers; *American Scientist* 255: 179-190 (1986).

Balasubramanian, A V, Vijayalakshmi, K, Sridhar, S, Arumugasamy, S; Modern Dilemmas and Traditional Insights; pp 74–83; In: Haverkort, B et. al., (Eds); *Ancient Roots, New Shoots; Endogenous Development in Practice*; Zed Books; London (2003).

Bard, A J, Fox, M A; *Accounts of Chemical Research* 28: 141–145 (1995).

Barrett, M; Low Carbon Energy Scenarios for the European Union; Sept 2007; Swedish Environmental Protection Agency (2007).

Bartone, C R, Bernstein, J D; Improving Municipal Solid Waste Management in Third World Countries; *Resources, Conservation and Recycling* 8: 43–54 (1993).

Bauer, C E; Environmental Management of Regional Development; *Water Resources Development*; 4(4): 243–250 (1988).

Baumann, M, Bell, J, Koechlin, F, Pimbert, S (Eds); *The Life Industry: Biodiversity, People and Profits*; Intermediate Technical Publications; London (1996).

Beamish, T D; Silent Spill: The Organization of an Industrial Crisis; MIT Press, Cambridge; Massachusetts (2002).

Bell, G; Measuring the Cost of Reproduction I: The Correlation Structure of the Life Table of a Plankton Rotifer; *Evolution* 38: 300–313 (1984).

Berger, J J; *Environment Restoration: Science and Strategies for Restoring the Earth; Island Press*; New York (1990).

Berkhout, F, Howes, R; The Adoption of Life-cycle Approaches by Industry: Patterns and Impacts; *Resources, Conservation and Recycling* 20: 71–94 (1997).

Berry, W; *Sex, Economy, Freedom and Community: Eight Essays*; Pantheon Books; New York (1992).

Berryman, A A; *Population System: A General Introduction*; Plenum Press; New York (1981).

Berryman, A A, Valenti, M A, Harris, M J, Fulton, D C; Ecological Engineering: An Idea whose Time has come?; *TREE* 7: 268–270 (1992).

Berryman, T; Relieving Modern Day Atlas of an Illusory Burden: Abandoning the Hypermodern Fantasy of an Education to manage the Globe; pp 88–96; In Jarnet, A, Jickling, B, Sauvé, L, Wals, A, Clarkin, P (Eds); *The Future of Environmental Education in a Postmodern World?* (A Colloquium); Proc. of On-line Colloquium held on Oct 19, 1998 at Yukon College, Canada (2000).

Betts, K S; Keeping Drugs out of Drinking Water; *Environmental Science Technology* 36: 377A–378A (2002).

Bhatia, C R Serving Human Needs: Nuclear Technology for Sustainable Development; *Current Science* 81: 1397–1399 (2001).

Birkett, J W, Lester, J N (Eds); *Endocrine Disrupters in Wastewater and Sludge Treatment*; IWA Publishing (2002).

Blaauwbroek, J; CSR in the Netherlands: Changing Consumption and Production Patterns; *UNEP Industry and Environment* 26(4): 10–12 (Oct–Dec 2003).

Blackmore, C, Smyth, J C; Systemic Approaches to Learning in the Context of Agenda 21; 4th Australia and New Zealand Systems Conference; University of Western Sydney (6–10 October, 1998).

Boyhan, W S; Approaches to Eliminating Chlorofluorocarbon Use in Manufacturing; *PNAS* (USA) 89: 812–814 (1992).

Bradshaw, A D, Chadwick, M J; *The Restoration of Land*; Blackwell; Oxford (1980).

Bratby, J; *Coagulation and Flocculation*; Uplands Press; Croydon; Cambridge (1980).

Bridgeman, J; Public Perception towards Water Recycling in California; *Water and Environmental Journal* 18: 150–154 (2004).

Bruinsma, J (Ed); *World Agriculture: Towards 2015/2030: A FAO Perspective*; Earthscan; London (2003).

Bruno, K, et. al., Greenhouse Gangsters vs Climate Justice (*www.corpwatch.org/press*) (1999).

Bui, X A, Rodriguez, L, Sarwatt, S V, Preston, T R; Installation and Performance of Low-cost Polyethylene Tube Biodigesters on Small-scale Farms; *World Animal Review* No. 88; FAO; Rome (1997).

Buijs, J; Shaping Biotechnological Developments in the Context of Resource-Poor Farming: A study of the Andhra Pradesh-Netherlands Biotechnology Programme in Andhra Pradesh, India; MSc Thesis; Wageningen University; Netherlands (2002).

Buonicore, A J, Davis, W T (Eds); *Air Pollution Engineering Manual*; Van Norstrand Reinhold; New York (1992).

Catton, W; *Overshoot: The Ecological Basis of Revolutionary Change*; University of Illinois Press; Urbana (1980).

Census of India, 2001; Ministry of Non-Conventional Energy Sources (2001).

CGIAR; *Shaping the CGIAR's Future: Summary of Proceedings and Decisions*; CGIAR International Centres Week; pp 52–53; 26–30 Oct 1998; CGIAR Secretariat; Washington DC (1998).

Christensen, F M; Pharmaceuticals in the Environment–A Human Risk?; *Regul Toxicol Pharmacol* 28: 212–221 (1998).

Citizens Fund; Poisons in our Neighbourhoods: Toxic Pollution in the United States; Citizens Fund; Washington (1991).

Clark, N, Juma, C; *Biotechnology for Sustainable Development*; ACTS Press; Nairobi; Kenya (1990).

Clini, C, Moody-Stuart, M; *Renewable Energy: Development that Lasts;* G8 Renewable Energy Task Force (2001).

COER (Committee on Environmental Research, Commission on Life Sciences); *National Research Council; Research to Protect, Restore and Manage the Environment*; National Academy Press; Washington DC (1993).

Conway, G; *The Doubly Green Revolution: Food for All in the 21st Century*; pp 4–5 and 44–65; Cornell University Press; Ithaca; New York (1998).

Corbey, D; Presidency Note on EU Fuel Quality Revision; *http://register.consilium. Europa.eu/pdf/en/07/st12/st12451.en07/pdf.* Also, *www.europarl.europa.eu.*

Corpwatch; Corporate Globalization Fact Sheet (*www.corpwatch.org/press*); (2001).

Costanza, R (Ed); *Ecological Economics: The Science and Management of Sustainability*; Columbia University Press; New York (1991).

Costanza, R et. al., The Value of the World's Ecosystem Services and Natural Capital; *Nature* 387: 253–260 (1997).

Critchley, W, Kiio, J, Kameti, S, Brommer, M; The Ututus: Four Families, Five Wells and a Windpump; *LEISA India* 7(1): 15 (March 2005).

Daily, G (Ed); *Nature's Services: Societal Dependence on Natural Ecosystems*; Island Press; Washington DC (1997).

Dale, T, Carter, V G; *Topsoil and Civilization*; University of Oklahoma Press; Norman; Oklahoma (1955).

Dangelis, D L, Post, W M, Travis, C C; *Positive Feedback in Natural Systems*; Springer; Berlin (1986).

Dasgupta, P S, Mody, A, Roy, S, Wheeler, D; *Environmental Regulation and Development: A Cross-country Empirical Analysis*; Policy Research Working Paper No. 1448; World Bank; Washington, DC (1995).

Derspeh, R; In: *Sustaining the Global Farm*; Stott, D E, Mohtar, R H, Steinhardt, G C (Eds); pp 248–254; International Soil Conservation Organization, USDA and Purdue University; West Lafayatte; Indiana (2001).

Dewes, W; Introduction to Traditional Knowledge and Sustainable Development, pp 3; In Davis, S H, Ebbe, K (Eds); Proceedings of the Conference held at the World Bank; Washington DC; Sept 27–28, 1993; Environmentally Sustainable Development Proceeding Series No. 4 (1993).

Dooge, J C I et. al., (Eds); An Agenda of Science for Environment and Development into the 21st Century; Cambridge University Press (1992).

DPC (DeLorme Publishing Company); *Eartha.* ME: DeLorme Mapping Company; Yarmouth; Maine (1998).

Dresselhaus, M S, Thomas, I L; Alternative Energy Technologies; *Nature* 414: 332–337 (2001).

Dreyfus, A Wals, A E J, Van Weelie, D; Biodiversity as a Postmodern Theme for Environmental Education; pp 176–185; In Jarnet, A et. al., (Eds); *The Future of Environmental Education in a Postmodern World?* Proc. On-line Colloquium, Oct 19, 1998; Yukon College; Canada (2000).

Duchin, F; Industrial Input–Output Analysis, Implications for Industrial Ecology; PNAS (USA) 89: 851–855 (1992).

Duchin, F, Lange, G M; *Technological Choice, Their Implications for the US Economy, 1963–2000: Report on the Construction Application of an Engineering/Input–Output Model Database;* Inst. Econ. Anal., New York (1991).

Duriappah, A K et. al., Land Tenure, Land Use, Environmental Degradation and Conflict Resolution: A PASIR Analysis for Narok District, Kenya; International Institute for Environment and Development; London; CREED Working Paper No. 33: 1–24 (2000).

Durieu, X; How Europe's Retail Sector helps Promote Sustainable Production and Consumption; *UNEP Industry and Environment* 26(1): 7–9 (March, 2003).

Dyer, L; Cybernetic Insect Outbreaks; *Ecology* 81: 3262–3263 (2000).

Easterbrook, G; *A Moment on the Earth: The Coming Age of Environmental Optimism*; Viking; Penguin (1995).

Easterling, K; *Tomorrow's Materials*; Institute of Metals; London (1988).

EC (European Union); *Towards Environmental Pressure Indicators for the EU*; Eurostat; Luxemburg (2000).

EIA (Energy Information Administration); Office of Energy Markets and End Use; *Annual Energy Review* 1999; US Department of Energy, Washington DC (2000) and *International Energy Annual* 1999 US Department of Energy; Washington DC (2001).

EPA; *Profile of the Nonferrous Metals Industry*; US Office of Enforcement and Compliance Assurance; US EPA (EPA/310-R-95-010); Washington DC (Sept, 1995).

EPA; *Report to Congress on Metal Recovery, Environmental Regulation and Hazardous Waste*; US EPA (EPA/530-R-93-018); Washington DC (Feb, 1994).

EPA (1992); *Toxic Release Inventory* (TRI) Public Data Release US EPA; Office of Pollution Prevention and Toxics (EPA/745-R94-001); Washington DC (April, 1994).

EPA; *Report to Congress on Special Wastes from Mineral Processing: Summary and Findings, Methods and Analysis*, Appendices; US EPA; Office of Solid Waste and Emergency Response (530-SW-90-070C) (1990).

EPRI; Efficient Electricity Use: Estimates of Maximum Energy Savings; Electric Power Research Institute; EPRI/CU–6746 (1990).

Erlenkotter, D; An Early Classic Misplaced: Ford W Harris's Economic Order Quantity Model of 1915; *Management Science* 35: 898–900 (1989).

Esteva; G Au-delà du Développement; In Sachs, W, Esteva, G (Eds); *Des Ruines du Développement*; pp 87–138; Ecosociété; Montreal (1994).

Falt, E; WSSD: "Workmanlike" Agreements on Water, Chemicals, Energy; *UNEP Industry and Environment* 25 (3–4); pp 101; UNEP; DTIE; Paris (2002).

FAO; *Agricultural Production Data and FAOSTAT 98*; FAO; Rome (1999).

FAO; *FISHSTAT PLUS and Forest Resources Assessment*; FAO; Rome (2000).

FAO; *World Review of the State of Food and Agriculture*; FAO; Rome (2001).

Feddema, R; South Korea Plans its Biotechnology Future; *Biotechnology & Development Monitor* 50: 8–13 (2003).

Feenberg, A; Critical Theory of Technology: An Overview; pp 47–64; In: *Tailoring Biotechnologies: Potentialities, Actualities and Spaces*; Ruivenkamp, G et. al., (Eds); Centre for Tailor-made Biotechnologies and Genomics; Wageningen (2005).

Fenhann, J; The Efficiency of the CDM Project Cycle is Improving; *E+ Energy, Climate and Sustainable Development*; pp 8–10 (Nov, 2005).

Fien, J; *Education for the Environment: Critical Curriculum Theorizing and Environmental Education*; Deakin University Press; Geelong (1993).

Fischer-Kowalski, M, Hüttler, W; *Journal of Industrial Ecology* 2: 107–137 (1998).

Fishbein, M, Ajzen, I; *Understanding Attitudes and Predicting Social Behavior*; Prentice Hall; Englewood Cliffs (1980).

Follett, P A, Duan, J J (Eds); *Nontarget Effects of Biological Control*; Kluwer Academic; Norwell; Massachusetts (2000).

Francis, M; Modeling: Driving Fuel Cells; *Materials Today* 34–39 (May, 2002).

Freeman, H M (Ed.); *Industrial Pollution Prevention Handbook*; McGraw-Hill; New York (1995).

Frosch, R A; Industrial Ecology and Sustainability; *American Scientist* 86: 2 (1998).

Frosch, R A; Industrial Ecology: A Physiological Introduction; *PNAS* (USA) 89: 800–803 (1992).

Frosch, R W, Gallopoulos, N E; *Toward an Industrial Ecology*; General Motors Research Labs; Warren; Michigan Publication No. GMR-6959 (1990).

Furuholt, E; Life Cycle Assessment of Gasoline and Diesel; *Resources, Conservation and Recycling* 14: 251–263 (1995).

Fussler, C; Eco-efficiency and Beyond: The Next Sources of Innovation; *UNEP Industry and Environment* 25(3–4), pp 78–80 (July–Dec, 2002).

Ganapathy, R S, Padmanabhan, G; *Towards a Strategy for Aluminium in India*; Department of Science & Technology; New Delhi (1992).

Geibler, J V, Kuhndt, M; Helping Small and Not-so-small Businesses Improve their Triple Bottom Line Performance; *UNEP Industry and Environment* 25(3–4): pp 63–66 (2002).

Geiser, K; What Next in Cleaner Production Technologies?; *UNEP Industry and Environment*; 25(3-4): pp 75–77 (July–Dec, 2002).

Geiser, K, Griener, T; Innovation and Adoption of Cleaner Production Technologies; In Forrant, R, Pyle, J, Lazonick, W, Levenstein, C (Eds); *Approaches to Sustainable Development*; University of Massachusetts Press; Amherst (2001).

Gereluk, W; The Social Dimension of Sustainable Development and the Retail Sector; *UNEP Industry and Environment* 26(1): 33–35 (2003).

Gold, W Ewing, K Banks, J Groom, M Hinckley, T Secord, D Schebitz, D; Collaborative Ecological Restoration; Science 312: 1880–1881 (2006).

Goodman, B; Can Celera Map Money into Genomics?; *Red Herring Business Magazine*; (15 Feb, 2001).

Goodland, R, Daly, H; The Missing Tools; In: Mungall, C, McLaren, D J (Eds); *Planet Under Stress: The Challenge of Global Change*; pp 269–284; Oxford University Press (1990).

Gough, A; *Education and the Environment: Policy, Trends and the Problems of Marginalization*; Australia Council for Education Research; Melbourne (1998).

Grätzel, M; Photoelectrochemical Cells; *Nature* 414: 338–344 (2001).

Green, R; Changing Production and Consumption Patterns: Progress made and remaining Challenges; *UNEP Industry and Environment*; pp 33–35 (July–Dec, 2002).

Greening, L A, Green, D L, Difiglio, C; Energy Efficiency and Consumption—The Rebound Effect; *Energy Policy* 286 (7) (2000).

GRI (Global Reporting Institute); *Sustainability Reporting Guidelines on Economic, Environmental and Social Performance*; Boston (2000).

Gupta, R, Ahuja, P, Khan, S, Saxena, R K, Mohapatra, H; Microbial Biosorbents: Meeting Challenges of Heavy Metal Pollution in Aqueous Solutions; *Current Science* 78: 967–973 (2000).

Hall, M; *Earth Repair: A Transatlantic History of Environmental Restoration*; University of Virginia Press, Charlottesville, Virginia (2005).

Hasenauer, H (Ed); *Sustainable Forest Management, Growth Models for Europe*; Springer (2006).

Haverkort, B, Millar, D, Gonese, C; Knowledge and Belief Systems in Sub Saharan Africa; pp 137–152; In: Haverkort, B, Vant Hooft, K, Hiemstra, W (Eds); *Ancient Roots, New Shoots*; Compass; Zed Books; London (2003).

Hawksworth, D L (Ed); *The Biodiversity of Microorganisms and Invertebrates: Its Role in Sustainable Agriculture*; CAB International; London (1991).

Hay, J E; Facilitating Uptake of Cleaner Production with Decision Support Tools, Learning Opportunities and Information Technologies; *UNEP Industry and Environment* 25(3–4) pp 72–75 (July–Dec, 2002).

Hazell, P B R; Agricultural Growth, Poverty Alleviation and Environmental Sustainability: Having it All; 2020 Brief No. 59, International Food Policy Research Institute; Washington DC (1999).

Heberer, T; Tracking Persistent Pharmaceutical Residues from Municipal Sewage to Drinking Water; *Journal of Hydrology* 266: 175–189 (2002).

Heberer, T, Stan, H J; Determination of Clofibric Acid and N-(Phenyl Sulfonyl) -Sarcosine in Sewage, River and Drinking Water; *International Journal of Environmental Analytical Chemistry* 67: 113–124 (1997).

Henrichs, R; Environmental Issues and the Law; *PNAS* (USA) 89: 856–859 (1992).

Herrera, C, Ramirez, S; Clean Energy for Chilling Milk; *LEISA India* 7(1): 18–19 (March 2005).

Hill, L J; *Comparison of Methods to Integrate DSM and Supply Resources in Electric Utility Planning*; ORNL/CON-341; Oak Ridge; Tennessee (Dec, 1991).

Hillary, R (Ed); *Small and Medium-sized Enterprises and the Environment: Business Imperatives*; Greenleaf Publishing; Sheffield (2000).

Himesh, S; Dilemma of Development and Environment: A Perspective; *Current Science* 80: 1101–1104 (2001).

Hodgson, E (Ed); *Review in Environmental Toxicology*; pp 85–94; Elsevier; Amsterdam (1987).

Hoffman, J S; Pollution Prevention as a Market-enhancing Strategy: A Storehouse of Economical and Environment Opportunities; *PNAS* (USA) 89: 832–834 (1992).

Hoffman, S M, Oliver-Smith, A (Eds); *Catastrophe and Culture: The Anthropology of Disaster*; School of American Research Press; Santa Fe (2002).

Holliday, C O, Schmidheiny, S, Watts, P; *Walking the Talk: The Business Case for Sustainable Development*;Greenleaf Publishing; Sheffield (2002).

Hu, S D; *Cogeneration*; Reston Publishing Co; Reston; USA (1985).

Huckle, J; Locating Environmental Education between Modern Capitalism and Postmodern Socialism: A Reply to Lucie Sauvé; pp 71–75; In Jarnet, A et. al., (Eds); *The Future of Environmental Education in a Postmodern World?* (A Colloquium); Proc. On-line Colloquium; Oct 19, 1998; Yukon College; Canada (2000).

Hughes, J, Anslow, M; Power On; *Ecologist* 37: 35–39 (Dec, 2007).

Hunt, R G, Sellers, J D, Franklin, W E; Resource and Environmental Profile Analysis: A Life Cycle Environmental Assessment for Products and Procedures; *Environmental Impact Assessment Review*; 12: 245–269 (1992).

IEA (International Energy Agency); *IEA World Energy Outlook 2002*; OECD; Paris (2002).

IEA; *Tracking Industrial Energy Efficiency and CO_2 Emissions*; International Energy Agency; *www.iea.org* (2007).

IEE; *India's Economic Development, Environmental Conservation and Energy Security*; Institute of Energy Economics (Japan) 7–9 (2001).

IFPRI; *A 2020 Vision for Food, Agriculture and the Environment: The Vision, Challenge and Recommended Action*; International Food Policy Research Institute; Washington DC (1995).

IIASA; Global Agro-ecological Zones 2000; International Institute for Applied System Analysis; Rome (2000).

ILO; *Chemical in the Working Environment*; *World Labour Report*; ILO; Rome (2000).

ILO; Wage Workers in Agriculture: Conditions of Employment and Work, Sectoral Activities Program; ILO; Geneva (1996).

INFORM; *Preventing Pollution Through Technical Assistance: One State's Experience*; Dorfman, M, Riggio; J INFORM; New York (1990).

IPCC; *Climate Change 2001: The Scientific Basis*; Cambridge University Press, Cambridge (2001).

IUCN; In: McNeely, J A (Ed); *Conservation and the Future: Trends and Options Toward the Year 2025*; The World Conservation Union Biodiversity Policy Coordination Division; Gland; Switzerland (1997).

Jackson, T; *Towards Clean Production: Concepts and Principles for Guiding Technological Choice Towards Sustainable Development*; Working Paper; Stockholm Environment Institute; Stockholm (1992).

Jackson, T; Waste Reduction and the Prevention of Marine Pollution; Working Paper 17 to the Second Ad-Hoc Group of Experts Meeting on the Annexes to the London Dumping Convention; International Maritime Organization; London (1990).

Jackson, T (Ed); Renewable Energy; *Energy Policy* 20: 861–883 (1992).

Jakpa, I, Lodolo, A, Miertus, S; A Overview of Soil Remediation Technologies; *Genetic Engineering and Biotechnology* UNIDO; Vienna; Issue No. 3/4; pp 1–11 (1998).

James, C; Global Review of Commercialized Transgenic Crops: 1998; ISAAA *Brief No. 8* (1999).

Jaworski, J, Minns, D; Technology Innovations and Cleaner Production: Possibilities and Limitations; *Industry and Environment* 24(1–2); pp 60–64 (Jan–June, 2001).

Jelinski, L W, Graedel, T E, Laudise, R A, McCall, D W, Patel, C K N; Industrial Ecology: Concepts and Approaches; *PNAS* (USA) 89: 793–797 (1992).

Jickling, B; Why I don't want my Children to be Educated for Sustainable Development?; *Journal of Environmental Education* 23(4): 5–8 (1992).

Jones, O A H, Lester, J N, Voulvoulis, N; Pharmaceuticals: A Threat to Drinking Water?; *TIBTECH* 23: 163–167 (2005).

Jones, O A H et. al., Analytical Method Development for the Simultaneous Determination of Five Human Pharmaceuticals in Water and Wastewater Samples by Gas Chromatography–Mass Spectrometry; *Chromatographia* 58: 471–477 (2003).

Jones, O A H et. al., Potential Ecological and Human Health Risks Associated with the Presence of Pharmaceutically Active Compounds in the Aquatic Environment; *Critical Reviews in Toxicology* 34: 335–350 (2004).

Joo, S H, Cheng, I F; *Nanotechnology for Environmental Remediation*; Springer (2006).

Joshi, U N, Luthra, Y P; An Overview of Heavy Metals: Impact and Remediation; *Current Science* 78: 773–774 (2000).

Kanniah, R; Cleaner Production in the Context of Sustainable Development; *UNEP Industry and Environment*; 25(3–4): pp 41–43 (July–Dec, 2002).

Kant, S, Munk, R A (Eds); *Economics, Sustainability and Natural Resources*; Springer; Berlin (2005).

Kaounides, L; New and Advanced Materials: Implications for Industrial Policy in Developing Countries; In: *UNIDO Report PPD. 141 "New Technologies and Global Industrialisation"Prospects for Developing Countries"* UNIDO; Vienna; pp 165–213 (13 Nov, 1989).

Kappeli, O, Auberson, L; The Science and Intricacy of Environmental Safety Evaluations; *TIBTECH* 15: 342–344 (1997).

Kates, R W, Turner, B L, Clark, W C; In Turner B L II et. al., (Eds); *The Earth as Transformed by Human Action*; pp 1–17; Cambridge University Press; Cambridge (1990).

Kato, H, Kudo, A; *The Journal of Physical Chemistry* B 106: 5029–5034 (2002).

Kendall, H W et. al., Meeting the Challenges of Population, Environment and Resources: The Costs of Inaction; A Report of the Senior Scientists' Panels; *Environmentally Sustainable Development Proceedings* Ser. 14; World Bank; Washington DC (1995).

Kennedy, P; *Preparing for the 21st Century*; Random House; New York (1993).

Kerski, A; Pulp, Paper and Power; *The Ecologist* 25: 142–149 (1995).

Khaladkar, P R, Hare, C H, Norsworthy R; In: Review; R W (Ed); *Uhlig's Corrosion Handbook*; pp 965–1069; Wiley; New York (2000).

Kim, C H, Hong, Y; An Optimal Production Run Length in Deteriorating Production Processes; *International Journal of Production Economics* 58: 183–189 (1999).

Kleiner, K; Promise Boiling Over; *Nature* 450: 934–935 (2007).

Kletz, T A; *Process Plants: A Handbook for Inherently Safer Design*; Taylor and Francis; Philadelphia (1998).

Klinkers, L, Van der Kooy, W, Wijen, H; Product-oriented Environmental Management provides New Opportunities and Directions for Speeding up Environmental Performance; Green. Manage. Internat. 26: (1999).

Köhler, R; Information für die strategische Planung von Produktinnovationen [Information for Strategic Planning of Product Innovations]; In Klein-Blenkers, F (Ed) *Distributionspolitik*; Cologne (1987).

Kolawole, O D; Local Knowledge Utilization and Sustainable Rural Development in the 21st Century; *Indigineous Knowledge Development Monitor* 9: 13–15 (2001).

Kornevall, C; Sustainability is Everybody's Business; *UNEP Industry and Environment*; pp 30–32 (July–Dec, 2002).

Kranz, C, Sagasser, I; How Chemical Industry Initiatives contribute to Environmental Safety and Health Protection in SMEs: An Example from BASF; *UNEP Industry and Environment* 26(4): 24–25 (Oct–Dec, 2003)

Kuhndt, M, Schäfer, J, Liedtke, C; Developing a System of Sectoral Sustainability Indicators for the European Aluminium Industry; *UNEP Industry and Environment* 25(3–4); pp 67–71 (2002).

Kuhndt, M, Geibler, J V, Liedtke, C; *Towards a Sustainable Aluminium Industry: Stakeholder Expectations and Core Indicators; Final Report for the GDA (Gesamtverband der Aluminiumindustrie) and the European Aluminium Industry*; Wuppertal Institute (*www.eco-efficiency.de*) (2002a).

Kuhndt, M, Von Geibler, J, Villar, A; Challenges for SMEs in a Globalized World Economy; *UNEP Industry and Environment* 26(4): 7–9 (Oct–Dec, 2003).

Kuisma, J; Practical Steps towards Sustainability in the Retail Trade: The Case of Finland's Kesko; *UNEP Industry and Environment* 26(1): 10–12 (2003).

Kumar, H D; *General Ecology*; Vikas; New Delhi (1995).

Kumar, H D Kumar, S; *Global and General Environment*; Anmol Publications; New Delhi (1997).

Kumar, H D; *A Textbook on Biotechnology*; Affil. East West Press, New Delhi, (1998).

Kumar, H D; *Environmental Pollution and Waste Management*; M D Publications; New Delhi (1998).

Kumar, H D; *Introductory Phycology*; 2nd Ed; Affil. East West Press, New Delhi (1999).

Kumar, H D; *Biodiversity and Sustainable Conservation*; Oxford & IBH; New Delhi (1999).

Kumar, H D; *Plant-Animal Interactions*; Affil. East West Press; New Delhi (2000).

Kumar, H D; *Sustainable Human Ecology*; Affil. East West Press; New Delhi (2001).

Kumar, H D; *Forest Resources: Conservation and Management*; Affil. East West Press; New Delhi (2001).

Kumar, H D; *Environmental Science: Economic, Social and Political Dimensions*; Daya Publishing House; New Delhi (2003 & 2004).

Kumar, H D; *Sustainability and Management of Aquaculture and Fisheries*; Daya Publishing House; New Delhi (2003).

Kumar, H D; *Agricultural Biotechnology*; Daya Publishing House; New Delhi (2006).

Kumar, H D; *Agricultural Ecology*; APH Publishing Corporation; New Delhi (2006).

Kumar, H D; *Water Woes: Conserving and Managing Our Future Lifeline*; Daya Publishing House; New Delhi (2006).

Kumar, H D; *Global Climate Change: Insights, Impacts and Concerns*; Vitasta Publishing; New Delhi (2006).

Kumar, H D; *Energy and Natural Resources: Sustainability and Management*; Vitasta Publishing; New Delhi (2008).

Kuta, C C, Koch, D G, Hildebrandt, C C, Janzen, D C; Improvement of Products and Packaging through the Use of Life Cycle Analysis; *Resources, Conservation and Recycling* 14: 185–198 (1995).

Landis, P H; *Rural Life in Process*; McGraw-Hill; New York (1940).

Larbalestier, D; High-T_6 Superconducting Materials for Electric Power Applications; *Nature* 414: 368–377 (2001).

LaRocco, P; A Business Model for Clean-energy SMEs: Small Companies' Role in Eradicating Energy Waste and Energy Poverty; *UNEP Industry and Environment* 26(4): 20–23 (Oct–Dec, 2003)

Larsen, T A et. al., How to Avoid Pharmaceuticals in the Aquatic Environment?; J Bacteriol; 113: 295–304 (2004).

Lawton, J H, May, R M (Eds); *Extinction Rates*; Oxford University Press; Oxford (1995).

Lederberg, J, Shope, R E, Oaks, S C Jr (Eds); *Emerging Infections: Microbial Threats to Health in the United States*; National Academy Press; Washington DC (1992).

Leisinger, K M; *Socio-political Effects on New Biotechnologies in Developing Countries*; Food, Agriculture and the Environment Discussion Paper No. 2; International Food Policy Research Institute; Washington DC (1995).

Leontief, W, Duchin, F; *The Future Impact of Automation on Workers*; Oxford University Press; New York (1986).

Lin, C S, Chen, C H, Kroll, D E; Integrated Production-inventory Models for Imperfect Production Processes under Inspection Schedules;*Computers and Industrial Engineering* 44: 633–650 (2003).

Lin, G C, Lin, H D; Determining a Production Run Time for an Imperfect Production–Inventory System with Scrap; *Journal of Scientific & Industrial Research* 66: 724–735 (2007).

Lindhqvist, T, Christiansen, K; *Collection and Sorting of Used Batteries*: Final Report for the Commission of the European Communities; TEM University of Lund; Sweden (1990).

Livingston, J A; Some Reflections on Integrated Wildlife and Forest Management; *The Trumpeter* 3(3): 24–29 (1986).

Logan, J A, Hall, E P (Eds); *Chaos and Insect Ecology*; Virginia Experimental Station; Blacksburg (1991).

Long, W; Economic Aspects of Transport and Disposal of Hazardous Wastes; *Marine Policy* 14(3) (1990).

Lowdermilk, W C; *Conquest of the Land through 7,000 Years*; US Department of Agriculture; Washington DC (1953).

Lubchenco, J; Entering the Century of the Environment: A New Social Contract for Science; *Science* 279: 491–497 (1998).

Luzier, W D; Materials Derived from Biomass/Biodegradable Materials; *PNAS* (USA) 89: 839–842 (1992).

Lynch, J; *Education for Citizenship in a Multicultural Society*; Cassell; London (1992).

Maeda, K et. al., *Journal of the American Chemical Society*; 127: 8286–8287 (2005).

Maeda, K et. al., *Journal of Physical Chemistry* B 109: 20504–20510 (2005a).

Maeda, K et. al., Photocatalyst releasing Hydrogen from Water; *Nature* 440: 295 (2006).

Magnaghi, A; Local Self-sustainable Development: Subjects of Transformation; pp 79-102; In *Tailoring Biotechnologies: Potentialities, Actualities and Spaces* (Ruivenkamp, G, et al., Eds); Centre for Tailor-made Biotechnologies and Genomics; Wageningen (2005).

Mander, J; Does Globalization help the Poor?; *IFG Bulletin* 1(3): 1–5 (Bulletin of International Forum on Globalization); San Francisco (2001).

Mander, J; The Environment and Globalization; *IFG Bulletin* 3(1): 1–14 (2002).

Mansouri, T, Guinebault, A; Passive Solar Architecture for Mountain Agriculture; *LEISA India* 7(1): 20–21 (March 2005).

Marecki, J; *Combined Heat and Power: Generating Systems*; Peter Peregrinus Ltd; London (1988).

Mariscal, J C, Degado, F, Perez, R; Indicators for Measuring Poverty; *Compass Magazine* 8: 16–19 (February 2005).

Marisol, E (Ed); *Learning from Change: Issues and Experiences in Participatory Monitoring and Evaluation*; Intermediate Technology Publications; London (2000).

Masel, R; Hydrogen Quick and Clean; *Nature* 442: 521–522 (2006).

Masel, R I, Gold, S, Zheng, N; In: *Encyclopedia of Chemical Processing*; Lee, S (Ed); pp 1643–1661; Taylor & Francis; New York (2005).

Masterton, G; Sustainable Cities—Who put the Civil into Civilisation; *Interdisciplinary Science Reviews* 27: 39–43 (2002).

Matthews et. al., *The Weight of Nations: Material Outflows from Industrial Economies*; World Resources Institute; Washington DC (2000).

McFarland, M; Investigation of the Environmental Acceptability of Fluorocarbon Alternative to Chlorofluorocarbons; *PNAS* (USA) 89: 807–811 (1992).

McInnes, G; The Impact of Trade on the Environment: Main Issues and Challenges; *UNEP Industry and Environment* 25(3–4); pp 92–95 (2002).

McMichael, A J, Haines, A, Slooff, R, Kovats, S; (Eds); *Climate Change and Human Health*; World Health Organization; Geneva (1996).

McNeely, J A, Miller, KR, Reid, WV, Mittermeier, R A, Werner, T B; *Conserving the World's Biological Diversity*; IUCN; Gland (1990).

Meadows, D H et. al., The Limits to Growth: A report for the Club of Rome's Project on the Predicament of Mankind; Universe Books; New York (1972).

Meadows, DH et. al., Beyond the Limits: Confronting Global Collapse, envisioning a Sustainable Future; Chelsea Green Publishing; White River Junction; Vermont (1992).

Means, J, Hinchee, R E; *Emerging Technology for Bioremediation of Metals*; Lewis Publishers; Boca Raton (1994).

Mebratu, D; *Strategy for Sustainable Industrial Development in Sub-Saharan Africa*; Lund University; Sweden (2000).

Mebratu, D; The Challenges of Industrial Development in Africa; *UNEP Industry and Environment* 25(3–4): 60–61 (July–Dec, 2002).

Mehlhorn, B; Better Transparency for a Cleaner Environment; *Issues in Science & Technology*; pp 19; (FALL, 2007).

Militzer, M; A Synchrotron Llook at Steel; *Science* 298: 975, 976 (2002).

Mitchell, J W; Alternative Starting Material for Industrial Processes; *PNAS* (USA) 89: 821–826 (1992).

Mitsch, W J, Jorgensen, S E; *Ecological Engineering: An Introduction to Ecotechnology*; Wiley; Chichester (1989).

Montgomery, D R; Soil Erosion and Agricultural Sustainability; *PNAS* (USA) 104: 13268–13272 (2007).

Montgomery, D R; *Dirt: The Erosion of Civilization*; University of California Press; Berkeley; California (2007a).

Mooney, H A, Cushman, J H, Medina, E, Sala, O E, Schulze, E–D (Eds); *Functional Roles of Biodiversity: A Global Perspective*; Wiley; New York (1996).

Morton, R, Palermo, M; Development of Procedures to Manage and Monitor Capping of Contaminated Dredged Materials; Paper to the *8th International Ocean Disposal Symposium*; Dubrovnik; Yugoslavia (1989).

Myers, N, Kent, J; *Perverse Subsidies: How Misused Tax Dollars Harm the Environment and the Economy*; Island Press; Washington DC (2001).

Naganagouda, R, Shuijin, Z, Patil, VC; Planting to Catch more Sunlight; *LEISA India* 7(1): 7 (March 2005).

NAS (National Academy of Science); Energy for Rural Development: Renewable Resources and Alternatives Technologies for Developing Countries; Washington DC (1976).

Natesh, S, Govil, S (Eds); *Innovative Environmental Biotechnologies: From Research to Application*; Department of Biotechnology; New Delhi (2003).

National Research Council; *Alternative Agriculture*; National Academy Press; Washington DC (1989).

NEA; *Feasibility of Disposal of High Level Radioactive Waste into the Seabed*; Nuclear Energy Agency; OECD; Paris (1988).

Newell, J, Metry, A, Neilson, R; Applications of Thermal Technologies for Decontaminating Soil; In: Maltezou, SA, Metry, A, Irwin, W; *Industrial Risk Management and Clean Technology*; Verlag Orac; Vienna (1990).

Nordstrom, H, Vaughan, S; *Trade and the Environment* (Special Studies 4); WTO; Geneva (1999).

NWPPC (Northwest Power Planning Council); *Northwest Conservation and Electric Power Plan*; Northwest Power Planning Council Portland; Oregon (1991).

Odum, E P; *Ecology: A Bridge Between Science and Society*; Sinauer; Sunderland (1997).

Odum, H T; *Environment, Power and Society*; Wiley; Chichester (1971).

OECD; *Technology for Cleaner Production and Products*; Organization of Economic Cooperation and Development; Paris (1995).

Olson, S L; In Western, D, Pearl, M C (Eds); Conservation for the 21st Century; pp 50; Oxford University Press; Oxford (1989).

Orellana, I, Fauteux, S; Environmental Education: Tracing the High Points of its History; pp 2–11; In Jarnet, A et. al., (Eds); *The Future of Environmental Education in a Postmodern World?;* Proc. On-line Colloquium Oct 19, 1998; Yukon College; Canada (2000).

Orr, D; *Earth in Mind: On Education, Environment and the Human Prospect*; Island Press; Washington DC (1994).

Orr, D; *Ecological Literacy: Education and the Transition to a Postmodern World*; State University of New York Press; Albany (1992).

Osorio, L G; Plants Protecting other Plants; *LEISA* Magazine 17(4): 23–24 (Dec, 2001).

Osorio, L G; Improving Organic Fertilizers; *LEISA India* 7(1): 13–14 (March, 2005).

OTA; Advanced Materials by Design; Office of Technology Assessment; Washington (June, 1988).

Padmanaban, G; Growth of Biotechnology in India; *Current Science* 85: 712–719 (2003).

Palmer, J, Goldstein, W, Curnow, A (Eds); *Planning Education to Care for the Earth*; pp 95–102; IUCN; Gland; Switzerland (1995).

PARCOM; *On the Use of the Best Available Technology*; Parcom Recommendation 89/1; Paris Commission of the Convention for the Prevention of Marine Pollution from Land-based Sources; London (1989).

Parikh, J K, Reddy, B S, Banerjee, R; *Planning for Demand Side Management in Electricity Sector*; 112–117; Tata Mc-Graw Hill; New Delhi (1994).

Parikh, J K, Reddy, B S, Banerjee, R, Koundinya, S; DSM Survey in India: Awareness, Barrier and Implementability; *Energy* 21: 98–107 (1996).

Parry, B; *Trading the Genome: Investigating the Commodification of Bio-Information*; Columbia University Press; New York (2004).

Parry, B; From the Corporeal to the Informational: Exploring the Scope of Benefit Sharing Agreements and their Applicability to Sequence Databases; In: Theile, F; Ashcroft, R E (Eds); *Bioethics in a Small World*; Springer–Verlag; Berlin (2005).

Parry, B; New Spaces of Biological Commodification: The Dynamics of Trade in

Genetic Resources and 'Bioinformation'; *Interdisciplinary Science Reviews* 31: 19–31 (2006).

Patel, C K N; Industrial Ecology; *PNAS* (USA) 89: 789–790 (1992).

Patterson, W; *Keeping the Lights On—Towards Sustainable Electricity*; Earthscan; London (2007).

Pauly, D et. al., Science 279: 860–863 (1998).

Pauly, D, Christensen, V; *Nature* 374: 255–257 (1995).

PCSD (President's Council on Sustainable Development); *Sustainable America: A New Consensus for Prosperity, Opportunity and a Healthy Environment for the Future*; GPO; Washington DC (1996).

Pearce, D; Auditing the Earth; *Environment* 40(2): 23–28 (1998).

Pearce, D W, Turner, K; *Economics of Natural Resources and the Environment*; Harvester Wheatsheaf (1990).

Pearce, D W, Turner, R K; Packaging Waste and the Polluter Pays Principle: Taxation Solution; Centre for Social and Economic Research on Global Environment (CSERGE); Discussion Paper; WM 91–101; University of East Anglia, Norwich and University of College, London (1991).

Pearce, F; Consuming Myths; *New Scientist* 159/2150 (1998).

Pennisi, E; Microbes for Environmental Cleanup; *ASM News* 392 (1995).

Penny, G; Energy, Industrial Ecology and the Cost of Change; *Water & Atmosphere* 11(1): 26–27 (2003).

Perelli, A, Flematti, F, Ruivenkamp, G L; 'Agribusiness Multinazionale; *La Questione Agraria* No. 15; Franco Angeli Editore; Milan (1984).

Perlin, J; *A Forest Journey: The Role of Wood in the Development of Civilization*; Harvard University Press; Cambridge; Massachusetts (1989).

Perrings, C, Folke, C, Maler, K G; The Ecology and Economics of Biodiversity Loss; *Ambio* 21: 201–211 (1992).

Perrow, C; *Normal Accidents*; Princeton University Press; Princeton; New Jersey (1999).

Pimentel, D, Pimentel, M; *Food, Energy and Society*; Colorado University Press; Niwot (1996).

Pimentel, D, Pimentel, M; Energy Use in Agriculture: An Overview; *LEISA India*, 7(1): 5–7 (March 2005).

Pimentel, D, Pimentel, M, Karpenstein-Machan, M; Energy Use in Agriculture: An Overview; *CIGR Electronic Journal (www.agen.tamu.edu/cigr)* (1999).

Pitkethly, M; Surfing the Nanotechnology Wave; *Nanotoday* 2(5): 6 (2007).

Poliakoff, M, Licence, P; Green Chemistry; *Nature* 450: 810–812 (2007).

Pollution Probe; *Profit from Pollution Prevention*; Campbell, M, Glenn, W (Eds); Pollution Probe; Toronto; Canada (1982).

Pommez, P; Life-cycle Assessment; *UNEP Industry and Environment*; pp 38–40 (2000).

Postel, S; *Defusing the Toxics Threat: Controlling Pesticides and Industrial Waste*; Worldwatch Institute; Washington DC (1987).

Postel, S L, Daily, G C, Ehrlich, P R; *Science* 271: 785 (1996).

Postman, N; *Technopoly: The Surrender of Culture to Technology*; Vintage Press; New York (1992).

Postman, N; *The End of Education: Redefining the Value of School*; Vintage Press; New York (1995).

Prasad, P N, Mark, E, Fai, T J (Eds); *Advanced Turbulent Drag Reducing and Flocculating Materials based on Polysaccharides in Polymers and other Advanced Materials: Emerging Technologies and Business Opportunities*; Plenum Press; pp 227–249; New York (1995).

Prasad, R; Rural Energy Transitions—A Successful Case of Community Participation; *LEISA India* 7(1): 24–25 (March, 2005).

Preston, T R; Biodigesters in Ecological Farming Systems; *LEISA India* 7(1): 8–9 & 12 (March, 2005).

Rajvanshi, A K; Electric and Improved Cycle Rickshaw as a Sustainable Transport System for India; *Current Science* 83: 703–707 (2002).

Rajvanshi, A K; *Human Power* 49: pp 15–18 (Winter 1999–2000).

Ramprasad, V, Krishnaprasad, G, Manasi, S; The Path of Rediscovery; In: Haverkort, B, van't Hooft, K, Hiemstra, W (Eds); *Ancient Roots, New Shoots: Endogenous Development in Practice*; pp 89–101; ETC/Compass; Zed Books; London (2003).

Rhoades, R, Bebbington, A; Farmers who Experiment: An Untapped Resource for Agricultural Research and Development; pp 269–307; In Warren, DM, Slikkerveer, LJ, Brokensha, D (Eds); *The Cultural Dimension of Indigenous Knoweldge Systems*; Intermediate Technology Publications; London (1995).

Rifkin, J; *The Biotech Century*; Tarcher/Putnam; New York (1998).

Rodale, R; *Regenerative Agriculture and the Weed Problem*; North Central Weed Science Society; Lexin; USA (1988).

Rosegrant, M; Current Water Policy: A Threat to Global Supply; *Report*; International Food Policy Research Institute; Washington DC (2002).

Rosenblatt, M J, Lee, H L; A Comparative Study of Continuous and Periodic Inspection Policies in Deteriorating Production Systems; *IIE Trans.* 18: 2–9 and 18: 48–55 (1986).

Ross, M; Efficient Energy Use in Manufacturing; *PNAS* (USA) 89: 827–831 (1992).

Roszak, T, Gomes, M E, Kanner, A D; *The Ecopsychology Reader*; Sierra Club Books; San Francisco (1995).

Röth, G; The Position of Farmers' Local Knowledge within Agricultural Extension, Research and Development Cooperation; *Indigenous Knowledge and Development Monitor* 9: 10–11 (2001).

Ruivenkamp, G; Tailor-made Biotechnologies: Between Bio-power and Sub-politics; pp 11–46; In *Tailoring Biotechnologies: Potentialities, Actualities and Spaces*; Ruivenkamp, G et. al., (Eds); 1(1); Centre for Tailormade Biotechnologies and Genomics, Wageningen (2005).

Ruivenkamp, G; Access to Food Through Tailor-Made Biotechnologies; TAO Document; Wageningen (2001).

Ruivenkamp, G; Tailor-made Biotechnologies for Endogenous Developments and the Creation of New Networks and Knowledge Means; *Biotechnology and Development Monitor*; 50: 14–16 (2003).

Sachs, W, Esteva, G; *Des Ruines du Développement*; Écosociété; Montreal (1996).

Sampson, G P; *Trade, the Environment and WTO: The Post-Seattle Agenda;* Policy Essay No. 27; Overseas Development Council; Johns Hopkins University Press; Baltimore; Maryland (2000).

Sarkis, J (Ed); *Greening the Supply Chain*; Springer (2006).

Sauvé, L; Convergence and Divergence: A Rejoinder to John Huckle; In Jarnet et. al., 76–77 (2000a).

Sauvé, L; Environmental Education and Sustainable Development; *Canad. J. Environ. Education* 1: 7–35 (1996).

Sauvé, L; Environmental Education between Modernity and Postmodernity; *Canad. J. Environ. Education* 4: 9–35 (1999).

Sauvé, L; Environmental Education between Modernity and Postmodernity: Searching for an Integrating Educational Framework; pp 44–56; In: Jarnet, A et. al., (Eds); *The Future of Environmental Education in a Postmodern World?*; Proc. On-line Colloquium; Oct 19, 1998; Yukon College; Canada (2000).

Sayre, E; Human Ascent: Exploration into the Complex Nature of Human Needs and Need Satisfaction; PhD Dissertation, University of Philippines, Los Banos (1991).

Schimel, D S et. al., pp 39–71; In: Houghton, J T et. al., (Eds); *Climate Change 1994: Radiative Forcing of Climate Change*; Cambridge University Press; Cambridge (1995).

Schlapbach, L (Ed); Hydrogen in Intermetallic Compounds I; *Electronic, Thermodynamic and Crystallographic Properties, Preparation*; Springer; Berlin (1988).

Schlapbach, L (Ed); Hydrogen in Intermetallic Compounds II; *Surface and Dynamic Properties, Applications*; Springer; Berlin (1992).

Schlapbach, L, Züttel, A; Hydrogen-storage Materials for Mobile Applications; *Nature* 414: 353–358 (2001).

Scholl-Buckwald, S; The First World; *Global Pesticide Campaigner* 12(3): 2 (Dec, 2002).

Schowalter, D; *Insect Ecology: An Ecosystem Approach*; Academic Press; San Diego (2000).

Schreuder, D R; Delusion of Progress: A Case of Reconceptualizing Environmental Education; *South African Journal of Environmental Education* 15: 18–25 (1995).

Schreuder, D R, Reddy, C P S, le Grange, L; Science and Sustainability: Alternative Understandings of Environmental Education and Sustainability; 170–175; In: Jarnet, A et. al., (Eds); *The Future of Environmental Education in a Postmodern World?*; Proc. On-line Colloquium; Oct 19, 1998; Yukon College; Canada (2000).

Schrödinger, E; *What is Life?*; Cambridge University Press; Cambridge (1944).

Schulman, P; Lessons from a Slow Leak; *Science* 296: 1403–1404 (2002).

Seaforth, W; Five Years after Habitat II: Successes and Set-backs; UNCHS *Habitat Debate* 7(1): pp 1–6 (March, 2001).

SEI (Stockholm Environmental Institute); *Conventional Worlds: Technical Description of Bending the Curve Scenarios*; PolStar Series Report No. 8; Stockholm Environmental Institute; Stockholm (1998).

Selby, D; Global Education: Towards a Quantum Model of Environmental Education; pp 139–146; In: Jarnet, A. et. al., (Eds); *The Future of Environmental Education in a Postmodern World?*; Proc. On-line Colloquium; Oct 19, 1998; Yukon College; Canada (2000).

SER (Society for Ecological Restoration); *The SER Primer on Ecological Restoration*; Society for Ecological Restoration; Science Policy Work Group; Tucson; Arizona (2002).

Serageldin, I; Biotechnology and Food Security in the 21st Century; *Science* 285: 387–389 (1999).

Serageldin, I, Collins, W (Eds); *Biotechnology and Biosafety*; Proc. Workshop; Environmentally and Socially Sustainable Development Series; pp 1–214; World Bank; Washington DC (1999).

Shaler, N S; *Man and the Earth*; Fox; Duffield; New York (1905).

Shao, G, Reynolds, K M; *Computer Applications in Sustainable Forest Management*; Springer (2006).

Shaw, R W, Öberg, S; *Science of the Total Environment* 149: 193–214 (1994).

Shrestha, L K, Shrestha, G R, Munankami, R; Improving Traditional Water Mills; *LEISA India* 7(1): 16–17 (March, 2005).

Silver, E A, Pyke, D F, Peterson, R; *Inventory Management, Production Planning and Scheduling* (3 Ed); pp 170–179; Wiley; New York (1998).

Simmons, I G; *Interpreting Nature: Cultural Constructions of the Environment*; Routledge; London (1993).

Singh, K; Selected Data on Corporate Power and Profits; Presented at 3rd APRN Conference on Corporate Power or Peoples' Power; Sydney; 27–29 (Sept 2001).

Singh, R P et. al., Novel Biodegradable Flocculants based on Polysaccharides; *Current Science* 78: 798–803 (2000).

Smart, B; Industry as a Metabolic Activity; *PNAS* (USA) 89: 804–806 (1992).

Smyth, J; Is There a Future for Education Consistent with Agenda 21?; pp 27–33; In: Jarnet, A et. al., (Eds); *The Future of Environmental Education in a Postmodern World?*; Proc. On-line Colloquium; Oct 19, 1998; Yukon College; Canada (2000).

Smyth, J C, Blackmore, C, Harvey, T E; Education for Sustainability at the United Nations: Making progress?; *The Environmentalist* 17(3): 173–179 (1997).

Smyth, J C, Stapp, W B; Learning to Survive with the Biosphere; In N Polunin and J Burnett (Eds); *Surviving with the Biosphere*; pp 244–252; Edinburgh University Press; Edinburgh (1993).

Speth, J G; The Transition to a Sustainable Society; *PNAS* (USA) 89: 870–872 (1992).

Stapp, W B, Wals, A E J, Stankorb, S; *Environmental Education for Empowerment: Action Research and Community Problem Solving*; Kendall/Hunt Publishing; Dubuque; Iowa (1996).

Starch Research Group; *The Thermoplastic Processing of Starch*; Massachusetts Institute of Technology; Cambridge (1991).

Steele, B C H, Heinzel, A; Materials for Fuel-cell Technologies; *Nature* 414: 345–352 (2001).

Stein, R S; Polymer Recycling: Opportunities and Limitations; *PNAS* (USA) 89: 835–838 (1992).

Straughan, R; Analysis of Ethical Principles Arising from the Workshop; pp 173–180; In: *Ethics and Equity*; Proc. Workshop CGIAR; 21–25 April 1997; Foz do Iguacu; Brazil (1997).

Strauss, M; Faecal Sludge Treatment and Management—Research, Extension and Dissemination; *SANDEC News* (EAWAG, Dubendorf) No. 5: 3 (June, 2002).

Stren, R E; Social Development and Eradication of Poverty; UNCHS *Habitat Debate* 7(1): 10–11 (2001).

Suter, M J F, Giger, W; Trace Determinants of Emerging Water Pollutants; Endocrine Disruptors, Pharmaceuticals and Speciality Chemicals; *Chimia (Aarau)* 54: 13–16 (2001).

Swisher, J N, Jannuzzi, G M, Redlinger, R Y; *Tools and Methods for Integrated Resource Planning: Improving Energy Efficiency and Protecting the Environment*; UNEP Collaborating Centre on Energy and Environment; Denmark (1997).

Sy-Palanca, I; Keynote Speeches; *UNEP Industry and Environment*; pp 10 (July–Dec, 2002).

Takacs, D; *The Idea of Biodiversity: Philosophies of Paradise*; Johns Hopkins University Press; Baltimore (1996).

Tam, H; *Communitarianism: A New Agenda for Politics and Citizenship*; Macmillan; London (1998).

Tang, S L Y, Smith, R L, Poliakoff, M; *Green Chem.* 7: 761–762 (2005).

Tarascon, J-M, Armand, M; Issues and Challenges facing Rechargeable Lithium Batteries; Nature 414: 359–367 (2001).

Tauber, R; *Quantitative Analysis of Pharmaceuticals in Drinking Water from Ten Canadian Cities*; Enviro-Test Laboratories; Xenos Division; Ontario; Canada (2003).

Tauscher, W, Pollak, K; The Reduction of the Greenhouse Effect and the Possibilities of the Mineral Oil Industry; *Natural Resources and Development* 39: 39–51 (1994).

Thomashow, M; *Ecological Identity: Becoming a Reflective Environmentalist*; MIT Press; Cambridge Massachusetts (1995).

Thomashow, M; The Ecopsychology of Global Environmental Change; pp 128–138; In: Jarnet, A et. al., (Eds); *The Future of Environmental Education in a Postmodern World?*; Proc. On-line Colloquium; Oct 19, 1998; Yukon College; Canada (2000).

Tilbury, D; Environmental Education for Sustainability: Defining the New Focus of Environmental Education in the 1990s; *Environmental Education Research*; 1(2): 195–212 (1995).

Tréllez Solis E, Wilches-Chaux, G, Torres, M; *Education Ambiental Para un Futuro*

Sustenible en America Latina y el Caribe: Documento; Lima; Popayan; Santafé de Bogotá (1998).

Trimble, S W, Crosson, P; *Science* 289: 248 (2000).

Troxel, D E; Educating and Training Industrial Ecologists for the 1990s; *PNAS* (USA) 89: 862–863 (1992).

Tsukahara, M et. al., Hydrogen Storage and Electorde Properties of V-based Solid Solution Type Alloys Prepared by a Thermic Process; *Journal of The Electrochemical Society* 147: 2941–2944 (2000).

Turner, B M; *Man-Made Disasters*; Wykeham; London (1978).

TWN (Third World Network); Some Critical Environmental Issues after Rio; *Third World Resurgence* 81/82 (May/June, 1997).

UN; *Recasting Education for Sustainable Development*; World Congress on Environmental and Development Education and Communication; ECO–ED; Toronto (1992).

UNCHS/UNEP; Environmental Management; UNCHS *Habitat Debate* 7(1): 12–21 (2001).

UNDESA (United Nations Department of Economic and Social Affairs); *Johannesburg Declaration on Sustainable Development and Plan of Implementation of the World Summit on Sustainable Development*; 26 Aug–4 Sept, 2002; Johannesburg; United Nations; New York (2003).

UNDP (United Nations Development Programme); *Human Development Report* 1998; Oxford University Press; pp 19; New York (1998).

UNECA; *Growth Strategies for Africa: Lessons and Proposals*; Addis Ababa (1999).

UNECE; *Report on the Seminar on Low-waste Technology; Senior Advisors to ECE Governments on Environmental Protection*; Environmental Seminar No. 15/2; Paris; France (1984).

UNECE; *Ministerial Statement for the World Summit on Sustainable Development; Regional Ministerial Meeting for the World Summit on Sustainable Development*; Economic Commission for Europe (UNECE); Geneva (24–25 Sept, 2001).

UNEP and Consumers International; *Tracking Progress: Implementing Sustainable Consumption Policies*; Nairobi (2002).

UNEP DTIE; *Division of Technology, Industry and Economics; Developing Better Systems for Communicating Environmental Best Practice in Business—Final Report* Paris (1997).

UNEP; *Global Environment Outlook 2000*; Oxford University Press; New York (1999).

UNESC (UN Economic and Social Council); *Implementing Agenda 21; Report of the Secretary-General; Commission on Sustainable Development Acting as the Preparatory Committee for the World Summit on Sustainable Development*; Second Preparatory Session; Advance Unedited Text; pp 40–41 (2001).

UNESCO; *Eduquer pour un Avenir Viable: Une Vision Transdisciplinaire Pour l'action Concertée*; International Conference on Environment and Society; Thessaloniki; Greece (December 8–12, 1997).

UNESCO; *Éduquer pour un Avenir Viable: Une Vision Transdisciplinaire pour l' action Concertée*; Conférence Internationale de Thessaloniki; EPD–97/CONF.401/CLD.1 (Nov, 1997a).

UNESCO; *Projet de déclaration de Thessalonique; Conférence Internationale–Environment et société*; Éducation et Sensibilisation du Public à la Viablité; UNESCO-EPD/CONF.401/CLD.2 (1997b).

UNESCO/UNEP; Population: Working for Equitable and Sustainable Development in Harmony with the Environment; *Connexion*; Vol. XIX, No. 4, EE Bulletin; December (1994).

UNESCO-UNEP; Sustainable Development via Environmental Education; *Connect* 13(2): 1–3 (June, 1988).

UNIDO; African Industry 2000: The Challenges of Going Global; Vienna (1999).

UNIDO; *International Yearbook of Industrial Statistics*; Vienna (2001).

UNIDO; *Corporate Social Responsibility: Implications for Small and Medium Enterprises in Developing Countries*; UNIDO; Vienna (2002).

US Office of Technology Assessment; *Serious Reduction of Hazardous Wastes: For Pollution Prevention and Industrial Efficiency*; Office of Technology Assessment; US Congress; Washington DC (1986).

Vaillancourt, J-G; Le Développement Durable ou le "Compromis" de la Commission Brundtland; In Collectif. L'avenir d'un monde fini; *Cahiers de la Recherche Ethique* (pp 17–44); Fides; Montréal (1992).

Van Bueren, E L, Osman, A; Stimulating GMO–Free Breeding for Organic Agriculture: A View from Europe; *LEISA Magazine* 17(4): 12–14 (2001).

Van den Akker, F; Recycling and Clean Technologies: The Challenge for the 21st Century; In: Maltezou, S, Metry, A, Irwin, W (Eds); *Industrial Risk Management and Clean Technology*; Verlag Orac; Vienna (1990).

Van den Bosch, R, Messenger, P S, Gutieprez, A P; In: *Introduction to Biological Control*; Plenum Press; New York (1982).

Van der Maarel, E; *Biodiversity: From Babel to Biosphere Management*; Opulus Press; Uppsala (1997).

Van Dijk-Looijaard, A M, Van Genderen, J; Levels of Exposure from Drinking Water; *Food and Chemical Toxicology* 38: S37–S40 (2000).

Van Etten, J, Van den Dool, L; Building Capacity to Improve Urban Governance; UNCHS *Habitat Debate* 7(1): 24–25 (2001).

Venkaiah, M, Kaushik, S C, Dewangan, M L; Policies and Measures for Economic Efficiency and Energy Security and Environment Protection in India; *Journal of Scientific and Industrial Research*; 66: 928–934 (2007).

Visser, B; Biotechnology: A Basket of Options; *LEISA* Magazine 17 (4): 9–11 (2001).

Vitousek, P M, Ehrlich, P R, Ehrlich, A H, Matson, P A; *BioScience* 34: 368–373 (1986).

Vitousek, P M, Mooney, H A, Lubchenco, J, Melillo, J M; *Science* 277: 494 (1997).

Volesky, B (Ed); *Biosorption of Heavy Metals*; CRC Press; Boca Raton (1990).

Von Weizsaecker, E U, Liedtke, C, Seiler-Hausmann, J D (Eds); *Eco-Efficiency and Beyond: Towards the Sustainable Enterprise*; Greenleaf Publishing; Sheffield (2003).

Wackernagel, M et. al., *Ambio* 28: 604–612 (1999a).

Wackernagel, M et. al., *Ecological Economics* 29: 375–390 (1999).

Wackernagel, M et. al., Tracking the Ecological Overshoot of the Human Economy; *PNAS* (USA) 99: 9266–9271 (2002).

Wals, A E J, Van der Leij, T; Alternatives to National Standards in Environmental Education: Process-based Quality Assessment; *Canada Journal of Environmental Education* 2: 7–28 (1997).

Warren, D M; Using Indigenous Knowledge in Agricultural Development; World Bank; Washington DC (1991).

Warren, D M; The Role of Indigenous Knowledge and Biotechnology in Sustainable Agricultural Development; Keynote Address; Southwestern Nigerian Regional Workshop on Indigenous Knowledge and Biotechnology; Obafemi Awolowo University; Ile-Ife; Osun State; Nigeria; 30 July (1996).

Wasserscheid, P, Welton, T (Eds); *Ionic Liquids in Synthesis* 2 Ed; Wiley–VCH; Weinheim (2007).

WCED (World Commission on Environment and Development); *Our Common Future*; Oxford University Press; Oxford (1987).

Webb, S et. al., Indirect Human Exposure to Pharmaceuticals via Drinking Water; *Toxicology Letters* 142: 157–167 (2003).

Wei, S H, Zunger, A; Band-gap Narrowing in Ordered and Disordered Semiconductor Alloys; *Applied Physics Letters* 56: 662–664 (1990).

Weizsäcker, E, Lovins, A B, Hunter Lovins, L; *Factor Four Doubling Wealth—Halving Resource Use*; Earthscan; London (1997).

Welbourne A; How Women see their Lives Changing?; *ILEIA Newsletter*1/92: 6–7 (March, 1992).

Westra, L; Biotechnology and Transgenics in Agriculture and Aquaculture: The Perspective from Ecosystem Integrity; *Environmental Values* 7: 79–86 (1998).

Wilhite, B A, Weiss, S E, Ying, J Y, Schmidt, M A, Jensen, K F; *Advanced Materials* 18: 1701–1704 (2006).

Williams, M; *Deforesting the Earth: From Prehistory to Global Crisis*; University of Chicago Press; Chicago (2003).

Winter, E F; *Clean Technology Digest: A Proposal*; UNIDO; Vienna IPCT; 123 (SPEC) (28 August, 1990).

Winter, E F; Some Novel Agroindustrial CleanTechnologies for an Ecological Integrative and Commercially Intensive Mega Food Production System; In: *UNIDO Report* 10, 50 (SPEC); pp 33–90; Vienna (6 Nov, 1990).

Wischmeier, W H, Smith, D D; *Predicting Rainfall Erosion Losses—A Guide to Conservation Planning*; US Department of Agriculture; US Government Printing Office; Agricultural Handbook 537; Washington DC (1978).

Wood, P M; Biodiversity as the Source of Biological Resources: A New Look at Biodiversity Values; *Environmental Values* 6: 251–268 (1997).

World Bank; *Trade and the Environment: A View from the World Bank*; Washington DC (1999).

WRI (World Resources Institute); *World Resources Report* 1991–92; Oxford University Press; Oxford (1992).

WRI; The Weight of Nations: Material Outflows from Industrial Economics (*www.wri.org/materials/weightofnations.htm*) (2000).

WRI; Tomorrow's Markets: Global Trends and the Implications for Business (*www.wri.org/press/tomorrow_market.ptml*) (2002).

WRI; World Resources 2000–2001; *People and Ecosystems: The Fraying Web of Life*; OUP; Oxford (2000).

WRI; World Resources 2000–2001; *People and Ecosystems: The Fraying Web of Life*; World Resources Institute/Oxford University Press; New York (2001).

Wright, B D; Crop Genetic Resource Policy: Towards a Research Agenda; Environment and Production Technology Division Discussion Paper No. 19; International Food Policy Research Institute; Washington DC (1996).

Wright, R; World Pulp Market: Forecasts and Prospects as at Mid-1992; *Paper and Packaging Analyst* 14: 13–19 (1993).

WWF (World Wild Fund); Windows on the Wild—Biodiversity Basics Draft; Unpublished Draft Materials (1997).

Zogg, B; Switzerland's Coop: Working Closely with Suppliers; *UNEP Industry and Environment* 26(1): 16–19 (2003).

Zurbrugg, C, Drescher, S; Solid Waste Management—Biological Treatment of Municipal Solid Waste; SANDEC News (EAWAG, Dubendorf) No. 5: 6 (June, 2002).

Zwetsloot, G I J M, Ashford, N; *Towards Inherently Safer Production: A Feasibility Study on Implementation of an Inherent Safety Opportunity Audit and Technology Options Analysis in European Firms*; TNO Report R990341, TNO Work and Employment; Hoofdorp (1999).

Zwetsloot, G I J M, Ashford, N A; Inherently Safer Production: A Natural Complement to Cleaner Production; *UNEP Industry and Environment* 25(3–4); pp 84–88 (July–Dec, 2002).

Zwillich, T; A Tentative Comeback for Bioremediation; *Science* 289: 2266–2267 (2000).

Index

F

G

H

I

K

L

M

N

O

P

Q

R

S

T

U

V

W

Z